FORENSIC DNA TYPING

FORENSIC DNA TYPING

BIOLOGY & TECHNOLOGY BEHIND STR MARKERS

John M. Butler

ACADEMIC PRESS

A Harcourt Science and Technology Company

San Diego   San Francisco   New York   Boston
London   Sydney   Tokyo

ACADEMIC PRESS
A Harcourt Science and Technology Company
Harcourt Place, 32 Jamestown Road, London NW1 7BY, UK
http://www.academicpress.com

ACADEMIC PRESS
A Harcourt Science and Technology Company
525 B Street, Suite 1900, San Diego, California 92101-4495, USA
http://www.academicpress.com

ISBN 0-12-147951-X

A catalogue record for this book is available from the British Library

Typeset by Kenneth Burnley, Wirral, Cheshire
Printed in Spain by Grafos SA Arte Sobre Papel, Barcelona
01 02 03 04 05 06 GF 9 8 7 6 5 4 3 2 1

CONTENTS

FOREWORD

The advent of DNA typing in the mid-1980s has had an enormous effect on the ability of crime laboratories to identify individuals uniquely by testing a variety of their body fluids. In the past 15 years, technologies for individual identification have moved at a breathtaking pace. The first forensic samples to be typed by DNA procedures required at least 25–100 times more sampled DNA than is currently needed for a result. The incorporation of modern molecular biological techniques in the crime laboratory has resulted, at a remarkably increasing rate, in the identification of criminals and the exoneration of the innocent.

In this book, Dr Butler has addressed the biology and technology pertaining to a powerful and relatively new manner of performing forensic DNA typing. The primary focus is on the major molecular biological technique currently being used throughout the world: the use of molecular amplification to isolate and visualize short segments of DNA in the human genome. This technology, known as short tandem repeat (STR) testing, is the main emphasis of the book. By focusing on this technology, the author has developed and uses a wide array of illustrations and examples that help make the tools of molecular biology easy to comprehend. The book will help the reader understand the process of STR DNA typing. It will be of use to the neophyte or law enforcement/legal specialist who wants to know more about STR technology and its applications. It will provide a wealth of information and will be a valuable resource for the scientist at the laboratory bench. Finally, it will be of great use in the classroom for teaching the principles of forensic DNA testing.

While there are many books that discuss the principles of molecular biology and forensic testing, none have dealt solely with the biology, technology, and applications of DNA typing in such a comprehensive fashion as this one. Dr Butler has a unique perspective on DNA typing. His background in analytical chemistry, work and research at the FBI's Forensic Science and Research Training Center, postdoctoral studies in capillary electrophoresis at the National Institute of Standards and Technology, and industrial research in mass spectrometry uniquely qualify him as an expert in the forensic field.

His numerous publications and scholarship are reflected in a very readable text and his graphical presentations are helpful in providing clear explanations of complex processes.

DENNIS J. REEDER, PH.D.
April 2000

INTRODUCTION

The advent of modern DNA technology has resulted in the increased ability to perform human identity testing. Individual identification is desirable in a number of situations including the determination of perpetrators of violent crime such as murder and rape, resolving unestablished paternity, and identifying remains of missing persons or victims of mass disasters.

In the past few years, the general public has become more familiar with the power of DNA typing as the media has covered the O.J. Simpson murder trial, the President Clinton–Monica Lewinsky scandal, and the identification of the remains in the Tomb of the Unknown Soldier. In addition, our perceptions of history have been changed with DNA evidence that revealed Thomas Jefferson may have fathered a child by one of his slaves.

These cases have certainly attracted widespread media attention in recent years; however, they are only a small fraction of the thousands of forensic DNA and paternity cases that are conducted each year by public and private laboratories around the world. The technology for performing DNA typing has evolved rapidly during the 1990s to the point where it is now possible to obtain results in a few hours on samples with only the minutest amount of biological material.

This book will examine the science of current forensic DNA typing methods by focusing on the biology and technology behind short tandem repeat (STR) markers and the most common forensic DNA analysis methods used today. The materials in this book are intended primarily for two audiences: forensic scientists who want to gain a better understanding of STRs, and professionals in the law enforcement and legal communities who find it hard to comprehend the complexities of DNA profiling.

This book is also intended to aid forensic DNA laboratories in meeting the training requirements stated in the new DNA Advisory Board Quality Assurance Standards. These standards are striving to improve the quality of work performed in forensic laboratories by requiring technical managers and DNA examiners to have training in biochemistry, genetics and molecular biology in order to gain a basic understanding of the foundation of forensic DNA analysis. See Standard 5.2.1 and 5.3.1 in Appendix III of this book.

OVERVIEW OF BOOK CHAPTERS

The book has been divided into two primary sections covering the biology and technology of STR markers. Within each section, the chapters progress from basic introductory information to ongoing 'cutting-edge' research. The first few chapters in particular are meant as introductory material for those readers who might be less familiar with DNA or as a review of useful materials for more advanced readers. The biology section covers Chapters 2 through 8 and the technology section involves Chapters 9 through 16. The final chapter combines all of the information developed in the book and reviews the DNA testing performed in high-profile cases such as the O.J. Simpson case and the Thomas Jefferson evidence.

BIOLOGY SECTION

The book begins with an overview and history of DNA and its use in human identification. An actual criminal investigation where DNA evidence proved crucial is used to illustrate the value of this technology to law enforcement. Chapter 2 provides some basic information on DNA structure and function, while Chapter 3 covers the processes involved in preparing samples for DNA amplification via the polymerase chain reaction, which is discussed in Chapter 4. Chapter 5 focuses on the 13 commonly used STR markers in the United States today with details about naming of alleles and unique characteristics of each marker. Chapter 6 goes into the biology of STR markers including stutter products, non-template addition, microvariants, and null alleles. These aspects can complicate data interpretation if they are not understood properly. Chapter 7 discusses issues that are unique to the forensic DNA community, namely mixtures, degraded DNA samples, PCR inhibition, and contamination, all of which impact forensic casework since many samples do not come from a pristine, controlled environment. Chapter 8, the last chapter in the biology section, discusses additional markers in use today with STRs to aid in human identification. These markers include amelogenin for gender identification (sex typing), mitochondrial DNA for situations involving highly degraded DNA or cases where tracking maternal inheritance is useful, and Y-chromosome markers for specifically identifying the male contributor or paternal lineage of a sample. We also touch on the use of non-human DNA to aid forensic investigations and new developments such as the ability to obtain DNA profiles from fingerprint residue.

TECHNOLOGY SECTION

The technology portion of the book begins in Chapter 9 with a discussion of DNA separations using slab gel and capillary electrophoresis. Fluorescent detection methods are the primary topic of Chapter 10. This chapter has a number of colorful figures featuring the fluorescent dyes in use today. The DNA analysis instruments used in a majority of forensic laboratories are the topics of Chapters 11 and 12. Chapter 11 covers the ABI Prism 310 Genetic Analyzer while Chapter 12 reviews the Hitachi FMBIO II Fluorescence Imaging System. Issues surrounding genotyping of STR results are the focus of Chapter 13. Laboratory validation and quality assurance of DNA analysis is covered in Chapter 14. New DNA analysis technologies such as mass spectrometry and microchips are reviewed in Chapter 15. The final chapter in the technology section, Chapter 16, discusses the use of computer DNA databases to solve crimes. Large national DNA databases will continue to benefit law enforcement for many years to come by connecting violent crimes and serial criminal activity.

HIGH-PROFILE DNA CASES

The book's final chapter covers the DNA information involved in high-profile cases. The O.J. Simpson trial evidence is reviewed as is the famous blue dress in the President Clinton–Monica Lewinsky affair. The use of DNA information in identifying the remains of the Romanov family and the Vietnam soldier in the Tomb of the Unknown Soldier is also covered. To recognize the increasing role that DNA information is playing in mass disaster victim identification, we discuss here the use of STRs to aid in the identification of individuals who died in the Waco Branch Davidian fire (April 1993) and the airline crash of Swissair Flight 111 (September 1998). Finally, the Thomas Jefferson–Sally Hemings affair is reviewed in terms of the DNA information uncovered by this interesting investigation.

APPENDICES

There are four appendices at the back of the book that provide valuable supplemental material. Appendix I describes all reported alleles for the 13 CODIS STR loci as of January 2000. Sequence information, where available, has been included along with the reference that first described the noted allele. As most laboratories now use either a Promega GenePrint® STR kit or a PE Applied Biosystems AmpFlSTR® kit for PCR amplification, we have listed the expected size for each allele based on the sequence information. Appendix II includes the genotypes from a family inheritance study that illustrate how even closely related individuals can be differentiated using the 13 CODIS STR markers. Appendix III contains the DNA Advisory Board Quality Assurance Standards that pertain to forensic DNA testing laboratories and convicted offender DNA databasing laboratories in the United States. These standards are important for laboratory validation and maintaining high-quality results as DNA testing becomes more prevalent. Appendix IV is a compilation of companies and organizations that are suppliers of DNA analysis equipment, products, and services. A total of 65 companies are listed along with their addresses, phone numbers, internet web pages, and a brief description of their products and/or services.

ACKNOWLEDGEMENTS

We express a special thanks to colleagues and fellow researchers who kindly provided important information and supplied some of the figures for this book. These individuals include Dan Ehrlich, Nicky Fildes, Ron Fourney, Lee Fraser, Chip Harding, Debbie Hobson, Bill Hudlow, Margaret Kline, Steve Lee, Bruce McCord, Randy Nagy, Steve Niezgoda, Jim Schumm, Melissa Smrz, and Lois Tully.

Several other people deserve specific recognition for their support of this endeavor. The information reported in this book was in large measure made possible by a comprehensive collection of references on the STR markers used in forensic DNA typing. For this collection, now numbering over a thousand references, I am indebted to Christian Ruitberg for tirelessly collecting and cataloging these papers. A complete listing of these references may be found at http://www.cstl.nist.gov/biotech/strbase. Christian was also a great help in gathering background information on the O.J. Simpson case and the Unknown Soldier investigation.

Dr Dennis Reeder has been a model mentor offering consistent encouragement and support throughout my career and particularly at the time of this endeavor. Nick Fallon, my contact and editor at Academic Press, has been very enthusiastic of this project from the start and very patient with my efforts.

My wife Terilynne, who carefully reviewed the manuscript and made helpful suggestions, was always a constant support in the many hours that this project took away from my family. As the initial editor of all my written materials, Terilynne helped make the book more coherent and readable.

Since I was first exposed to forensic DNA typing in 1990 when a friend gave me a copy of Joseph Wambaugh's *The Blooding* to read, I have watched with wonder as the forensic DNA community has rapidly evolved. DNA testing that once took weeks can now be performed in a matter of hours. I enjoy being a part of the developments in this field and hope that this book will help many others come to better understand the principles behind the biology, technology, and genetics of STR markers.

This book is dedicated to my father,

who inspired me to write

CHAPTER 1

OVERVIEW AND HISTORY OF DNA TYPING

In the darkness of the early morning hours of 26 August 1999, a young University of Virginia student awoke to find a gun pointed at her head. The assailant forced her and a male friend spending the night to roll over on their stomachs. Terrorized, they obeyed their attacker. After robbing the man of some cash, the intruder put a pillow over the man's head and raped the female student. The female was blindfolded with her own shirt and led around the house while the intruder searched for other items to steal.

Throughout the entire ordeal, the intruder kept his gun to the back of the male student's head, daring him to look at him and telling him if he tried he would blow his head off. The assailant forced the young woman to take a shower in hopes that any evidence of the crime would be washed away. After helping himself to a can of beer, the attacker left before dawn taking with him the cash, the confidence, and the sense of safety of his victims. Even though the assailant had tried to be careful and clean up after the sexual assault, he had left behind enough of his personal body fluids to link him to this violent crime.

The police investigating the crime collected some saliva from the beer can. In addition, evidence technicians found some small traces of semen on the bed sheets that could not be seen with the naked eye. These samples were submitted to the Virginia Department of Forensic Sciences in Richmond along with control samples from other occupants of the residence where the crime occurred. The DNA profiles from the beer can and the bed sheets matched each other, but no suspect had been developed yet. Because of intense darkness and then the blindfold, the only description police had from the victims was that the suspect was black, medium height, and felt heavy set.

A suspect list was developed by the Charlottesville Police Department that contained over 40 individuals, some from the sex offender registry and some with extensive criminal histories who were stopped late at night in the area of the home invasion. Unfortunately, no further leads were available, leaving the victims as well as other University of Virginia students and their parents suspicious and fearful. The police were at the end of their rope and considered asking many of the people on the suspect list to voluntarily donate blood samples for purposes of a DNA comparison. The top suspects were systematically eliminated by DNA evidence, leaving the police frustrated.

Then, on 5 October, 6 long weeks after the crime had been committed, the lead detective on the case, Lieutenant J.E. 'Chip' Harding of the Charlottesville Police Department, received a call that he describes as being 'one of the most exciting phone calls in my 22 years of law enforcement.' A match had been obtained from the crime scene samples to a convicted offender sample submitted to the Virginia DNA Database several years before. The DNA sample for Montaret D. Davis of Norfolk, Virginia, was among 8000 samples added to the Virginia DNA Database at the beginning of October 1999. (Since 1989, a Virginia state law has required all felons and juveniles 14 and older convicted of serious crimes to provide blood samples for DNA testing.)

A quick check for the whereabouts of Mr Davis found him in the Albemarle–Charlottesville Regional Jail. Ironically, because of a parole violation, he had been court ordered weeks before to report to jail on what turned out to be the same day as the rape. Amazingly enough he had turned himself in at 6 p.m. just 14 hours after committing the sexual assault! Unless he would have bragged about his crime, it is doubtful that Mr Davis would ever have made it on the suspect list without the power of DNA testing and an expanding DNA database. At his jury trial in April 2000, Mr Davis was found guilty of rape, forcible sodomy, and abduction among other charges and sentenced to a 90-year prison term.

DNA typing, since it was introduced in the mid-1980s, has revolutionized forensic science and the ability of law enforcement to match perpetrators with crime scenes. Thousands of cases have been closed and innocent suspects freed with guilty ones punished because of the power of a silent biological witness at the crime scene. This book will explore the science behind DNA typing and the biology, technology, and genetics that make DNA typing the most useful investigative tool to law enforcement since the development of fingerprinting 100 years ago.

HISTORY OF FORENSIC DNA ANALYSIS

'DNA fingerprinting,' or DNA typing (profiling) as it is now known, was first described in 1985 by an English geneticist named Alec Jeffreys. Dr Jeffreys found that certain regions of DNA contained DNA sequences that were repeated over and over again next to each other. He also discovered that the number of repeated sections present in a sample could differ from individual to individual. By developing a technique to examine the length variation of these DNA repeat sequences, Dr Jeffreys created the ability to perform human identity tests.

These DNA repeat regions became known as VNTRs, which stands for variable number of tandem repeats. The technique used by Dr Jeffreys to examine the VNTRs was called restriction fragment length polymorphism (RFLP) because it involved the use of a restriction enzyme to cut the regions of DNA surrounding the VNTRs. This RFLP method was first used to help in an English immigration case and shortly thereafter to solve a double homicide case. Since that time, human identity testing using DNA typing methods has been widespread. The past 15 years have seen tremendous growth in the use of DNA evidence in crime scene investigations as well as paternity testing. Today over 100 public forensic laboratories and several dozen private paternity testing laboratories conduct hundreds of thousands of DNA tests annually in the United States. In addition, most countries in Europe and Asia have forensic DNA programs. The number of laboratories around the world conducting DNA testing will continue to grow as the technique gains in popularity within the law enforcement community.

COMPARISON OF DNA TYPING METHODS

Technologies used for performing forensic DNA analysis differ in their ability to differentiate two individuals and in the speed with which results can be obtained. The speed of analysis has dramatically improved for forensic DNA analysis. DNA testing that previously took 6 or 8 weeks can now be performed in a few hours.

The human identity testing community has used a variety of techniques including single-locus probe and multi-locus probe RFLP methods and more recently PCR (polymerase chain reaction)-based assays. Numerous advances have been made in the last 15 years in terms of sample processing speed and sensitivity. Instead of requiring large blood stains with well-preserved DNA, minute amounts of sample, as little as a single cell in some cases, can yield a useful DNA profile.

The gambit of DNA typing technologies used over the past 15 years for human identity testing are compared in Figure 1.1. The various DNA markers have been divided into four quadrants based on their power of discrimination, i.e. their ability to discern the difference between individuals, and the speed at which they can be analyzed. New and improved methods have developed over the years such that tests with a high degree of discrimination can now be performed in a few hours.

An ABO blood group determination, which was the first genetic tool used for distinguishing between individuals, can be performed in a few minutes but is not very informative. There are only four possible genotype groups – A, B, AB, and O – and 40% of the population is type O. Thus, while the ABO blood

Figure 1.1

Comparison of DNA typing technologies. Forensic DNA markers are arbitrarily plotted in relationship to four quadrants defined by the power of discrimination for the genetic system used and the speed at which the analysis for that marker may be performed. Note that this diagram does not reflect the usefulness of these markers in terms of forensic cases.

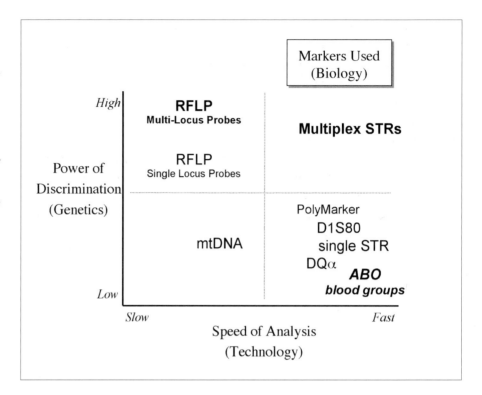

groups are useful for excluding an individual from being the source of a crime scene sample, the test is not very useful when an inclusion has been made, especially if the sample is type O.

On the other extreme, multi-locus RFLP probes are highly variable between individuals but require a great deal of labor, time, and expertise to produce a DNA profile. Analysis of multi-locus probes (MLP) cannot be easily automated, a fact that makes them undesirable as the demand for processing large numbers of DNA samples has increased. Deciphering sample mixtures, which are common in forensic cases, is also a challenge with MLP RFLP methods, which is the primary reason that laboratories went to single-locus RFLP probes used in serial fashion.

The best solution including a high power of discrimination and a rapid analysis speed has been achieved with short tandem repeat (STR) DNA markers, shown in the upper right quadrant of Figure 1.1. Also because STRs by definition are short, they can be analyzed three or more at a time. Multiple STRs can be examined in the same DNA test, or 'multiplexed.' Multiplex STRs are valuable because they can produce highly discriminating results (Chapter 5) and can successfully measure sample mixtures and biological materials containing degraded DNA molecules (Chapter 7). In addition, the detection of multiplex STRs can be automated, which is an important benefit as demand for DNA testing increases.

It should be noted, however, that Figure 1.1 does not fully reflect the usefulness of these markers in terms of forensic cases. Mitochondrial DNA (mtDNA), which is shown in the quadrant with the lowest power of discrimination and longest sample processing time, can be very helpful in forensic cases involving severely degraded DNA samples or when associating maternally related individuals (Chapter 8). In many situations, multiple technologies may be used to help resolve an important case (Chapter 17).

Over the past 15 years, there has been a gradual evolution in adoption of the various DNA typing technologies shown in Figure 1.1. When early methods for DNA analysis are superseded by new technologies, there is usually some overlap as forensic laboratories implement the new technology. Validation of the new methods is crucial to maintaining high-quality results (Chapter 14). Table 1.1 lists some of the major historical events in forensic DNA typing. The implementation of new methods by the FBI Laboratory has been listed in this historical timeline because the DNA casework protocols used by the FBI create an important trend within the United States and around the world.

STEPS IN DNA SAMPLE PROCESSING

This book contains a review of the steps involved in processing forensic DNA samples with short tandem repeat markers. STRs are a smaller version of the VNTR sequences first described by Dr Jeffreys. Samples obtained from a crime scene or a paternity investigation are subjected to defined processes involving biology, technology, and genetics (Figure 1.2).

BIOLOGY

The DNA is first extracted from its biological source material and then measured to evaluate the quantity of DNA recovered (Chapter 3). After isolating the DNA from its cells, specific regions are copied with a technique known as the polymerase chain reaction (Chapter 4). PCR produces millions of copies for each starting DNA molecule and thus permits very minute amounts of DNA to be examined. Multiple STR regions can be examined simultaneously to increase the informativeness of the DNA test (Chapter 5).

TECHNOLOGY

The resulting PCR products are then separated and detected in order to characterize the STR region being examined. The separation methods used today include slab gel and capillary electrophoresis (CE) (Chapter 9). Fluorescence detection methods have greatly aided the sensitivity and ease of measuring

Figure 1.2

Overview of biology, technology, and genetic components of DNA typing using short tandem repeat (STR) markers.

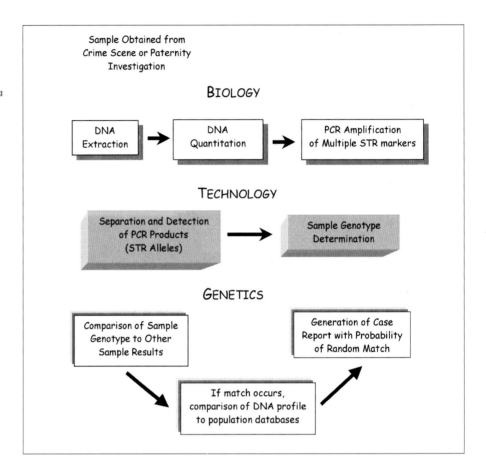

PCR-amplified STR alleles (Chapter 10). The two primary instrument platforms used in the United States for fluorescence detection of STR alleles are the ABI 310 Genetic Analyzer (Chapter 11) and the Hitachi FMBIO II (Chapter 12). After detecting the STR alleles, the number of repeats in a DNA sequence is determined, a process known as sample genotyping (Chapter 13).

GENETICS

The resulting DNA profile for a sample, which is a combination of individual STR genotypes, is compared to other samples. In the case of a forensic investigation, these other samples would include known reference samples such as the victim or a suspect that are compared to the crime scene evidence. With paternity investigations, the child's genotype would be compared to his or her mother's and the alleged father(s) under investigation. If there is no match between the questioned sample and the known sample, then the samples may be considered to have originated from different sources. The term for failure to match between two DNA profiles is 'exclusion.'

If a match or 'inclusion' results, then a comparison of the DNA profile is made to a population database, which is a collection of DNA profiles obtained from unrelated individuals of a particular ethnic group. For example, due to genetic variation between the groups, African-Americans and Caucasians have different population databases for comparison purposes. Finally a case report or paternity test result is generated. This report typically includes the random match probability for the match in question. This random match probability is the chance that a randomly selected individual from a population will have an identical STR profile or combination of genotypes at the DNA markers tested.

STR MULTIPLEX EXAMPLE

An example of DNA profiles obtained from two different individuals using STR markers is shown in Figure 1.3. In a single amplification reaction, unique sites on ten different chromosomes were probed with this DNA test to provide a random match probability of approximately 1 in 3 trillion. Note that every single site tested produces a different result between these two DNA samples. For example, marker A has two peaks in the top panel and only one peak in the bottom panel. Likewise, marker J produces two peaks in both samples but they result in different patterns due to different sizes at the site measured in the two DNA samples. These results can be reliably obtained in as little as a few hours from a very small drop of blood or blood stain.

Each STR allele is distinguished from the others in the amplification reaction by separating it based on its length and color. The color results from a fluores-

Figure 1.3

Comparison of the DNA profiles for two individuals obtained with multiple short tandem repeat markers. STR length variation at unique sites on ten different chromosomes are probed with this DNA test to provide a random match probability of approximately 1 in 3 trillion. A gender identification test also indicates that the top sample is from a male while the bottom sample is from a female individual. These results were obtained from a spot of blood the size of a pin head in less than 5 hours. The DNA size range in base pairs is shown across the top of the plot. Results from each DNA marker are indicated by the letters A–J.

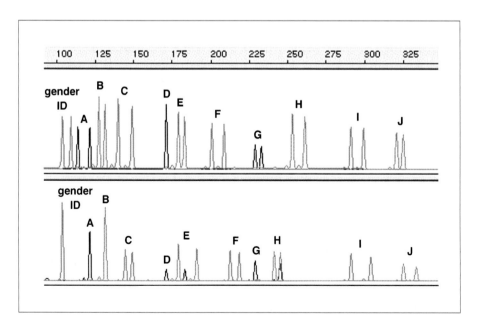

cent dye that is attached during the amplification reaction. In this example, DNA markers B, E, H, and J are labeled with a blue colored dye, markers A, D, and G are labeled with a yellow dye, and markers C, F, I, and the gender identification (ID) are labeled in green. The gender ID results in two peaks for a male sample and a single peak for a female sample.

COMPARISONS TO COMPUTER TECHNOLOGY

In order to obtain a better feel for how rapidly forensic DNA analysis methods have progressed in the last decade or so, a comparison to computer technology may be helpful. The use of computers at home and in the workplace has increased dramatically since personal computers became available in the mid-1980s. These computers become faster and more powerful every year. It is almost inconceivable that the internet, which has such a large impact on our daily lives, was just an idea a few years ago.

When multi-locus RFLP probes were first reported in 1985, the average computer operating speed was less than 25 MHz. Fifteen years later in the year 2000, computers with computing speeds of 1000 MHz (1 GHz) are now common. Computer processing speeds and capabilities have increased rapidly every year. Likewise, the ability of laboratories to perform DNA typing methods has improved dramatically due to the rapid progress in the areas of biology, technology, and understanding of genetic theories. In addition, the power of discrimination for DNA tests has steadily increased in the late 1990s (see Table 5.3).

Some interesting parallels can be drawn between Microsoft Corporation, the company that has led the computer technology revolution, and the timing for advancements in the field of forensic DNA typing (Table 1.1). In 1985, the year that Alec Jeffreys first published his work with multi-locus RFLP probes, Microsoft shipped its first version of Windows software to serve as a computer operating system. In 1986, as DNA testing began to 'go public' in the United States with Cellmark and Lifecodes performing multi-locus RFLP, Microsoft went public with a successful initial public offering.

In the late 1980s, single-locus RFLP probes began to be used by the FBI Laboratory in DNA casework. Owing to issues over the use of statistics for population genetics and the quality of results obtained in forensic laboratories, RFLP methods were questioned by the legal community in 1989 and the early 1990s. At this same time, Microsoft had quality problems of their own with the Windows 3.0 operating system. However, they 'turned the corner' with their product release of Windows 3.1 in 1991. In the same year, improved methods for DNA typing were introduced, namely fluorescent STR markers and Chelex extraction.

The popularity of Microsoft products improved in 1995 with the release of

Table 1.1 (facing)

Major historical events in forensic DNA typing shown by year. The events relating to forensic DNA (first column) are described in context with parallel developments in biotechnology (second column) and key events relating to Microsoft Corporation, which have impacted the computer age (final column).

Year	Forensic DNA Science and Application	Parallel Developments in Biotechnology	Microsoft Corporation Chronology
1985	Alec Jeffreys develops multi-locus RFLP probes	PCR process first described	First version of Windows shipped
1986	DNA testing goes public with Cellmark and Lifecodes in United States	Automated DNA sequencing with 4-colors first described	Microsoft goes public
1988	FBI begins DNA casework with single-locus RFLP probes		
1989	TWGDAM established; *NY v. Castro* case raises issues over quality assurance of laboratories	DNA detection by gel silver-staining, slot blot, and reverse dot blots first described	
1990	Population statistics used with RFLP methods are questioned; PCR methods start with DQA1	Human Genome Project begins with goal to map all human genes	Windows 3.0 released (quality problems); exceeds $1 billion in sales
1991	Fluorescent STR markers first described; Chelex extraction		Windows 3.1 released
1992	NRC I Report; FBI starts casework with PCR-DQA1	Capillary arrays first described	
1993	First STR kit available; sex-typing (amelogenin) developed	First STR results with CE	
1994	Congress authorizes money for upgrading state forensic labs; 'DNA wars' declared over; FBI starts casework with PCR-PM	Hitachi FMBIO and Molecular Dynamics gel scanners; first DNA results on microchip CE	
1995	O.J. Simpson saga makes public more aware of DNA; DNA Advisory Board setup; UK DNA Database established; FBI starts using D1S80/amelogenin	ABI 310 Genetic Analyzer and TaqGold DNA polymerase introduced	Windows 95 released
1996	NRC II Report; FBI starts mtDNA testing; first multiplex STR kits become available	STR results with MALDI-TOF and GeneChip mtDNA results demonstrated	
1997	13 core STR loci defined; Y-chromosome STRs described		Internet Explorer begins to overtake Netscape
1998	FBI launches national Combined DNA Index System; Thomas Jefferson and Bill Clinton implicated with DNA	2000 SNP hybridization chip described	Windows 98 released; anti-trust trial with US Justice Department begins
1999	Multiplex STR kits are validated in numerous labs; FBI stops testing DQA1/PM/D1S80	ABI 3700 96-capillary array for high-throughput DNA analysis; chromosome 22 fully sequenced	
2000	FBI and other labs stop running RFLP cases and convert to multiplex STRs	First copy of human genome completed	Bill Gates steps down as Microsoft CEO

Windows 95. During this same year, forensic DNA methods gained public exposure and popularity due to the O.J. Simpson trial. The United Kingdom also launched a National DNA Database that has revolutionized the use of DNA as an investigative tool. The United States launched their national Combined DNA Index System (CODIS) in 1998, concurrent with the release of Windows 98.

Finally, to aid sample throughput and processing speed, the FBI Laboratory and many other forensic labs have stopped running RFLP cases as of the year 2000. On 13 January 2000, Bill Gates stepped down as the CEO of Microsoft in order to help his company move into new directions.

We recognize that, owing to the rapid advances in the field of forensic DNA typing, some aspects of this book may be out of date by the time it is published, much like a computer is no longer the latest model by the time it is purchased. However, a reader should be able to gain a fundamental understanding of forensic DNA typing from the following pages. While we cannot predict the future with certainty, short tandem repeat DNA markers have had and will continue to have an important role to play in forensic DNA typing due to their use in DNA databases.

The match on Mr Davis described at the beginning of this chapter was made with eight STR markers. These eight STRs are a subset of 13 STR markers described in detail throughout this book that will most likely be used in DNA databases around the world for many years to come. Perhaps with the odds of getting caught becoming greater than ever before, violent criminals like Mr Davis will think twice before carrying out such heinous actions.

BIOLOGY

CHAPTER 2

DNA BIOLOGY REVIEW

BASIC DNA PRINCIPLES

The basic unit of life is the cell, which is a miniature factory producing the raw materials, energy, and waste removal capabilities necessary to sustain life. Thousands of different proteins, called enzymes, are required to keep these cellular factories operational. An average human being is composed of approximately 100 trillion cells, all of which originated from a single cell. Each cell contains the same genetic programming. Within the nucleus of our cells is a chemical substance known as DNA that contains the informational code for replicating the cell and constructing the needed enzymes. Because the DNA resides in the nucleus of the cell, it is often referred to as nuclear DNA. (As will be discussed in Chapter 8, some minor extranuclear DNA exists in human mitochondria, which are the cellular powerhouses).

Deoxyribonucleic acid, or DNA, is sometimes referred to as our genetic blueprint because it stores the information necessary for passing down genetic attributes to future generations. Residing in every cell of our body (with the exception of red blood cells, which lack nuclei), DNA provides a 'computer program' that determines our physical features and many other attributes. The complete set of instructions for making an organism, i.e. all the DNA in a cell, is referred to collectively as its genome.

DNA has two primary purposes: (1) to make copies of itself so cells can divide and carry on the same information; and (2) to carry instructions on how to make proteins so cells can build the machinery of life. Information encoded within the DNA structure itself is passed on from generation to generation with one-half of a person's DNA information coming from their mother and one-half coming from their father.

DNA STRUCTURE AND DEFINITIONS

Nucleic acids including DNA are composed of nucleotide units that are made up of three parts: a nucleobase, a sugar, and a phosphate (Figure 2.1). The nucleobase or 'base' imparts the variation in each nucleotide unit while the phosphate and sugar portions form the backbone structure of the DNA molecule.

The DNA alphabet is composed of only four characters representing the four nucleobases: A (adenine), T (thymine), C (cytosine), and G (guanine). The various combinations of these four letters, known as nucleotides or bases, yield the diverse biological differences among human beings and all living creatures. Humans have approximately three billion nucleotide positions in their

Figure 2.1

Basic components of nucleic acids: (a) phosphate sugar backbone with bases coming off the sugar molecules, (b) chemical structure of phosphates and sugar molecules illustrating numbering scheme on the sugar carbon atoms. DNA sequences are conventionally written from 5′ to 3′.

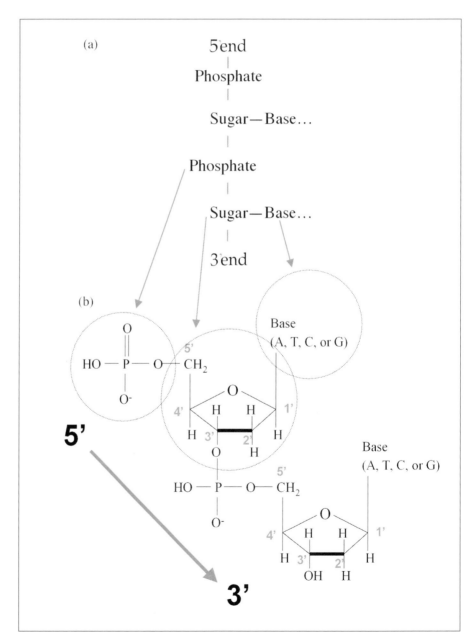

genomic DNA. Thus, with four possibilities (A, T, C, or G) at each position, literally trillions of combinations are possible. The informational content of DNA is encoded in the order (sequence) of the bases just as computers store binary information in a string of ones and zeros.

Directionality is provided when listing a DNA sequence by designating the '5'-end' and the '3'-end.' This numbering scheme comes from the chemical structure of DNA and refers to the position of carbon atoms in the sugar ring of the DNA backbone structure (Figure 2.1). A sequence is normally written (and read) from 5' to 3' unless otherwise stated. DNA polymerases, the enzymes that copy DNA, only 'write' DNA sequence information from 5' to 3', much like we read words and sentences from left to right.

BASE PAIRING AND HYBRIDIZATION OF DNA STRANDS

In its natural state in the cell, DNA is actually composed of two strands that are linked together through a process known as *hybridization*. Individual nucleotides pair up with their 'complementary base' through hydrogen bonds that form between the bases. The base pairing rules are such that adenine can only hybridize to thymine and cytosine can only hybridize to guanine (Figure 2.2). There are two hydrogen bonds between the adenine–thymine base pair and three hydrogen bonds between the guanine–cytosine base pair. Thus, GC base pairs are stuck together a little stronger than AT base pairs. The two DNA strands form a double helix due to this 'base-pairing' phenomenon (Figure 2.2).

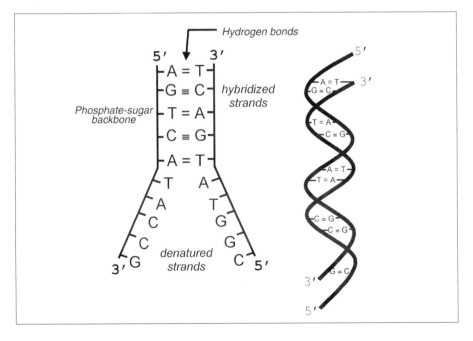

Figure 2.2

Base pairing of DNA strands to form a double-helix structure.

The two strands of DNA are 'anti-parallel', that is one strand is in the 5′ to 3′ orientation and the other strand lines up in the 3′ to 5′ direction relative to the first strand. By knowing the sequence of one DNA strand, its complementary sequence can easily be determined based on the base pairing rules of A with T and G with C. These combinations are sometimes referred to as Watson–Crick base pairs for James Watson and Francis Crick who discovered this structural relationship in 1953.

Hybridization of the two strands is a fundamental property of DNA. However, the hydrogen bonds holding the two strands of DNA together through base pairing may be broken by elevated temperature or by chemical treatment, a process known as *denaturation*. A common method for denaturing double-stranded DNA is to heat it to near boiling temperatures. The DNA double helix can also be denatured by placing it in a salt solution of low ionic strength or by exposing it to chemical denaturants such as urea or formamide, which destabilize DNA by forming hydrogen bonds with the nucleotides and preventing their association with a complementary DNA strand.

Denaturation is a reversible process. If a double-stranded piece of DNA is heated up, it will separate into its two single strands. As the DNA sample cools, the single DNA strands will find their complementary sequence and rehybridize or anneal to each other. The process of the two complementary DNA strands coming back together is referred to as *renaturation* or *reannealing*.

CHROMOSOMES, GENES, AND DNA MARKERS

There are approximately three billion base pairs in a single copy of the human genome. Obtaining a complete catalog of the genes contained in the human genome is the focus of the Human Genome Project, which is an international effort that has been ongoing since 1990. The information from the Human Genome Project will benefit medical science as well as forensic human identity testing and help us better understand our genetic makeup.

Within human cells, DNA found in the nucleus of the cell (nuclear DNA) is divided into chromosomes, which are dense packets of DNA and protection proteins called histones. The human genome consists of 22 matched pairs of autosomal chromosomes and two sex determining chromosomes. Thus, normal human cells contain 46 different chromosomes or 23 pairs of chromosomes. Males are designated XY because they contain a single copy of the X chromosome and a single copy of the Y chromosome, while females contain two copies of the X chromosome and are designated XX. Most human identity testing is performed using markers on the autosomal chromosomes, and gender determination is done with markers on the sex chromosomes.

Chromosomes in all body (somatic) cells are in a *diploid* state; they contain two sets of each chromosome. On the other hand, gametes (sperm or egg) are in a *haploid* state; they have only a single set of chromosomes. When an egg cell and a sperm cell combine during conception, the resulting zygote becomes diploid again. Thus, one chromosome in each chromosomal pair is derived from each parent at the time of conception.

Mitosis is the process of nuclear division in somatic cells that produces daughter cells, which are genetically identical to each other and to the parent cell. *Meiosis* is the process of cell division in sex cells or gametes. In meiosis, two consecutive cell divisions result in four rather than two daughter cells, each with a haploid set of chromosomes.

The DNA material in chromosomes is composed of 'coding' and 'non-coding' regions. The coding regions are known as *genes* and contain the information necessary for a cell to make proteins. A gene usually ranges from a few thousand to tens of thousands of base pairs in size. Approximately 50 000–100 000 genes exist in the human genome, a number we will not know exactly until the completion of the Human Genome Project.

Genes consist of *exons* (protein-coding portions) and *introns* (the intervening sequences). Genes only make up ~5% of human genomic DNA. Non-protein coding regions of DNA make up the rest of our chromosomal material. Because these regions are not related directly to making proteins they are sometimes referred to as 'junk' DNA. Markers used for human identity testing are found in the non-coding regions either between genes or within genes (i.e. introns) and thus do not code for genetic variation.

Polymorphic (variable) markers that differ among individuals can be found throughout the non-coding regions of the human genome. The chromosomal position or location of a gene or a DNA marker in a non-coding region is commonly referred to as a *locus* (plural: *loci*). Thousands of loci have been characterized and mapped to particular regions of human chromosomes through the worldwide efforts of the Human Genome Project.

Pairs of chromosomes are described as *homologous* because they are the same size and contain the same genetic structure. A copy of each gene resides at the same position (locus) on each chromosome of the homologous pair. One chromosome in each pair is inherited from an individual's mother and the other from his or her father. The DNA sequence for each chromosome in the homologous pair may or may not be identical since mutations may have occurred over time.

The alternative possibilities for a gene or genetic locus are termed *alleles*. If the two alleles at a genetic locus on homologous chromosomes are different, they are termed *heterozygous* and, if the alleles are identical at a particular locus, they are termed *homozygous*. Detectable differences in alleles at corresponding loci are essential to human identity testing.

A *genotype* is a characterization of the alleles present at a genetic locus. If there are two alleles at a locus, A and a, then there are three possible genotypes: AA, Aa, and aa. The AA and aa genotypes are homozygous while the Aa genotype is heterozygous. A *DNA profile* is the combination of genotypes obtained for multiple loci. DNA typing or DNA profiling is the process of determining the genotype present at specific locations along the DNA molecule. Multiple loci are typically examined in human identity testing to reduce the possibility of a random match between unrelated individuals.

NOMENCLATURE FOR DNA MARKERS

The nomenclature for DNA markers is fairly straightforward. If a marker is part of a gene or falls within a gene, the gene name is used in the designation. For example, the short tandem repeat (STR) marker TH01 is from the human tyrosine hydroxylase gene located on chromosome 11. The '01' portion of TH01 comes from the fact that the repeat region in question is located within intron 1 of the tyrosine hydroxylase gene. Sometimes the prefix HUM- is included at the beginning of a locus name to indicate that it is from the human genome. Thus, the STR locus TH01 would be correctly listed as HUMTH01.

DNA markers that fall outside of gene regions may be designated by their chromosomal position. The STR loci D5S818 and DYS19 are examples of markers that are not found within gene regions. In these cases, the 'D' stands for DNA. The next character refers to the chromosome number, 5 for chromosome 5 and Y for the Y chromosome. The 'S' refers to the fact that the DNA marker is a single copy sequence. The final number indicates the order in which the marker was discovered and categorized for a particular chromosome. Sequential numbers are used to give uniqueness to each identified DNA marker. Thus, for the DNA marker D16S539:

> D: DNA
> 16: chromosome 16
> S: single copy sequence
> 539: 539th locus described on chromosome 16

DESIGNATING PHYSICAL CHROMOSOME LOCATIONS

The basic regions of a chromosome are illustrated in Figure 2.3. The center region of a chromosome, known as the *centromere*, controls the movement of the chromosome during cell division. On either side of the centromere are 'arms' that terminate with *telomeres* (Figure 2.3). The shorter arm is referred to as 'p' while the longer arm is designated 'q'.

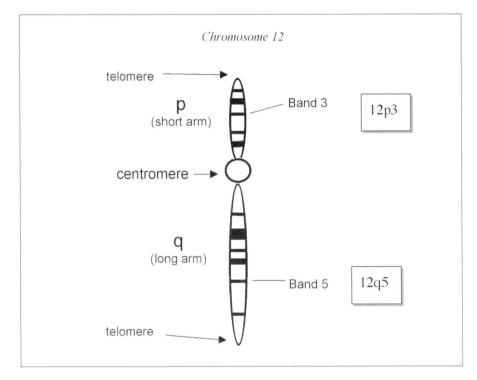

Chromosome 12

telomere

p
(short arm)

Band 3

12p3

centromere

q
(long arm)

Band 5

12q5

telomere

Figure 2.3

Basic chromosome structure and nomenclature. The centromere is a distinctive feature of chromosomes and plays an important role during mitosis. On either side of the centromere are 'arms' that extend to terminal regions, known as telomeres. The short arm of a chromosome is designated as 'p' while the long arm is referred to as 'q'. The band nomenclature refers to physical staining with a Giemsa dye (G-banded). Band localization is determined by G-banding the image of a metaphase spread during cell division. Bands are numbered outward from the centromere with the largest values near the telomeres.

Human chromosomes are numbered based on their overall size, with chromosome 1 being the largest and chromosome 22 the smallest. The complete sequence of chromosome 22 was reported in December 1999 to be over 33 million nucleotides in length. When the Human Genome Project completes its monumental effort, we will know the sequence and length of all 23 pairs of human chromosomes.

During most of a cell's life cycle, the chromosomes exist in an unraveled linear form. Prior to cell division, during the metaphase step of mitosis, the chromosomes condense into a more compact form that can be observed under a microscope following chromosomal staining. Chromosomes are visualized under a light microscope as consisting of a continuous series of light and dark bands when stained with different dyes. The pattern of light and dark bands results because of different amounts of A and T versus G and C bases across the chromosomes.

A common method for staining chromosomes to obtain a banding pattern is the use of a Giemsa dye mixture that results in so-called 'G-bands' via the 'G-staining' method. These G-bands serve as signposts on the chromosome highway to help determine where a particular DNA sequence or gene is located compared to other DNA markers. The differences in chromosome size and banding patterns allow the 24 chromosomes (22 autosomes and X and Y) to be distinguished from one another, an analysis called a *karotype*.

A DNA or genetic marker is physically mapped to a chromosome location using banding patterns on the metaphase chromosomes. Bands are classified according to their relative positions on the short arm (p) or the long arm (q) of specific chromosomes (Figure 2.3). Thus, the chromosomal location 12p1 means band 1 on the short arm (p) of chromosome 12. The band numbers increase outward from the centromere to the telomere portion of the chromosome. For example, band 32 is closer to the telomere than band 20. For DNA markers close to the terminal ends of the chromosome, the nomenclature 'ter' is often used as a suffix to the chromosome arm designation. The location of a DNA marker might therefore be listed as 15qter, meaning the terminus of the long arm of chromosome 15. Sometimes a DNA marker is not yet mapped with a high degree of accuracy, in which case the chromosomal location would be listed as being in a particular range, i.e. 2p23-pter or somewhere between band 23 and the terminus of the short arm on chromosome 2.

POPULATION VARIATION

The vast majority of our DNA molecules (over 99.7%) is the same between people. It is the small fraction of our DNA (0.3% or ~one million nucleotides) that differs between people and makes us unique individuals. These variable regions of DNA provide the capability of using DNA information for human identity purposes. Methods have been developed to locate and characterize this genetic variation at specific sites in the human genome.

TYPES OF DNA POLYMORPHISMS

DNA variation is exhibited in the form of different alleles, or various possibilities at a particular locus. Two forms of variation are possible at the DNA level: sequence polymorphisms and length polymorphisms (Figure 2.4).

Figure 2.4

Two primary forms of variation exist in DNA: (a) sequence polymorphisms and (b) length polymorphisms. The short tandem repeat DNA markers discussed in this book are length polymorphisms.

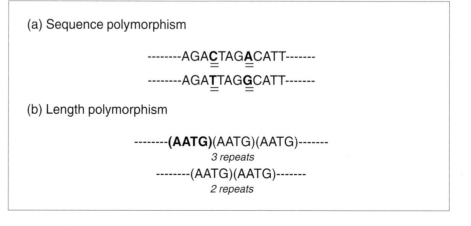

(a) Sequence polymorphism

--------AGA**C**TAGA**A**CATT-------

--------AGA**T**TAGG**G**CATT-------

(b) Length polymorphism

--------**(AATG)**(AATG)(AATG)-------
3 repeats
--------(AATG)(AATG)-------
2 repeats

As discussed earlier, a genotype is an indication of a genetic type or allele state. A sample containing two alleles, one with 13 and the other with 18 repeat units, would be said to have a genotype of '13,18'. This shorthand method of designating the alleles present in a sample makes it easier to compare results from multiple samples.

In DNA typing, multiple markers or loci are examined. The more DNA markers examined and compared, the greater the chance that two unrelated individuals will have different genotypes. Alternatively, each piece of matching information adds to the confidence in connecting two matching DNA profiles from the same individual. If each locus is inherited independent of the other loci, then a calculation of a DNA profile frequency can be made by multiplying each individual genotype frequency together. This is known as the *product rule*.

Owing to the fact that it is currently not feasible in terms of time and expense to evaluate an individual's entire DNA sequence, multiple discrete locations are evaluated (Figure 2.5). The variability that is observed at these locations is used to include or exclude samples, i.e. do they match or not. Because absolute certainty in DNA identification is not possible in practice, the next best thing is to claim virtual certainty due to the extreme small probabilities of a coincidental (random) match.

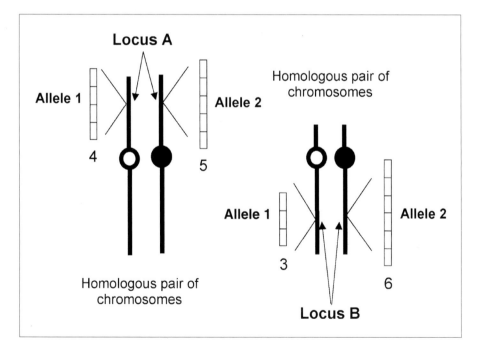

Figure 2.5

Schematic representation of two different STR loci on different pairs of homologous chromosomes. The chromosomes with the open circle centromeres are paternally inherited while the solid centromere chromosomes are maternally inherited. Thus, this individual received the four repeat allele at locus A and the three repeat allele at locus B from their father, and the five repeat allele at locus A and the six repeat allele at locus B from their mother.

DNA searches can be narrowed down by gathering more data points in a manner analogous to how the US Postal Service delivers the mail. The entire United States has over 260 million individuals but by including the zip code, state, city, street, street number, and name on an envelope, a letter can be delivered to a single, unique individual. Likewise, the use of more and more information from DNA markers can be used to narrow a search down to a single individual. If marker 1, marker 2, marker 3, and so on match on a DNA profile between crime scene evidence and a suspect, one can become more confident that the two DNA types are from the same source. The likelihood increases with each marker match.

GENETIC VARIABILITY

Large amounts of genetic variability exist in the human population. This is shown by the fact that, with the exception of identical twins, we all appear different from each other. Hair color, eye color, height, and shape all represent alleles in our genetic makeup. To gain a better appreciation for how the number of alleles present at a particular locus impacts the variability, let us consider the ABO blood group. Three alleles are possible: A, B, and O. These three alleles can be combined to form three possible homozygous genotypes (AA, BB, and OO) and three heterozygous genotypes (AO, BO, and AB). Thus, with three alleles there are six possible genotypes.

With larger numbers of alleles for a particular DNA marker, a greater number of genotypes result. In general, if there are n alleles, there are n homozygous genotypes and $n(n-1)/2$ heterozygous ones. Thus, a locus with ten possible alleles would exhibit $10 + (10 \times 9)/2 = 55$ genotypes. A locus with 20 possible alleles would exhibit $20 + (20 \times 19)/2 = 210$ genotypes. A combination of ten loci with 10 alleles in each locus would have over 2.5×10^{17} possible genotypes ($55 \times 55 \times 55 \times \ldots$). Whereas the use of four loci with 30 alleles in each locus would have 465 genotypes each and 4.7×10^{10} possible genotypes ($465 \times 465 \times 465 \times 465$).

RECOMBINATION: SHUFFLING OF GENETIC MATERIAL

Recombination is the process by which progeny derive a combination of genes different from that of either parent. During the process of meiosis or gamete cell production, each reproductive cell receives at random one representative of each pair of chromosomes, or 23 in all. Since there are two chromosomes in each pair, meiosis results in 2^{23}, or about 8.4 million, different possible combinations of chromosomes in human eggs or sperm cells. The union of egg and sperm cells therefore results in over 70 trillion ($2^{23} \times 2^{23}$) different possible combinations – each one representing half of the genetic material from the father and half from the mother. In this manner, human genetic material is effectively shuffled with each generation producing the diversity seen in the world today.

GENBANK: A DATABASE OF DNA SEQUENCES

Genetic variation from DNA sequence information around the world is cataloged in a large computer database known as GenBank. GenBank is maintained by the National Center for Biotechnology Information (NCBI), which is part of the National Library of Medicine with the US National Institutes of Health. NCBI was established in 1988 as a national resource for molecular biology information to improve understanding of molecular processes affecting human health and disease. As of August 1999, GenBank contained over 3.4 billion nucleotide bases from 4.6 million different records. This repository of DNA sequence information is not from humans alone. Over 55 000 different species are represented in GenBank. GenBank DNA sequences may be viewed and retrieved over the internet via the NCBI home page at http://www.ncbi.nlm.nih.gov.

METHODS FOR MEASURING DNA VARIATION

Techniques used by forensic DNA laboratories for human identity testing purposes are based on the same fundamental principles and methods used for medical diagnostics and gene mapping. A person's genetic makeup can be directly determined from very small amounts of DNA present in blood stains, saliva, bone, hair, semen, or other biological material. Because all the cells in the human body descend by successive divisions from a single fertilized egg, the DNA material is (barring mutations) identical between any cells collected from that individual and therefore provides the same forensic information.

   The two primary approaches for performing DNA typing are restriction fragment length polymorphism (RFLP) methods and polymerase chain reaction (PCR)-based methods. Some of the characteristics of these techniques are compared in Table 2.1. PCR-based methods have rapidly overtaken RFLP methods due to the ability of PCR to handle forensic samples that are of low quantity and of poor quality. The desire for a rapid turnaround time and the capabilities for high-volume sample processing have also driven the acceptance of PCR-based methods and markers. The most recent and probably most rapidly accepted forensic DNA markers are short tandem repeats due to a number of advantages.

ADVANTAGES OF STR MARKERS

This book covers the use of short tandem repeat DNA markers for human identity testing. These markers have become popular for forensic DNA typing because they are PCR-based and work with low-quantity DNA templates or

Table 2.1

Comparison of RFLP and PCR-based DNA typing methods.

Characteristic	RFLP Methods	PCR Methods
Time required to obtain results	6–8 weeks with radioactive probes; ~1 week with chemiluminescent probes	1–2 days
Amount of DNA needed	50–500 ng	0.1–1 ng
Condition of DNA needed	High molecular weight, intact DNA	May be highly degraded
Capable of handling sample mixtures	Yes (single locus probes)	Yes
Allele identification	Binning required	Discrete alleles obtained
Power of discrimination	~1 in 1 billion with 6 loci	~1 in 1 billion with 8–13 loci (requires more loci)
Automatable and capable of high-volume sample processing	No	Yes
Commonly used DNA markers	D1S7, D2S44, D4S139, D5S110, D7S467, D10S28, D17S79	DQA1, D1S80, PolyMarker (LDLR, GYPA, HBGG, Gc, D7S8), TH01, VWA, numerous STR loci

degraded DNA samples. STR typing methods are amenable to automation and involve sensitive fluorescent detection, which enables scientists to collect data quickly from these markers. When sites on multiple chromosomes are examined, STRs are highly discriminating between unrelated and even closely related individuals. Finally, discrete alleles make results easier to interpret and to compare through the use of computerized DNA databases than RFLP-based systems where similar DNA sizes were grouped together.

ADDITIONAL READING

Lee, H.C., Ladd, C., Bourke, M.T., Pagliaro, E. and Tirnady, F. (1994) *American Journal of Forensic Medicine and Pathology*, 15, 269–282.

National Research Council (1996) *The Evaluation of Forensic DNA Evidence.* Washington, DC: National Academy Press.

Primrose, S.B. (1998) *Principles of Genome Analysis: A Guide to Mapping and Sequencing DNA from Different Organisms*, 2nd edn. Malden, MA: Blackwell Science.

Tagliaferro, L. and Bloom, M.V. (1999) *The Complete Idiot's Guide to Decoding Your Genes.* New York: Alpha Books.

CHAPTER 3

SAMPLE COLLECTION AND PREPARATION (DNA EXTRACTION AND QUANTIFICATION)

Before a DNA test can be performed on a sample, it must be collected and the DNA isolated and put in the proper format for further characterization. This chapter covers the important topics of sample collection, DNA extraction, and DNA quantification. Each of these steps is vital to obtain a successful result regardless of the DNA typing procedure used. If the samples are not handled properly in the initial stages of an investigation, then no amount of hard work in the final analytical or data interpretation steps can compensate.

SAMPLE COLLECTION

DNA SAMPLE SOURCES

DNA is present in every nucleated cell and is therefore present in biological materials left at crime scenes. DNA has been successfully isolated and analyzed from a variety of biological materials. Introduction of the polymerase chain reaction (PCR) has extended the range of possible DNA samples that can be successfully analyzed because many copies are made of the DNA markers to be examined (see Chapter 4). Some of the biological materials that have been tested with PCR-based DNA typing methods are included in Table 3.1. The most common materials tested in forensic laboratories are blood and semen, or bloodstains and semen stains.

BIOLOGICAL EVIDENCE AT CRIME SCENES

The different types of biological evidence discussed in the previous section can be used to associate or to exclude an individual from involvement with a crime. In particular, the direct transfer of DNA from one individual to another individual or to an object can be used to link a suspect to a crime scene. As noted by Dr Henry Lee (Lee *et al.* 1991, Lee 1996), this direct transfer could involve:

1   the suspect's DNA deposited on the victim's body or clothing;
2   the suspect's DNA deposited on an object;

3 the suspect's DNA deposited at a location;

4 the victim's DNA deposited on the suspect's body or clothing;

5 the victim's DNA deposited on an object;

6 the victim's DNA deposited at a location;

7 the witness' DNA deposited on victim or suspect; or

8 the witness' DNA deposited on an object or at a location.

DNA evidence collection from a crime scene must be performed carefully and a chain of custody established in order to produce DNA profiles that are meaningful and legally accepted in court. DNA testing techniques have become so sensitive that biological evidence too small to be easily seen with the naked eye can be used to link suspects to crime scenes. The evidence must be carefully collected, preserved, stored, and transported prior to any analysis conducted in a forensic DNA laboratory. The National Institute of Justice has produced a brochure entitled 'What Every Law Enforcement Officer Should Know About DNA Evidence' that contains helpful hints for law enforcement personnel who are the first to arrive at a crime scene.

Table 3.1

Sources of biological materials used for PCR-based DNA typing.

Material	Reference
Blood and blood stains	Budowle *et al.* (1995)
Semen and semen stains	Budowle *et al.* (1995)
Bones	Gill *et al.* (1994)
Teeth	Alvarez Garcia *et al.* (1996)
Hair with root	Higuchi *et al.* (1988)
Hair shaft	Wilson *et al.* (1995)
Saliva (with nucleated cells)	Sweet *et al.* (1997)
Urine	Benecke *et al.* (1996)
Feces	Hopwood *et al.* (1996)
Debris from fingernails	Wiegand *et al.* (1993)
Muscle tissue	Hochmeister (1998)
Cigarette butts	Hochmeister et al. (1991)
Postage stamps	Hopkins *et al.* (1994)
Envelope sealing flaps	Word and Gregory (1997)
Dandruff	Herber and Herold (1998)
Fingerprints	Van Oorschot and Jones (1997)
Personal items: razor blade, chewing gum, wrist watch, ear wax, toothbrush	Tahir *et al.* (1996)

EVIDENCE COLLECTION AND PRESERVATION

The importance of proper DNA evidence collection cannot be overemphasized. If the DNA sample is contaminated from the start, obtaining unambiguous information becomes a challenge at best and an important investigation can be compromised. Samples for collection should be carefully chosen as well to prevent needless redundancy in the evidence for a case. The following suggestions may be helpful during evidence collection to preserve it properly:

- Avoid contaminating the area where DNA might be present by not touching it with your bare hands, or sneezing and coughing over the evidence.
- Use clean latex gloves for collecting each item of evidence. Gloves should be changed between handling of different items of evidence.
- Each item of evidence must be packaged separately.
- Bloodstains, semen stains, and other types of stains must be thoroughly air-dried prior to sealing the package.
- Samples should be packaged in paper envelopes or paper bags after drying. Plastic bags should be avoided because water condenses in them, especially in areas of high humidity and water can speed the degradation of DNA molecules. Packages should be clearly marked with case number, item number, collection date, and initialed across the package seal in order to maintain a proper chain of custody.
- Stains on unmovable surfaces (such as table or floor) may be transferred with sterile cotton swabs and distilled water. Rub the stained area with the moist swab until the stain is transferred to the swab. Allow the swab to air dry without touching any others. Store each swab in a separate paper envelope.

STORAGE AND TRANSPORT OF DNA EVIDENCE

Carelessness or ignorance of proper handling procedures during storage and transport of DNA from the crime scene to the laboratory can result in a specimen unfit for analysis. For example, bloodstains should be thoroughly dried prior to transport. DNA can be stored as non-extracted tissue or as fully extracted DNA. DNA samples are not normally extracted though until they reach the laboratory.

Most biological evidence is best preserved when stored dry and cold. These conditions reduce the rate of bacterial growth and degradation of DNA. Samples should be packaged carefully and hand carried or shipped using overnight delivery to the forensic laboratory conducting the DNA testing. A nice evidence collection cardboard box was recently described for shipping and handling bloodstains and other crime scene evidence (Hochmeister *et al.* 1998). Inside the laboratory, DNA samples are either stored in a refrigerator at

4°C or a freezer at –20°C. For long periods of time, extracted DNA samples may even be stored at –70°C.

DNA EXTRACTION

A biological sample obtained from a crime scene in the form of a bloodstain or semen stain, or a liquid blood sample from a suspect or a paternity case contains a number of substances besides DNA. DNA molecules must be separated from other cellular material before they can be examined. Cellular proteins that package and protect DNA in the environment of the cell can inhibit the ability to analyze the DNA. Therefore, DNA extraction methods have been developed to separate proteins and other cellular materials from the DNA molecules. In addition, the quantity and quality of DNA often need to be measured prior to proceeding further with analytical procedures to ensure optimal results.

There are three primary techniques for DNA extraction used in today's forensic DNA laboratory: organic extraction, Chelex extraction, and FTA paper (Figure 3.1). The exact extraction or DNA isolation procedure varies depending on the type of biological evidence being examined. For example, whole blood must be treated differently from a bloodstain or a bone fragment.

Organic extraction, sometimes referred to as phenol chloroform extraction, has been in use for the longest period of time and may be used for situations where either RFLP or PCR typing is performed. High molecular weight DNA, which is essential for RFLP methods, may be obtained most effectively with organic extraction.

The Chelex method of DNA extraction is more rapid than the organic extraction method. In addition, Chelex extraction involves fewer steps and thus fewer opportunities for sample-to-sample contamination. However, it produces single-stranded DNA as a result of the extraction process and therefore is only useful for PCR-based testing procedures.

All samples must be carefully handled regardless of the DNA extraction method to avoid sample-to-sample contamination or introduction of extraneous DNA. The extraction process is probably where the DNA sample is more susceptible to contamination in the laboratory than at any other time in the forensic DNA analysis process. For this reason, laboratories usually process the evidence samples at separate times and sometimes even different locations from the reference samples.

A popular method for preparation of reference samples is to make a bloodstain by applying a drop of blood on to a cotton cloth, referred to as a swatch, to produce a spot about 1 cm² in area. Ten microliters of whole blood, about the size of a drop, contains approximately 70 000–80 000 white blood cells and should yield approximately 500 ng of genomic DNA. The actual yield will vary

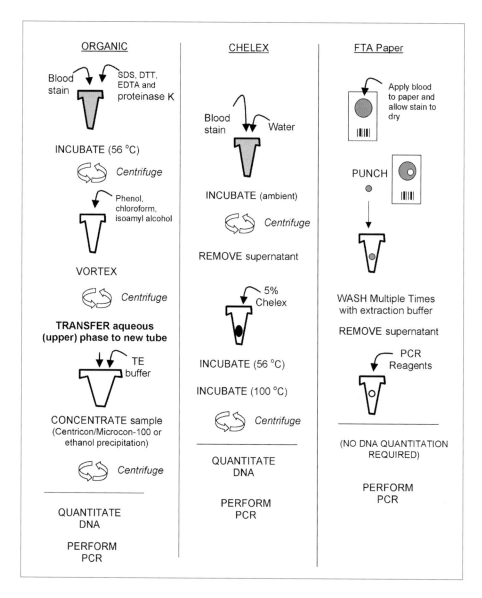

Figure 3.1

Schematic of commonly used DNA extraction processes.

with the number of white blood cells present in the sample and the efficiency of the DNA extraction process.

Extracted DNA is typically stored at $-20°C$, or even $-80°C$ for long-term storage, to prevent nuclease activity. Nucleases are enzymes (proteins) found in cells that degrade DNA to allow for recycling of the nucleotide components. Nucleases need magnesium to work properly so one of the measures to prevent them from digesting DNA in blood is the use of purple-topped tubes containing a blood preservative known as EDTA. The EDTA chelates, or binds up, all of the free magnesium and thus prevents the nucleases from destroying the DNA in the collected blood sample.

ORGANIC (PHENOL–CHLOROFORM) EXTRACTION

Organic extraction involves the serial addition of several chemicals. First sodium dodecyl sulfate (SDS) and proteinase K are added to break open the cell walls and to break down the proteins that protect DNA molecules while they are in chromosomes. Next a phenol/chloroform mixture is added to separate the proteins from the DNA. The DNA is more soluble in the aqueous portion of the organic–aqueous mixture. Some protocols involve a Centricon 100 (Amicon, Beverly, MA) dialysis and concentration step in place of the ethanol precipitation to remove heme inhibitors (Comey *et al.* 1994). While the organic extraction method works well for recovery of high molecular weight DNA, it is time consuming, involves the use of hazardous chemicals, and requires the sample to be transferred between multiple tubes (a fact that increases the risk of error or contamination).

CHELEX EXTRACTION

An alternative procedure for DNA extraction that has become popular among forensic scientists is the use of a chelating-resin suspension that can be added directly to the sample (e.g. blood, bloodstain, or semen). Introduced in 1991 to the forensic DNA community, Chelex® 100 (Bio-Rad Laboratories, Hercules, CA) is an ion-exchange resin that is added as a suspension to the samples (Walsh *et al.* 1991). Chelex is composed of styrene divinylbenzene copolymers containing paired iminodiacetate ions that act as chelating groups in binding polyvalent metal ions such as magnesium. By removing the magnesium from the reaction, DNA destroying enzymes known as nucleases are inactivated and the DNA molecules are thus protected.

In most protocols, biological samples, such as bloodstains, are added to a 5% Chelex suspension and boiled for several minutes to break open the cells and release the DNA. An initial, prior wash step is helpful to remove possible contaminants and inhibitors such as heme and other proteins (Willard *et al.* 1998). The exposure to 100°C temperatures denatures the DNA as well as disrupting the cell membranes and destroying the cell proteins. After a quick spin in a centrifuge to pull the Chelex resin to the bottom of the tube, the supernatant is removed and can be added directly to the PCR amplification reaction.

Chelex extraction procedures for recovering DNA from bloodstains or semen-containing stains are not effective for RFLP typing because Chelex denatures double-stranded DNA and yields single-stranded DNA from the extraction process. Thus, it can only be followed by PCR-based analyses. However, Chelex extraction is an advantage for PCR-based typing methods because it removes inhibitors of PCR and uses only a single tube for the

DNA extraction, which reduces the potential for laboratory-induced contamination.

The addition of too much whole blood or too large a bloodstain to the Chelex extraction solution can result in some PCR inhibition. The AmpFlSTR kit manuals recommend 3 µL whole blood or a bloodstain approximately 3 mm × 3 mm (Perkin Elmer Corporation 1998).

FTA™ PAPER

A relatively new approach to DNA extraction involves the use of FTA™ paper. In the late 1980s, FTA™ paper was developed by Lee Burgoyne at Flinders University in Australia as a method for storage of DNA (Burgoyne *et al.* 1994). FTA™ paper is an absorbent cellulose-based paper that contains four chemical substances to protect DNA molecules from nuclease degradation and preserve the paper from bacterial growth (Burgoyne 1996). As a result, DNA on FTA™ paper is stable at room temperature over a period of several years.

Use of FTA paper simply involves adding a spot of blood to the paper and allowing the stain to dry. The cells are lysed upon contact with the paper and DNA from the white blood cells is immobilized within the matrix of the paper. A small punch of the paper is removed from the FTA card bloodstain and placed into a tube for washing. The bound DNA can then be purified by washing it with a solvent to remove heme and other inhibitors of the PCR reaction. This purification of the paper punch can be seen visually because, as the paper is washed, the red color is removed with the supernatant. The clean punch is then added directly to the PCR reaction. Alternatively, some groups have performed a Chelex extraction on the FTA paper punch and used the supernant in the PCR reaction (Lorente *et al.* 1998).

A major advantage of FTA paper is that consistent results may be obtained without quantification. Furthermore, the procedure may be automated on a robotic workstation (Belgrader and Marino 1997). For situations where multiple assays need to be run on the same sample, a bloodstained punch may be reused for sequential DNA amplifications and typing (Del Rio *et al.* 1996).

A disposable toothbrush may also be used for collecting buccal cells in a non-threatening manner (Burgoyne 1997). This method can be very helpful when samples need to be collected from children. After the buccal cells have been collected by gently rubbing a wet toothbrush across the inner check, the brush can be tapped on to the surface of FTA™ paper for sample storage and preservation.

DIFFERENTIAL EXTRACTION

Differential extraction is a modified version of the organic extraction method that separates epithelial and sperm cells. Differential extraction was first described in 1985 (Gill *et al.* 1985) and is commonly used today by the FBI Laboratory and other forensic crime laboratories to isolate the female and male fractions in sexual assault cases that contain a mixture of male and female DNA. By separating the male fraction away from the victim's DNA profile, it is much easier to interpret the perpetrator's DNA profile in a rape case.

The differential extraction procedure involves preferentially breaking open the female epithelial cells with an incubation in a SDS/proteinase K mixture. Sperm nuclei are subsequently lysed by treatment with a SDS/proteinase K/dithiothreitol (DTT) mixture. The DTT breaks down the protein disulfide bridges that make up sperm nuclear membranes (Gill *et al.* 1985). Differential extraction works because sperm nuclei are impervious to digestion without DTT. The major difference between the regular version of organic extraction described earlier and differential extraction is the initial incubation in SDS/proteinase K without DTT present.

Differential extraction works well in most sexual assault cases to separate the female and male fractions from one another. Unfortunately, some perpetrators of sexual assaults have had a vasectomy in which case there is an absence of spermatozoa. Azoospermic semen, i.e. without sperm cells, cannot be separated from the female fraction with differential extraction. In the case of azoospermic perpetrators, the use of Y chromosome specific markers permit male DNA profiles to be deduced in the presence of excess female DNA (see Chapter 8).

OTHER METHODS FOR DNA EXTRACTION

Several other DNA extraction methods have been used to isolate DNA successfully prior to further sample processing. Microwave extraction has been used to shorten the conventional organic extraction method by several hours and to yield genomic DNA that could be PCR amplified (Lee *et al.* 1994). QIAamp spin columns have also proven effective as a means of DNA isolation (Greenspoon *et al.* 1998). The addition of 6 M NaCl to a proteinase K-digested cell extract followed by vigorous shaking and centrifugation results in a simple precipitation of the proteins (Miller *et al.* 1988). The supernatant containing the DNA portion of cell extract can then be added to a PCR reaction. A simple alkaline lysis with 0.2 M NaOH for 5 minutes at room temperature has been shown to work as well (Rudbeck and Dissing 1998). While each of these methods is effective for extracting most DNA samples, the forensic community has traditionally relied on the three main methods mentioned: organic extraction, Chelex extraction, and FTA paper.

DNA QUANTIFICATION

Only after DNA in a sample has been isolated can its quantity and quality be accurately determined. Determination of the amount of DNA in a sample is essential for most PCR-based assays because a narrow concentration range works best. For example, the ABI Profiler Plus and COfiler multiplex STR kits specify the addition of 1–2.5 ng of template DNA for optimal results (Perkin Elmer Corporation 1998). Promega STR kits also work best in a similar DNA concentration range. Too much DNA can result in peaks that are off-scale for the measurement technique. Too little DNA template may result in allele 'drop-out' because the PCR reaction fails to amplify the DNA properly. This phenomenon is sometimes referred to as stochastic fluctuation (see Chapter 4).

Early methods for DNA quantification typically involved either absorbance at 260 nm wavelength or fluorescence after staining a yield gel with ethidium bromide. Unfortunately, because these approaches are not very sensitive, they consume valuable forensic specimens that are irreplaceable. In addition, absorbance measurements are not specific for DNA and contaminating proteins or phenol left over from the extraction procedure can give falsely high signals. To overcome these problems, several methods have been developed for DNA quantification purposes. These include the slot blot procedure and fluorescence-based microtiter plate assays.

SLOT BLOT QUANTIFICATION

Probably the most popular method in forensic laboratories today for genomic DNA quantification is the so-called 'slot-blot' procedure. This test is specific for human and other primate DNA due to a 40 base pair (bp) probe that is complementary to a primate-specific alpha satellite DNA sequence D17Z1 located on chromosome 17 (Waye *et al.* 1989, Walsh *et al.* 1992). The slot blot assay was first described with radioactive probes (Waye *et al.* 1989), but has since been modified and commercialized with chemiluminescent or colorimetric detection formats (Walsh *et al.* 1992).

Slot blots involve the capture of genomic DNA on a nylon membrane followed by addition of a human-specific probe. Chemiluminescent or colorimetric signal intensities are compared between a set of standards and the samples (Figure 3.2). Slot blot quantification is a relative measurement involving the comparison of unknown samples to a set of standards that are prepared usually via a serial dilution from a DNA sample of known concentration. Typically about 30 samples are tested on a slot blot membrane with 6–8 standard samples run on each side of the membrane for comparison purposes. For example, the standards might be a serial dilution of human DNA starting

Figure 3.2

Illustration of a human DNA quantification result with the slot-blot procedure. A serial dilution of a human DNA standard is run on either side of the slot-blot membrane for comparison purposes. The quantity of each of the unknown samples is estimated by visual comparison to the calibration standards. For example, the sample indicated by the arrow is closest in appearance to the 2.5 ng standard.

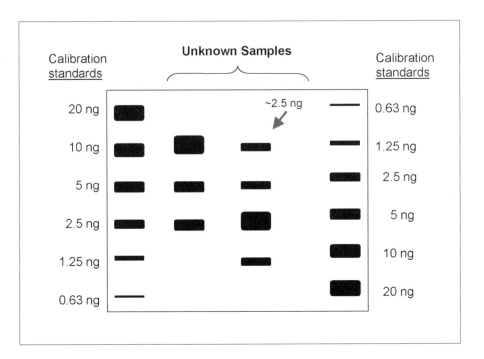

with 20 ng, 10 ng, 5 ng, 2.5 ng, etc. Only 5 μL of DNA extract is used for this quantification test.

The assay takes several hours to perform but is fairly sensitive as it can detect both single-stranded and double-stranded DNA down to levels of approximately 150 pg or about 50 copies of human genomic DNA. A 150 pg DNA standard can be detected after only a 15 minutes exposure to X-ray film (Walsh *et al.* 1992). With chemiluminescent detection, the sensitivity can be extended below 150 pg by performing longer exposures to the X-ray film and blotting additional low-dilution DNA standards on the membrane. Levels of 10–20 pg have been reported with a 3-hour exposure (Walsh *et al.* 1992).

The slot blot assay is available through two commercial products: QuantiBlot Human DNA Quantification Kit from PE Biosystems (Foster City, CA) and ACES 2.0+ Human DNA Quantification System from Life Technologies (Rockville, MD). Both kits use the same DNA probe from chromosome 17 and are thus useful for determining the level of human DNA present in a sample.

PICOGREEN MICROTITER PLATE ASSAY

As higher throughput methods for DNA determination are being developed, more automated procedures are needed for rapid assessment of extracted DNA quantity prior to DNA amplification. To this end, the Forensic Science Service has developed a PicoGreen assay that is capable of detecting as little as

0.25 ng/mL of double-stranded DNA in a 96-well microtiter plate format (Hopwood *et al.* 1997). PicoGreen is a fluorescent interchelating dye whose fluorescence is greatly enhanced when bound to double-stranded DNA.

To perform this microtiter plate assay, 5 µL of sample are added to 195 µL of a solution containing the PicoGreen dye. Each sample is placed into an individual well on a 96-well plate and then examined with a fluorometer. A 96-well plate containing 80 individual samples and 16 calibration samples can be analyzed in under 30 minutes (Hopwood *et al.* 1997). The DNA samples are quantified against a standard curve. This assay has been demonstrated to be useful for the adjustment of input DNA into the amplification reaction of STR multiplexes (Hopwood *et al.* 1997). It has been automated on a robotic workstation as well. Unfortunately, this assay quantifies all DNA in a sample and is not specific for human DNA.

Another approach to DNA quantification prior to PCR amplification is the use of a single STR locus (Kihlgren *et al.* 1998). Based on the signal intensities resulting from the amplification of a single STR marker, the level of DNA can be adjusted prior to amplifying the multiplex set of DNA markers in order to obtain the optimal results (see Chapters 5 and 6). This method is a functional test because it also monitors the level of PCR inhibitors present in the sample (see Chapter 7). In the end, each of the DNA quantification methods described here has advantages and disadvantages, and could be used depending on the equipment available and the needs of the laboratory.

DNA QUANTITIES USED IN FLUORESCENCE-BASED STR TYPING

PCR amplification is dependent on the quantity of template DNA molecules added to the reaction. Based on the DNA quantification results obtained using either the slot blot procedure or some other test, the extracted DNA for each sample is adjusted to a level that will work optimally in the PCR amplification reaction. Most commercial STR typing kits work best with an input DNA template of around 1 ng.

A quantity of 1 ng of human genomic DNA corresponds to approximately 333 copies of each locus that will be amplified (Focus box 3.1). There are approximately 6 pg (one million one millionth of a gram or 10^{-12} g) of genomic DNA in each cell containing a single diploid copy of the human genome. Thus, a range of typical DNA quantities from 0.1 ng to 25 ng would involve approximately 30–8330 copies of every DNA sequence.

Focus Box 3.1

Calculation of DNA quantities in genomic DNA.

Important values for calculations:

1 bp = 618 g/mol   A: 313 g/mol; T: 304 g/mol; AT base pairs = 617 g/mol
G: 329 g/mol; C: 289 g/mol; GC base pairs = 618 g/mol

1 genome copy = $\sim 3 \times 10^9$ bp = 23 chromosomes (one member of each pair)

1 mole = 6.02×10^{23} molecules

Standard DNA typing protocols with PCR amplification of STR markers typically ask for 1 ng of DNA template. How many actual copies of each STR locus exist in 1 ng?

1 genome copy = $(\sim 3 \times 10^9$ bp$) \times (618$ g/mol/bp$) = 1.85 \times 10^{12}$ g/mol

$= (1.85 \times 10^{12}$ g/mol$) \times (1$ mole$/6.02 \times 10^{23}$ molecules$)$

$= 3.08 \times 10^{-12}$ g = **3.08 pg**

Since a diploid human cell contains two copies of each chromosome, then *each diploid human cell contains ~6 pg genomic DNA*

Therefore 1 ng genomic DNA (1000 pg) = ~333 copies of each locus
(2 per 167 diploid genomes)

REFERENCES AND ADDITIONAL READING

Ahn, S.J., Costa, J. and Emanuel, J.R. (1996) *Nucleic Acids Research*, 24, 2623–2625.

Alvarez Garcia, A., Munoz, I., Pestoni, C., Lareu, M.V., Rodriguez-Calvo, M.S. and Carracedo, A. (1996) *International Journal of Legal Medicine*, 109, 125–129.

Andersen, J. (1998) In Lincoln, P.J. and Thomson, J. (eds) *Methods in Molecular Biology*, Vol. 98: *Forensic DNA Profiling Protocols*, pp. 33–38. Totowa, NJ: Humana Press.

Belgrader, P. and Marino, M.A. (1997) *Laboratory Robotics and Automation*, 9, 3–7.

Benecke, M., Schmitt, C. and Staak, M. (1996) *Proceedings of the First European Symposium on Human Identification*. Madison, Wisconsin: Promega Corporation, p. 148.

Budowle, B., Baechtel, F.S., Comey, C.T., Giusti, A.M. and Klevan, L. (1995) *Electrophoresis* 16, 1559–1567.

Burgoyne, L., Kijas, J., Hallsworth, P. and Turner, J. (1994) *Proceedings of the Fifth International Symposium on Human Identification*. Madison, Wisconsin: Promega Corporation, p. 163.

Burgoyne, L.A. (1996) Solid medium and method for DNA storage. US Patent 5,496,562.

Burgoyne, L.A. (1997) *Proceedings of the Eighth International Symposium on Human Identification*. Madison, Wisconsin: Promega Corporation, p. 153.

Comey, C.T., Koons, B.W., Presley, K.W., Smerick, J.B., Sobieralski, C.A., Stanley, D.M. and Baechtel, F.S. (1994) *Journal of Forensic Sciences*, 39, 1254–1269.

Del Rio, S.A. (1997) *Proceedings of the Eighth International Symposium on Human Identification*. Madison, Wisconsin: Promega Corporation, pp. 64–69.

Del Rio, S.A., Marino, M.A. and Belgrader, P. (1996) *BioTechniques,* 20, 970–974.

Gill, P., Jeffreys, A.J. and Werrett, D.J. (1985) *Nature,* 318, 577–579.

Gill, P., Ivanov, P.L., Kimpton, C., Piercy, R., Benson, N., Tully, G., Evett, I., Hagelberg, E. and Sullivan, K. (1994) *Nature Genetics,* 6, 130–135.

Greenspoon, S.A., Scarpetta, M.A., Drayton, M.L. and Turek, S.A. (1998) *Journal of Forensic Sciences,* 43, 1024–1030.

Herber, B. and Herold, K. (1998) *Journal of Forensic Sciences*, 43, 648–656.

Higuchi, R., von Beroldingen, C.H., Sensabaugh, G.F. and Erlich, H.A. (1988) *Nature,* 332, 543–546.

Hochmeister, M.N. (1998) In Lincoln, P.J. and Thomson, J. (eds) *Methods in Molecular Biology*, Vol. 98: *Forensic DNA Profiling Protocols*, pp. 19–26. Totowa, NJ: Humana Press.

Hochmeister, M.N., Budowle, B., Jung, J., Borer, U.V., Comey, C.T. and Dirnhofer, R. (1991) *International Journal of Legal Medicine,* 104, 229–233.

Hochmeister, M., Rudin, O., Meier, R., Eisenberg, A., Nagy, R., Gehrig, C. and Dirnhofer, R. (1998) *Progress in Forensic Genetics*, 7, 24.

Hopkins, B., Williams, N.J., Webb, M.B.T., Debenham, P.G. and Jeffreys, A.J. (1994) *Journal of Forensic Sciences,* 39, 526–532.

Hopwood, A.J., Mannucci, A. and Sullivan, K.M. (1996) *International Journal of Legal Medicine,* 108, 237–243.

Hopwood, A., Oldroyd, N., Fellows, S., Ward, R., Owen, S.-A. and Sullivan, K. (1997) *BioTechniques*, 23, 18–20.

Kihlgren, A., Beckman, A. and Holgersson, S. (1998) *Progress in Forensic Genetics*, 7, 31–33.

Kobilinsky, L. (1992) *Forensic Science Reviews*, 4, 67–87.

Lee, H.C. (1996) *Proceedings of the Seventh International Symposium on Human Identification*. Madison, Wisconsin: Promega Corporation, pp. 39–45.

Lee, H.C., Gaensslen, R.E., Bigbee, P.D. and Kearney, J.J. (1991) *Journal of Forensic Identification, 41*, 344–356.

Lee, S.B., Ma, M., Worley, J.M., Sprecher, C., Lins, A.M., Schumm, J.W. and Mansfield, E.S. (1994) *Proceedings of the Fifth International Symposium on Human Identification.* Madison, Wisconsin: Promega Corporation, pp. 137–145.

Lorente, J.A., Lorente, M., Lorente, M.J., Alvarez, J.C., Entrala, C., Lopez-Munoz, J. and Villanueva, E. (1998) *Progress in Forensic Genetics*, 7, 114–116.

Miller, S.A., Dykes, D.D. and Polesky, H.F. (1988) *Nucleic Acids Research,* 16, 1215.

Perkin Elmer Corporation (1998) *AmpFlSTR® Profiler Plus™ PCR Amplification Kit User's Manual.* Foster City, CA: Perkin Elmer Corporation.

Pfeiffer, H., Huhne, J., Seitz, B. and Brinkmann, B. (1999) *International Journal of Legal Medicine*, 112, 142–144.

Rudbeck, L. and Dissing, J. (1998) *BioTechniques*, 25, 588–592.

Schmerer, W.M., Hummel, S. and Herrmann, B. (1999) *Electrophoresis*, 20, 1712–1716.

Sweet, D., Lorente, M., Lorente, J.A., Valenzuela, A. and Villanueva, E. (1997). *Journal of Forensic Sciences,* 42, 320–322.

Tahir, M.A., Sovinski, S.M. and Novick, G.E. (1996) *Proceedings of the Seventh International Symposium on Human Identification.* Madison, Wisconsin: Promega Corporation, p. 176.

Vandenberg, N., van Oorschot, R.A.H. and Mitchell, R.J. (1997) *Electrophoresis*, 18, 1624–1626.

Van Oorschot, R.A.H. and Jones, M.K. (1997) *Nature*, 387, 767.

Walsh, P.S., Metzger, D.A. and Higuchi, R. (1991) *BioTechniques*, 10, 506–513.

Walsh, P.S., Varlaro, J. and Reynolds, R. (1992) *Nucleic Acids Research,* 20, 5061–5065.

Waye, J.S., Presley, L.A., Budowle, B., Shutler, G.G. and Fourney, R.M. (1989) *BioTechniques*, 7, 852–855.

Wiegand, P., Bajanowski, T. and Brinkmann, B. (1993) *International Journal of Legal Medicine*, 106, 81–83.

Willard, J.M., Lee, D.A. and Holland, M.M. (1998) *Methods in Molecular Biology*, Vol. 98: *Forensic DNA Profiling Protocols*, pp. 9–18.

Wilson, M.R., Planskey, D., Butler, J., DiZinno, J.A., Replogle, J. and Budowle, B. (1995) *BioTechniques,* 18, 662–669.

Word, C.J. and Gregory, S. (1997) *Proceedings of the Eighth International Symposium on Human Identification.* Madison, Wisconsin: Promega Corporation, p. 143.

CHAPTER 4

THE POLYMERASE CHAIN REACTION (DNA AMPLIFICATION)

Forensic science and DNA typing laboratories have greatly benefited from the discovery of a technique known as the polymerase chain reaction or PCR. First described in 1985 by Kary Mullis and members of the Human Genetics group at the Cetus Corporation (now Roche Molecular Systems), PCR has revolutionized molecular biology with the ability to make millions of copies of a specific sequence of DNA in a matter of only a few hours. The impact of PCR has been such that its inventor, Kary Mullis, received the Nobel Prize in Chemistry in 1993 – less than 10 years after it was first described.

Without the ability to make copies of DNA samples, many forensic samples would be impossible to analyze. DNA from crime scenes is often limited in both quantity and quality and obtaining a cleaner, more concentrated sample is normally out of the question (most perpetrators of crimes are not surprisingly unwilling to donate more evidence material). The PCR DNA amplification technology is well suited to analysis of forensic DNA samples because it is sensitive, rapid, and not limited by the quality of the DNA as the restriction fragment length polymorphism (RFLP) methods are.

POLYMERASE CHAIN REACTION PROCESS

PCR is an enzymatic process in which a specific region of DNA is replicated over and over again to yield many copies of a particular sequence (Saiki *et al.* 1988, Reynolds *et al.* 1991). This molecular 'xeroxing' process involves heating and cooling samples in a precise thermal cycling pattern over ~30 cycles (Figure 4.1). During each cycle, a copy of the target DNA sequence is generated for every molecule containing the target sequence (Figure 4.2). The boundaries of the amplified product are defined by oligonucleotide primers that are complementary to the 3′ ends of the sequence of interest.

Theoretically after 30 cycles approximately a billion copies of the target region on the DNA template have been generated (Table 4.1). This PCR product, sometimes referred to as an 'amplicon', is then in sufficient quantity that it can be easily measured by a variety of techniques, which are discussed in more detail in the technology section.

Figure 4.1

Thermal cycling temperature profile for the polymerase chain reaction. Thermal cycling typically involves three different temperatures that are repeated over and over again 25–35 times. At 94°C, the DNA strands separate, or 'denature'. At 60°C, primers bind or 'anneal' to the DNA template and target the region to be amplified. At 72°C, the DNA polymerase extends the primers by copying the target region using the deoxynucleotide triphosphate building blocks. The entire PCR process is about 3 hours in duration with each cycle taking ~5 minutes on conventional thermal cyclers: 1 minute each at 94°C, 60°C, and 72°C and about 2 minutes ramping between the three temperatures.

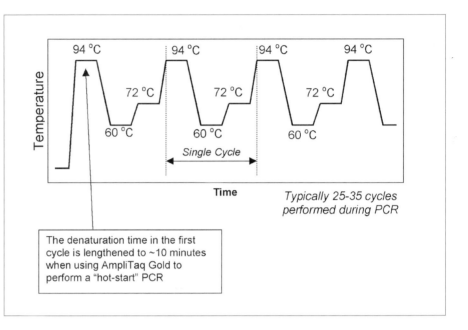

Figure 4.2

DNA amplification process with the polymerase chain reaction. In each cycle, the two DNA template strands are first separated (denatured) by heat. The sample is then cooled to an appropriate temperature to bind (anneal) the oligonucleotide primers. Finally the temperature of the sample is raised to the optimal temperature for the DNA polymerase so that the polymerase can extend the primers to produce a copy of each DNA template strand. For each cycle, the number of DNA molecules (with the sequence between the two PCR primers) doubles.

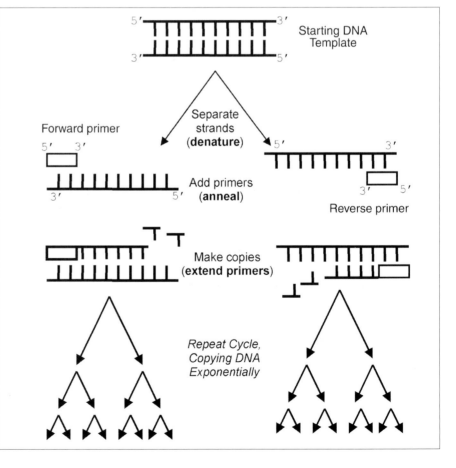

Cycle Number	Number of Double-stranded Target Molecules (Specific PCR Product)
1	0
2	0
3	2
4	4
5	8
6	16
7	32
8	64
9	128
10	256
11	512
12	1 024
13	2 048
14	4 096
15	8 192
16	16 384
17	32 768
18	65 536
19	131 072
20	262 144
21	524 288
22	1 048 576
23	2 097 152
24	4 194 304
25	8 388 608
26	16 777 216
27	33 544 432
28	67 108 864
29	134 217 728
30	268 435 456
31	536 870 912
32	1 073 741 824

Table 4.1

Number of target DNA molecules created by PCR amplification (if reaction is working at 100% efficiency). The target PCR product is not completely defined by the forward and reverse primers until the third cycle.

PCR is commonly performed with a sample volume in the range of 5–100 μL. At such low volumes, evaporation can be a problem and accurate pipetting of the reaction components can become a challenge. On the other hand, larger solution volumes lead to thermal equilibrium issues for the reaction mixture. It takes longer for an external temperature change to be transmitted to the center of a larger solution than a smaller one. Therefore, longer hold times are needed at each temperature, which leads to longer overall thermal cycling times. Most molecular biology protocols for PCR are thus in the 20–50 μL range.

The sample is pipetted into a variety of reaction tubes designed for use in PCR thermal cyclers. The most common tube in use with 20–50 μL PCR reactions is a thin-walled 0.2 mL tube. These 0.2 mL tubes can be purchased as individual tubes with and without attached caps or as 'strip-tubes' with 8 or 12 tubes connected together in a row. In higher throughput laboratories, 96-well or 384-well plates are routinely used for PCR amplification.

PCR has been simplified in recent years by the availability of reagent kits that allow a forensic DNA laboratory to simply add a DNA template to a pre-made PCR mix containing all the necessary components for the amplification reaction. These kits are optimized through extensive research efforts on the part of commercial manufacturers. The kits are typically prepared so that a user adds an aliquot of the kit solution to a particular amount of genomic DNA. The best results with these commercial kits are obtained if the DNA template is added in an amount that corresponds to the concentration range designed for the kit.

PCR COMPONENTS

A PCR reaction is prepared by mixing several individual components and then adding deionized water to achieve the desired volume and concentration of each of the components. Commercial kits with pre-mixed components may also be used for PCR. These kits have greatly simplified the use of PCR in forensic DNA laboratories.

The most important components of a PCR reaction are the two primers, which are short DNA sequences that precede or 'flank' the region to be copied. A primer acts to identify or 'target' the portion of the DNA template to be copied. It is a chemically synthesized oligonucleotide that is added in a high concentration relative to the DNA template to drive the PCR reaction. Some knowledge of the DNA sequence to be copied is required in order to select appropriate primer sequences.

The other components of a PCR reaction consist of template DNA that will be copied, building blocks made up of each of the four nucleotides, and a DNA polymerase that adds the building blocks in the proper order based on the template DNA sequence. The various components and their optimal concentrations are listed in Table 4.2. Thermal stable polymerases that do not fall apart

Table 4.2

Typical components for PCR amplification.

Reagent	Optimal Concentration
Tris–HCl, pH 8.3 (25°C)	10–50 mM
Magnesium chloride	1.2–2.5 mM
Potassium chloride	50 mM
Deoxynucleotide triphosphates (dNTPs)	200 μM each dATP, dTTP, dCTP, dGTP
DNA polymerase, thermal stable[a]	0.5–5 U
Bovine serum albumin (BSA)	100 μg/mL
Primers	0.1–1.0 μM
Template DNA	1–10 ng genomic DNA

[a]*Taq* and *Taq*Gold are the two most common thermal stable polymerases used for PCR.

during the near-boiling denaturation temperature steps have been important to the success of PCR (Saiki *et al.* 1988). The most commonly used thermal stable polymerase is *Taq*, which comes from a bacterium named *Thermus aquaticus* that inhabits hot springs.

When setting up a set of samples that contain the same primers and reaction components, it is common to prepare a 'master mix' that can then be dispensed in equal quantities to each PCR tube. This procedure helps to insure that there is more homogeneity between samples. Also by setting up a larger number of reactions at once, small pipetting volumes can be avoided, which improves the accuracy of adding each component (and thus the reproducibility of one's method). When performing a common test on a number of different samples, the goal should be to examine the variation in the DNA samples *not* variability in the reaction components used and the sample preparation method.

CONTROLS USED TO MONITOR PCR

Controls are used to monitor the effectiveness of the chosen experimental conditions and/or the technique of the experimenter. These controls typically include a 'negative control', which is the entire PCR reaction mixture without any DNA template. The negative control usually contains water or buffer of the same volume as the DNA template, and is useful to assess whether or not any of the PCR components have been contaminated by DNA (e.g. someone else in your lab). An extraction 'blank' is also useful to verify that the reagents used for DNA extraction are free from any extraneous DNA templates (Presley and Budowle 1994).

A 'positive control' is also a valuable indicator of whether or not any of your PCR components have failed or were not added during the reaction setup phase of your experiments. A standard DNA template with good-quality DNA should be used for the positive control. This DNA template should be amplified with the same PCR primers as used on the rest of the samples in the batch that is being amplified. The purpose of a positive control is to ensure confidence that the reaction components and thermal cycling parameters are working for amplifying a specific region of DNA.

STOCHASTIC EFFECTS FROM LOW LEVELS OF DNA TEMPLATE

Forensic DNA specimens often possess low levels of DNA. When amplifying very low levels of DNA template, a phenomenon known as *stochastic fluctuation* can occur. Stochastic effects, which are an unequal sampling of the two alleles present from a heterozygous individual, result when only a few DNA molecules are used to initiate PCR (Walsh *et al.* 1992). PCR reactions involving DNA template levels below approximately 100 pg of DNA, or about 17 diploid copies of genomic DNA, have been shown to exhibit allele dropout (Fregeau and Fourney 1993, Kimpton *et al.* 1994). False homozygosity results if one of the alleles fails to be detected. The problem of stochastic effects can be avoided by adjusting the cycle number of the PCR reaction such that approximately 20 or more copies of target DNA are required to yield a successful typing result (Walsh *et al.* 1992).

THERMAL CYCLING PARAMETERS

A wide range of PCR cycling protocols have been used for various molecular biology applications. To serve as an example of PCR cycling conditions commonly used by forensic DNA laboratories, Table 4.3 contains the parameters used with the GenePrint® STR kits from Promega Corporation and the AmpFlSTR® kits from PE Applied Biosystems. The primary reason that PCR protocols vary is that different primer sequences have different hybridization properties and thus anneal to the DNA template strands at different rates.

THERMAL CYCLERS

The instrument that heats and cools a DNA sample in order to perform the PCR reaction is known as a thermal cycler. Precise and accurate sample heating and cooling is crucial to PCR in order to guarantee consistent results. There are a wide variety of thermal cycler options available from multiple manufacturers. These instruments vary in the number of samples that can be handled at a time,

Table 4.3

Thermal cycling parameters used to amplify short tandem repeat DNA markers with commercially available PCR amplification kits. Cycling parameters differ because reaction components, in particular the primer concentrations and sequences, vary between the different manufacturers' kits.

Step in Protocol	AmpFlSTR® Kits (PE Biosystems)	GenePrint® STR Kits (Promega Corporation)
Initial incubation	95°C for 11 minutes	95°C for 11 minutes
Thermal cycling	28 cycles	30 cycles[a]
Denature	94°C for 1 minute	94°C for 30 seconds (cycle 1–10)
		90°C for 30 seconds (cycle 11–30)
Anneal	59°C for 1 minute	60°C for 30 seconds
Extend	72°C for 1 minute	70°C for 45 seconds
Final extension	60°C for 45 minutes	60°C for 30 minutes
Final soak	25°C (until samples removed)	4°C (until samples removed)

[a]The first ten cycles are run with a denaturation temperature of 94°C and the last 20 cycles are run at 90°C instead. The Promega PowerPlex 1.1 and 2.1 kits also use specific ramp times between the different temperature steps that differ from the conventional 1°C/second.

the size of the sample tube and volume of reagents that can be handled, and the speed at which the temperature can be changed. Prices for thermal cycling devices range from a few thousand dollars to over 10 000 dollars.

Perhaps the most prevalent thermal cycler in forensic DNA laboratories is the GeneAmp® PCR System 9600 from PE Biosystems. The '9600' can heat and cool 96 samples in an 8×12-well microplate format at a rate of approximately 1°C per second. The 9600 uses 0.2 mL tubes with tube caps. These tubes may be attached together in strips of 8 or 12, in which case they are referred to as 'strip-tubes'.

Modern thermal cyclers use a heated lid to keep the PCR reagents from condensing at the top of the tube during the temperature cycling. However, there are some forensic laboratories that still use an older model thermal cycler called the DNA Thermal Cycler '480'. Samples amplified in the 480 require an overlay of a drop of mineral oil on top of the PCR reaction mix in order to prevent evaporation since there is no heated lid.

Thermal cyclers capable of amplifying 384 samples or more at one time are now available. The Dual 384-well GeneAmp® PCR System 9700 can run 768 reactions simultaneously on two 384-well sample blocks. Thermal cyclers capable of high sample volume processing are valuable in production settings but are not widely used in forensic DNA laboratories.

HOT START PCR

Regular DNA polymerases exhibit some activity below their optimal temperature, which for *Taq* polymerase is 72°C. Thus, primers can anneal non-specifically to the template DNA at room temperature when PCR reactions are being set up and non-specific products may result. It is also possible at a low temperature for the primers to bind to each other creating products called 'primer dimers'. These are a particular problem because their small size relative to the PCR products means that they will be preferentially amplified.

Once low-temperature non-specific priming occurs, these undesirable products will be efficiently amplified throughout the remaining PCR cycles. Because the polymerase is busy amplifying these competing products, the target DNA region will be amplified less efficiently. If this happens, you will obtain less of what you are looking for and you may not have enough specific DNA to run your other tests.

Low-temperature mispriming can be avoided by initiating PCR at an elevated temperature, a process usually referred to as 'hot start' PCR. Hot start PCR may be performed by introducing a critical reaction component, such as the polymerase, after the temperature of the sample has been raised above the desired annealing temperature (e.g. 60°C). This minimizes the possibility of mispriming and misextension events by not having the polymerase present during reaction setup. However, this approach is cumbersome and time consuming when working with large numbers of samples. Perhaps a more important disadvantage is the fact that the sample tubes must be opened at the thermal cycler to introduce the essential component, which gives rise to a greater opportunity for cross-contamination between samples. As will be discussed in the next section, a modified form of *Taq* DNA polymerase has been developed that requires thermal activation and thus enables a closed-tube hot start PCR. This enzyme, named AmpliTaq Gold, has greatly benefited the specificity of PCR amplifications.

AMPLITAQ GOLD DNA POLYMERASE

AmpliTaq Gold™ DNA polymerase is a chemically modified enzyme that is rendered inactive until heated (Birch *et al.* 1996). An extended pre-incubation of 95°C, usually for 10 or 11 minutes, is used to activate the AmpliTaq Gold. (The chemical modification involves a derivitization of the epsilon-amino groups of the lysine residues (Innis and Gelfand 1999). At a pH below 7.0 the chemical modification moieties fall off and the activity of the polymerase is restored.) The Tris buffer in the PCR reaction is pH sensitive with temperature variation, and higher temperatures cause the solution pH to go down by approximixately 0.02 pH units with every 1°C (Innis and Gelfand 1990). A Tris buffer with pH 8.3 at 25°C will go down to pH ~6.9 at 95°C. Thus, not only is the template DNA well denatured but the polymerase is activated just when it is needed, and not in a situation where primer dimers and mispriming can occur as easily.

It is important to note that AmpliTaq Gold is not compatible with the pH 9.0 buffers used for regular AmpliTaq DNA polymerases (Moretti *et al.* 1998). This is because the pH does not become low enough to remove the chemical modifications on Taq Gold and thus the enzyme remains inactive. Tris buffers with a pH 8.0 or 8.3 at 25°C work the best with TaqGold.

PCR PRIMER DESIGN

Well-designed primers are probably the most important components of a good PCR reaction. The target region on the DNA template is defined by the position of the primers. PCR yield is directly affected by the annealing characteristics of the primers. For the PCR to work efficiently, the two primers must be specific to the target region, possess similar annealing temperatures, not interact significantly with each other or themselves to form 'primer dimers', and be structurally compatible. Likewise, the sequence region to which the primers bind

Parameter	Optimal Values
Primer length	18–30 bases
Primer T_m (melting temperature)	55–72°C
Percentage GC content	40–60%
No self-complementarity (hairpin structure)	≤3 contiguous bases
No complementarity to other primer (primer dimer)	≤3 contiguous bases (especially at the 3′-ends)
Distance between two primers on target sequence	<2000 bases apart
Unique oligonucleotide sequence	Best match in BLAST[a] search
T_m difference between forward and reverse primers in pair	≤5°C
No long runs with the same base	<4 contiguous bases

Table 4.4

General guidelines for PCR primer design.

[a]BLAST search examines similarity of the primer to other known sequences that may result in multiple binding sites for the primer and thus reduce the efficiency of the PCR amplification reaction. BLAST searches may be conducted via the internet: http://www.ncbi.nlm.nih.gov/BLAST.

must be fairly well conserved because, if the sequence changes from one DNA template to the next, then the primers will not bind appropriately. The general guidelines to optimal PCR primer design are listed in Table 4.4 (see also Dieffenbach *et al.* 1993).

A number of primer design software packages are commercially available including Gene Runner (Hastings Software, Hastings, NY), Primer Express (PE Applied Biosystems, Foster City, CA), and Oligo (Molecular Biology Insights, Cascade, CO). These programs use thermodynamic 'nearest neighbor' calculations to predict annealing temperatures and primer interactions with themselves or other possible primers (Mitsuhashi 1996).

The internet has become a valuable resource for tools that aid primer selection. For example, a primer design program called Primer 3 is available on the World Wide Web through the Whitehead Institute (http://www.genome.wi.mit.edu/cgi-bin/primer/primer3_www.cgi). With Primer 3, the user inputs a DNA sequence and specifies the target region within that sequence to be amplified. Parameters such as PCR product size, primer length and desired annealing temperature may also be specified by the user. The program then ranks the best PCR primer pairs and passes them back to the user over the internet. Primer 3 works well for quickly designing singleplex primer pairs that amplify just one region of DNA at a time.

MULTIPLEX PCR

The polymerase chain reaction permits more than one region to be copied simultaneously by simply adding more than one primer set to the reaction

Figure 4.3

Schematic of multiplex PCR. A multiplex PCR makes use of two or more primer sets within the same reaction mix. Three sets of primers, represented by arrows, are shown here to amplify three different loci on a DNA template (a). The primers were designed so that the PCR products for locus A, locus B, and locus C would be different sizes and therefore resolvable with a size-based separation system (b).

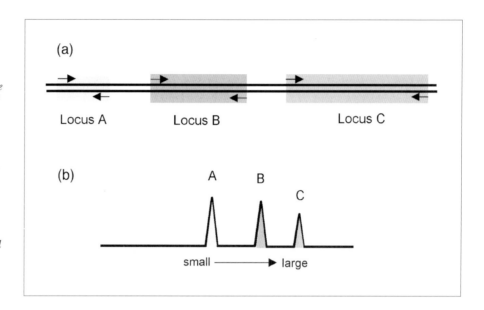

mixture (Edwards and Gibbs 1994). The simultaneous amplification of two or more regions of DNA is commonly known as multiplexing or multiplex PCR (Figure 4.3). For a multiplex reaction to work properly, the primer pairs need to be compatible. In other words, the primer annealing temperatures should be similar and excessive regions of complementarity should be avoided to prevent the formation of primer-dimers that will cause the primers to bind to one another instead of the template DNA. The addition of each new primer in a multiplex PCR reaction exponentially increases the complexity of possible primer interactions.

Each new PCR application is likely to require some degree of optimization in either the reagent components or thermal cycling conditions. Multiplex PCR is no exception. In fact, multiplex PCR optimization is more of a challenge than singleplex reactions because so many primer annealing events must occur simultaneously without interfering with each other. Extensive optimization is normally required to obtain a good balance between the amplicons of the various loci being amplified (Kimpton *et al.* 1996).

The variables that are examined when trying to obtain optimal results for a multiplex PCR amplification include many of the reagents listed in Table 4.2 as well as the thermal cycling temperature profile. Primer sequences and concentrations along with magnesium concentrations are usually the most crucial to multiplex PCR. Extension times during thermal cycling are often increased for multiplex reactions in order to give the polymerase time to fully copy all of the DNA targets. Obtaining successful co-amplification with well-balanced PCR product yields sometimes requires redesign of primers and tedious experiments with adjusting primer concentrations.

Primer design for the short tandem repeat (STR) DNA markers that are discussed in Chapter 5 include some additional challenges. Primers need to be adjusted on the STR markers to achieve good size separation between loci labeled with the same fluorescent dye. In addition, the primers must produce robust amplifications with good peak height balance between loci as well as specific amplification with no non-specific products that might interfere with proper interpretation of a sample's DNA profile. Finally, primers should produce a maximal non-template-dependent A addition to all PCR products (see Chapter 6).

PRECAUTIONS AGAINST CONTAMINATION

The sensitivity of PCR necessitates constant vigilance on the part of the laboratory staff to ensure that contamination does not affect DNA typing results. Contamination of PCR reactions is always a concern because the technique is very sensitive to low amounts of DNA. A scientist setting up the PCR reaction can inadvertently add his or her own DNA to the reaction if he or she is not careful. Likewise, the police officer or crime scene technician collecting the evidence can contaminate the sample if proper care is not taken. For this reason, each piece of evidence should be collected with clean tweezers or handled with disposable gloves that are changed frequently.

To aid discovery of laboratory contamination, everyone in a forensic DNA laboratory is typically genotyped in order to have a record of possible contaminating DNA profiles. Laboratory personnel should be appropriately gowned during interactions with samples prior to PCR amplification. The appropriate covering includes lab coats and gloves as well as facial masks and hairnets to prevent skin cells or hair from falling into the amplification tubes. These precautions are especially critical when working with minute amounts of sample or sample that has been degraded.

Some tips for avoiding contamination with PCR reactions in a laboratory setting include:

- Pre- and post-PCR sample processing areas should be physically separated. Usually a separate room or a containment cabinet is used for setting up the PCR amplification reactions (Perkin Elmer 1998).
- Equipment, such as pipettors, and reagents for setting up PCR should be kept separate from other laboratory supplies, especially those used for analysis of PCR products.
- Disposable gloves should be worn and changed frequently.
- Reactions may also be set up in a laminar flow hood, if available.
- Aerosol-resistant pipet tips should be used and changed on every new sample to prevent cross-contamination during liquid transfers.

- Reagents should be carefully prepared to avoid the presence of any contaminating DNA or nucleases.
- Ultraviolet irradiation of laboratory PCR setup space when the area is not in use, and cleaning workspaces and instruments with isopropanol and/or 10% bleach solutions help to insure that extraneous DNA molecules are destroyed prior to DNA extraction or PCR setup (Kwok and Higuchi 1989, Prince and Andrus 1992).

PCR product carryover results from amplified DNA contaminating a sample that has not yet been amplified. Because the amplified DNA is many times more concentrated than the unamplified DNA template, it will be preferentially copied during PCR and the unamplified sample will be masked. The inadvertent transfer of even a very small volume of a completed PCR amplification to an unamplified DNA sample can result in the amplification and detection of the 'contaminating' sequence. For this reason, the evidence samples are typically processed through a forensic DNA laboratory prior to the suspect reference samples to avoid any possibility of contaminating the evidence with the suspect's amplified DNA.

Pipet tips should never be reused. Even a small drop of PCR product left in a pipet tip contains as many as a billion copies of the amplifiable sequence. By comparison, a nanogram of human genomic DNA contains only about 300 copies of single-copy DNA markers.

ADVANTAGES AND DISADVANTAGES OF PCR WITH FORENSIC SPECIMENS

We conclude this chapter by reviewing the advantages and disadvantages of PCR amplification for forensic DNA analysis. The advantages of PCR amplification for biological evidence include the following:

- Minute amounts of DNA template may be used from as little as a single cell.
- DNA degraded to fragments only a few hundred base pairs in length can serve as effective templates for amplification.
- Large numbers of copies of specific DNA sequences can be amplified simultaneously with multiplex PCR reactions.
- Contaminant DNA, such as fungal and bacterial sources, will not amplify because human-specific primers are used.
- Commercial kits are now available for easy PCR reaction setup and amplification.

There are three potential pitfalls that could be considered disadvantages of PCR:

1   the target DNA template may not amplify due to the presence of PCR inhibitors in the extracted DNA (see Chapter 7 discussion on PCR inhibition);

2   amplification may fail due to sequence changes in the primer binding region of the genomic DNA template (see Chapter 6 discussion on null alleles); and

3   contamination from other human DNA sources besides the forensic evidence at hand or previously amplified DNA samples is possible without careful laboratory technique and validated protocols (see Chapter 7 discussion on PCR contamination and Chapter 14 on laboratory validation).

REFERENCES

Birch, D.E., Kolmodin, L., Wong, J., Zangenberg, G.A., Zoccoli, M.A., McKinney, N., Young, K.K.Y. and Laird, W.J. (1996) *Nature*, 381, 445–446.

Dieffenbach, C.W., Lowe, T.M.J. and Dveksler, G.S. (1993) *PCR Methods and Applications*, 3, S30–S37.

Edwards, M.C. and Gibbs, R.A. (1994). *PCR Methods and Applications*, 3, S65–S75.

Fregeau, C.J. and Fourney, R.M. (1993) *BioTechniques*, 15, 100–119.

Innis, M.A. and Gelfand, D.H. (1990) In Innis, M.A. (ed.) *PCR Protocols: A Guide to Methods and Applications*. San Diego: Academic Press.

Innis, M.A. and Gelfand, D.H. (1999) In Innis, M.A., Gelfand, D.H. and Sninsky, J.J. (eds) *PCR Applications: Protocols for Functional Genomics*. San Diego: Academic Press.

Kimpton, C., Fisher, D., Watson, S., Adams, M., Urquhart, A., Lygo, J. and Gill, P. (1994) *International Journal of Medicine*, 106, 302–311.

Kimpton, C.P., Oldroyd, N.J., Watson, S.K., Frazier, R.R.E., Johnson, P.E., Millican, E.S., Urquhart, A., Sparkes, B.L. and Gill, P. (1996) *Electrophoresis*, 17, 1283–1293.

Kwok, S. and Higuchi, R. (1989) *Nature*, 339, 237–238.

Mitsuhashi, M. (1996) *Journal of Laboratory Analysis*, 10, 285–293.

Moretti, T., Koons, B. and Budowle, B. (1998) *BioTechniques* 25, 716–722.

Perkin Elmer Corporation (1998) *AmpFlSTR® Profiler Plus™ PCR Amplification Kit User's Manual*. Foster City: PE Biosystems.

Presley, L.A. and Budowle, B. (1994) In Griffin, H.G. and Griffin, A.M. (eds) *PCR Technology: Current Innovations*, pp. 259–276. Boca Raton: CRC Press Inc.

Prince, A.M. and Andrus, L. (1992) *BioTechniques*, 12, 358.

Reynolds, R., Sensabaugh, G. and Blake, E. (1991) *Analytical Chemistry*, 63, 1–15.

Saiki, R.K., Gelfand, D.H., Stoffel, S., Scharf, S.J., Higuchi, R., Horn, G.T., Mullis, K.B. and Erlich, H.A. (1988) *Science*, 239, 487–491.

Walsh, P.S., Erlich, H.A. and Higuchi, R. (1992) *PCR Methods and Applications*, 1, 241–250.

CHAPTER 5

COMMONLY USED
SHORT TANDEM REPEAT MARKERS

REPEATED DNA

Eukaryotic genomes are full of repeated DNA sequences. These repeated DNA sequences come in all types of sizes, and are typically designated by the length of the core repeat unit and the number of contiguous repeat units or the overall length of the repeat region. Long repeat units may contain several hundred to several thousand bases in the core repeat.

These regions are often referred to as *satellite* DNA and may be found surrounding the chromosomal centromere. The term satellite arose due to the fact that frequently one or more minor satellite bands were seen in early experiments involving equilibrium density gradient centrifugation (Primrose 1998).

The core repeat unit for a medium-length repeat, sometimes referred to as a *minisatellite* or a VNTR (variant number of tandem repeats), is in the range of approximately 10–100 bases in length. The forensic DNA marker D1S80 is a minisatellite with a 16 bp repeat unit and contains alleles spanning the range of 16–41 repeat units (Kasai *et al.* 1990).

DNA regions with repeat units that are 2–6 bp in length are called *microsatellites*, simple sequence repeats (SSRs), or short tandem repeats (STRs). STRs have become popular DNA repeat markers because they are easily amplified by the polymerase chain reaction (PCR) without problems of differential amplification. This is due to the fact that both alleles from a heterozygous individual are similar in size since the repeat size is small. The number of repeats in STR markers can be highly variable among individuals which makes them effective for human identification purposes.

Literally thousands of polymorphic microsatellites have been identified in human DNA. STR markers are scattered throughout the genome and occur on average every 10 000 nucleotides (Edwards *et al.* 1991). A large number of STR markers have been characterized by academic and commercial laboratories for use in disease gene location studies. For example, the Marshfield Medical Research Foundation in Marshfield, Wisconsin, has gathered genotype data on over 8000 STRs that are scattered across the 23 pairs of human chromosomes for the purpose of developing human genetic maps (Broman *et al.* 1998).

Figure 5.1

Schematic of minisatellite and microsatellite (STR) DNA markers. PCR primers are designed to target invariant flanking sequence regions. The number of tandem repeat units in the repeat regions varies among individuals making them useful markers for human identification.

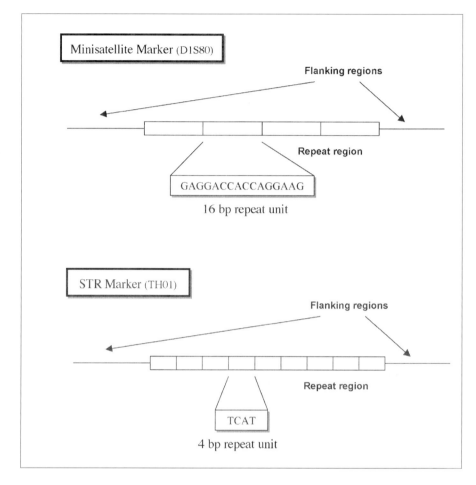

ISOLATION AND TYPES OF STR MARKERS

In order to perform analysis on STR markers, the flanking regions surrounding the repeats must be determined. Once the flanking sequences are known then PCR primers can be designed and the repeat region amplified for analysis. New STR markers are usually identified in one of two ways: (1) searching DNA sequence databases such as GenBank for regions with more than six or so contiguous repeat units (Weber and May 1989); or (2) performing molecular biology isolation methods (Edwards *et al.* 1991).

STR repeat sequences are named by the length of the repeat unit. Dinucleotide repeats have two nucleotides repeated next to each other over and over again. Trinucleotides have three nucleotides in the repeat unit, tetranucleotides have four, pentanucleotides have five, and hexanucleotides have six repeat units in the core repeat. Theoretically, there are 4, 16, 64, 256, 1024, 4096 possible motifs for mono-, di-, tri-, tetra-, penta-, and hexanucleotide

Focus Box 5.1

*List of possible
microsatellite motifs*

Theoretically, there are 4, 16, 64, 256, 1024, 4096 possible motifs for mono-, di-, tri-, tetra-, penta-, and hexanucleotide repeats, respectively. However, because microsatellites are tandemly repeated, some motifs are actually equivalent to others. Two rules can be used to identify whether motif A is equivalent to motif B. Motif A is considered equivalent to motif B when (1) motif A is inversely complementary to motif B, or (2) motif A is different from motif B or the inversely complementary sequence of motif B by frameshift. For example, $(GAAA)_n$ is equivalent to $(AGAA)_n$ or $(AAGA)_n$, to $(AAAG)_n$ or $(TTTC)_n$, to $(TTCT)_n$ or $(TCTT)_n$, or to $(CTTT)_n$. In other words, the eight motifs are equivalent. Note that $(AGAG)_n$ is considered a dinucleotide repeat instead of a tetranucleotide motif (Jin *et al.* 1994).

Because of this equivalence in repeat motif structure, there are only 2, 4, 10, 33, 102, and 350 possible motifs for for mono-, di-, tri-, tetra-, penta-, and hexanucleotide repeats, respectively (see below).

Mononucleotide repeats (2):

A   C

Dinucleotide repeats (4):

AC   AG   AT   CG

Trinucleotide repeats (10):

AAC   AAG   AAT   ACC   ACG   ACT   AGC   AGG   ATC   CCG

Tetranucleotide repeats (33):

AAAC	AAAG	AAAT	AACC	AACG	AACT	AAGC	AAGG	AAGT	AATC
AATG	AATT	ACAG	ACAT	ACCC	ACCG	ACCT	ACGC	ACGG	ACGT
ACTC	ACTG	**AGAT**	AGCC	AGCG	AGCT	AGGC	AGGG	ATCC	ATCG
ATGC	CCCG	CCGG							

AGAT or GATA motif is the most common for STR loci used by forensic scientists

Penta- (102) and hexanucleotide (350) repeats are not shown due to the sheer number of motifs possible.

repeats, respectively (Jin *et al.* 1994). However, because microsatellites are tandemly repeated, some motifs are actually equivalent to others (Focus box 5.1). For reasons that will be discussed below, tetranucleotide repeats have become the most popular STR markers for human identification.

STR sequences not only vary in the length of the repeat unit and the number of repeats, but also in the rigor with which they conform to an incremental repeat pattern. STRs are often divided into several categories based on the repeat pattern. *Simple repeats* contain units of identical length and sequence, *compound repeats* comprise two or more adjacent simple repeats, and *complex repeats* may contain several repeat blocks of variable unit length as well as variable intervening sequences (Urquhart *et al.* 1994). *Complex hypervariable repeats* also exist with numerous non-consensus alleles that differ in both size and sequence, and are therefore challenging to genotype reproducibly (Urquhart *et al.* 1993, Gill *et al.* 1994). This last category of STR markers is not commonly used in forensic DNA typing due to difficulties with allele nomenclature and measurement variability between laboratories.

Not all alleles for a STR locus contain complete repeat units. Even simple repeats can contain non-consensus alleles that fall in between alleles with full repeat units. *Microvariants* are alleles that contain incomplete repeat units. Perhaps the most common example of a microvariant is the allele 9.3 at the TH01 locus, which contains nine tetranucleotide repeats and one incomplete repeat of three nucleotides because the seventh repeat is missing a single adenine out of the normal AATG repeat unit (Puers *et al.* 1993).

DESIRABLE CHARACTERISTICS OF STRs USED IN FORENSIC DNA TYPING

For human identification purposes it is important to have DNA markers that exhibit the highest possible variation or a number of less polymorphic markers that can be combined in order to obtain the ability to discriminate between samples. As will be discussed further in Chapter 7, forensic specimens are often challenging to PCR amplification because the DNA in the samples may be severely degraded (i.e. broken up into small pieces). Mixtures are prevalent as well in some forensic samples, such as those obtained from sexual assault cases containing biological material from both the perpetrator and victim.

The small size of STR alleles (~100–400 bp) compared to minisatellite VNTR alleles (~400–1000 bp) make the STR markers better candidates for use in forensic applications where degraded DNA is common. PCR amplification of degraded DNA samples can be accomplished better with smaller product sizes (see Chapter 7). Allelic dropout of larger alleles in minisatellite markers caused by preferential amplification of the smaller allele is also a significant problem with minisatellites (Tully *et al.* 1993). Furthermore, single base resolution of DNA fragments can be obtained more easily with sizes below 500 bp using denaturing polyacrylamide gel electrophoresis (see Chapter 9). Thus, for both biology and technology reasons the smaller STRs are advantageous to the larger minisatellite VNTRs.

Among the various types of STR systems, tetranucleotide repeats have become more popular than di- or trinucleotides. Penta- and hexanucleotide repeats are less common in the human genome but are being examined by some laboratories (Bacher *et al.* 1999). As will be discussed in Chapter 6, a biological phenomenon known as 'stutter' results when STR alleles are PCR amplified. Stutter products are amplicons that are typically one or more repeat units less in size than the true allele and arise during PCR because of strand slippage (Walsh *et al.* 1996). Depending on the STR locus, stutter products can be as large as 15% of the allele product quantity with tetranucleotide repeats. With di- and trinucleotides, the stutter percentage can be much higher (30% or more), making it difficult to interpret sample mixtures (see Chapter 7). In addition, the four-base spread in alleles with tetranucleotides makes closely spaced heterozygotes easier to resolve with size-based electrophoretic separations (see Chapter 9) compared to alleles that could be two or three bases different in size with dinucleotides and trinucleotide markers, respectively.

Thus, to summarize, the advantages of using tetranucleotide STR loci in forensic DNA typing over VNTR minisatellites or di- and trinucleotide repeat STRs include:

- a narrow allele size range that permits multiplexing;
- a narrow allele size range that reduces allelic dropout from preferential amplification of smaller alleles;
- the capability of generating small PCR product sizes that benefit recovery of information from degraded DNA specimens; and
- reduced stutter product formation compared to dinucleotide repeats that benefit the interpretation of sample mixtures.

In the past decade, a number of tetranucleotide STRs have been explored for application to human identification. The types of STR markers that have been sought out have included short STRs for typing degraded DNA materials, STRs with low stuttering characteristics for analyzing mixtures, and male-specific Y chromosome STRs for analyzing male–female mixtures from sexual crimes (Carracedo and Lareu 1998). The selection criteria for candidate STR loci in human identification applications include the following characteristics (Gill *et al.* 1996, Carracedo and Lareu 1998):

- high discriminating power, usually >0.9, with observed heterozygosity >70%;
- separate chromosomal locations to ensure that closely linked loci are not chosen;
- robustness and reproducibility of results when multiplexed with other markers;
- low stutter characteristics;
- low mutation rate; and
- predicted length of alleles that fall in the range of 90–500 bp with smaller sizes better suited for analysis of degraded DNA samples.

In order to take advantage of the product rule, STR markers used in forensic DNA typing are typically chosen from separate chromosomes to avoid any problems with linkage between the markers.

A COMMON NOMENCLATURE FOR STR ALLELES

To aid in inter-laboratory reproducibility and comparisons of data, a common nomenclature has been developed in the forensic DNA community. DNA results cannot be effectively shared unless all parties are speaking the same language and referring to the same conditions. (It would do little good to describe the recipe for baking a cake in a language that is not understood by both the recipe giver and the chef. For example, if the recipe says to turn the oven on to 450° Fahrenheit and the chef uses 450 Kelvin (~250°F), the results would be vastly different.) Likewise if one laboratory calls a sample 15 repeats at a particular STR locus and the same sample is designated 16 repeats by another laboratory, a match would not be considered, and the samples would be assumed to come from separate sources. As will be discussed in Chapter 16, the advent of national DNA databases with many laboratories worldwide contributing information has made it crucial to have internationally accepted nomenclature for designating STR alleles.

A repeat sequence is named by the structure (base composition) of the core repeat unit and the number of repeat units. However, because DNA has two strands which may be used to designate the repeat unit for a particular STR marker, more than one choice is available and confusion can arise without a standard format. Also, where an individual starts counting the number of repeats can make a difference. With double-stranded DNA sequences being read in the 5′ to 3′ direction (see Chapter 2), the choice of the strand impacts the sequence designation. For example, the 'top' strand for an STR marker may be 5′-. . . (GATA)$_n$ . . . -3′, while the 'bottom' strand for the same sequence would be 5′-. . . (TATC)$_n$ . . . -3′. Depending on the sequence surrounding the repeat region, the core repeat could be shifted relative to the other strand (Figure 5.2).

Recognizing the need for standardization in STR repeat nomenclature, a committee of forensic DNA scientists, known as the DNA Commission of the

Figure 5.2

Example of the DNA sequence in a STR repeat region. Note that using the top strand versus the bottom strand results in different repeat motifs and starting positions. In this example, the top strand has six TCTA repeat units while the bottom strand has six TGAA repeat units. Under ISFH recommendations (Bar et al. 1997), the top strand from GenBank should be used. Thus, this example would be described as having [TCAT] as the repeat motif. Repeat numbering, indicated above and below the sequence, proceeds in the 5′ to 3′ direction as illustrated by the arrows.

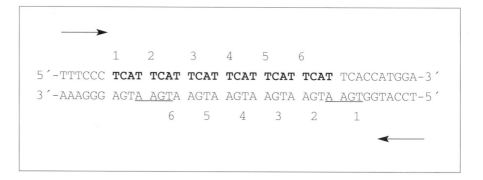

International Society of Forensic Haemogenetics (ISFH), issued guidelines for designating STR alleles in 1994 (Bar *et al.* 1994) and again in 1997 (Bar *et al.* 1997). The ISFH 1994 recommendations focused on allelic ladders and designation of alleles that contain partial repeat sequences. The ISFH 1997 guidelines discuss the sequence and repeat designation of STRs.

When reviewing the STR literature prior to 1997, an individual should keep in mind that repeat nomenclatures often differ from the ISFH 1997 guidelines. This fact can lead to some confusion if one is not careful. For example, early descriptions of the STR locus TH01 by the Forensic Science Service label the repeat TCAT (Kimpton *et al.* 1993), while Caskey and co-workers described the TH01 repeat as AATG (Edwards *et al.* 1991).

The latest ISFH (Bar *et al.* 1997) recommendations are reviewed below.

Choice of the Strand

- For STRs within protein coding regions (as well as in the intron of the genes), the coding strand should be used. This would apply to STRs such as VWA (GenBank: M25716), TPOX (GenBank: M68651), and CSF1PO (GenBank: X14720).

- For repetitive sequences without any connection to protein coding genes like many of the D#S### loci, the sequence originally described in the literature of the first public database entry shall become the standard reference (and strand) for nomenclature. Examples here include D18S51 (GenBank: L18333) and D21S11 (GenBank: M84567).

- If the nomenclature is already established in the forensic field but not in accordance with the aforementioned guideline, the nomenclature shall be maintained to avoid unnecessary confusion. This recommendation applies to the continued use by some laboratories of the 'AATG repeat' strand for the STR marker TH01. The GenBank sequence for TH01 uses the coding strand and therefore contains the complementary 'TCAT repeat' instead.

Choice of the Motif and Allele Designation

- The repeat sequence motif should be defined so that the first 5´-nucleotides that can define a repeat motif are used. For example, 5´-GG TCA TCA TCA TGG-3´ could be seen as having $3 \times TCA$ repeats or $3 \times CAT$ repeats. However, under the recommendations of the ISFH committee, only the first one ($3 \times TCA$) is correct because it defines the first possible repeat motif.

- Designation of incomplete repeat motifs should include the number of complete repeats and, separated by a decimal point, the number of base pairs in the incomplete repeat. Examples of 'microvariants' with incomplete repeat units include allele 9.3 at the TH01 locus. TH01 allele 9.3 contains nine tetranucleotide AATG repeats and one incomplete ATG repeat of three nucleotides (Puers *et al.* 1993). Another microvariant example is allele 22.2 at the FGA locus, which contains 22 tetranucleotide repeats and one incomplete repeat with two nucleotides (Barber *et al.* 1996).

■ Allelic ladders containing sequenced alleles that are named according to the recommendations listed above should be used as a reference for allele designation in unknown samples. Allelic ladders may be commercially obtained or prepared in house and should contain all common alleles.

ALLELIC LADDERS

An allelic ladder is an artificial mixture of the common alleles present in the human population for a particular STR marker (Sajantila *et al.* 1992). They are generated with the same primers as tested samples and thus provide a reference DNA size for each allele included in the ladder. Allelic ladders have been shown to be important for accurate genotype determinations (Smith 1995). These allelic ladders serve as a standard, such as a measuring stick, for each STR locus. They are necessary to adjust for different sizing measurements obtained from different instruments and conditions used by various laboratories.

Allelic ladders are constructed by combining genomic DNA or locus-specific PCR products from multiple individuals in a population which possess alleles that are representative of the variation for the particular STR marker (Sajantila *et al.* 1992, Baechtel *et al.* 1993). The samples are then co-amplified to produce an artificial sample containing the common alleles for the STR marker (Figure 5.3). Allele quantities are balanced by adjusting the input amount of each component so that the alleles are fairly equally represented in the ladder. For example, to produce a ladder containing five alleles with 6, 7, 8, 9, and 10 repeats, individual samples with genotypes of (6,8), (7,10), and (9,9) could be combined. Alternatively, the combination of genotypes could be (6,9), (7,8), and (10,10) or (6,6), (7,7), (8,8), (9,9), and (10,10).

Figure 5.3

Principle of allelic ladder formation. STR alleles from a number of samples are separated on a polyacrylamide gel and compared to one another. Samples representing the common alleles for the locus are combined and re-amplified to generate an allelic ladder. Each allele in the allelic ladder is sequenced since it serves as the reference material for STR genotyping. Allelic ladders are included in commercially available STR kits.

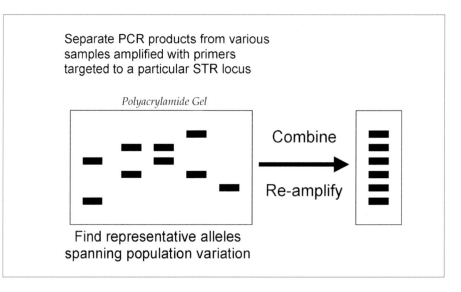

Separate PCR products from various samples amplified with primers targeted to a particular STR locus

Polyacrylamide Gel

Combine

Re-amplify

Find representative alleles spanning population variation

Additional quantities of the same allelic ladder (second- and third-genera-
tion ladders) may be produced by simply diluting the original ladder
1/1000–1/1 000 000 parts with deionized water and then re-amplifying it using
the same PCR primers (Baechtel *et al.* 1993). It is imperative that allelic ladders
be generated with the same PCR primers as used to amplify unknown samples
so that the allele 'rungs' on the ladder will accurately reflect the repeat number
of the unknown sample when the unknown is compared to the ladder. As will be
seen in the next section, commercial manufacturers now provide allelic ladders
in their STR typing kits so that individual laboratories do not have to produce
their own allelic ladders.

CHOICE OF MARKERS USED BY THE FORENSIC DNA TYPING COMMUNITY

For DNA typing markers to be effective across a wide number of jurisdictions, a
common set of standardized markers must be used. The STR loci that are
commonly used today were initially characterized and developed either in the
laboratory of Dr Thomas Caskey at the Baylor College of Medicine (Edwards *et
al.* 1991, Hammond *et al.* 1994) or at the Forensic Science Service in England
(Kimpton *et al.* 1993, Urquhart *et al.* 1994). Promega Corporation (Madison,
WI) commercialized many of the Caskey markers, while PE Applied Biosystems
(Foster City, CA) picked up on the Forensic Science Service (FSS) STR loci as
well as developing some new markers.

Today both PE Applied Biosystems and Promega Corporation have STR kits
that address the needs of the DNA typing community and cover a common set
of STR loci. The availability of STR kits that permit robust multiplex amplification of eight or more STR markers has truly revolutionized forensic DNA.
Matching probabilities that exceed one in a billion are possible in a single
amplification with 1 ng (or less) of DNA sample. Just as impressive is the fact
that results can be obtained today in only a few hours compared to the weeks
that restriction fragment length polymorphism (RFLP) methods took just a few
years ago.

One of the first STR multiplexes to be developed was a quadruplex developed
by the Forensic Science Service comprising the four loci TH01, FES/FPS, VWA,
and F13A1 (Kimpton *et al.* 1994). This so-called 'first-generation multiplex' had
a matching probability of approximately 1 in 10 000. The FSS followed with a
second-generation multiplex (SGM) made up of six polymorphic STRs and a
gender identification marker (Gill *et al.* 1996, Sparkes *et al.* 1996). The six STRs
in SGM are TH01, VWA, FGA, D8S1179, D18S51, and D21S11 and provide a
matching probability of approximately 1 in 50 million. The gender identification marker amelogenin will be described in more detail in Chapter 8.

The first commercially available STR kit capable of multiplex amplification became available from Promega Corporation in 1994 for silver stain analysis. This kit consisted of the STR loci CSF1PO, TPOX, and TH01 and is often referred to as the 'CTT' triplex using the first letter in each locus. The CTT triplex only had a matching probability of ~1 in 500 but was still widely used in the United States as it was the first available STR multiplex kit and could be performed with a fairly low start-up cost.

THE 13 CODIS STR LOCI

In the United States, utilization of STRs initially lagged behind that of Europe, especially the efforts of the Forensic Science Service in the United Kingdom. However, beginning in 1996, the FBI Laboratory sponsored a community-wide forensic science effort to establish core STR loci for inclusion within the national DNA database known as CODIS (Combined DNA Index System). Chapter 16 covers CODIS and DNA databases in more detail. This STR Project beginning in April 1996 and concluding in November 1997 involved 22 DNA typing laboratories and the evaluation of 17 candidate STR loci. The evaluated STR loci were CSF1PO, F13A01, F13B, FES/FPS, FGA, LPL, TH01, TPOX, VWA, D3S1358, D5S818, D7S820, D8S1179, D13S317, D16S539, D18S51, and D21S11.

At the STR Project meeting on 13–14 November 1997, 13 core STR loci were chosen to be the basis of the future CODIS national DNA database (Budowle *et al.* 1998). The 13 CODIS core loci are CSF1PO, FGA, TH01, TPOX, VWA, D3S1358, D5S818, D7S820, D8S1179, D13S317, D16S539, D18S51, and D21S11. Table 5.1 lists the original references in the literature for these 13 STRs. When all 13 CODIS core loci are tested, the average random match probability is rarer than one in a trillion among unrelated individuals (Chakraborty *et al.* 1999).

The three most polymorphic markers are FGA, D18S51, and D21S11, while TPOX shows the least variation between individuals. A summary of information on the 13 STRs is contained in Table 5.2, which describes the chromosomal location, the repeat motif, allele range, and GenBank accession number where the DNA sequence for a reference allele may be found. We have included detailed allele sequence information and PCR product sizes with commercially available STR kits in Appendix I.

Using the previously described classification scheme for categorizing STR repeat motifs (Urquhart *et al.* 1994), the 13 CODIS core STR loci may be divided up into four categories:

1   simple repeats consisting of one repeating sequence: TPOX, CSF1PO, D5S818, D13S317, D16S539;

2   simple repeats with non-consensus alleles: TH01, D18S51, D7S820;

3   compound repeats with non-consensus alleles: VWA, FGA, D3S1358, D8S1179; and

4   complex repeats: D21S11.

Locus Name	Reference
CSF1PO	Hammond, H.A., Jin, L., Zhong, Y., Caskey, C.T. and Chakraborty, R. (1994) Evaluation of 13 short tandem repeat loci for use in personal identification applications. *American Journal of Human Genetics,* 55, 175–189.
FGA	Mills, K.A., Even, D. and Murray, J.C. (1992) Tetranucleotide repeat polymorphism at the human alpha fibrinogen locus (FGA). *Human Molecular Genetics,* 1, 779.
TH01	Polymeropoulos, M.H., Xiao, H., Rath, D.S. and Merril, C.R. (1991) Tetranucleotide repeat polymorphism at the human tyrosine hydroxylase gene (TH). *Nucleic Acids Research,* 19, 3753.
TPOX	Anker, R., Steinbrueck, T. and Donis-Keller, H. (1992) Tetranucleotide repeat polymorphism at the human thyroid peroxidase (hTPO) locus. *Human Molecular Genetics,* 1, 137.
VWA	Kimpton, C.P., Walton, A. and Gill, P. (1992) A further tetranucleotide repeat polymorphism in the vWF gene. *Human Molecular Genetics ,* 1, 287.
D3S1358	Li, H., Schmidt, L., Wei, M.-H., Hustad, T., Lerman, M.I., Zbar, B. and Tory, K. (1993) Three tetranucleotide polymorphisms for loci: D3S1352, D3S1358, D3S1359. *Human Molecular Genetics,* 2, 1327.
D5S818	Cooperative Human Linkage Center GATA3F03.512.
D7S820	Cooperative Human Linkage Center GATA3F01.511.
D8S1179	Cooperative Human Linkage Center GATA7G07.37564.
D13S317	Cooperative Human Linkage Center GATA7G10.415.
D16S539	Cooperative Human Linkage Center GATA11C06.715.
D18S51	Staub, R.E., Speer, M.C., Luo, Y., Rojas, K., Overhauser, J., Otto, L. and Gilliam, T.C. (1993) A microsatellite genetic linkage map of human chromosome 18. *Genomics,* 15, 48–56.
D21S11	Sharma, V. and Litt, M. (1992) Tetranucleotide repeat polymorphism at the D21S11 locus. *Human Molecular Genetics,* 1, 67.
Amelogenin	Sullivan, K.M., Mannucci, A., Kimpton, C.P. and Gill, P. (1993) A rapid and quantitative DNA sex test: fluorescence-based PCR analysis of X-Y homologous gene amelogenin. *BioTechniques,* 15, 637–641.

Cooperative Human Linkage Center information is available via the internet: http://lpg.nci.nih.gov/CHLC/

Table 5.1

Original references describing each of the 13 CODIS STR loci and the gender identification marker amelogenin

Table 5.2

Summary information on the 13 CODIS core STR loci.

Locus Name	Chromosomal Location	Repeat Motif ISFH Format	GenBank Accession[a]	Allele in GenBank	Allele Range[b]	Number of Alleles Seen[c]
CSF1PO	5q33.3–34	TAGA	X14720	12	6–16	15
FGA	4q28	CTTT	M64982	21	15–51.2	69
TH01	11p15.5	TCAT	D00269	9	3–14	20
TPOX	2p23–pter	GAAT	M68651	11	6–13	10
VWA	12p12–pter	[TCTG][TCTA]	M25858	18	10–24	28
D3S1358	3p	[TCTG][TCTA]	Not available[d]	—	9–20	20
D5S818	5q21–31	AGAT	G08446	11	7–16	10
D7S820	7q11.21–22	GATA	G08616	12	6–15	22
D8S1179	8	[TCTA][TCTG]	G08710	12	8–19	13
D13S317	13q22–31	TATC	G09017	13	5–15	14
D16S539	16q24–qter	GATA	G07925	11	5–15	10
D18S51	18q21.3	AGAA	L18333	13	7–27	43
D21S11	21q21	Complex [TCTA][TCTG]	AP000433	29	24–38	70

[a] GenBank sequence information for a particular STR locus may be accessed on the World Wide Web (http://www2.ncbi.nlm.nih.gov/cgi-bin/genbank) by entering the accession number shown here.
[b] Numbers in this column refer to the number of repeat units present in the alleles. More detail on alleles that have been observed and their PCR products with commercially available STR kits may be found in Appendix I.
[c] See Appendix I.
[d] D3S1358 sequence information may be found on the STRBase web site (http://www.cstl.nist.gov/biotech/strbase), since it is presently not available through GenBank.

COMMERCIALLY AVAILABLE STR KITS

A number of kits are available for single or multiplex PCR amplification of STR markers used in DNA typing. Two primary vendors for STR kits used by the forensic DNA community exist: Promega Corporation located in Madison, WI, and PE Applied Biosystems located in Foster City, CA. These companies have expended a great deal of effort in the past few years to bring new STR markers to forensic scientists.

The technology has evolved quickly in the late 1990s for more sensitive, rapid, and accurate measurements of STR alleles. At the same time, the number of STRs that can be simultaneously amplified has increased from three or four with silver-stained systems to over ten STRs using multiple-color fluorescent tags (see Chapter 10). A list of commercially available STR multiplexes and when they were released as products is shown in Table 5.3.

Table 5.3

Information on commercially available STR multiplexes (fluorescently labeled).

Name	Source	Release Date	STR Loci Included	Power of Discrimination[a]
TH01, TPOX, CSF1PO monoplexes (silver stain)	Promega	Feb 1993	TH01, TPOX, CSF1PO	1:410
AmpFlSTR® Blue	PE Applied Biosystems	Oct 1996	D3S1358, VWA, FGA	1:5000
AmpFlSTR® Green I	PE Applied Biosystems	Jan 1997	Amelogenin, TH01, TPOX, CSF1PO	1:410
CTTv	Promega	Jan 1997	CSF1PO, TPOX, TH01, VWA (vWF)	1:6600
FFFL	Promega	Jan 1997	F13A1, FES/FPS, F13B, LPL	1:1500
GammaSTR	Promega	Jan 1997	D16S539, D13S317, D7S820, D5S818	$1:1.8 \times 10^4$
PowerPlex™ (version 1.1 and 1.2 later)	Promega	Jan 1997 Sept 1998	CSF1PO, TPOX, TH01, VWA, D16S539, D13S317, D7S820, D5S818	$1:1.2 \times 10^8$
AmpFlSTR® Profiler	PE Applied Biosystems	May 1997	D3S1358, VWA, FGA, Amelogenin, TH01, TPOX, CSF1PO, D5S818, D13S317, D7S820	$1:3.6 \times 10^9$
AmpFlSTR® Profiler Plus	PE Applied Biosystems	Dec 1997	D3S1358, VWA, FGA, Amelogenin, D8S1179, D21S11, D18S51, D5S818, D13S317, D7S820	$1:9.6 \times 10^{10}$
AmpFlSTR® COfiler	PE Applied Biosystems	May 1998	D3S1358, D16S539, Amelogenin, TH01, TPOX, CSF1PO, D7S820	$1:8.4 \times 10^5$
AmpFlSTR® SGM Plus	PE Applied Biosystems	Feb 1999	D3S1358, VWA, D16S539, D2S1338, Amelogenin, D8S1179, D21S11, D18S51, D19S433, TH01, FGA	$1:3.3 \times 10^{12}$
PowerPlex™ 2.1	Promega	June 1999	D3S1358, TH01, D21S11, D18S51, VWA, D8S1179, TPOX, FGA, Penta E	$1:8.5 \times 10^{10}$
PowerPlex™ 16	Promega	2000	CSF1PO, FGA, TPOX, TH01, VWA, D3S1358, D5S818, D7S820, D8S1179, D13S317, D16S539, D18S51, D21S11, Penta D, Penta E, amelogenin	$1:1.8 \times 10^{17}$

[a]Caucasian population (rounded to two significant figures).

The adoption of the 13 core loci for CODIS in the United States has led to development of STR multiplexes that cover these markers. As of early 2000, two PCR reactions are required to obtain information from all the 13 STRs: either PowerPlex™ 1.1 and PowerPlex™ 2.1 or Profiler Plus™ and COfiler™. The STR markers amplified in each kit are described in Figure 5.4. As an internal check to reduce the possibility of mixing up samples, both manufacturers have included overlapping loci in their kits that should produce concordant data between samples amplified from the same biological material. The Profiler Plus™ and COfiler™ kits have the loci D3S1358 and D7S820 in common, while the PowerPlex™ 1.1 and PowerPlex™ 2.1 have the loci TH01, TPOX, and VWA in common (Figure 5.4).

Figure 5.4

Commercially available STR kit solutions for the 13 CODIS core loci. Currently two PCR reactions are required, either Profiler Plus™ and COfiler™ or PowerPlex™ 1.1 and 2.1. General size ranges and dye-labeling strategies are indicated. Loci with darker color boxes around them are present in both kits and serve to confirm that no mixing of samples occurred during sample preparation.

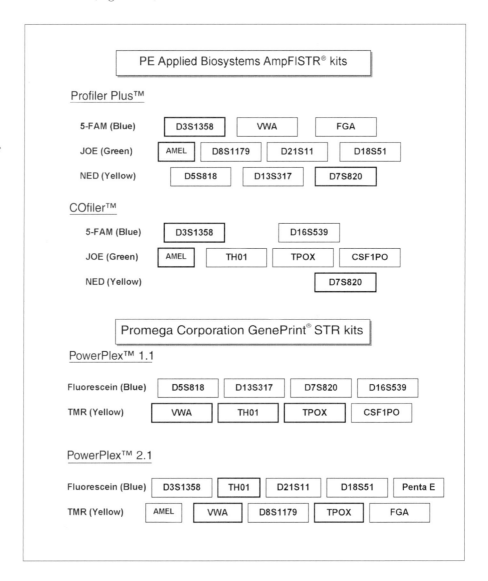

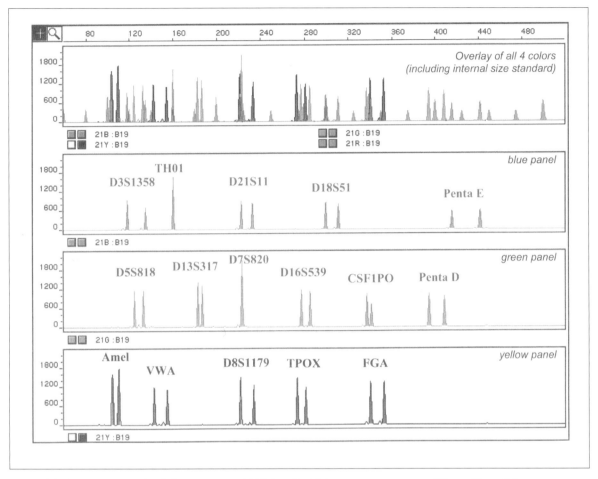

Work is in progress at both Promega and PE Applied Biosystems to co-amplify all 13 STRs in a single PCR reaction along with the amelogenin sex-typing marker and two additional STR loci. The result from a prototype of PowerPlex™ 16.2 may be seen in Figure 5.5.

As will be discussed in the Technology section, two primary methods are used in modern forensic DNA laboratories to separate and detect fluorescently labeled STR alleles. The PowerPlex reactions have been balanced to work with the Hitachi FMBIO II scanner (see Chapter 12), while the Profiler Plus and COfiler reaction are typically analyzed on an ABI Prism 310 Genetic Analyzer capillary electrophoresis system (see Chapter 11) or an ABI Prism 377 slab gel system.

Commercial manufacturers of STR kits have spent a great deal of research effort defining which markers would be included in each kit as well as verifying if primer pairs are compatible and will work well in combination with each other during multiplex PCR conditions. These developed primers are considered proprietary and have not been revealed at this time. Commercially

Figure 5.5

PowerPlex™ 16.2 prototype. Figure courtesy of Randy Nagy, Promega Corporation.

available kits quickly dictate which STRs will be used by the vast majority of forensic laboratories.

Most laboratories do not have the time or resources to design primers, optimize PCR multiplexes, and quality control primer synthesis. The convenience of using ready-made kits is also augmented by the fact that widely used primer sets and conditions allow improved opportunities for sharing data between laboratories without fear of possible null alleles (see Chapter 6). Available STR multiplex sets vary based on which STR loci are included, the fluorescent dye combinations, the DNA strand that is labeled, allelic ladders present in kits, and most importantly, the primer sequences utilized for PCR amplification.

COMMERCIAL ALLELIC LADDERS

Each manufacturer of STR kits provides allelic ladders that may be used for accurate genotyping. It is important to note that kits from Promega Corporation and PE Applied Biosystems for comparable STR markers often contain different alleles in their allelic ladders. For example, the PowerPlex™ 1.1 kit from Promega contains alleles 7–15 in its D5S818 allelic ladder, while the Profiler Plus™ kit from PE Applied Biosystems contains alleles 7–16 in its D5S818 allelic ladder. By having the allele present in the ladder, a laboratory can be more confident of a call from an unknown sample that is being analyzed. In the D5S818 example listed here, one would be more confident typing an observed allele 16 when using the PE Applied Biosystems kit than the Promega kit because the D5S818 allelic ladder has an allele 16 in the ABI kit. The alleles present in the two sources of commercially available multiplex STR kits are reviewed and contrasted in Table 5.4.

Some of the more recent kits come with an amazing number of alleles in their ladders. For example, the SGM Plus™ kit from PE Applied Biosystems contains 159 alleles (Figure 5.6). Putting together and mass-producing such a large set of alleles is an impressive feat. The Promega PowerPlex™ 16.2 kit will have over 200 alleles in its allelic ladders.

DETAILS ON ALLELES PRESENT IN THE 13 CODIS STR LOCI

Table 5.4 (facing)

Comparison of represented alleles in commercially available STR allelic ladders.

Each of the 13 core STR loci has unique characteristics, either in terms of the number of alleles present, the type of repeat sequence, or the kinds of microvariants that have been observed. This section reviews some of the basic details on each of the 13 core STR loci. We have included in Appendix I a detailed summary of the alleles that have been reported in the literature for the

CSF1PO

PPlex 1.1	COfiler
6	6
7	7
8	8
9	9
10	10
11	11
12	12
13	13
14	14
15	15
10 alleles	**10 alleles**

TPOX

PPlex 1.1	COfiler
6	6
7	7
8	8
9	9
10	10
11	11
12	12
13	13
8 alleles	**8 alleles**

D3S1358

PPlex 2.1	ProPlus
12	12
13	13
14	14
15	15
16	16
17	17
18	18
19	19
20	
9 alleles	**8 alleles**

D5S818

PPlex 1.1	ProPlus
7	7
8	8
9	9
10	10
11	11
12	12
13	13
14	14
15	15
	16
9 alleles	**10 alleles**

FGA

PPlex 2.1	ProPlus	SGM Plus
17	17	17
18	18	18
19	19	19
20	20	20
21	21	21
22	22	22
23	23	23
24	24	24
25	25	25
26	26	26
	26.2	26.2
27	27	27
28	28	28
29	29	29
30	30	30
		30.2
31.2		31.2
		32.2
		33.2
		42.2
43.2		43.2
44.2		44.2
45.2		45.2
46.2		46.2
		47.2
		48.2
		50.2
		51.2
19 alleles	**14 alleles**	**28 alleles**

TH01

PPlex 1.1	COfiler	SGM Plus
		4
5	5	5
6	6	6
7	7	7
8	8	8
9	9	9
	9.3	9.3
10	10	10
11		11
		13
7 alleles	**7 alleles**	**10 alleles**

D7S820

PPlex 1.1	ProPlus
6	6
7	7
8	8
9	9
10	10
11	11
12	12
13	13
14	14
	15
9 alleles	**10 alleles**

D18S51

PPlex 2.1	ProPlus	SGM Plus
		7
8		8
9	9	9
10	10	10
10.2	10.2	10.2
11	11	11
12	12	12
13	13	13
13.2	13.2	13.2
14	14	14
	14.2	14.2
15	15	15
16	16	16
17	17	17
18	18	18
19	19	19
20	20	20
21	21	21
22	22	22
23	23	23
24	24	24
25	25	25
26	26	26
27		27
22 alleles	**21 alleles**	**23 alleles**

VWA

PPlex 2.1	ProPlus	SGM Plus
10		
11	11	11
12	12	12
13	13	13
14	14	14
15	15	15
16	16	16
17	17	17
18	18	18
19	19	19
20	20	20
21	21	21
22		22
		23
		24
13 alleles	**11 alleles**	**14 alleles**

D13S317

PPlex 1.1	ProPlus
7	
8	8
9	9
10	10
11	11
12	12
13	13
14	14
15	15
9 alleles	**8 alleles**

D21S11

PPlex 2.1	ProPlus	SGM Plus
24		24
24.2	24.2	24.2
25	25	25
25.2		
26	26	26
27	27	27
28	28	28
28.2	28.2	28.2
29	29	29
29.2	29.2	29.2
30	30	30
30.2	30.2	30.2
31	31	31
31.2	31.2	31.2
32	32	32
32.2	32.2	32.2
33	33	33
33.2	33.2	33.2
34	34	34
34.2	34.2	34.2
35	35	35
35.2	35.2	35.2
36	36	36
37		37
38	38	38
25 alleles	**22 alleles**	**24 alleles**

D8S1179

PPlex 2.1	ProPlus
7	
8	8
9	9
10	10
11	11
12	12
13	13
14	14
15	15
16	16
17	17
18	18
	19
12 alleles	**12 alleles**

D16S539

PPlex 1.1	COfiler
5	5
6	6
7	7
8	8
9	9
10	10
11	11
12	12
13	13
14	14
15	15
9 alleles	**9 alleles**

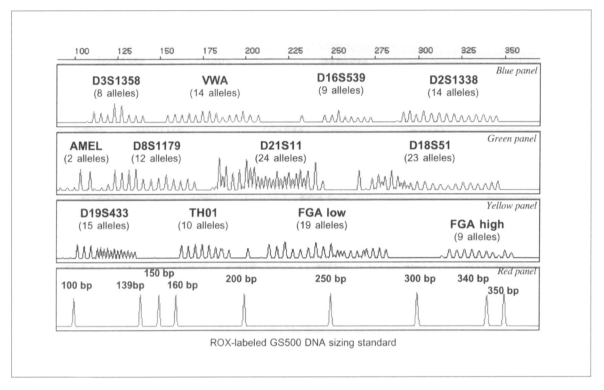

Figure 5.6
AmpFISTR® SGM Plus™
allelic ladders (PE
Applied Biosystems).
A total of 159 alleles are
included in this set of
allelic ladders used for
genotyping a multiplex
PCR reaction involving
ten STR loci and the
amelogenin sex-typing
test.

13 core STR loci along with their expected sizes using the various kits that are available from Promega or PE Applied Biosystems. The size difference in the PCR products produced by the different STR kits is important because a large difference is more likely to lead to null alleles when comparing results between two kits (see Chapter 6).

CSF1PO is a simple tetranucleotide repeat found in the c-*fms* proto-oncogene for the CSF-1 receptor on the long arm of chromosome 5. Common alleles contain an AGAT core repeat and range in size from 6 to 15 repeats. PCR products from Promega's PowerPlex™ 1.1 STR kit are 11 bp larger than those generated with PE Biosystems kits for equivalent alleles.

FGA is a compound tetranucleotide repeat found in the third intron of the human alpha fibrinogen locus on the long arm of chromosome 4. FGA has also been referred to in the literature as FIBRA or HUMFIBRA. The locus contains a CTTT repeat flanked on either side by degenerate repeats. The spread in allele sizes is larger for FGA than any of the other core STR loci. Reported alleles range in size from 15 repeats to 51.2 repeats, spanning over 35 repeats! A 2 bp deletion, from the loss of a CT, in the region just prior to the core repeat motif is responsible for the x.2 microvariant alleles that are very prevalent in this STR system. PCR products from Promega's PowerPlex™ 2.1 STR kit are 112 bp larger than those generated with PE Biosystems kits for equivalent alleles. The size difference between the two primer sets is the largest of any of the 13 core loci.

TH01 is a simple tetranucleotide repeat found in intron 1 of the tyrosine hydroxylase gene on the short arm of chromosome 11. The locus name arises from the initials for tyrosine hydroxylase and intron 1 (i.e. 01). The locus is sometimes incorrectly referred to as 'THO1' with an 'O' instead of a 'zero'. In the literature, TH01 has also been referred to as TC11 and HUMTH01.

TH01 has a simple tetranucleotide sequence with a repeat motif of TCTA on the upper strand in the GenBank reference sequence. The repeat motif is commonly referenced as AATG, which is correct for the complementary (bottom) strand to the GenBank reference sequence. A common microvariant allele that exists in Caucasians contains a single base deletion from allele 10 and is designated allele 9.3. Other x.3 alleles have been reported such as 8.3, 10.3, and 13.3 (Griffiths *et al.* 1998). TH01 has probably been the most studied of the 13 core loci with well over 400 population studies reported in the literature using this DNA marker. PCR products from Promega's PowerPlex™ 1.1 STR kit are 11 bp larger than those generated with PE Biosystems kits for equivalent alleles. The PowerPlex™ 1.1 and PowerPlex™ 2.1 STR kits produce amplicons that are 19 bp different in size.

TPOX is a simple tetranucleotide repeat found in intron 10 of the human thyroid peroxidase gene on the short arm of chromosome 2. TPOX has also been referred to in the literature as hTPO. This STR locus possesses a simple AATG repeat and is the least polymorphic of the 13 core loci. PCR products from Promega's PowerPlex™ 1.1 STR kit are 7 bp larger than those generated with PE Biosystems kits for equivalent alleles. The PowerPlex™ 1.1 and PowerPlex™ 2.1 STR kits produce amplicons that are 38 bp different in size.

VWA is a compound tetranucleotide repeat found in intron 40 of the von Willebrand Factor gene on the short arm of chromosome 12. VWA has also been referred to in the literature as vWF and vWA. It possesses a TCTA repeat interspersed with a TCTG repeat. The VWA marker targeted by STR multiplex kits is only one of three repeats present in that region of the von Willebrand Factor. The other two have not been found to be as polymorphic (Kimpton *et al.* 1992). PCR products from Promega's PowerPlex™ 1.1 STR kit are 29 bp smaller than those generated with PE Biosystems kits for equivalent alleles. The PowerPlex™ 1.1 and PowerPlex™ 2.1 STR kits overlap at three STRs including VWA. Both kits produce amplicons that are equivalent in size for VWA alleles.

D3S1358 is a compound tetranucleotide repeat found on the short arm of chromosome 3. This locus possesses both AGAT and AGAC repeat units (Mornhinweg *et al.* 1998). The D3 marker is common to PE Biosystems STR multiplexes Profiler, Profiler Plus, COfiler, and SGM Plus. PCR products from Promega's PowerPlex™ 2.1 STR kit are 2 bp larger than those generated with PE Biosystems kits for equivalent alleles.

D5S818 is a simple tetranucleotide repeat found on the long arm of chromosome 5. The locus possesses AGAT repeat units with alleles ranging in size from 7 to 16 repeats. In both Promega and PE Biosystems STR kits, D5S818 is one of the smaller sized loci and as such should appear more than some of the other loci in degraded DNA samples. Few, if any, microvariants have been reported at this STR marker. PCR products from Promega's PowerPlex™ 1.1 STR kit are 15 bp smaller than those generated with PE Biosystems kits for equivalent alleles.

D7S820 is a simple tetranucleotide repeat found on the long arm of chromosome 7. The locus possesses primarily a GATA repeat. However, a number of new D7 microvariant alleles have been reported recently indicating that a partial repeat may exist in some populations (see Appendix I). PCR products from Promega's PowerPlex™ 1.1 STR kit are 42 bp smaller than those generated with PE Biosystems kits for equivalent alleles.

D8S1179 is a compound tetranucleotide repeat found on chromosome 8. In early publications by the Forensic Science Service, D8S1179 is listed as D6S502 because of a labeling error in the Cooperative Human Linkage Center database from which this STR was chosen (Oldroyd *et al.* 1995, Barber and Parkin 1996). The locus consists primarily of alleles containing TCTA, although a TCTG repeat unit enters the motif for all alleles larger than 13 repeats, usually at the second or third position from the 5′-end of the repeat region (Barber and Parkin 1996). PCR products from Promega's PowerPlex™ 2.1 STR kit are 80 bp larger than those generated with PE Biosystems kits for equivalent alleles.

D13S317 is a simple GATA tetranucleotide repeat found on the long arm of chromosome 13. Common alleles contain between 7 and 15 repeat units. PCR products from Promega's PowerPlex™ 1.1 STR kit are 36 bp smaller than those generated with PE Biosystems kits for equivalent alleles.

D16S539 is a simple tetranucleotide repeat found on the long arm of chromosome 16. Nine common alleles exist that possess a core repeat unit of AGAT. These include an allele with five repeats and consecutive alleles ranging from 8 to 15 repeat units in length. PCR products from Promega STR kits are 31 bp larger than those generated with PE Biosystems kits for equivalent alleles.

D18S51 is a simple tetranucleotide repeat found on the long arm of chromosome 18. It has a repeat motif of AGAA. A number of x.2 allele variants exist due to a 2 bp deletion from a loss of AG in the 3′-flanking region (Barber and Parkin 1996). More than 40 alleles have been reported for D18S51 making it one of the more polymorphic of the 13 core loci. PCR products from Promega's PowerPlex™ 2.1 STR kit are 22 bp larger than those generated with PE Biosystems kits for equivalent alleles.

D21S11 is a complex tetranucleotide repeat found on chromosome 21. A variable number of TCTA and TCTG repeat blocks surround a constant 43 bp section made up of the sequence {[TCTA]₃ TA [TCTA]₃ TCA [TCTA]₂ TCCA TA}. The x.2 microvariant alleles arise primarily from a 2 bp (TA) insertion on the 3´-end of the repeat region (Brinkmann *et al.* 1996). PCR products from Promega's PowerPlex™ 2.1 STR kit are 17 bp larger than those generated with PE Biosystems kits for equivalent alleles.

Early papers in the literature by the Forensic Science Service had alleles named based on the dinucleotide subunit CV, where the V represents either an A, T, or G (Urquhart *et al.* 1994), while other authors adopted a different allele naming scheme based on the primary tetranucleotide repeat (Moller *et al.* 1994). As outlined in the European DNA Profiling Group interlaboratory study on D21S11 (Gill *et al.* 1997), a simple formula can be used to convert the Urquhart (U) designation into the Moller (M) equivalent:

$$M = \frac{1}{2} \times (U - 5) \tag{5.1}$$

Today most laboratories use the Moller allele notation since it fits the ISFH allele designation recommendation (Bar *et al.* 1997).

D21S11 is far more polymorphic than can be easily detected with sized-based length separations. A careful search of the literature has revealed more than 70 reported alleles, many of which are the same length (see Appendix I). Fine differences in the D21S11 allele structures can only be determined by DNA sequencing since so many of the alleles have the same length but different internal sequence structure because some of the repeat units are switched around. For example, there are four different alleles designated as 30 repeats.

The three most polymorphic of the 13 loci are D21S11, FGA, and D18S51. These loci contain numerous microvariant alleles that are being uncovered as more and more samples are examined around the world.

ADDITIONAL STR LOCI COMMONLY USED

The 13 core loci used within the United States for CODIS are effective DNA markers for human identification and will most likely continue to be used for some time. However, these 13 markers are by no means the only STRs that have been evaluated or used by forensic laboratories around the world. Dozens of other markers have been used, some quite extensively.

PE Applied Biosystems has created the AmpFlSTR® SGM Plus™ kit that co-amplifies ten STR loci including two new STRs: D19S433 and D2S1338. With the adoption of the SGM Plus kit by the Forensic Science Service and much of Europe, the amount of population data on the STR loci D19S433 and D2S1338 will continue to grow. Likewise, Promega Corporation has included two penta-nucleotide STR loci, Penta E and Penta D, in their GenePrint® PowerPlex™ 2.1 and PowerPlex™ 16 kits. Because these markers are included in the STR multiplexes in conjunction with the 13 core loci for developing DNA databases, they will become more prevalent as the number of samples in the databases grow.

Promega also has a multiplex commonly referred to as FFFL that is used in many laboratories and amplifies the four STRs F13A01, F13B, FES/FPS, and LPL. Table 5.5 includes a listing of these markers as well as many others that have appeared in the literature along with useful information such as the

Locus Name	Chromosomal Location	GenBank Accession	Repeat ISFH Format	Allele Range	Amplicon Size Range (bp)	Reference
ARA	Xcen–q13	M21748	CAG	14–32	255–315	Hammond *et al.* (1994)
APOAI1	11q23–qter	J00048	AAAG	Complex	263–291	Dupuy and Olaisen (1997)
ACTBP2	5/6	V00481	AAAG	Complex	233–333	Dupuy and Olaisen (1997)
CD4	12p12–pter	M86525	TTTTC	6–16	125–175	Hammond *et al.* (1994)
CYAR04	15q21.1	M30798	AAAT	5–12	173–201	Hammond *et al.* (1994)
F13A01	6p24.3–25.1	M21986	GAAA	3.2–16	281–331	Hammond *et al.* (1994)
F13B	1q31–q32.1	M64554	TTTA	6–12	169–193	Promega
FABP	4q28–31	M18079	ATT	10–15	199–220	Hammond *et al.* (1994)
FES/FPS	15q25–qter	X06292	ATTT	7–14	222–250	Hammond *et al.* (1994)
HPRTB	Xq26.1	M26434	TCTA	6–17	259–303	Hammond *et al.* (1994)
LPL	8p22	D83550	TTTA	7–14	105–133	Promega
Penta D	21q	Not present	AAAGA	2.2–17	376–441	**PowerPlex 16**
Penta E	15q	Not present	AAAGA	5–24	379–474	**PowerPlex 2.1**
PLA2A1	12q23–qter	M22970	AAT		118–139	Hammond *et al.* (1994)
RENA4	1q32	M10151	ACAG		255–275	Hammond *et al.* (1994)
D1S1656	1pter–qter	G07820	(TAGA) (TAGG)	9–19.3	125–168	Wiegand *et al.* (1999)
D2S1242	2pter–qter	L17825	(GAAA) (GAAG)	10–18	141–175	Reichenpfader *et al.* (1999)
D2S1338	2q35–37.1	G08202	(TGCC) (TTCC)	15–28	289–341	**SGM Plus**
D3S1359	3p	AA306290	TCTA	11–25.3	196–255	Poltl *et al.* (1998)
D3S1744	3q24	G08246	GATA	14–22	150–182	Lifecodes
D6S477	6pter–qter	G08543	TCTA	13.2–22	206–240	Carracedo and Lareu (1998)
D7S809	7pter–qter	X73290	(AGGA) (AGGC)	9 alleles	241–289	Tamaki *et al.* (1996)
D8S347	8q22.3–24.3	L12268	AGAT	16–28	340–388	Poltl *et al.* (1997)
D8S639	8p21–p11	L24797	(AGAT) (AGGT)	20–33.3	316–371	Seidl *et al.* (1999)
D9S302	9q31–33	G08746	ATCT	17 alleles	255–353	Carracedo and Lareu (1998)
D10S2325	10pter–qter	G08790	TCTTA	6–17	113–168	Wiegand *et al.* (1999)
D11S488	11q24.1–25	L04732	(AAAG) (GAAG)	26–41	242–302	Seidl *et al.* (1999)
D11S554	11p11.2–12	M87277	AAAG	Complex	176–286	Dupuy and Olaisen (1997)
D12S391	12	G08921	(AGAT) (AGAC)	15–26	209–253	Lareu *et al.* (1996)
D12S1090	12q12	Not found	GATA	9–33	212–306	Lifecodes
D18S535	18pter–qter	G07985	GATA	9–16	130–158	Wiegand *et al.* (1999)
D18S849	18q12–q21	G07992	GATA	9–20	93–133	Lifecodes
D19S433	19q12–13.1	G08036	AAGG	9–17.2	106–140	**SGM Plus**
D20S161	20pter–qter	L16405	TAGA	14–22	156–187	Hou *et al.* (1999)
D22S683	22pter–qter	G08086	(TA) (TATC)	12–21.2	168–206	Carracedo and Lareu (1998)
DXS6807	Xpter–p22.2	G09662	GATA	11–17	251–275	Edelmann and Szibor (1999)

GenBank accession number, references, and size ranges with a reported set of PCR primers. In particular, the Y chromosome STRs are becoming increasingly popular due to their ability to aid sexual assault investigations (see Chapter 8).

STRBASE: A DYNAMIC SOURCE OF INFORMATION ON STR MARKERS

The rapid growth of the human identification applications for STR loci insures that static written materials, such as this book, will quickly become out of date. New alleles are constantly being discovered (including 'off-ladder' microvariant alleles), additional STR markers are being developed, and population data increase with each month of published journals. Indeed, a growing list of publications describing the application of STR loci to forensic DNA typing has exceeded 1000 references.

The growth of the World Wide Web now permits dynamic sources of information to be widely available. Several years ago a web site was created to enable forensic scientists to keep abreast with the rapidly evolving field of DNA typing. In anticipation of the impact of STR markers on DNA typing and the need for a common source of information that could evolve as the process improved, an internet-accessible informational database was created in early 1997. STRBase was officially launched in July 1997 and is maintained by the DNA Technologies Group of the National Institute of Standards and Technology (Butler *et al.* 1997). STRBase may be reached via the World Wide Web using the following URL: http://www.cstl.nist.gov/biotech/strbase. The home page for STRBase is shown in Figure 5.7.

STRBase contains a number of useful elements. Continually updated information includes the listing of references related to STRs and DNA typing (over 1000 references), addresses for scientists working in the field, and previously unreported microvariant or 'off-ladder' STR alleles. Other information that is updated less frequently includes STR fact sheets (with allele information similar to that given in Appendix I), links to other web pages, a review of technology used for DNA typing as well as published primer sequence information, and population data for STR markers.

STR markers have become important tools for human identity testing. Commercially available STR kits are now widely used in forensic and paternity testing laboratories. The adoption of the 13 CODIS core loci for the US national DNA database ensures that these STR markers will be used for many years to come. However, as we will see in the next two chapters, results from STR markers require careful interpretation in order to be effective tools for law enforcement.

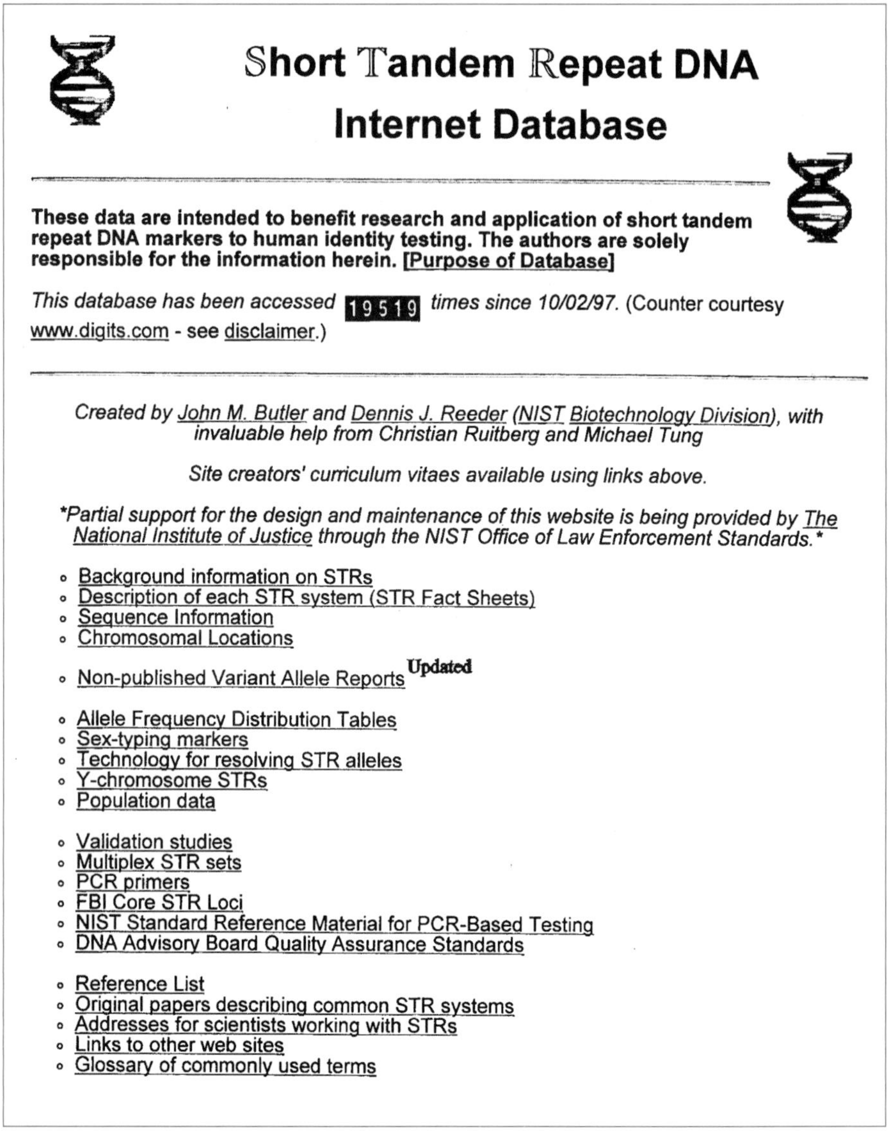

Figure 5.7

Homepage for STRBase, an internet-accessible database of information on STR markers used in forensic DNA typing. STRBase may be accessed via the URL: http://www.cstl.nist.gov/ biotech/strbase/ and contains among other things a comprehensive listing of all papers relating to STR typing for human identity testing purposes now numbering over 1000 references.

Short **T**andem **R**epeat DNA
Internet Database

These data are intended to benefit research and application of short tandem repeat DNA markers to human identity testing. The authors are solely responsible for the information herein. [Purpose of Database]

This database has been accessed `19519` *times since 10/02/97.* (Counter courtesy www.digits.com - see disclaimer.)

Created by John M. Butler and Dennis J. Reeder (NIST Biotechnology Division), with invaluable help from Christian Ruitberg and Michael Tung

Site creators' curriculum vitaes available using links above.

Partial support for the design and maintenance of this website is being provided by The National Institute of Justice through the NIST Office of Law Enforcement Standards.

- Background information on STRs
- Description of each STR system (STR Fact Sheets)
- Sequence Information
- Chromosomal Locations

- Non-published Variant Allele Reports **Updated**

- Allele Frequency Distribution Tables
- Sex-typing markers
- Technology for resolving STR alleles
- Y-chromosome STRs
- Population data

- Validation studies
- Multiplex STR sets
- PCR primers
- FBI Core STR Loci
- NIST Standard Reference Material for PCR-Based Testing
- DNA Advisory Board Quality Assurance Standards

- Reference List
- Original papers describing common STR systems
- Addresses for scientists working with STRs
- Links to other web sites
- Glossary of commonly used terms

REFERENCES

Bacher, J.W., Hennes, L.F., Gu, T., Tereba, A., Micka, K.A., Sprecher, C.J., Lins, A.M., Amiott, E.A., Rabbach, D.R., Taylor, J.A., Helms, C., Donis-Keller, H. and Schumm, J.W. (1999) *Proceedings of the Ninth International Symposium on Human Indentification*. Madison, WI: Promega Corporation, pp. 24–37.

Baechtel, F.S., Smerick, J.B., Presley, K.W. and Budowle, B. (1993) *Journal of Forensic Sciences*, 38, 1176–1182.

Bar, W., Brinkmann, B., Lincoln, P., Mayr, W.R. and Rossi, U. (1994) *International Journal of Legal Medicine*, 107, 159–160.

Bar, W., Brinkmann, B., Budowle, B., Carracedo, A., Gill, P., Lincoln, P., Mayr, W.R. and Olaisen, B. (1997) *International Journal of Legal Medicine*, 110, 175–176.

Barber, M.D. and Parkin, B.H. (1996) *International Journal of Legal Medicine*, 109, 62–65.

Barber, M.D., McKeown, B.J. and Parkin, B.H. (1996) *International Journal of Legal Medicine*, 108, 180–185.

Brinkmann, B., Meyer, E. and Junge, A. (1996) *Human Genetics*, 98, 60–64.

Broman, K.W., Murray, J.C., Sheffield, V.C., White, R.L. and Weber, J.L. (1998) *American Journal of Human Genetics*, 63, 861–869.

Budowle, B., Moretti, T.R., Niezgoda, S.J. and Brown, B.L. (1998) *The Second European Symposium on Human Identification*. Madison, WI: Promega Corporation, pp. 73–88.

Butler, J.M., Ruitberg, C.M. and Reeder, D.J. (1997) *Proceedings of the Eighth International Symposium on Human Identification*. Madison, WI: Promega Corporation, pp. 38–47.

Carracedo, A. and Lareu, M.V. (1998) *Proceedings of the Ninth International Symposium on Human Identification*. Madison, WI: Promega Corporation, pp. 89–107.

Chakraborty, R., Stivers, D.N., Su, Y. and Budowle, B. (1999) *Electrophoresis*, 20, 1682–1696.

Dupuy, B.M. and Olaisen, B. (1997) *Forensic Science International*, 86, 207–227.

Edelmann, J. and Szibor, R. (1999) *Electrophoresis*, 20, 2844–2846.

Edwards, A., Civitello, A., Hammond, H.A. and Caskey, C.T. (1991) *American Journal of Human Genetics*, 49, 746–756.

Gill, P., Kimpton, C.P., d'Aloja, E., Andersen, J.F., Bar, W., Brinkmann, B., Holgersson, S., Johnsson, V., Kloosterman, A.D., Lareu, M.V., Nellemann, L., Pfitzinger, H., Phillips, C.P., Schmitter, H., Schneider, P.M. and Stenersen, M. (1994) *Forensic Science International*, 65, 51–59.

Gill, P., Urquhart, A., Millican, E.S., Oldroyd, N.J., Watson, S., Sparkes, R. and Kimpton, C.P. (1996) *International Journal of Legal Medicine*, 109, 14–22.

Gill, P., d'Ajola, A., Andersen, J., Dupuy, B., Jangblad, M., Johnsson, U., Kloosterman, A.D., Kratzer, A., Lareu, M.V., Meldegaard, M., Philips, C., Pfitzinger, H., Rand, S., Sabatier, M., Scheithauer, P., Schmitter, H., Schneider, P.M. and Vide, M.C. (1997) *Forensic Science International*, 86, 25–33.

Griffiths, R.A.L., Barber, M.D., Johnson, P.E., Gillbard, S.M., Haywood, M.D., Smith, C.D., Arnold, J., Burke, T., Urquhart, A.J. and Gill, P. (1998) *International Journal of Legal Medicine*, 111, 267–272.

Hammond, H.A., Jin, L., Zhong, Y., Caskey, C.T. and Chakraborty, R. (1994) *American Journal of Human Genetics*, 55, 175–189.

Hou, Y., Jin, Z.M., Li, Y.B., Wu, J., Walter, H., Kido, A. and Prinz, M. (1999) *International Journal of Legal Medicine*, 112, 400–402.

Jin, L., Zhong, Y. and Chakraborty, R. (1994) *American Journal of Human Genetics*, 55, 582–583.

Kasai, K., Nakamura, Y. and White, R. (1990) *Journal of Forensic Sciences*, 35, 1196–1200.

Kimpton, C., Walton, A. and Gill, P. (1992) *Human Molecular Genetics*, 1, 287.

Kimpton, C.P., Gill, P., Walton, A., Urquhart, A., Millican, E.S. and Adams, M. (1993) *PCR Methods and Applications*, 3, 13–22.

Kimpton, C.P., Fisher, D., Watson, S., Adams, M., Urquhart, A., Lygo, J. and Gill, P. (1994) *International Journal of Legal Medicine*, 106, 302–311.

Lareu, M.V., Pestoni, C., Schurenkamp, M., Rand, S., Brinkmann, B. and Carracedo, A. (1996) *International Journal of Legal Medicine*, 109, 134–138.

Moller, A., Meyer, E. and Brinkmann, B. (1994) *International Journal of Legal Medicine*, 106, 319–323.

Mornhinweg, E., Luckenbach, C., Fimmers, R. and Ritter, H. (1998) *Forensic Science International*, 95, 173–178.

Oldroyd, N.J., Urquhart, A.J., Kimpton, C.P., Millican, E.S., Watson, S.K., Downes, T. and Gill, P.D. (1995) *Electrophoresis*, 16, 334–337.

Poltl, R., Luckenbach, C., Fimmers, R. and Ritter, H. (1997) *Electrophoresis*, 18, 2871–2873.

Poltl, R., Luckenbach, C. and Ritter, H. (1998) *Forensic Science International*, 95, 163–168.

Primrose, S.B. (1998) *Principles of Genome Analysis: A Guide to Mapping and Sequencing DNA from Different Organisms*, 2nd edn. Malden, MA: Blackwell Science.

Puers, C., Hammond, H.A., Jin, L., Caskey, C.T. and Schumm, J.W. (1993) *American Journal of Human Genetics*, 53, 953–958.

Reichenpfader, B., Zehner, R. and Klintschar, M. (1999) *Electrophoresis*, 20, 514–517.

Sajantila, A., Puomilahti, S., Johnsson, V. and Ehnholm, C. (1992) *BioTechniques*, 12, 16–21.

Seidl, C., Muller, S., Jager, O. and Seifried, E. (1999) *International Journal of Legal Medicine*, 112, 355–359.

Smith, R.N. (1995) *BioTechniques*, 18, 122–128.

Sparkes, R., Kimpton, C., Gibard, S., Carne, P., Andersen, J., Oldroyd, N., Thomas, D., Urquhart, A. and Gill, P. (1996) *International Journal of Legal Medicine*, 109, 195–204.

Tamaki, K., Huang, X.-L., Nozawa, H., Yamamoto, T., Uchihi, R., Katsumata, Y. and Armour, J.A.L. (1996) *Forensic Science International*, 81, 133–140.

Tully, G., Sullivan, K.M. and Gill, P. (1993) *Human Genetics*, 92, 554–562.

Urquhart, A., Kimpton, C.P. and Gill, P. (1993) *Human Genetics*, 92, 637–638.

Urquhart, A., Kimpton, C.P., Downes, T.J. and Gill, P. (1994) *International Journal of Legal Medicine*, 107, 13–20.

Walsh, P.S., Fildes, N.J. and Reynolds, R. (1996) *Nucleic Acids Research*, 24, 2807–2812.

Weber, J.L. and May, P.E. (1989) *American Journal of Human Genetics*, 44, 388–396.

Wiegand, P., Lareu, M.V., Schurenkamp, M., Kleiber, M. and Brinkmann, B. (1999) *International Journal of Legal Medicine*, 112, 360–363.

CHAPTER 6

BIOLOGY OF STRs: STUTTER PRODUCTS, NON-TEMPLATE ADDITION, MICROVARIANTS, NULL ALLELES, AND MUTATION RATES

During polymerase chain reaction (PCR) amplification of short tandem repeat (STR) alleles, a number of artifacts can arise that may interfere with the clear interpretation and genotyping of the alleles present in the DNA template. In this chapter, we will focus on those PCR products that give rise to additional peaks besides the true, major allele peak(s). These artifacts include stutter products and non-template nucleotide addition. Other factors that impact STR typing, including microvariants, allele dropout, and mutations, will also be covered.

STUTTER PRODUCTS

A close examination of electropherograms containing STR data typically reveals the presence of small peaks several bases smaller than each STR allele peak (Figure 6.1). These 'stutter product' peaks result from the PCR process when STR loci are copied by a DNA polymerase. In the literature, this stutter product has also been referred to as a shadow band or a DNA polymerase slippage product (Hauge and Litt 1993).

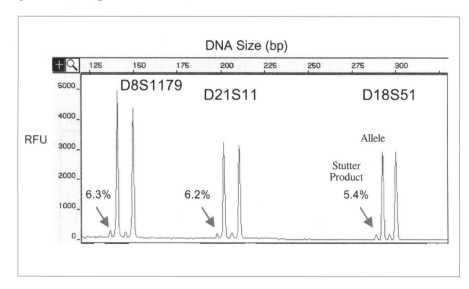

Figure 6.1

STR alleles shown with stutter products (indicated by arrows). Only the stutter percentage for the first allele from each locus is noted.

Sequence analysis of stutter products from the tetranucleotide repeat locus VWA has shown that they contain one repeat unit less than the corresponding main allele peak (Walsh *et al.* 1996). Stutter products that are larger in size by one repeat unit than the corresponding alleles have not been observed in commonly used tetranucleotide repeat STR loci.

Stutter products have been reported in the literature since STRs (microsatellites) were first described. The primary mechanism that has been proposed to explain the existence of stutter products is slipped-strand mispairing (Hauge and Litt 1993, Walsh *et al.* 1996). In the slipped-strand mispairing model, a region of primer-template complex becomes unpaired during primer extension allowing slippage of either primer or template strand such that one repeat forms a non-base-paired loop (Hauge and Litt 1993). The consequence of this one-repeat loop is a shortened PCR product that is less than the primary amplicon (STR allele) by a single repeat unit.

IMPACT OF STUTTER PRODUCTS ON DATA INTERPRETATION

Stutter products impact interpretation of DNA profiles, especially in cases where two or more individuals may have contributed to the DNA sample (see Chapter 7). Because stutter products are the same size as actual allele PCR products, it can be challenging to determine whether a small peak is a real allele from a minor contributor or a stutter product of an adjacent allele.

Mixture interpretation requires a good understanding of the behavior of stutter products in single source samples. Often a laboratory will quantify the percentage of stutter product peak heights compared to their corresponding allele peak heights. The percentage of stutter product formation for an allele is determined simply by dividing the stutter peak height by the corresponding allele peak height.

A plot of the alleles from each of the 13 standard STR loci reveals variation in the percentage of stutter for each locus as well as alleles from the same locus (Figure 6.2). Such a plot illustrates several important principles. First, each locus has a different amount of stutter product formation. Second, longer alleles for a STR locus exhibit a greater degree of stutter than smaller alleles for the same locus. Third, stutter percentage with the standard tetranucleotide repeats is less than 15% for all 13 CODIS core STR loci.

REDUCED STUTTER PRODUCTION FORMATION

The amount of stutter product formation may be reduced when using STR markers with longer repeat units, STR alleles with imperfect repeat units, and DNA polymerases with faster processivity. Several pentanucleotide repeat loci

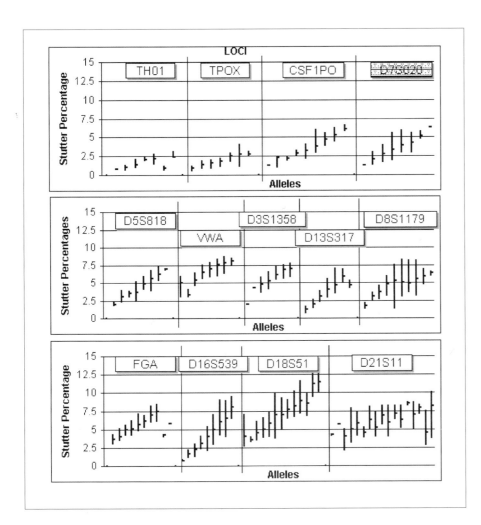

Figure 6.2
Stutter percentages for 13 CODIS STR loci (data adapted from AmpFISTR manuals). Alleles for each STR locus are shown from smallest to largest.
Each locus has a different average stutter percentage but all loci show the trend of increasing stutter with larger alleles (longer repeats).

have been developed in an effort to produce STR markers that exhibit low amounts of stutter products to aid in mixture interpretation (Bacher and Schumm 1998). The first seven loci have been labeled Penta A through Penta G. Penta E has been incorporated in the GenePrint® PowerPlex™ 2.1 system and reportedly exhibits an average stutter percentage of less than 1% (Bacher *et al.* 1999).

Alleles for a STR locus that contain variations on the common repeat motif exhibit a smaller amount of stutter product formation. For example, the common repeat motif for the STR marker TH01 is AATG. However, with allele 9.3, there is an ATG nucleotide sequence present in the middle of the repeat region (Puers *et al.* 1993). When the core repeat sequence has been interrupted, stutter product formation is reduced compared to alleles that are similar in length but possess uninterrupted core repeat sequences. This fact has been demonstrated with sequencing results from several VWA alleles (Walsh *et al.* 1996).

The amount of stutter may be related to the DNA polymerase processivity, or how rapidly it copies the template strand. Stutter products have been shown to increase relative to their corresponding alleles with a slower polymerase (Walsh *et al.* 1996). If thermal stable DNA polymerases become available in the future that are faster than the current 50–60 base processivity of *Taq* DNA polymerase, then it may be possible to reduce the stutter product formation. A faster polymerase would be able to copy the two DNA strands before they could come apart and re-anneal out of register during primer extension.

A summary of stutter product formation is listed below:

- primarily one repeat unit smaller than corresponding main allele peak;
- typically less than 10% of corresponding allele peak height;
- quantity of stutter depends on locus as well as PCR conditions and polymerase used;
- propensity for stutter decreases with longer repeat units (pentanucleotide repeats<tetra-<tri-<dinucleotides);
- quantity of stutter is greater for large alleles within a locus;
- quantity of stutter is less if sequence of repeats is imperfect.

NON-TEMPLATE ADDITION

DNA polymerases, particularly the *Taq* polymerase used in PCR, often add an extra nucleotide to the 3′-end of a PCR product as they are copying the template strand (Clark 1988, Magnuson *et al.* 1996). This non-template addition is most often adenosine and is therefore sometimes referred to as 'adenylation' or the 'plus A' form of the amplicon. Non-template addition results in a PCR product that is one base pair longer than the actual target sequence.

Addition of the 3′ A nucleotide can be favored by adding a final incubation step at 60°C or 72°C after the temperature cycling steps in PCR (Clark 1988, Kimpton *et al.* 1993). However, the degree of adenylation is dependent on the sequence of the template strand, which in the case of PCR results from the 5′-end of the reverse primer (Figure 6.3). If the forward primer is labeled with a fluorescent dye to amplify the STR allele, then only the top strand is detected by the fluorescent measurement. Since the sequence at the 3′-end of the top (labeled) strand serves as a template for polymerase extension, then the terminal nucleotide of the labeled strand is determined by the 5′-end of the reverse primer used in generating the complementary unlabeled strand (Magnuson *et al.* 1996). One study found that if the 5′-terminus of the primer is a guanosine, then a complete addition is favored by the polymerase (Brownstein *et al.* 1996). Thus, every locus will have slightly different adenylation properties because the primer sequences differ.

Now why is all of this important? From a measurement standpoint, it is better

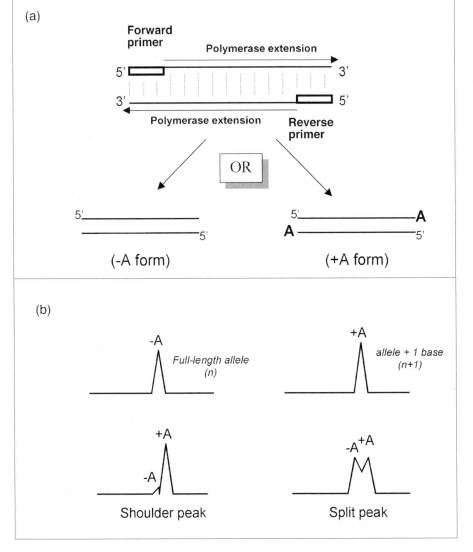

(a)

Forward primer

Polymerase extension

5' ▭

3'

3'

5'

Polymerase extension   Reverse primer

OR

5'

5'

(-A form)

5'

A

A

5'

(+A form)

(b)

-A
Full-length allele
(n)

+A
allele + 1 base
(n+1)

+A
-A

Shoulder peak

-A ⁺A

Split peak

Figure 6.3

Schematic of non-template nucleotide addition shown (a) with illustrated measurement result (b). DNA polymerases add an extra nucleotide beyond the 3'-end of the target sequence extension product. The amount of non-template addition is dependent on the sequence of the 5'-end of the opposing primer. In the case of dye labeled PCR products where the fluorescent dye is on the forward primer, the reverse primer sequence is the critical one.

to have all of the molecules as similar as possible for a particular allele. Partial adenylation, where some of the PCR products do not have the extra adenine (i.e. –A peaks) and some do (i.e. +A peaks), can contribute to peak broadness if the separation system's resolution is poor. Sharper peaks improve the likelihood that a system's genotyping software can make accurate calls. In addition, variation in the adenylation status of an allele across multiple samples can have an impact on accurate sizing and genotyping potential microvariants. For example, a non-adenylated TH01 10 allele would be the same size as a fully adenylated TH01 9.3 allele because they contain an identical number of base pairs. Therefore, it is beneficial if all PCR products for a particular amplification are either +A or –A rather than a mixture of +/– A products. Table 6.1 lists some of the methods that have been used to convert PCR products into either the –A or +A form.

During PCR amplification most STR protocols include a final extension step to give the DNA polymerase extra time to adenylate all double-stranded PCR products completely.

Table 6.1

Ways to convert STR allele peaks to either –A or +A forms.

Method	Result	Reference
Conversion to fully adenylated products (+A form)		
Final extension at 60°C or 72°C for 30–45 minutes	Promotes full adenylation of all products	Kimpton *et al.* 1993, Perkin-Elmer Corporation 1999
Addition of sequence GTTCTT on the 5´-end of reverse primers ('PIG-tailing')	Promotes nearly 100% adenylation of the 3´ forward strand	Brownstein *et al.* 1996
Conversion to blunt-ended products (–A form)		
Restriction enzyme site built into reverse primer	Makes blunt end fragments following restriction enzyme digestion	Edwards *et al.* 1991
Enzymatic removal of one base overhang	Exonuclease activity of *Pfu* or T4 DNA polymerase removes +A	Ginot *et al.* 1996
Use of modified polymerase without terminal transferase activity	Polymerase does not add 3´ A nucleotide	Butler and Becker 1999

For example, the standard AmpFlSTR® kit amplication parameters include a final extension at 60°C for 45 minutes at the end of thermal cycling (Perkin-Elmer Corporation 1999). In order to make correct genotype calls, it is important that the allelic ladder and the sample have the same adenylation status for a particular STR locus. For all commercially available STR kits, this means that the STR alleles are all in the +A form.

Amplifying higher quantities of DNA than the optimal amount suggested by the manufacturer's protocols can result in incomplete 3´ A nucleotide addition and therefore split peaks. The addition of 10 ng of template DNA to a PCR reaction with AmpFlSTR Profiler Plus results in split peaks compared to using only 2 ng of the same template DNA (Figure 6.4). Thus, quantifying the amount of DNA prior to PCR and adhering to the manufacturer's protocols will produce improved STR typing results when using commercial STR kits.

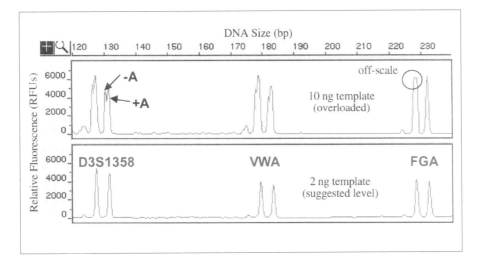

Figure 6.4

Incomplete non-template addition with high levels of DNA template. In the top panel, partial adenylation (both −A and +A forms of each allele) is seen because the polymerase is overwhelmed due to an abundance of DNA template. Note also that the peaks in the top panel are off-scale and flat-topped in the case of the smaller FGA allele. When the suggested level of DNA template is used, all alleles are fully adenylated (bottom panel).

MICROVARIANTS AND 'OFF-LADDER' ALLELES

Rare alleles are encountered in the human population that may differ from common allele variants at tested DNA markers by one or more base pairs. Sequence variation between STR alleles can take the form of insertions, deletions, or nucleotide changes. Alleles containing some form of sequence variation compared to more commonly observed alleles are often referred to as *microvariants* because they are only slightly different from full repeat alleles. Because microvariant alleles often do not size the same as consensus alleles present in the reference allelic ladder, they are referred to as 'off-ladder' alleles.

One example of a common microvariant is allele 9.3 at the STR locus TH01. The repeat region of TH01 allele 9.3 contains nine full repeats (AATG) and a partial repeat of three bases (ATG). The 9.3 allele differs from the 10 allele by a single base deletion of adenine in the seventh repeat (Puers *et al.* 1993).

Microvariants exist for most STR loci and are being identified in greater numbers as more samples are being examined around the world. In a recent study, 42 apparent microvariants were seen in over 10 000 samples examined at the CSF1PO, TPOX, and TH01 loci (Crouse *et al.* 1999). Microvariants are most commonly found in more polymorphic STR loci, such as FGA, D21S11, and D18S51, which possess the largest and most complex repeat structures compared to simple repeat loci, such as TPOX and CSF1PO (see Appendix I).

DETERMINING THE PRESENCE OF A MICROVARIANT ALLELE

Suspected microvariants can be fairly easily seen in heterozygous samples where one allele lines up with the fragment sizes in the allelic ladder and one does not

(Figure 6.5). In the example shown here, the sample contains a peak that lines up with allele 25 from the FGA allelic ladder and a second peak that is labeled as an 'off-ladder allele' and lines up between the 28 and 28.2 shaded virtual bins created by the ladder. Each peak is labeled with its calculated size in base pairs determined by reference to the internal GS500 sizing standard (see Chapter 13). The relative size difference between the questioned sample and an allelic ladder marker run under the same electrophoretic conditions is then used to determine if the allele is truly a microvariant (Gill *et al.* 1996).

Figure 6.5

Detection of a microvariant allele at the STR locus FGA. The sample in the bottom panel is compared to the allelic ladder shown in the top panel using Genotyper 2.5 software. Peaks are labeled with the allele category and the calculated fragment sizes using the internal sizing standard GS500-ROX.

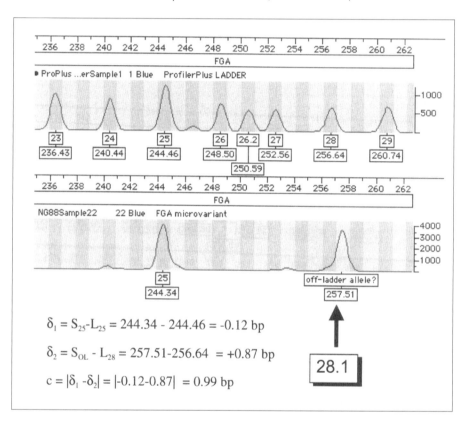

In Figure 6.5, the size difference between the sample allele 25 and the ladder allele 25 is –0.12 bp (δ_1) while the 'off-ladder allele' differs from the ladder allele 28 by +0.87 bp (δ_2). The relative peak shift between the two alleles in this heterozygous sample is 0.99 bp ($|\delta_1 - \delta_2|$) and therefore the 'off-ladder' allele is 1 bp larger than allele 28 making it a true 28.1 microvariant at the FGA locus.

The presence of a STR microvariant at a particular locus usually becomes evident following a comparison to an allelic ladder made up of characterized alleles for that locus. However, not all alleles (particularly rare microvariant alleles) can be incorporated into the standard allelic ladder used for genotyping STR markers. Therefore, interpolation of data from peaks that migrate between two characterized alleles or extrapolation of data from peaks that fall outside the expected allele range may be performed.

If an allele peak falls in between the nominal alleles present in the allelic ladder, the sample is designated by the allele number followed by a '.*x*' (Crouse *et al.* 1999). For example, the larger FGA allele shown in Figure 6.5 would be designated as a '28.*x*' allele. If an allele migrates above or below the defined allelic ladder, the allele is described as '>' or '<' than the nearest allele (Crouse *et al.* 1999).

SAME LENGTH BUT DIFFERENT SEQUENCE ALLELES

Complex repeat sequences, such as those found in D21S11, can contain variable repeat blocks in which the order is switched around for alleles that are the same length. For example, the STR locus D21S11 has four alleles that are all 210 bp when amplified with the Profiler Plus™ kit (Appendix I). While these alleles would be sized based on length to be 'allele 30', they contain repeat blocks of 4-6-CR-12, 5-6-CR-11, 6-5-CR-11, and 6-6-CR-10 for the pattern [TCTA]-[TCTG]-constant region (CR)-[TCTA]. In such cases, variant alleles would only be detectable with complete sequence analysis.

PEAKS OUTSIDE THE ALLELIC LADDER RANGE AND THREE-BANDED PATTERNS

Occasionally new rare alleles may fall outside the allele range spanned by the locus allelic ladder. If these peaks fall between two STR loci in a multiplex set, they can be challenging to assign to a particular locus without amplification using individual locus-specific primer sets.

Three-banded patterns are sometimes observed at a single locus in a multiplex STR profile. These extra peaks are not a result of a mixture but are reproducible artifacts of the sample. Extra chromosomal occurrences or primer point mutations have been known to happen and result in a three-banded pattern (Crouse *et al.* 1999). For example, a three-banded pattern has been observed in the 9948 cell line at CSF1PO and in the K562 cell line at D21S11 (see Focus box 7.1).

The three peaks seen at a particular locus may or may not be equal in intensity. While the TPOX three-banded patterns reported by Crouse and co-workers (1999) were equal in intensity, they are not always so as seen in Figure 6.6. In this example, the other STR loci besides D18S51 have two peaks of similar intensity, which confirms that a sample mixture is not likely (see Chapter 7). Three-banded patterns have been seen at TPOX, CSF1PO, FGA, D5S818, D21S11, and D18S51 among other loci.

Figure 6.6

Three-banded pattern at D18S51. The DNA sample was amplified with the Profiler Plus™ STR kit, separated on the ABI Prism 310 Genetic Analyzer and viewed with Genotyper® 2.5 software. The allele calls are listed under each peak. Only the green dye-labeled PCR products are shown here for simplicity's sake.

Figure 6.7

Possible sequence variation in or around STR repeat regions and the impact on PCR amplification. The asterisk symbolizes a DNA difference (base change, insertion or deletion of a nucleotide) from a typical allele for a STR locus. In situation (a), the variation occurs within the repeat region and should have no impact on the primer binding and the subsequent PCR amplification (although the overall amplicon size may vary slightly). In situation (b), the sequence variation occurs just outside the repeat in the flanking region but interior to the primer annealing sites. Again, PCR should not be effected, although the size of the PCR product may vary slightly. However, in situation (c) the PCR can fail due to a disruption in the annealing of a primer because the primer no longer perfectly matches the DNA template sequence.

ALLELE DROPOUT AND NULL ALLELES

When amplifying DNA fragments that contain STR repeat regions, it is possible to have a phenomenon known as *allele dropout*. Sequence polymorphisms are known to occur within or around STR repeat regions. These variations can occur in three locations (relative to the primer binding sites): within the repeat region, in the flanking region, or in the primer-binding region (Figure 6.7).

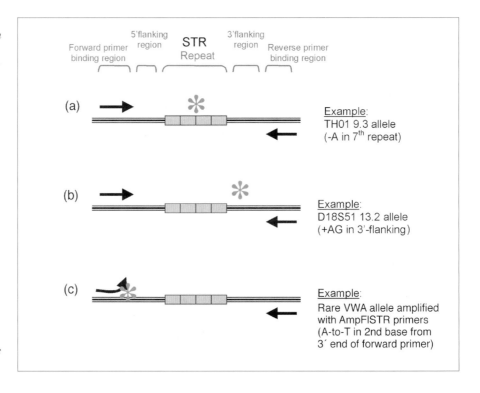

If a base pair change occurs in the DNA template at the PCR primer binding region, the hybridization of the primer can be disrupted, resulting in a failure to amplify, and therefore failure to detect an allele that exists in the template DNA. More simply, the DNA template exists for a particular allele but fails to amplify during PCR due to primer hybridization problems. This phenomenon results in what is known as a *null allele*. Fortunately null alleles are rather rare because the flanking sequence around STR repeats is fairly stable and consistent between samples.

DISCOVERY OF NULL ALLELES

Null alleles have been 'discovered' by the observation of different typing results when utilizing independent STR primer sets. During a comparison of STR typing results on 600 population samples at the VWA locus, one sample typed 16,19 with Promega's PowerPlex kit and 16,16 with PE Applied Biosystem's AmpFlSTR® Blue kit (Kline *et al.* 1998). In this case, VWA allele 19 dropped out with the AmpFlSTR® VWA primer set due to a sequence polymorphism near the 3′-end of the forward primer (Walsh 1998).

Allele dropout may occur due to mutations (variants) at or near the 3′-end of a primer and thus produce little or no extension during PCR. In this case, the VWA allele 19 was present in the sample but failed to be amplified by one of the primer sets. It was later reported that the null allele resulted from a rare A–T nucleotide change in the DNA template at the second base from the 3′-end of the AmpFlSTR® VWA forward primer (Walsh 1998).

Potential null alleles resulting from allele dropout can be predicted by statistical analysis of the STR typing data. The observed number of homozygotes can be compared to the expected number of homozygotes based on Hardy–Weinberg equilibrium (Chakraborty *et al.* 1992). An abnormally high level of homozygotes would indicate the possible presence of null alleles. Thus, each set of population data should be carefully examined when new STR markers are being tested in a forensic DNA laboratory.

SOLUTIONS TO NULL ALLELES

If a null allele is detected at a STR locus, there are several possible solutions. First, the problem PCR primer could be redesigned and moved away from the problematic site. This approach was taken early in the development of the D7S820 primers for the Promega PowerPlex kit (Schumm *et al.* 1996). However, this solution could result in the new primer interfering with another one in the multiplex set of primers or call for new PCR reaction optimization experiments. Clearly this solution is undesirable because it is time consuming and labor intensive.

A second solution is to simply drop the STR locus from the multiplex mix rather than attempting to redesign the PCR primers to avoid the site. This approach is only desirable when early in the development cycle of a multiplex STR assay. The Forensic Science Service dropped the STR locus D19S253 from consideration in their prototype second-generation multiplex when a null allele was discovered (Urquhart *et al.* 1994).

A third, and more favorable, solution is to add a 'degenerate' primer that contains the known sequence polymorphism. This extra primer will then amplify alleles containing the problematic primer binding site sequence variant. However, if the sequence variation at the primer binding site is extremely rare, it may not be worth the effort to add an additional primer to the multiplex primer mix.

A fourth possible solution to correct for allele dropout that will work for some problematic primer binding sites is to re-amplify the sample with a lower annealing temperature and thereby reduce the stringency of the primer annealing. If the primer is only slightly destabilized, as detected by a peak height imbalance with a heterozygous sample (Figure 6.8), then it may be possible to correct the peak height imbalance by lowering the annealing temperature during PCR.

Figure 6.8

Impact of a sequence polymorphism in the primer binding site illustrated with a hypothetical heterozygous individual. Heterozygous allele peaks may be well-balanced (a), imbalanced (b), or exhibit allele dropout (c).

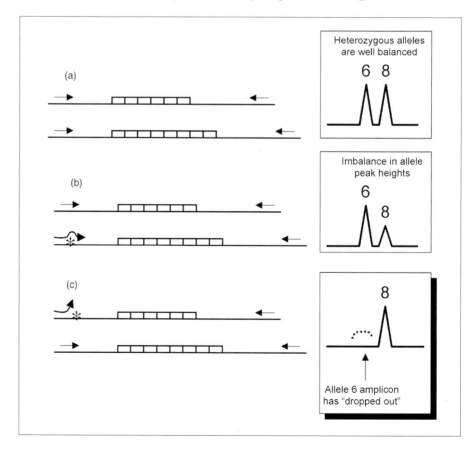

No primer set is completely immune to the phenomenon of null alleles. However, when identical primer sets are used to amplify evidence samples and suspect reference samples, full concordance is expected from biological materials originating from a common source. If the DNA templates and PCR conditions are identical between two samples from the same individual, then identical DNA profiles should result regardless of how well or poorly the PCR primers amplify the DNA template.

The potential of null alleles is not a problem within a laboratory that uses the same primer set to amplify a particular STR marker. However, with the emergence of national and international DNA databases, which store only the genotype information for a sample, allele dropout could potentially result in a false-negative or incorrect exclusion of two samples that come from a common source. To overcome this potential problem, the matching criteria in database searches can be made less stringent when searching a crime stain sample against the DNA database of convicted offender profiles (see Chapter 16). That is, the database search might be programmed to return any profiles with a match at 25 out of 26 alleles instead of 26 out of 26.

When primers are selected for amplification of STR loci, candidate primers are evaluated carefully to avoid primer binding site mutations (Schumm *et al.* 1996). Sequence analysis of multiple alleles in performed, family inheritance studies are conducted, within-locus peak signal ratios for heterozygous samples are examined, apparent homozygous samples are re-amplified with lower annealing temperatures, and statistical analysis of observed versus expected homozygosity is performed on population databases (Walsh 1998). It is truly a challenge to design multiplex STR primer sets in which primer binding sites are located in sequence regions that are as highly conserved as possible and yet do not interfere with primers amplifying other loci.

MUTATIONS AND MUTATION RATES

As with any region of DNA, mutations can and do occur at STR loci. By some mechanism that is not completely characterized, STR alleles can change over time. Theoretically, all of the alleles that exist today for a particular STR locus have resulted from only a few 'founder' individuals by slowly changing over tens of thousands of years (Wiegand *et al.* 2000). The mutational event may be in the form of a single base change or in the length of the entire repeat. The molecular mechanisms by which STRs mutate are thought to involve replication slippage or defective DNA replication repair (Nadir *et al.* 1996).

DISCOVERY OF STR ALLELE MUTATIONS

Estimation of mutational events at a DNA marker may be achieved by comparison of genotypes from offspring to those of their parents. Genotype data from paternity trios involving a father, a mother, and at least one child is examined. The discovery of an allele difference between the parents and the child is seen as evidence for a possible mutation (Figure 6.9). The search for mutations in STR loci involves examining many, many parent–child allele transfers because the mutation rate is rather low in most STRs.

Figure 6.9

Mutational event observed in family trios. Normal transmission of alleles from a STR locus (a) is compared here to mutation of paternal allele 14 into the child's allele 13 (b).

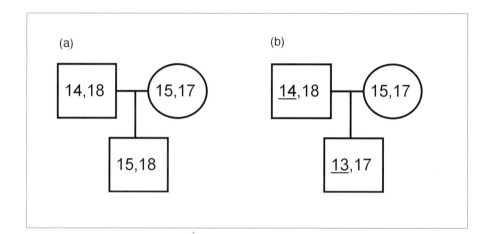

The majority of STR mutations involve the gain or loss of a single repeat unit. Thus, a VWA allele with 14 repeats would show up as a 13 or a 15 in the next generation following a mutational event (Figure 6.9). Paternal mutations appear to be more frequent than maternal ones for STR loci (Sajantila *et al.* 1999, Henke and Henke 1999). However, depending on the genotype combinations, it can be difficult to ascertain from which parent the mutant allele was inherited.

MEASURING THE MUTATION RATE

Since the average mutation rate is below 0.1%, approximately 1000 parent–offspring allele transfers would have to be observed before one mutation would be seen in some STR markers (Weber and Wong 1993). Brinkman and co-workers (1998) examined 10 844 parent–child allele transfers at nine STR loci and observed 23 mutations. No mutations were observed at three of the loci (TH01, F13B, CD4). Sajantila *et al.* (1999) studied 29 640 parent–child allele transfers at five STRs and four minisatellites, and observed only 18 mutational events (11 in 3 STR loci: D3S1359, VWA, and TH01). Two of the STRs, TPOX and FES/FPS, had no detectable mutations.

The mutation rates for the 13 core STR loci have been gathered from a number of studies in the literature and are summarized in Table 6.2. Most of these mutation rates are on the order of 1–5 mutations per 1000 allele transfers or generational events. The STR loci with the lowest observed mutation rates

Locus	Observed Mutation Rate	Reference	Mutation Rate
CSF1PO	0/237 maternal 0/165 paternal	Henke and Henke 1999 Henke and Henke 1999	$0/402 = <2.5 \times 10^{-3}$
FGA	5/1246 meioses 0/307 maternal 3/218 paternal	Brinkmann *et al.* 1998 Henke and Henke 1999 Henke and Henke 1999	$8/1771 = 4.5 \times 10^{-3}$
TH01	0/2008 meioses 1/5918 meioses 0/394 maternal 0/301 paternal	Brinkmann *et al.* 1998 Sajantila *et al.* 1999 Henke and Henke 1999 Henke and Henke 1999	$1/8621 = 1.2 \times 10^{-4}$
TPOX	0/2457 meioses 0/240 maternal 0/167 paternal	Sajantila *et al.* 1999 Henke and Henke 1999 Henke and Henke 1999	$0/2864 = <3.5 \times 10^{-4}$
VWA	4/2013 meioses 5/3684 meioses 1/258 maternal 0/178 paternal	Brinkmann *et al.* 1998 Sajantila *et al.* 1999 Henke and Henke 1999 Henke and Henke 1999	$10/6133 = 1.6 \times 10^{-3}$
D3S1358	0/257 maternal 0/176 paternal 1/390 maternal 1/390 paternal 1/130 meioses	Henke and Henke 1999 Henke and Henke 1999 Szibor *et al.* 1998 Szibor *et al.* 1998 Mornhinweg *et al.* 1998	$3/1343 = 2.2 \times 10^{-3}$
D5S818	0/258 maternal 0/178 paternal	Henke and Henke 1999 Henke and Henke 1999	$0/436 = <2.3 \times 10^{-3}$
D7S820	0/256 maternal 2/176 paternal	Henke and Henke 1999 Henke and Henke 1999	$2/432 = 4.6 \times 10^{-3}$
D8S1179	0/213 maternal 0/149 paternal	Henke and Henke 1999 Henke and Henke 1999	$0/362 = <2.8 \times 10^{-3}$
D13S317	0/258 maternal 0/178 paternal 1/317 maternal	Henke and Henke 1999 Henke and Henke 1999 Lins *et al.* 1998	$1/753 = 1.3 \times 10^{-3}$
D16S539	2/156 meioses 0/300 meioses	Thomson *et al.* 1999 Lins *et al.* 1998	$2/456 = 4.4 \times 10^{-3}$
D18S51	0/286 maternal 2/205 paternal	Henke and Henke 1999 Henke and Henke 1999	$2/491 = 4.1 \times 10^{-3}$
D21S11	1/557 meioses 1/267 maternal 3/189 paternal	Brinkmann *et al.* 1998 Henke and Henke 1999 Henke and Henke 1999	$5/1013 = 4.9 \times 10^{-3}$

Table 6.2

Observed mutation rates for the 13 core STR loci. The reported mutation rates are broken out into maternal or paternal when that information is available. The final mutation rate column is a summation of all available data.

are CSF1PO, TH01, TPOX, D5S818, and D8S1179. Not surprisingly, the STR loci with the highest mutation rates – D21S11, FGA, D7S820, D16S539, and D18S51 – are among the most polymorphic with the highest number of observed alleles (Appendix I).

IMPACT OF MUTATION RATES ON PATERNITY TESTING

Low mutation rates are especially critical for paternity testing. This is because links are being made between the child and the alleged father based on the assumption that alleles remain the same when they are passed from one generation to the next. Parent–offspring allele transfer information tests for germline mutations. Additionally, genotypes from different kinds of tissues from the same individual are examined to demonstrate that no somatic mutations occur.

Mutations have practical consequences for paternity testing and mass disaster investigations as well as population genetics where conclusions are being drawn from genetic data across one generation or many generations. In paternity testing situations, a high mutation rate for a STR marker could result in a false exclusion at that locus. With regards to population evolution studies, the mutation process must be subtracted from population demography and population history in order to address the population genetic questions being asked accurately. Any time a family reference sample is used to try to match recovered remains during a mass disaster investigation, mutations become an important issue because an exact match cannot be made when a mutation is present.

REFERENCES

Bacher, J. and Schumm, J.W. (1998) *Profiles in DNA* (Promega Corporation) 2 (2), 3–6.

Bacher, J.W., Hennes, L.F., Gu, T., Tereba, A., Micka, K.A., Sprecher, C.J., Lins, A.M., Amiott, E.A., Rabbach, D.R., Taylor, J.A., Helms, C., Donis-Keller, H. and Schumm, J.W. (1999) *Proceedings of the Ninth International Symposium on Human Indentification*. Madison, WI: Promega Corporation, pp. 24–37.

Brinkmann, B., Klintschar, M., Neuhuber, F., Huhne, J. and Rolf, B. (1998) *American Journal of Human Genetics*, 62, 1408–1415.

Brownstein, M.J., Carpten, J.D. and Smith, J.R. (1996) *BioTechniques*, 20, 1004–1010.

Butler, J.M. and Becker, C.H. (1999) Improved analysis of DNA short tandem repeats with time-of-flight mass spectrometry. Final Report on NIJ Grant 97-LB-VX-0003. Washington, DC: National Institute of Justice.

Chakraborty, R., de Andrade, M., Daiger, S.P. and Budowle, B. (1992) *American Journal of Human Genetics*, 56, 45–57.

Clark, J.M. (1988) *Nucleic Acids Research*, 16, 9677–9686.

Crouse, C., Rogers, S., Amiott, E., Gibson, S. and Masibay, A. (1999) *Journal of Forensic Sciences*, 44, 87–94.

Edwards, A., Civitello, A., Hammond, H.A. and Caskey, C.T. (1991) *American Journal of Human Genetics*, 49, 746–756.

Gill, P., Urquhart, A., Millican, E.S., Oldroyd, N.J., Watson, S., Sparkes, R. and Kimpton, C.P. (1996) *International Journal of Legal Medicine*, 109, 14–22.

Ginot, F., Bordelais, I., Nguyen, S. and Gyapay, G. (1996) *Nucleic Acids Research*, 24, 540–541.

Hauge, X.Y. and Litt, M. (1993) *Human Molecular Genetics*, 2, 411–415.

Henke, J. and Henke, L. (1999) *American Journal of Human Genetics*, 64, 1473.

Kimpton, C.P., Gill, P., Walton, A., Urquhart, A., Millican, E.S. and Adams, M. (1993) *PCR Methods and Applications*, 3, 13–22.

Kline, M.C., Jenkins, B. and Rogers, S. (1998) *Journal of Forensic Sciences*, 43, 250.

Lins, A.M., Micka, K.A., Sprecher, C.J., Taylor, J.A., Bacher, J.A., Rabbach, D.R., Bever, R.A., Creacy, S.D., and Schumm, J.W. (1998) *Journal of Forensic Sciences*, 43, 1178–1190.

Magnuson, V.L., Ally, D., Nylund, S.J., Karanjawala, Z.E., Rayman, J.B., Knapp, J.I., Lowe, A.L., Ghosh, S. and Collins, F.S. (1996) *BioTechniques*, 21, 700–709.

Meldgaard, M. and Morling, N. (1997) *Electrophoresis*, 18, 1928–1935.

Mornhinweg, E., Luckenbach, C., Fimmers, R. and Ritter, H. (1998) *Forensic Science International*, 95, 173–178.

Nadir, E., Margalit, H., Gallily, T. and Ben-Sasson, S.A. (1996) *Proceedings of the National Academy of Sciences USA*, 93, 6470–6475.

Perkin-Elmer Corporation (1999) AmpFlSTR® SGM Plus™ PCR Amplification Kit User's Manual, P/N 4309589. Foster City: PE Applied Biosystems.

Puers, C., Hammond, H.A., Jin, L., Caskey, C.T. and Schumm, J.W. (1993) *American Journal of Human Genetics*, 53, 953–958.

Sajantila, A., Lukka, M. and Syvanen, A.-C. (1999) *European Journal of Human Genetics*, 7, 263–266.

Schumm, J.W., Lins, A.M., Micka, K.A., Sprecher, C.J., Rabbach, D.R. and Bacher, J.W. (1996) *Proceedings of the Seventh International Symposium on Human Identification*. Madison, WI: Promega Corporation, pp. 70–88.

Szibor, R., Lautsch, S., Plate, I., Bender, K. and Krause, D. (1998) *International Journal of Legal Medicine*, 111, 160–161.

Thomson, J.A., Pilotti, V., Stevens, P., Ayres, K.L. and Debenham, P.G. (1999) *Forensic Science International*, 100, 1–16.

Urquhart, A., Chiu, C.T., Clayton, T., Downes, T., Frazier, R., Jones, S., Kimpton, C., Lareu, M.V., Millican, E., Oldroyd, N., Thompson, C., Watson, S., Whitaker, J. and Gill, P. (1994) *Proceedings of the Fifth International Symposium on Human Identification*. Madison, WI: Promega Corporation, pp. 73–83.

Walsh, P.S. (1998) *Journal of Forensic Sciences*, 43, 1103–1104.

Walsh, P.S., Fildes, N.J. and Reynolds, R. (1996) *Nucleic Acids Research*, 24, 2807–2812.

Weber, J.L. and Wong, C. (1993) *Human Molecular Genetics*, 2, 1123–1128.

Wiegand, P., Meyer, E. and Brinkmann, B. (2000) *Electrophoresis*, 21, 889–895.

CHAPTER 7

FORENSIC ISSUES: DEGRADED DNA, PCR INHIBITION, CONTAMINATION, AND MIXED SAMPLES

UNIQUE NATURE OF FORENSIC SAMPLES

A forensic DNA laboratory often has to deal with DNA samples that are less than ideal. The biological material serving as evidence of a crime may have been left exposed to a harsh environment for days, months, or even years, such as in the case of the investigation of a missing person. The victims of homicides are typically taken to out of the way places where they remain until their bodies are discovered. Instead of being preserved in a freezer away from caustic chemicals that can break it down, the DNA molecules may have been left in direct sunlight or in damp woods.

Regardless of the situation, the DNA molecules from a crime scene come from a less than pristine environment that is normally found in molecular biology laboratories. Just as important is the fact that the retrieved biological sample may be limited in quantity. Thus, accurate sample analysis is critical since a forensic scientist may only obtain enough evidence for one attempt at analysis. In this chapter, we will explore the forensic issues surrounding the analysis of short tandem repeats (STRs), including handling degraded DNA samples, avoiding contamination, overcoming polymerase chain reaction (PCR) inhibition, and interpreting mixtures, which are prevalent in forensic cases, especially those involving sexual assault.

DEGRADED DNA

Environmental exposure degrades DNA molecules by randomly breaking them into smaller pieces. Enemies to the survival of intact DNA molecules include water and enzymes called nucleases that chew up DNA. Both are ubiquitous in nature. With older technologies such as restriction fragment length polymorphism (RFLP), these severely degraded DNA samples would have been very difficult if not impossible to analyze. High molecular weight DNA molecules need to be present in the sample in order to detect large VNTR (variable number of tandem repeats) alleles (e.g. 20 000 bp) with RFLP techniques.

An ethidium bromide-stained agarose 'yield gel' may be run to evaluate the quality of a DNA sample. Typically high molecular weight, high-quality genomic DNA runs as a relatively tight band of approximately 20 000 bp relative to an appropriate molecular weight marker. On the other hand, degraded DNA appears as a smear of DNA that is much less than 20 000 bp in size.

Modern-day PCR methods, such as multiplex STR typing, are powerful because minute amounts of DNA can be measured by amplifying them to a level where they may be detected. Less than 1 ng of DNA can now be analyzed with multiplex PCR amplification of STR alleles compared to 100 ng or more that might have been required with RFLP only a few years ago. However, this sensitivity to low levels of DNA also brings the challenge of avoiding contamination from the police officer or crime scene technician who collects the biological evidence.

In order for PCR amplification to occur, the DNA template must be intact where the two primers bind as well as between the primers so that full extension can occur. Without an intact DNA strand that surrounds the STR repeat region to serve as a template strand, PCR will be unsuccessful because primer extension will halt at the break in the template. The more degraded a DNA sample becomes, the more breaks occur in the template and fewer and fewer DNA molecules contain the full length needed for PCR amplification.

BENEFITS OF STR MARKERS WITH DEGRADED DNA SAMPLES

Fortunately, because STR loci can be amplified with fairly small product sizes, there is a greater chance for the STR primers to find some intact DNA strands for amplification. In addition, the narrow size range of STR alleles benefits analysis of degraded DNA samples because allele dropout via preferential amplification of the smaller allele is less likely to occur since both alleles in a heterozygous individual are similar in size.

A number of experiments have shown that there is an inverse relationship between the size of the locus and successful PCR amplification from degraded DNA samples, such as those obtained from a crime scene or a mass disaster (Whitaker et al. 1995, Sparkes et al. 1996, Takahashi et al. 1997). The STR loci with larger sized amplicons in a multiplex amplification, such as D18S51 and FGA, are the first to drop out of the DNA profile when amplifying extremely degraded DNA samples.

In one of the first studies demonstrating the value of multiplex STR analysis with degraded DNA samples, the Forensic Science Service was able successfully to type a majority of 73 duplicate pathological samples obtained from the Waco disaster with four STR markers (Whitaker et al. 1995). They observed no allele dropout and obtained concordant results on all samples where alleles were scored. A correlation was observed between successful typing at a locus and the average length of the alleles at that locus. The FES/FPS locus, which has alleles in the size range of 212–240 bp, only yielded 91 successful amplifications while the VWA locus, with alleles ranging from 130–169 bp, had 115 successful amplifications. Thus, loci with the larger alleles failed first. In addition, amelogenin amplicons (106 or 112 bp) were obtained on all 24 samples examined as part of the Waco identification program.

The potential for analysis of degraded DNA samples is an area where multiplex STR systems really shine over previously used DNA markers. STRs are more sensitive than single locus probe RFLP methods, less prone to allelic dropout than VNTR systems (AmpFLPs) such as D1S80, and more discriminating than other PCR-based typing methods, such as HLA-DQA1 and AmpliType PolyMarker.

PCR INHIBITION

Another important challenge to amplifying DNA samples from crime scenes is the fact that the PCR amplification process can be affected by inhibitors present in the samples themselves. Occasionally materials such as textile dyes or hemoglobin from red blood cells can remain with the DNA throughout the sample preparation process and interfere with the polymerase to prevent successful PCR amplification (Akane *et al.* 1994, DeFanchis *et al.* 1988).

The result of amplifying a DNA sample containing an inhibitor such as hematin is a loss of the alleles from the larger sized STR loci. The results look similar to a degraded DNA sample (Perkin Elmer Corporation 1998). Thus, the failure to amplify the larger STR loci for a sample can be either due to degraded DNA, where there are not enough intact copies of the DNA template, or due to the presence of a sufficient level of PCR inhibitor to reduce the activity of the polymerase.

SOLUTIONS TO PCR INHIBITION

PCR inhibitors may be removed or their effects reduced by one or more of the following solutions. The genomic DNA template may be diluted, which also dilutes the PCR inhibitor, and re-amplified in the presence of less inhibitor. Alternatively, more DNA polymerase can be added to overcome the inhibitor. With this approach some fraction of the *Taq* polymerase binds to the inhibiting molecule(s) and removes them from the reaction so that the rest of the *Taq* can do its job and amplify the DNA template.

In addition, additives such as bovine serum albumin (BSA) have been shown to prevent or minimize the inhibition of PCR (Comey *et al.* 1994). More recently, a sodium hydroxide treatment of DNA has been shown to neutralize inhibitors of *Taq* polymerase (Bourke *et al.* 1999). Finally, a separation step may be performed prior to PCR to separate the extracted DNA from the inhibiting compound. Centricon-100 and Microcon-100 filters have been used for this purpose (Comey *et al.* 1994).

CONTAMINATION ISSUES

The sensitivity of PCR with its ability to amplify low quantities of DNA can be a problem if proper care is not taken. Validated laboratory protocols must be adhered to so that contamination from higher concentrations of DNA, such as those of the DNA analyst, can be avoided. However, it is important to keep in mind that, if contamination does occur, it will most likely result in an 'exclusion' or 'inconclusive' result and be in favor of the defendant.

Contamination implies the accidental transfer of DNA. There are three potential sources of contamination when performing PCR: sample contamination with genomic DNA from the environment, contamination between samples during preparation, and contamination of a sample with amplified DNA from a previous PCR reaction (Lygo *et al.* 1994). The first source of contamination is largely dependent on sample collection at the crime scene and the care taken there by the evidence collection team (see Chapter 3). Environmental contamination can be monitored only in a limited sense by 'substrate controls' (Gill 1997). The latter two sources of contamination can be controlled and even eliminated by using appropriate laboratory procedures and designated work areas (see Chapter 4).

The possibility of laboratory contamination is addressed with 'negative controls' that test for contamination of PCR reagents and tubes. Basically, a negative control involves running a blank sample through the entire process in parallel with the forensic case evidence. The same volume of purified water as DNA template in the other samples is added to a negative control PCR reaction. If any detectable PCR products are observed in the negative control, then sources of contamination should be sought out and eliminated before proceeding further.

In a systematic examination of possible sources of PCR contamination, Henry Lee and co-workers found that under the circumstances normally encountered during casework analysis, PCR contamination was never noted (Scherczinger *et al.* 1999). Using reverse dot blot detection of AmpliType PM and DQA1 systems (the same PCR principles apply as with STR markers detected using fluorescence), they examined four general aspects of PCR during which contamination might occur: PCR amplification setup, handling the PCR products, aerosolization, and DNA storage. In these studies, detectable contamination occurred only when gross deviations from basic preventative protocols were employed. They concluded that contamination could not be generated by simple acts of carelessness (Scherczinger *et al.* 1999).

The genotypes of laboratory personnel are typically stored for comparison purposes so that any contamination by an individual in the laboratory can be picked up. Only in the case of gross laboratory error, would a mixture of two DNA types result (i.e. that of the analyst and the sample being examined). These types of errors would most likely be sorted out by comparing the result with genotypes of laboratory personnel when the mixture analysis is performed (see discussion on mixtures below).

To avoid contamination problems during the laboratory examination of DNA samples, all pre-PCR and post-PCR amplification reactions should be kept physically separate (see Chapter 4). However, if the original DNA sample has been contaminated during the collection process (see Chapter 3), then the DNA profile would be a mixture and the results would need to be interpreted as described in the next section.

MIXTURES

Mixtures arise when two or more individuals contribute to the sample being tested. Mixtures can be challenging to detect and interpret without extensive experience and careful training. As detection technologies have become more sensitive with PCR sensitivity coupled with fluorescent measurements, the ability to see minor components in the DNA profile of mixed samples has improved vastly over what was available with RFLP methods only a few years ago. Likewise, the theoretical aspects of statistical calculations for mixture interpretation have been examined more thoroughly (Curran *et al.* 1999).

VALUE OF HIGHLY POLYMORPHIC MARKERS IN DEALING WITH MIXTURES

The probability that a mixture will be detected improves with the use of more loci and genetic markers that have a high incidence of heterozygotes. The detectability of multiple DNA sources in a single sample relates to the ratio of DNA present from each source, the specific combinations of genotypes, and the total amount of DNA amplified. In other words, some mixtures will not be as easily detectable as other mixtures.

Using highly polymorphic STR markers with more possible alleles translates to a greater chance of seeing differences between the two components of a mixture. For example, D18S51 has 27 possible alleles, while TPOX has only eight common alleles, making D18S51 a more useful marker for detecting mixtures. Likewise, the more markers examined (e.g. by using a multiplex STR amplification), the greater the chance to observe multiple components in the mixture.

The quantity of each component in a mixture makes a difference in the ability to detect all contributors to the mixed sample. For example, if the two DNA sources are in similar quantities, they will be much easier to detect than if one is present at only a fraction of the other. The minor component of a mixture is usually not detectable for mixture ratios below the 5% level or 1:20 (Perkin Elmer Corporation 1998, Cotton 1995). The AmpFlSTR kits recommend that the minor component be above 35 pg in quantity to obtain a reliable genotype result (Perkin Elmer Corporation 1998).

QUANTITATIVE INFORMATION FROM FLUORESCENCE MEASUREMENTS

The ability to obtain quantitative information from peaks in an electropherogram, either using the ABI 310 or 377 platform (see Chapter 11) or a fluorescence scanner such as the FMBIO II (see Chapter 12), now permits relative peak heights or areas of STR alleles to be measured. This peak information can then be used to decipher the possible genotypes of the contributors to the mixed sample. Owing to peak shape variation, peak areas have been advocated as being superior to peak heights when comparing allele peak information (Gill *et al.* 1998a). However, peak heights are successfully used in some laboratories for mixture interpretation.

Figure 7.1 illustrates how typical single-source samples differ from mixed samples in their STR profiles. STR allele peak patterns for heterozygous samples will generally have stutter products that are less than 15% of the associated allele peak height/area. In addition, the peak height ratio, as measured by dividing the height of the lower quantity peak in relative fluorescence units by the height of the higher quantity allele peak, should be greater than approximately 70% in a single source sample (Perkin Elmer Corporation 1998, Gill *et al.* 1997). Thus, if peaks fall in the region between 15% and 70% of the highest peak at a particular STR locus, a mixed sample that has resulted from two or more contributors is probable.

DISTINGUISHING GENOTYPES IN A MIXED SAMPLE

Several clues exist to help determine that a mixture is present. Answers to the following questions can help ascertain the genotypes that make up the composite DNA profile of the mixture:

- Do any of the loci show more than two peaks in the expected allele size range?
- Is there a severe peak height imbalance between heterozygous alleles at a locus?
- Does the stutter product appear abnormally high (e.g. >15–20%)?

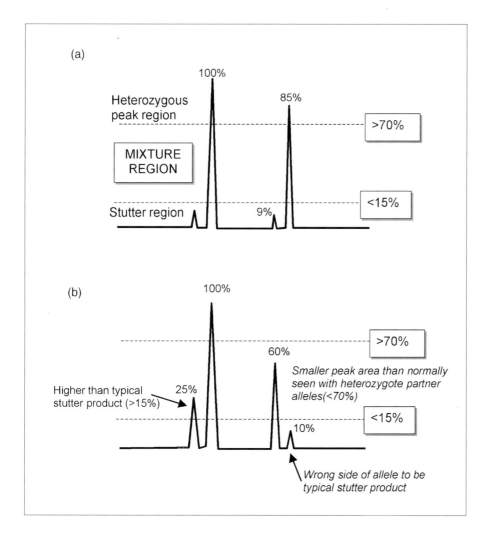

Figure 7.1

Illustration of typical single-source (a) versus mixed-sample (b) heterozygote peak patterns. The relative peak areas due to the measured fluorescent signal are useful indicators to decipher the presence of a sample mixture. If the highest peak at a locus is set at 100%, then heterozygous alleles should have peak areas and peak heights that are greater than 70% of the highest alleles. Stutter products are typically less than 15% of their corresponding allele peak and shorter by four base pairs for tetranucleotide repeats.

If the answer to any one of these three questions is 'yes', then the DNA profile may very well have resulted from a mixed sample. Mixture interpretation has been examined extensively by the Forensic Science Service (Clayton *et al.* 1998, Gill *et al.* 1998a, 1998b) and many of their strategies have been incorporated into this section's material.

Usually a mixture is first identified by the presence of three or more prominent peaks at one or more loci. At a single locus, a sample containing DNA from two sources can exhibit one, two, three, or four peaks due to the possible genotype combinations listed below.

Four peaks:

■   Heterozygote + heterozygote, no overlapping alleles (genotypes are unique).

Three peaks:

■ Heterozygote + heterozygote, one overlapping allele.

■ Heterozygote + homozygote, no overlapping alleles (genotypes are unique).

Two peaks:

■ Heterozygote + heterozygote, two overlapping alleles (genotypes are identical).

■ Heterozygote + homozygote, one overlapping allele.

■ Homozygote + homozygote, no overlapping alleles (genotypes are unique).

Single peak:

■ Homozygote + homozygote, overlapping allele (genotypes are identical).

When two contributors to a mixed stain share one or more alleles, the alleles are 'masked' and the contributing genotypes may not be easily decipherable. For example, if two individuals at the FGA locus have genotypes 23,24 and 24,24, then a mixture ratio of 1:1 will produce a ratio of 1:3 for the 23:24 peak areas. In this particular case, the mixture could be interpreted as a homozygous allele with a large stutter product without further information. However, by examining the STR profiles at other loci that have unshared alleles, i.e. three or four peaks per locus, this sample may be able to be dissected properly into its components.

In an effort to see if it was possible for masking to occur at every locus in a multiplex, the Forensic Science Service conducted a simulated mixture study with 120 000 individual STR profiles in their Caucasian database (Gill *et al.* 1997). They found that the vast majority of these artificial mixtures showed 15–22 peaks across a six-plex STR marker multiplex. The maximum number in a mixture of two heterozygous individuals with no overlapping alleles at six STRs would be 24 peaks. Thus, in this example with unrelated individuals, simple mixtures can be identified by the presence of three or more alleles at several loci. Out of more than 212 000 pairwise comparisons, there were only four examples where one or two alleles were observed at each locus in the six-plex, and these could be designated mixtures because of peak imbalances (Gill *et al.* 1997).

MIXTURE INTERPRETATION

This next section will review the principles outlined by Gill *et al.* (1998b) and Clayton *et al.* (1998) for interpreting mixed forensic stains using STR typing

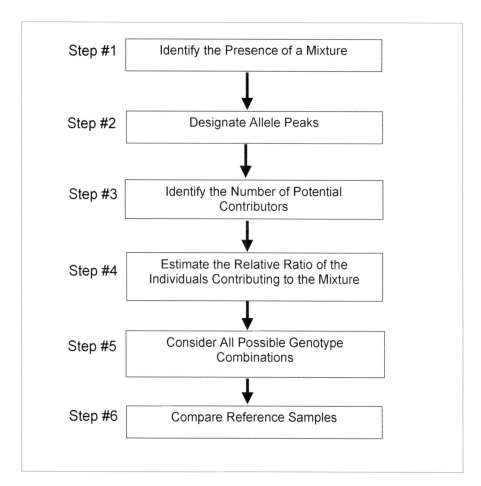

results. Their six primary steps for interpreting mixtures are outlined in Figure 7.2. The interpretation steps will first be discussed and then an example mixture will be reviewed to put these steps into the context of a real sample.

An understanding of how non-mixtures behave is essential to being able to proceed with mixture interpretation. Mixed DNA profiles need to be interpreted against a background of biological and technological artifacts. Chapter 6 reviewed some of the prominent biological artifacts that exist for STR markers. These include stutter products and null alleles. In addition, chromosomal abnormalities, such as three-banded patterns resulting from trisomy (the presence of three chromosomes instead of the normal two), and non-specific amplification products can occur and must be considered prior to making an attempt to decipher a mixed profile. Issues surrounding technological artifacts from fluorescence detection will be covered in Chapters 10 and 13.

Stutter products represent the greatest challenge in confidently interpreting a mixture and designating the appropriate alleles. It is not always possible to exclude stutters since they are allelic products and differ from their associated allele by a single repeat unit. The general guideline for stutter identification of one repeat unit less than the corresponding allele and less than 15% of that allele's peak area is typically a useful one and can be used to mark suspected stutter products. The introduction of pentanucleotide repeat markers with stutter products of less than 1–2% may greatly simplify mixture interpretation (Bacher *et al.* 1999).

After a mixture has been identified as such and all of the alleles have been called, the next step (Figure 7.2, step #3) is to identify the number of potential contributors. For a two-person mixture, the maximum number of alleles at any given locus is four if both individuals are heterozygous and there is no allele overlap. Thus, if more than four alleles are observed then a complex mixture consisting of more than two individuals is possible. Fortunately, the overwhelming majority of mixtures encountered in forensic casework involve two-person mixtures (Clayton *et al.* 1998).

Mixtures can range from equal proportions of each component to one component being greatly in excess. The varying proportions of a mixture are usually referred to in a ratio format (e.g. 1:1 or 1:5). Mixtures of known quantities of DNA templates have shown that the mixture ratio is approximately preserved during PCR amplification. Thus, the peak areas and heights observed in an electropherogram can be related back to the amount of DNA template components included in the mixed sample.

An approximate mixture ratio can be best determined by considering the profile as a whole and looking at all of the information from each locus. The ratio of mixture components is most easily determined when there are no shared alleles at a locus. Thus, it is best to first examine loci with four alleles as a starting point for estimating the relative ratio of the two individuals contributing to the mixture. Determining the ratio when there are shared alleles is more complex because there may be more than one possible combination of alleles that could explain the observed peak patterns (Clayton *et al.* 1998).

The possible combination of alleles for two, three, and four allele peak patterns are listed in Table 7.1. For four alleles at a locus, there are three possible pairwise comparisons that exist, if one does not worry about the reciprocal cases, i.e. which allele combinations belong to the minor contributor and which belong to the major contributor. For three alleles at a locus, there are six possible pairwise combinations and for two alleles at a locus there are four possible pairwise combinations (Table 7.1).

Amelogenin, the sex-typing marker, is an effective marker for deciphering the contributions of genetically normal male and female individuals. The predicted X and Y allele peak ratios for a number of possible male and female mixture ratios are listed in Table 7.2. The amelogenin X and Y peak areas are especially useful in determining whether the major contributor to the mixture is male or female.

Four Alleles (A,B,C,D)		Three Alleles (A,B,C)		Two Alleles (A,B)	
A, B	C,D	A,A	B,C	A,A	A,B
A,C	B,D	B,B	A,C	A,B	A,B
A,D	B,C	C,C	A,B	A,A	B,B
		A,B	A,C	A,B	B,B
		B,C	A,C		
		A,B	B,C		

Table 7.1

Pairwise comparisons of two, three and four allele peak patterns. Reciprocal combinations are not shown.

Mixture Ratio		Allele Combination		Ratio of X:Y Peak Areas
Female (X,X)	Male (X,Y)	X	Y	X:Y
20	1	41	1	41:1
10	1	21	1	21:1
5	1	11	1	11:1
4	1	9	1	9:1
3	1	7	1	7:1
2	1	5	1	5:1
1	1	3	1	3:1
1	**2**	**4**	**2**	**2:1**
1	3	5	3	1.7:1
1	4	6	4	1.5:1
1	5	7	5	1.4:1
1	10	12	10	1.2:1
1	20	22	20	1.1:1

Table 7.2

Possible amelogenin X and Y allele peak ratios with varying quantities of DNA. The 2:1 peak area ratio for the X and Y alleles observed in Figure 7.3 and calculated in Table 7.3 matches a mixture ratio of one part female to two parts male as indicated by the numbers underlined. Thus, there is twice as much male DNA compared to female DNA in the mixed sample shown in Figure 7.3.

The next step in examining a mixture is to consider all possible genotype combinations at each locus (Figure 7.2, step #5). Peaks representing the allele calls at each locus are labeled with the designations A, B, and so forth. The possible pairwise combinations from Table 7.1 are considered using the peak areas for each called allele. Each particular combination of alleles at the different loci is considered in light of the information determined previously regarding the mixture ratio for the sample under investigation (step #4). By stepping through each STR locus in this manner, the genotypes of the major and minor contributors to the mixture can be deciphered. In the example shown in Figure 7.3 and Table 7.3, some of these calculations are demonstrated.

The final step in the interpretation of a mixture is to compare the resultant genotype profiles for the possible components of the mixture with the genotypes of reference samples (Figure 7.2, step #6). In a sexual assault case, this reference sample could be the suspect and/or the victim. If the DNA profiles from the suspect's reference sample matches the major or minor component of the mixture, then that person cannot be eliminated as a possible contributor to the mixed stain (Clayton et al. 1998).

AN EXAMPLE MIXTURE

An example mixture will now be examined to demonstrate how the steps illustrated in Figure 7.2 may be used to interpret a mixture. Figure 7.3 shows a mixed sample that is a combination of male and female DNA, typical of what might be seen in a sexual assault investigation. The STR markers for the mixture are separated into three panels based on their dye label in order to visualize each STR locus more easily.

Figure 7.3

Mixture of male and female DNA typical of what might be seen in a forensic case involving mixed samples. Profiler Plus™ multiplex STR data are displayed here with GeneScan® 3.1. Sample mixture indicators include an imbalance in the amelogenin X and Y alleles as well as greater than two peaks at multiple STR markers.

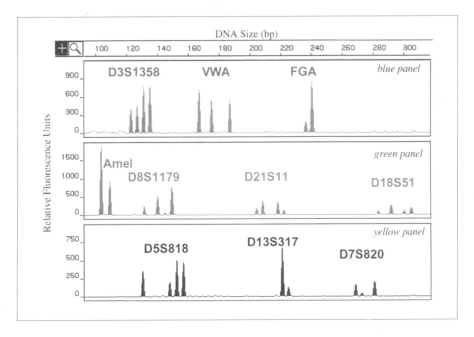

The first thing that is obvious in this example is the presence of more than two peaks at a majority of the loci. For example, D3S1358 contains four peaks and VWA has three peaks. There is also an imbalance in the X and Y alleles of the amelogenin sex-typing marker (see Chapter 8 for more information on amelogenin).

With the presence of a mixture established, the alleles are determined. Because there are a maximum of four peaks at any one locus, it is unlikely that there are more than two contributors to this example mixture. Each of the called alleles is labeled with a letter: 'A', 'B', 'C', or 'D'. These universal designations are used to track possible allele combinations through the rest of the mixture calculations.

The relative ratio of the individuals contributing to this example mixture is then estimated by examining loci with four peaks. The green panel STR data from Figure 7.3 is shown in Figure 7.4 with labeled peak areas. There are four peaks present at both the D21S11 and D18S51 loci. Since the peak areas of the

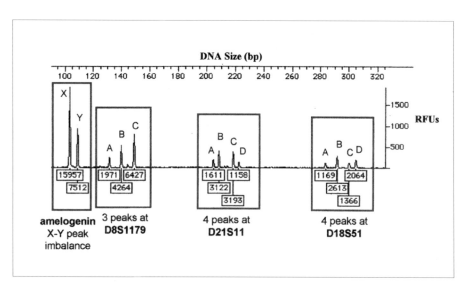

Figure 7.4

Peak areas for green panel data from example mixture in Figure 7.3. Mixture ratio calculations for these STR markers are shown in Table 7.3. RFUs = relative fluorescent units.

Table 7.3

Peak information for four loci from the data displayed in Figure 7.4. The mixture ratio is determined by comparing the peak areas for the appropriate peak combinations. The original source genotypes are also listed for the male and female components of the mixture, along with the expected number of peaks at each locus.

Locus	Component	Allele Call	Peak Area	Possible Combinations		Mixture Ratio
D21S11	A	29	1611	AD	BC	$\dfrac{B+C}{A+D} = \dfrac{3122+3193}{1611+1158} = 2.3$
	B	30	3122			
	C	32.2	3193	↓	↓	
	D	33.2	1158			**~2:1**
				29,33.2	30,32.2	
D18S51	A	12	1169	AC	BD	$\dfrac{B+D}{A+C} = \dfrac{2613+2064}{1169+1366} = 1.8$
	B	14	2613			
	C	16	1366	↓	↓	
	D	17	2064			**~2:1**
				12,16 and	14,17	
D8S1179	A	10	1971	AA	BC	
	B	12	4264	BB	AC	
	C	14	6427	CC	AB	
				AB	AC	Based on peak profile appearance for 2:1 mixture (see Figures 7.4 and 7.5)
				BC	AC ◄—	
				AB	BC	
Amel	X	X	15957	2X:1Y		$\dfrac{X}{Y}$ $\dfrac{15957}{7512} = 2.1$
	Y	Y	7512	2 parts male to 1 part female		

	D3	VWA	FGA	Amel	D8	D21	D18	D5	D13	D7
Male	17,18	14,19	24,24	X,Y	12,14	30,32.2	14,17	12,13	12,12	9,12
Female	15,16	16,16	23,24	X,X	10,14	29,33.2	12,16	7,11	12,13	10,12
Mixture										
# Peaks	4	3	2	2	3	4	4	4	2	3
Major	CD	AC	BB	XY	BC	BC	BD	CD	AA	AC
Minor	AB	BB	AB	XX	AC	AD	AC	AB	AB	BC

Original source genotypes for Figure 7.3 mixed sample example.

D21S11 A and the D alleles are similar, and the peak areas of the B and the C alleles are similar to each other, we can assume the AD and BC represent the best possible combination of alleles to explain the data. Likewise, the D18S51 A and C alleles have similar peak areas and can be grouped together so that the best possible combination of alleles at this locus is AC and BD (Table 7.3)

The mixture ratio for the D21S11 alleles is calculated to be 2.3, or approximately 2:1, by dividing the sum of the larger alleles (B and C) by the sum of the smaller alleles (A and D). Thus, the major contributor to this mixture has about twice as much DNA present as the minor contributor. Using the same approach, the D18S51 mixture ratio is calculated to be 1.8 or approximately 2:1 for the major contributor (Table 7.3). These mixture ratios will not always be exact due to the influence of stutter products and imbalances in heterozygote peak areas.

Calculating mixture ratios is much easier at loci with four observed alleles than at loci where one or more of the alleles are shared. D8S1179 in this example represents such a situation. Three peaks are present at D8S1179 with one of these peaks representing an allele from both the major and the minor contributor. Each possible combination of alleles is therefore carefully considered to determine which one best fits the observed data.

Expected peak patterns for each of the possible 2:1 mixture combinations are displayed in Figure 7.5. The observed data for D8S1179 (Figure 7.4) fits the scenario of BC and AC allele combinations with BC belonging to the major contributor. Thus, in this case allele C, or 14, is shared. The major contributor's genotype is therefore 12,14 at D8S1179 while the minor contributor's genotype is 10,14.

The major contributor in this example mixture was the male individual at a ratio of two times that of the female DNA in the mixture (Table 7.3). This fact was determined by examining the peak areas for the X and Y alleles and comparing them to the information found in Table 7.2. Thus, in this example it was possible to decipher that the major contributor was a male and that the D21S11 alleles 30 and 32.2, D18S51 alleles 14 and 17, and D8S1179 alleles 12 and 14 belonged to him. By continuing through all of the loci in the manner indicated above, the genotype profile of the major and minor contributors can be distinguished.

Mixture ratios cannot always be calculated at every locus with complete confidence, especially those with two or three peaks that have shared alleles between the contributors. Note that in Figure 7.5, when a homozygous individual is the minor component of a mixture, all three scenarios have indistinguishable profiles of three fairly balanced peak signals (e.g. VWA in Figure 7.3). Of course, stutter products and imbalanced heterozygote peak signals make mixture ratios less accurate.

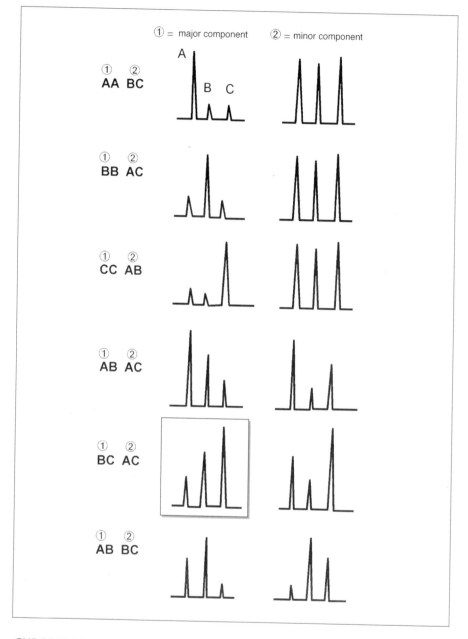

① = major component   ② = minor component

Figure 7.5

Expected peak profiles for 2:1 mixture combinations involving three peaks. These peak profiles assume no overlap with stutter products and homozygote alleles that possess twice the signal strength of each heterozygote allele.

CHROMOSOMAL ABNORMALITIES

Chromosomal abnormalities do exist and can give rise to extra allele peaks at a particular STR locus. Chromosomal translocations, somatic mutations and trisomies may occur in the cells of the donor of a forensic stain. However, the STR profile from the individual with the chromosomal abnormality would most likely show only a single extra band and the same pattern would be present in both the forensic stain and the reference sample from the matching suspect

Focus Box 7.1

*Abnormal STR peak
heights in K562 cell line
DNA profile.*

K562 genomic DNA is supplied as a control sample from Promega Corporation with their GenePrint® STR typing kits. However, as can be seen from the peak profiles below, some of the STR loci exhibit imbalanced heterozygous alleles and/or multiple peaks that would make the sample appear to come from more than one source of DNA. In this particular case, these extra peaks or peak imbalances are the result of an abnormal number of chromosomes present in the sample rather than a problem with the DNA typing system. K562 cells are derived from a female human subject with a diagnosis of chronic myelogeneous leukemia. Because mutant cells are present with chromosomes that possess somatic mutations that affect the number of repeats in various STR markers, the K562 cell line results do not possess the normal balance of chromosomal material seen in healthy individuals. Thus, balanced heterozygous allele peaks are not always seen. Shown below are six STR markers amplified from K562 genomic DNA that possess a significant variation in the balance of the STR allele peak heights.

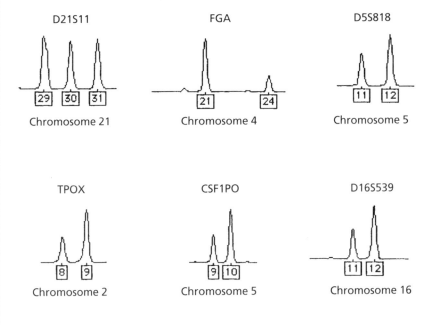

Genotyper 2.5 data from AmpFlSTR Profiler Plus and COfiler PCR amplifications with ABI 310 detection.

(Clayton *et al.* 1998). The rare cases where a chromosomal abnormality is observed can even help strengthen the final conclusions.

An excellent example of a chromosomal abnormality is found in the standard cell line K562. Three peaks are obtained at the D21S11 locus and at least five other STR loci have heterozygous peak patterns that are not balanced (Focus box 7.1). At first glance, one might suspect this sample to have arisen from more than one source rather than a sample with an abnormal number of chromosomes.

CONCLUSIONS ON INTERPRETING MIXTURES

Mixed sample stains are present in many forensic investigations and STR typing procedures have been demonstrated to be an effective means of differentiating components of a mixed sample. However, a case may contain multiple stains and not all of these will be mixtures. In fact, the proportions of a mixture can vary across the forensic stain itself. Thus, if additional samples can be tested that are easier to interpret, they should be sought after versus complicated mixtures (Gill *et al.* 1998b). As recommended by Peter Gill of the Forensic Science Service, the best advice is 'Don't do mixture interpretation unless you have to.'

Some forensic DNA laboratories may decide not to go through the trouble of fully deciphering the genotype possibilities and assigning them to the major and minor contributors. An easier approach is to simply include or exclude a suspect's DNA profile from the crime scene mixture profile. If all the alleles from a suspect's DNA profile are represented in the crime scene mixture, then the suspect cannot be excluded as contributing to the crime scene stain. Likewise, the alleles in a victim's DNA profile could be subtracted out of the mixture profile to simplify the alleles that need to be present in the perpetrator's DNA profile.

REFERENCES

Akane, A., Matsubara, K., Nakamura, H., Takahashi, S. and Kimura, K. (1994) *Journal of Forensic Sciences*, 39, 362–372.

Bacher, J.W., Hennes, L.F., Gu, T., Tereba, A., Micka, K.A., Sprecher, C.J., Lins, A.M., Amiott, E.A., Rabbach, D.R., Taylor, J.A., Helms, C., Donis-Keller, H. and Schumm, J.W. (1999) *Proceedings of the Ninth International Symposium on Human Indentification*. Madison, WI: Promega Corporation, pp. 24–37.

Banaschak, S., Moller, K. and Pfeiffer, H. (1998) *International Journal of Legal Medicine*, 111, 284–285.

Bourke, M.T., Scherczinger, C.A., Ladd, C. and Lee, H.C. (1999) *Journal of Forensic Sciences*, 44, 1046–1050.

Clayton, T.M., Whitaker, J.P., Sparkes, R. and Gill, P. (1998) *Forensic Science International*, 91, 55–70.

Comey, C.T., Koons, B.W., Presley, K.W., Smerick, J.B., Sobieralski, C.A., Stanley, D.M. and Baechtel, F.S. (1994) *Journal of Forensic Sciences*, 39, 1254–1269.

Cotton, R.W. (1995) *Proceedings of the Sixth International Symposium on Human Identification*. Madison, WI: Promega Corporation, pp. 112–115.

Curran, J.M., Triggs, C.M., Buckleton, J. and Weir, B.S. (1999) *Journal of Forensic Sciences*, 44, 987–995.

DeFranchis, R., Cross, N.C.P., Foulkes, N.S. and Cox, T.M. (1988) *Nucleic Acids Research*, 16, 10355.

Gill, P. (1997) *Forensic Science International*, 85, 105–111.

Gill, P., Sparkes, R. and Kimpton, C. (1997) *Forensic Science International*, 89, 185–197.

Gill, P., Sparkes, R., Pinchin, R., Clayton, T., Whitaker, J. and Buckleton, J. (1998a) *Forensic Science International*, 91, 41–53.

Gill, P., Sparkes, B., Clayton, T.M., Whittaker, J., Urquhart, A. and Buckleton, J.S. (1998b) *Proceedings of the Ninth International Symposium on Human Identification*. Madison, WI: Promega Corporation, pp. 7–18.

Lygo, J.E., Johnson, P.E., Holdaway, D.J., Woodroffe, S., Whitaker, J.P., Clayton, T.M., Kimpton, C.P. and Gill, P. (1994) *International Journal of Legal Medicine*, 107, 77–89.

Perkin Elmer Corporation (1998) AmpFlSTR Profiler Plus PCR Amplification Kit User's Manual. Foster City: PE Biosystems.

Sparkes, R., Kimpton, C.P., Watson, S., Oldroyd, N.J., Clayton, T.M., Barnett, L., Arnold, J., Thompson, C., Hale, R., Chapman, J., Urquhart, A. and Gill, P. (1996) *International Journal of Legal Medicine*, 109, 186–194.

Scherczinger, C.A., Ladd, C., Bourke, M.T., Adamowicz, M.S., Johannes, P.M., Scherczinger, R., Beesley, T. and Lee, H.C. (1999) *Journal of Forensic Sciences*, 44, 1042–1045.

Takahashi, M., Kato, Y., Mukoyama, H., Kanaya, H. and Kamiyama, S. (1997) *Forensic Science International*, 90, 1–9.

Whitaker, J.P., Clayton, T.M., Urquhart, A.J., Millican, E.S., Downes, T.J., Kimpton, C.P. and Gill, P. (1995) *BioTechniques*, 18, 670–677.

CHAPTER 8

ADDITIONAL DNA MARKERS: AMELOGENIN, Y-CHROMOSOME STRs, mtDNA, SNPs, Alu REPEATS

Research into the identification and validation of more and better marker systems for forensic analysis should continue with a view of making each profile unique.

(*NRC II Report*, p. 7, Recommendation 5.3)

ROLE OF ADDITIONAL GENETIC MARKERS IN FORENSIC SCIENCE

In this chapter, we will examine other DNA markers that are being used or being developed for forensic DNA typing purposes. The 13 core loci described in Chapter 5 are being extensively used today and will probably continue to be used for many years in the future because they are part of the DNA databases that are growing around the world. Yet forensic DNA scientists often use additional markers as the need arises to obtain further information about a particular sample.

Sex typing is performed in conjunction with available short tandem repeat (STR) kits to provide the gender of the individual who is the source of the DNA sample in question. Additionally, in cases where samples may be extremely degraded and fail to result in useful information with conventional STR multiplexes, mitochondrial DNA, which occurs in higher copy numbers per cell than nuclear DNA and thus more resistant to complete sample degradation, may be used.

Y-chromosome systems are becoming more popular as a means to extract information from the male portion of a sample mixture (e.g. evidence in rape cases). In this chapter, we have included a brief review of new markers that are being considered to add flexibility in forensic DNA analysis. Information from non-human DNA sources has already been used to solve forensic cases and will continue to grow in value as our knowledge of genomic DNA sequence diversity from human populations as well as other organisms improves. It is conceivable that, within a few years, a wide variety of validated marker sets and technologies will exist that will provide a forensic DNA laboratory with a smorgasbord of possibilities in their arsenal of weapons that may be used to solve crimes with biological evidence.

GENDER IDENTIFICATION WITH AMELOGENIN

The ability to designate whether a sample originated from a male or a female source is useful in sexual assault cases, where distinguishing between the victim and the perpetrator's evidence is important. Likewise, missing persons and mass disaster investigations can benefit from gender identification of the remains. Over the years a number of gender identification assays have been demonstrated using polymerase chain reaction (PCR) methods (Sullivan *et al.* 1993, Eng *et al.* 1994, Reynolds and Varlaro 1996). By far the most popular method for sex typing today is the amelogenin system as it can be performed in conjunction with STR analysis.

Amelogenin is a gene which codes for proteins found in tooth enamel. The British Forensic Science Service were the first to describe the particular PCR primer sets that are used so prevalently in forensic DNA laboratories today (Sullivan *et al.* 1993). These primers flank a 6 bp deletion within intron 1 of the amelogenin gene on the X homologue (Figure 8.1). PCR amplification of this area with their primers results in 106 bp and 112 bp amplicons from the X- and Y-chromosomes, respectively. Primers, which yield a 212 bp X-specific amplicon and a 218 bp Y-specific product by bracketing the same 6 bp deletion, were also

Figure 8.1

Schematic of the amelo-genin sex-typing assay. The X and Y chromosomes contain a high degree of sequence homology at the amelogenin locus. The primer sets depicted here target a 6 bp deletion that is present only on the X chromosome. The presence of a single peak indicates that the sample comes from a female while two peaks identifies the sample's source as male. The primers to amplify the 106/112 bp fragments are used in the AmpFlSTR kits while the PowerPlex 1.1 kit uses the larger primer set.

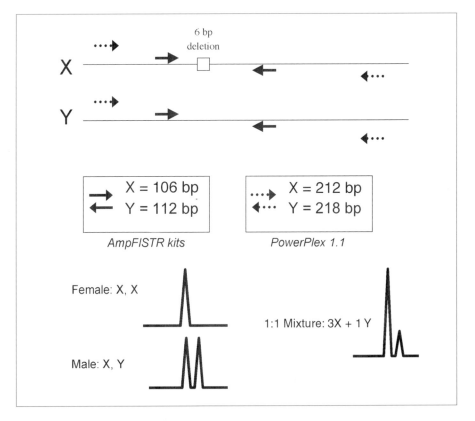

described in the original amelogenin paper (Sullivan *et al.* 1993) and have been used in conjunction with the D1S80 VNTR system (Budowle *et al.* 1996).

An advantage with the above approach, i.e. using a single primer set to amplify both chromosomes, is that the X chromosome product itself plays a role as a positive control. This PCR-based assay is extremely sensitive. Mannucci and co-workers were able to detect as little as 20 pg (~3 diploid copies) as well as sample mixtures where female DNA was in 100-fold excess of male DNA (Mannucci *et al.* 1994).

Other regions of the amelogenin gene have size differences between the X and Y homologues and may be exploited for sex-typing purposes. For example, Eng and co-workers (1994) used a single set of primers that generated a 977 bp product for the X chromosome and a 788 bp fragment for the Y chromosome. In this case, a 189 bp deletion in the Y relative to the X chromosome was used to differentiate the two chromosomes.

A recent study found that 19 regions of absolute homology, ranging in size from 22 to 80 bp, exist between the human amelogenin X and Y genes that can be used to design a variety of primer sets (Haas-Rochholz and Weiler 1997). Thus, by spanning various deletions of the X and/or Y chromosome, it is possible to generate PCR products from the X and Y homologues that differ in size and contain size ranges that can be integrated into future multiplex STR amplifications.

While amelogenin is an effective method for sex typing biological samples in most cases, the results are not foolproof. A rare deletion of the amelogenin gene on the Y chromosome can cause the Y chromosome amplicon to be absent (Santos *et al.* 1998). In such a case, a male sample would falsely appear as a female. However, a male sample with only the X amelogenin amplicon can be shown to be male using additional Y-chromosome markers, such as those described below.

LINEAGE MARKERS

Autosomal DNA markers, such as the 13 core STR loci, are shuffled with each generation because half of an individual's genetic information comes from their father and half from their mother. However, the Y chromosome and mitochondrial DNA markers that will be discussed in this next section represent 'lineage markers'. They are passed down from generation to generation without changing (except for mutational events). Maternal lineages can be traced with mitochondrial DNA sequence information, while paternal lineages can be followed with Y-chromosome markers.

With lineage markers, the genetic information from each marker is referred to as a haplotype rather than a genotype because there is only a single allele per individual. Because the Y-chromosome and mitochondrial DNA markers are linked on the same chromosome (i.e. they are not shuffled with each generation), the statistical calculations for a random match probability cannot involve the product rule. Therefore, haplotypes obtained from lineage markers can never be as effective in differentiating between two individuals as genotypes from autosomal markers that are unlinked and segregate separately from generation to generation. However, as will be discussed below, Y-chromosome and mitochondrial DNA markers do have an important role to play in forensic investigations.

Y-CHROMOSOME STRs

The Y chromosome is becoming a popular method for tracing human evolution through male lineages (Jobling and Tyler-Smith 1995) as well as application to male identification in forensic situations (Kayser *et al.* 1997a). The ability to separate and identify the male component of a mixture is valuable for many forensic situations. For example, evidence from sexual assaults contains a mixture of DNA from the male perpetrator and the female victim. Using Y-chromosome-specific primers can improve the chances of detecting low levels of the perpetrator's DNA in a high background of the female victim's DNA.

The use of Y-chromosome markers can also benefit paternity testing when a male offspring is in question. In addition, the ability of Y markers to trace paternal lineages was demonstrated in 1998 by linking modern-day descendants of Thomas Jefferson and Eston Hemmings (see Chapter 17).

However, until recently, use of the Y chromosome for forensic purposes was restricted by a lack of polymorphic markers. Since the Y chromosome is passed down from father to son without any recombination, it is not as variable between individuals and results from individual markers cannot be combined using the product rule. Thus, many markers are needed to obtain a high degree of discrimination. Within the last several years, however, a number of Y-chromosome STRs have been described and are being developed into multiplex assays (Redd *et al.* 1997, Prinz *et al.* 1997, Gusmao *et al.* 1999).

Table 8.1 contains a summary of 23 Y STRs that are being used in Y-chromosome studies. These markers range in degree of polymorphism and their ability to differentiate two unrelated male individuals. DYS385 is one of the most polymorphic markers in this set (Schneider *et al.* 1998). The top nine STRs in Table 8.1 have been the most widely studied.

In a small population study, all 70 males could be identified by an individual-specific Y-STR haplotype using nine Y-STR markers (Kayser *et al.* 1997b). More extensive male population studies have been reported for the Y-STRs DYS19, DYS389I, DYS389II, DYS390, DYS391, DYS392, and DYS393 (de Knijff *et al.*

Table 8.1

Y-chromosome STR markers.

Marker Name	GenBank Accession	Repeat Motif	Allele Range	PCR Product Sizes	Reference
DYS19	X77751	TAGA	8–16	178–210 bp	Roewer and Epplen (1992)
DYS385	Z93950	GAAA	10–22	252–300 bp	Schneider et al. (1998)
DYS388	G09695	ATT	12–17	128–143 bp	Kayser et al. (1997a)
DYS389 I	G09600	(TCTG) (TCTA)	I: 7–13	239–263 bp	Kayser et al. (1997a)
DYS389 II	G09600	(TCTG) (TCTA)	II: 23–31	353–385 bp	Kayser et al. (1997a)
DYS390	G09611	(TCTA) (TCTG)	18–27	191–227 bp	Kayser et al. (1997a)
DYS391	G09613	TCTA	8–13	275–295 bp	Kayser et al. (1997a)
DYS392	G09867	TAT	7–16	236–263 bp	Kayser et al. (1997a)
DYS393	G09601	AGAT	9–15	108–132 bp	Kayser et al. (1997a)
YCAIII	AC006370	CA	19–25	192–204 bp	Kayser et al. (1997a)
DYS434	AC002992	ATCT	8–11	110–122 bp	Ayub et al. (2000)
DYS435	AC002992	TGGA	9–13	210–228 bp	Ayub et al. (2000)
DYS436	AC005820	GTT	10–15	128–143 bp	Ayub et al. (2000)
DYS437	AC002992	TCTA	8–11	186–202 bp	Ayub et al. (2000)
DYS438	AC002531	TTTTC	6–12	203–233 bp	Ayub et al. (2000)
DYS439	AC002992	AGAT	9–14	238–258 bp	Ayub et al. (2000)
Y–GATA–A4	G42670	AGAT	11–14	242–254 bp	White et al. (1999)
Y–GATA–A7.1	G42675	ATAG	7–12	161–181 bp	White et al. (1999)
Y–GATA–A7.2	G42671	TAGA	8–12	174–190 bp	White et al. (1999)
Y–GATA–A8	G42672	TCTA	8–14	219–244 bp	White et al. (1999)
Y–GATA–A10	G42674	TATC	11–14	160–172 bp	White et al. (1999)
Y–GATA–C4	G42673	TATC	11–16	251–271 bp	White et al. (1999)
Y–GATA–H4	G42676	TAGA	10–13	362–370 bp	White et al. (1999)

1997). By means of a multicenter study, this group surveyed more than 4000 male DNA samples from 48 different subpopulation groups. An internet database containing population data on multiple Y-chromosome STR markers is accessible via the web site: http://ystr.charite.de.

MITOCHONDRIAL DNA

BACKGROUND INFORMATION

The vast majority of the human genome is located within the nucleus of each cell. However, mitochondria, which are located in the cytoplasm and provide the energy for the cell, contain a small circular genome. Mitochondrial DNA (mtDNA) has 16 569 base pairs and possesses 37 genes that code for products in the oxidative phosphorylation process. A non-coding 'control region', also known as the D-loop, exhibits a fair degree of variation between individuals and is therefore useful for human identity testing purposes.

Human mtDNA was first sequenced in 1981 in the laboratory of Frederick Sanger in Cambridge, England (Anderson et al. 1981). Today the original sequence (GenBank accession: M63933) is the reference sequence to which new sequences are compared and is commonly known as the Anderson sequence or the Cambridge reference sequence (Andrews et al. 1999).

Table 8.2

Comparison of human nuclear DNA and mitochondrial DNA markers.

Characteristics	Nuclear DNA (nucDNA)	Mitochondrial DNA (mtDNA)
Size of genome	~3 billion bp	16 569 bp
Copies per cell	2 (1 allele from each parent)	Can be >1000
Structure	Linear; packages in chromosomes	Circular
Inherited from	Father and mother	Mother
Generational recombination	Yes	No
Unique	Unique to individual (except identical twins)	Not unique to individual
Mutation rate	Low	At least 5–10 times nucDNA
Sequence	Being determined by the Human Genome Project	Described in 1981 by Anderson and co-workers

mtDNA is valuable to the forensic DNA community because it can be efficiently amplified from limited or severely degraded biological material. In cases where the amount of extracted DNA is very small, as in tissues such as bone, teeth, and hair, the probability of obtaining a DNA typing result from mtDNA is higher than that of polymorphic markers found in nuclear DNA (e.g. STRs). Table 8.2 compares and contrasts nuclear DNA and mitochondrial DNA.

Owing to the increased labor and expense compared to STR typing, mtDNA sequence comparisons are utilized primarily in forensic cases where nuclear DNA markers fail to obtain results, such as hair shafts or skeletal remains. There are more copies of mtDNA per cell, a fact that gives it an advantage over single-copy nuclear DNA when biological material is subjected to extreme environmental conditions. The high copy number of mtDNA increases the success rate of obtaining sufficient DNA from extremely old or degraded DNA samples (Holland and Parsons 1999).

Human mtDNA is inherited strictly from one's mother. The sperm brings with it no mitochondria when it fertilizes the egg to form the zygote. The zygote's cytoplasm, which contains the mitochondria, comes solely from the mother's egg. Barring mutation, siblings and maternal relatives have an identical mtDNA sequence. Thus, an individual's mtDNA type is not unique to them.

An example family pedigree is shown in Figure 8.2 to demonstrate the inheritance pattern of mtDNA. In this example, unique mtDNA types exist solely for individuals 1, 5, 7, and 12. Note that individual 16 will possess the same mtDNA type as 6 of the other represented individuals (e.g. 2, 3, 6, 8, 11, 13, and 15). This fact can be helpful in solving missing persons or mass disaster investiga-

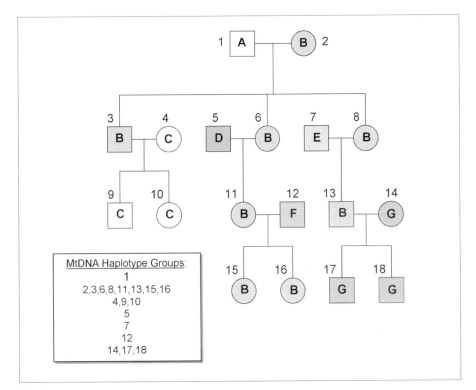

Figure 8.2

Illustration of maternal mitochondrial DNA inheritance. Squares represent males and circles females. Each unique mtDNA type is represented by a different letter.

tions but can reduce the significance of a match in forensic cases. In Chapter 17, we will discuss the value of mtDNA evidence in linking families and solving historical puzzles such as identifying the Vietnam Unknown Soldier and the Romanov family.

MARKERS AND METHODS USED FOR PROCESSING mtDNA SAMPLES

The most extensive mtDNA variations between individuals in the human population are found within the control region, or displacement loop (D-loop). Two regions within the D-loop known as hypervariable region I (HV1) and hypervariable region II (HV2) are normally examined by PCR amplification followed by sequence analysis. Approximately 610 bp are commonly evaluated – 342 bp from HV1 and 268 bp from HV2 (Figure 8.3). The numbering scheme refers to the nucleotide position on the Anderson reference sequence (Anderson *et al.* 1981).

The mtDNA control region has been estimated to vary about 1–3% (1–3 nucleotides out of every 100 is different) between unrelated individuals. This variation is scattered throughout the HV1 and HV2 regions and is therefore best measured with DNA sequence analysis (Butler and Levin 1998, MITOMAP). However, there are 'hot-spots' or regions where most of the

Figure 8.3

Schematic of the human mitochondrial DNA genome. The control region has been expanded to illustrate the regions used in forensic DNA typing. The base numbering system follows the standard reference sequence (Anderson et al. 1981), which begins arbitrarily near the middle of the control region. PCR primers are represented by the arrows and may be used to amplify the entire control region or the HV1 and HV2 regions separately.

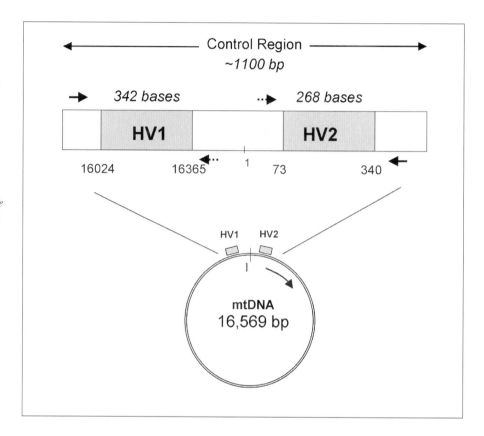

variation is clustered. Methods for rapidly screening mtDNA variation have been developed that may be used for excluding samples that do not match. These methods include using sequence-specific oligonucleotide probes (Stoneking *et al.* 1991), minisequencing (Tully *et al.* 1996), and denaturing gradient gel electrophoresis (Steighner *et al.* 1999) as well as a restriction digest assay for HV1 amplicons (Butler *et al.* 1998) and a reverse dot blot assay for HV2 amplicons (Comas *et al.* 1999).

The steps involved in performing mtDNA sequence comparisons are illustrated in Figure 8.4. Extraction of the mtDNA should be performed in a very clean laboratory environment because mtDNA is more sensitive to contamination than nuclear DNA since it is in a higher copy number per cell. Thus, it is preferable to analyze the reference samples after the evidence samples have been completely processed to avoid any potential contamination problems.

mtDNA typing results on samples from unknown sources are most useful if they are evaluated in comparison to a known sample or a database. Databases of more than 1000 unrelated individuals now exist and have been compiled from multiple population groups (Budowle *et al.* 1999). The size of the database is important because without recombination between mtDNA molecules, a

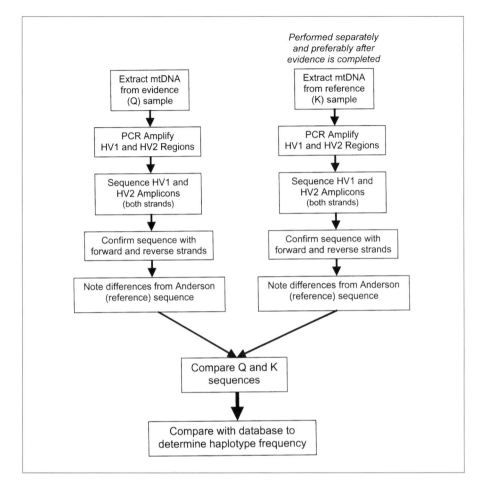

Figure 8.4

Process for evaluation of mtDNA samples. The evidence or question (Q) sample may come from a crime scene or a mass disaster. The reference or known (K) sample may be a maternal relative or the suspect in a criminal investigation.

mtDNA sequence is treated as a single locus (i.e. haplotype instead of genotype). The current practice of conveying the rarity of a mtDNA type among unrelated individuals is to count the number of times a particular haplotype (sequence) is seen in a database (Wilson *et al.* 1993). Thus, the larger number of unrelated individuals in the database, the better the statistics will be for a random match probability calculation.

HETEROPLASMY

The presence of more than one mtDNA type in an individual is known as heteroplasmy. Both sequence and length heteroplasmy are possible. Sequence heteroplasmy results in more than one base at a site in the mtDNA sequence (Figure 8.5). The level of heteroplasmy may not always be the same in different tissues particularly hair samples (Wilson *et al.* 1997). While heteroplasmy can sometimes complicate the interpretation of mtDNA results, the presence of

Figure 8.5

Example of mtDNA sequence heteroplasmy. The sequencing results for seven nucleotides, spanning positions 6368–6374 on the mtDNA genome, are shown here. The sample in the bottom panel has both C and T at the middle nucleotide (position 6371) while the top panel with a homoplasmic sequence has only a C at the same position. Figure courtesy of Lois Tully, NIST Biotechnology Division.

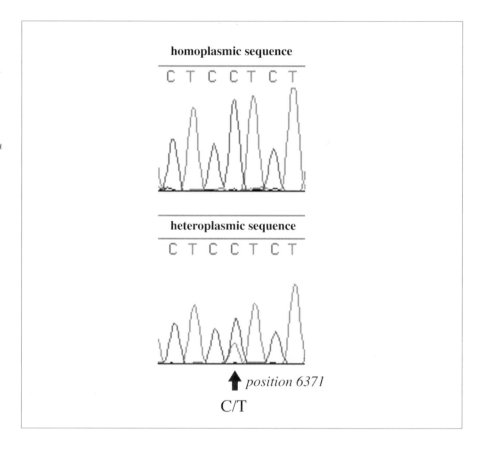

heteroplasmy at identical sites can improve the probability of a match, such as seen in the Romanov study (Ivanov *et al.* 1996).

ADDITIONAL POLYMORPHISM MARKERS

SINGLE NUCLEOTIDE POLYMORPHISMS

Sequence variation between individuals at a particular point in the genome is often referred to as a single nucleotide polymorphism (SNP). SNPs are abundant in the human genome and as such are being used for linkage studies to track genetic diseases. A million or more SNPs exist per individual. The analysis of SNPs therefore promises to be an important part of the future of differentiating between individuals. Table 8.3 compares and contrasts SNP and STR markers. A number of technologies are being developed to miniaturize and automate the procedure for SNP analysis. For example, a microchip-based SNP assay has been described where more than a thousand SNPs were examined simultaneously (Wang *et al.* 1998).

Characteristics	Short Tandem Repeats (STRs)	Single Nucleotide Polymorphisms (SNPs)
Occurrence in human genome	~1 in every 15 kb	~1 in every 1 kb
General informativeness	High	Low; only 20–30% as informative as STRs
Marker type	Di-, tri-, tetranucleotide repeat markers	Bi-allelic markers
Number of alleles per marker	Typically >5	Typically 2
Detection methods	Gel/capillary electrophoresis	Sequence analysis; microchip hybridization
Multiplex capability	>10 markers with multiple fluorescent dyes	Potential of 1000s on microchip

Table 8.3

Comparison of STR and SNP markers. SNPs are more common in the human genome than STRs but are not as polymorphic.

SNPs are appealing to the forensic DNA community for several reasons. First and foremost, there are no stutter artifacts, which means these markers have the potential to more easily discriminate between mixtures and single source samples. Second, they can be potentially multiplexed to a higher level than STRs. Third, the sample processing and data analysis may be more fully automated because a size-based separation is not needed. Finally, the PCR products from SNPs can be less than 100 bp in size, which means that these markers would be able to withstand degraded DNA samples better than STRs that have amplicons as large as 300–400 bp.

However, because each SNP locus possesses only two possible alleles, more markers are needed to obtain a high discriminatory power. Computational analyses have shown that on average 25–45 SNP loci are needed to yield equivalent random match probabilities as the 13 core STR loci (Chakraborty *et al.* 1999). The number of SNPs needed may vary because, in practice, different SNP loci have different allele frequencies.

SNPs can be population-specific because of their low mutation rate. Thus, in the future it may be possible to predict a perpetrator's ethnic origin with the analysis of a few population-specific SNP loci. In addition, a number of Y-chromosome SNP markers have been identified (Underhill *et al.* 1997) and may prove useful in combination with Y-STR markers for forensic evidence.

ALU INSERTION POLYMORPHISMS

Short, interspersed nuclear elements (SINEs) are another form of repeated DNA that has been investigated for population variation studies. The best-studied SINEs are *Alu* insertion polymorphisms, which were named for an *Alu*I restriction endonuclease site typical of the sequence. Alu units are found in

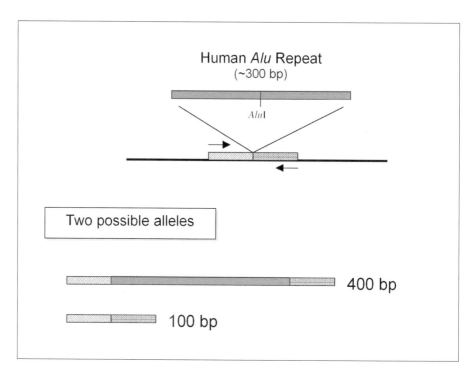

nearly a million copies per haploid genome (5–10% of the human genome) and can be found flanking genes or clustered with other interspersed repeated sequences (Primrose 1998).

The insertion of an *Alu* element at a particular locus can be regarded as a unique event. Once inserted, *Alu* elements are stable genetic markers and do not appear to be subject to loss or rearrangement. Human-specific *Alu* insertions may be typed in a bi-allelic fashion by using PCR, agarose gel electrophoresis, and ethidium bromide staining (Batzer *et al.* 1993). The presence of the Alu insertion will be indicated by a 400 bp PCR product while the absence of the insertion will result in a 100 bp amplicon (Figure 8.5). Commonly used *Alu* insertion polymorphisms include APO, PV92, TPA25, FXIIIB, D1, ACE, A25, and B65 (Sajantila 1998).

Alu repeats have the potential to yield information about the geographic/ethnic origin of the sample being tested (Batzer *et al.* 1993). Since many *Alu* sequences are unique to humans, it may be possible to design multiplex assays where contamination from most non-human DNA samples would not be a problem. However, *Alu* repeats exhibit less variation than multiplex STRs profiles and would therefore most likely be used to gain more information on an unknown sample rather than as an independent source of identification.

NEW AREAS OF RESEARCH

STR ANALYSIS FROM EXTREMELY LOW LEVELS OF HUMAN DNA

An exciting area of research that is ongoing in many laboratories is the ability to obtain DNA profiles from very small amounts of sample. In fact, fluorescent multiplexes have been used to obtain STR typing results from as little as a single buccal cell (Findlay *et al.* 1997). The number of PCR cycles is often increased to improve the amplification yield from samples containing extremely low levels of DNA template.

Remarkably, DNA profiles may be obtained from fingerprint residues due to cells that are left on the objects that are touched (van Oorschot and Jones 1997, van Hoofstat *et al.* 1998). DNA technology may permit the handles of tools used in crimes, such as knives or guns, to be effectively evaluated and used to link a perpetrator to his crime.

Crime scenes can contain insects that may be useful in linking a suspect to the crime in question. Several interesting studies have found that human DNA consumed by the insects may be extracted and successful identified. In particular, human crab louse feces have been reported as a source of human DNA (Replogle *et al.* 1994) as have mosquitoes (Kreike and Kampfer 1999). As demonstrated by these examples, the capability of obtaining a useful DNA profile is often only limited by the ability of the forensic investigator to find and collect the appropriate evidence.

NON-HUMAN DNA WORK

Human DNA is not the only source of DNA that may be useful in a criminal investigation (Sensabaugh and Kaye 1998). Domestic animals such as cats and dogs live in human habitats and deposit hair that may be used to place a suspect at the crime scene. For the purpose of demonstrating uniqueness of DNA profiles in forensic investigations, feline STR allele frequencies from domestic cats have been published (Menotti-Raymond *et al.* 1997) as have mtDNA sequences from domestic dogs (Savolainen *et al.* 1997).

Several interesting cases have used non-human DNA to link a suspect to a crime scene.

Two small seed pods from an Arizona Palo Verde tree found in the back of a pick-up truck were used to place an accused murderer at the crime scene (Yoon 1993). Genetic testing on the seeds showed that in a 'lineup' of 12 Palo Verde trees near the crime scene, DNA from the seeds matched only the tree under which the victim's body had been found. The jury found the accused guilty based in large measure on the plant DNA evidence.

REFERENCES

Anderson, S., Bankier, A.T., Barrell, B.G., de Bruijn, M.H.L., Coulson, A.R., Drouin, J., Eperon, I.C., Nierlich, D.P., Roe, B.A., Sanger, F., Schreier, P.H., Smith, A.J.H., Staden, R. and Young, I.G. (1981) *Nature*, 290, 457–465.

Andrews, R.M., Kubacka, I., Chinnery, P.F., Lightowlers, R.N., Turnbull, D.M. and Howell, N. (1999) *Nature Genetics*, 23, 147.

Ayub, Q., Mohyuddin, A., Qamar, R., Mazhar, K., Zerjal, T., Mehdi, S.Q. and Tyler-Smith, C. (2000) *Nucleic Acids Research*, 28, e8.

Batzer, M., Alegria-Hartman, M., Bazan, H., Kass, D.H., Shaikh, T.H., Novick, G.E., Ioannou, P.A., Boudreau, D.A., Scheer, W.D., Herrera, R.J., Stoneking, M. and Deininger, P.L. (1993) *Fourth International Symposium on Human Identification*. Madison, WI: Promega Corporation, pp. 49–57.

Budowle, B., Koons, B.W. and Errera, J.D. (1996) *Journal of Forensic Sciences*, 41, 660–663.

Budowle, B., Wilson, M.R., DiZinno, J.A., Stauffer, C., Fasano, M.A., Holland, M.M. and Monson, K.L. (1999) *Forensic Science International*, 103, 23–35.

Butler, J.M. and Levin, B.C. (1998) *Trends in Biotechnology*, 16, 158–162.

Butler, J.M., Wilson, M.R. and Reeder, D.J. (1998) *Electrophoresis*, 19, 119–124.

Chakraborty, R., Stivers, D.N., Su, B., Zhong, Y. and Budowle, B. (1999) *Electrophoresis*, 20, 1682–1696.

Comas, D., Reynolds, R. and Sajantila, A. (1999) *European Journal of Human Genetics*, 7, 459–468.

de Knijff, P., Kayser, M., Caglia, A., Corach, D., Fretwell, N., Gehrig, C., Graziosi, G., Heidorn, F., Herrmann, S., Herzog, B., Hidding, M., Honda, K., Jobling, M., Krawczak, M., Leim, K., Meuser, S., Meyer, E., Oesterreich, W., Pandya, A., Parson, W., Penacino, G., Perez-Lezaun, A., Piccinini, A., Prinz, M., Schmitt, C., Schneider, P.M., Szibor, R., Teifel-Greding, J., Weichhold, G.M. and Roewer, L. (1997) *International Journal of Legal Medicine*, 110, 134–140.

Eng, B., Ainsworth, P. and Waye, J.S. (1994) *Journal of Forensic Sciences*, 39, 1356–1359.

Findlay, I., Taylor, A., Quirke, P., Frazier, R. and Urquhart, A. (1997) *Nature*, 389, 555–556.

Gusmao, L., Gonzalez-Neira, A., Pestoni, C., Brion, M., Lareu, M.V. and Carracedo, A. (1999) *Forensic Science International*, 106, 163–172.

Haas-Rochholz, H. and Weiler, G. (1997) *International Journal of Legal Medicine*, 110, 312–315.

Holland, M.M. and Parsons, T.J. (1999) *Forensic Science Review*, 11, 21–50.

Ivanov, P.L., Wadhams, M.J., Roby, R.K., Holland, M.M., Weedn, V.W. and Parsons, T.J. (1996) *Nature Genetics*, 12, 417–420.

Jobling, M.A. and Tyler-Smith, C. (1995) *Trends in Genetics*, 11, 449–456.

Kayser, M., Caglia, A., Corach, D., Fretwell, N., Gehrig, C., Graziosi, G., Heidorn, F., Herrmann, S., Herzog, B., Hidding, M., Honda, K., Jobling, M., Krawczak, M., Leim, K., Meuser, S., Meyer, E., Oesterreich, W., Pandya, A., Parson, W., Penacino, G., Perez-Lezaun, A., Piccinini, A., Prinz, M., Schmitt, C., Schneider, P.M., Szibor, R., Teifel-Greding, J., Weichhold, G.M., de Knijff, P. and Roewer, L. (1997a) *International Journal of Legal Medicine*, 110, 125–133, Appendix 141–149.

Kayser, M., de Knijff, P., Dieltjes, P., Krawczak, M., Nagy, M., Zerjal, T., Pandya, A., Tyler-Smith, C. and Roewer, L. (1997b) *Electrophoresis*, 18, 1602–1607.

Kreike, J. and Kampfer, S. (1999) *International Journal of Legal Medicine*, 112, 380–382.

Mannucci, A., Sullivan, K.M., Ivanov, P.L. and Gill, P. (1994) *International Journal of Legal Medicine*, 106, 190–193.

Menotti-Raymond, M., David, V.A., Stephens, J.C., Lyons, L.A. and O'Brien, S.J. (1997) *Journal of Forensic Sciences*, 42, 1039–1051.

MITOMAP: A Human Mitochondrial Genome Database. Center for Molecular Medicine, Emory University, Atlanta, GA, USA. http://www.gen.emory.edu/mitomap.html

Primrose, S.B. (1998) *Principles of Genome Analysis: A Guide to Mapping and Sequencing DNA from Different Organisms.* Malden, MA: Blackwell Science.

Prinz, M., Boll, K., Baum, H. and Shaler, B. (1997) *Forensic Science International*, 85, 209–218.

Redd, A.J., Clifford, S.L. and Stoneking, M. (1997) *Biological Chemistry*, 378, 923–927.

Replogle, J., Lord, W.D., Budowle, B., Meinking, T.L. and Taplin, D. (1994) *Journal of Medical Entomology*, 31, 686–690.

Reynolds, R. and Varlaro, J. (1996) *Journal of Forensic Sciences*, 41, 279–286.

Roewer, L. and Epplen, J.T. (1992) *Forensic Science International*, 53, 163–171.

Sajantila, A. (1998) *Second European Symposium on Human Identification.* Madison, WI: Promega Corporation, pp. 1–5.

Santos, F.R., Pandya, A. and Tyler-Smith, C. (1998) *Nature Genetics*, 18, 103.

Savolainen, P., Rosen, B., Holmberg, A., Leitner, T., Uhlen, M. and Lundeberg, J. (1997) *Journal of Forensic Sciences*, 42, 593–600.

Schneider, P.M., Meuser, S., Waiyawuth, W., Seo, Y. and Rittner, C. (1998) *Forensic Science International*, 97, 61–70.

Sensabaugh, G. and Kaye, D.H. (1998) *Jurimetrics Journal*, 38, 1–16.

Steighner, R.J., Tully, L.A., Karjala, J.D., Coble, M.D. and Holland, M.M. (1999) *Journal of Forensic Sciences*, 44, 1186–1198.

Stoneking, M., Hedgecock, D., Higuchi, R.G., Vigilant, L. and Erlich, H.A. (1991) *American Journal of Human Genetics*, 48, 370–382.

Sullivan, K.M., Mannucci, A., Kimpton, C.P. and Gill, P. (1993) *BioTechniques*, 15, 637–641.

Tully, G., Sullivan, K.M., Nixon, P., Stones, R.E. and Gill, P. (1996) *Genomics*, 34, 107–113.

Underhill, P.A., Jin, L., Lin, A.A., Mehdi, Q., Jenkins, T., Vollrath, D., Davis, R.W., Cavalli-Sforza, L.L. and Oefner, P.J. (1997) *Genome Research*, 7, 996–1005.

Van Hoofstat, D.E.O., Deforce, D.L.D., Brochez, V., De Pauw, I., Janssens, K., Mestdagh, M., Millecamps, R., Van Geldre, E. and Van den Eeckhout, E.G. (1998) *Proceedings of the Second European Symposium on Human Identification*. Madison, WI: Promega Corporation, pp. 131–137.

Van Oorschot, R.A.H. and Jones, M.K. (1997) *Nature*, 387, 767.

Wang, D.G., Fan, J.-B., Siao, C.-J., Berno, A., Young, P., Sapolsky, R., Ghandour, G., Perkins, N., Winchester, E., Spencer, J., Kruglyak, L., Stein, L., Hsie, L., Topaloglou, T., Hubbell, E., Robinson, E., Mittmann, M., Morris, M.S., Shen, N., Kilburn, D., Rioux, J., Nusbaum, C., Rozen, S., Hudson, T.J., Lipshutz, R., Chee, M. and Lander, E.S. (1998) *Science*, 280, 1077–1082.

White, P.S., Tatum, O.L., Deaven, L.L. and Longmire, J.L. (1999) *Genomics*, 57, 433–437.

Wilson, M.R., Stoneking, M., Holland, M.M., DiZinno, J.A. and Budowle, B. (1993) *Crime Lab Digest*, 20, 68–77.

Wilson, M.R., Polanskey, D., Butler, J., DiZinno, J.A., Replogle, J. and Budowle, B. (1995) *BioTechniques*, 18, 662–669.

Wilson, M.R., Polanskey, D., Replogle, J., DiZinno, J.A. and Budowle, B. (1997) *Human Genetics*, 100, 167–171.

Yoon, C.K. (1993) *Science*, 260, 894–895.

TECHNOLOGY

CHAPTER 9

DNA SEPARATION METHODS: SLAB-GEL AND CAPILLARY ELECTROPHORESIS

INTRODUCTION

NEED FOR DNA SEPARATIONS

A polymerase chain reaction (PCR) reaction in which short tandem repeat (STR) alleles are amplified produces a mixture of DNA molecules that present a challenging separation problem. A multiplex PCR can produce 20 or more DNA fragments that must be resolved from one another. In addition, single base resolution is required to distinguish between closely spaced alleles (e.g. TH01 alleles 9.3 and 10). The typical separation size range where this single base resolution is needed is between 100 and 400 bp. Additionally, it is important that the separation method be reproducible and yield results that can be compared among laboratories.

In order to distinguish the various molecules from one another, a separation step is required to pull the different sized fragments apart. The separation is typically performed by a process known as electrophoresis and is either conducted in a slab-gel or capillary environment. This chapter will discuss the theory and background information on separation methods. Chapter 10 will cover how the bands in gel electrophoresis and the peaks in capillary electrophoresis are actually generated and detected. Chapters 11 and 12 will discuss specific techniques utilizing capillary electrophoresis and slab-gel electrophoresis that are widely used by forensic DNA typing laboratories.

ELECTROPHORESIS

PCR products from STR DNA must be separated in a fashion that allows each allele to be distinguished from other alleles. Heterozygous alleles are resolved in this manner with a sized-based separation method known as electrophoresis. The separation medium may be in the form of a slab gel or a capillary.

The word 'electrophoresis' comes from the Greek *electron* (charge) and the Latin *phore* (bearer). Thus, the process of electrophoresis refers to electrical charges carried by the molecules. In the case of DNA, the phosphate groups on the backbone of the DNA molecule have a negative charge. Nucleic acids are acids because the phosphate groups readily give up their H⁺ ions, making them negatively charged in most buffer systems. Under the influence of an electric field, DNA molecules will migrate away from the negative electrode, known as the cathode, and move towards the positive electrode, known as the anode. The higher the voltage, the greater the force felt by the DNA molecules and the faster the DNA moves.

The movement of ions in an electric field generates heat. This heat must be dissipated or it will be absorbed by the system. Excessive heat can cause a gel to generate bands that 'smile' or in very severe cases the gel can literally melt and fall apart. As will be described at the end of the chapter, performing electrophoresis in a capillary is an advantage because heat can be more easily dissipated from the capillary, which has a high surface area to volume ratio.

SLAB GELS

Slab gels consist of a solid matrix with a series of pores and a buffer solution through which the DNA molecules pass during electrophoresis. Gel materials are mixed together and poured into a mold to define the structure of the slab gel. A sample 'comb' is placed into the gel such that the teeth of the comb are imbedded in the gel matrix. After the gel has solidified, the comb is removed leaving behind wells that are used for loading the DNA samples. The basic format for a gel electrophoresis system is shown in Figure 9.1.

Figure 9.1

Schematic of a gel electrophoresis system. The horizontal gel is submerged in a tank full of electrophoresis buffer. DNA samples are loaded into wells across the top of the gel. These wells are created by a 'comb' placed in the gel while it is forming. When the voltage is applied across the two electrodes, the DNA molecules move towards the anode and separate by size. The number of lanes available on a gel is dependent on the number of teeth in the comb used to define the loading wells. At least one lane on each gel is taken up by a molecular weight size standard that is used to estimate the sizes of the sample bands in the other lanes.

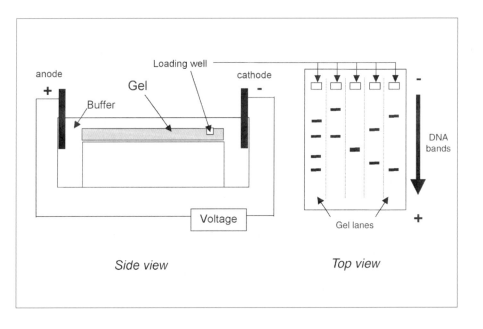

TYPES OF GELS

Two types of gels are commonly used in molecular biology and forensic DNA laboratories today to achieve DNA separations. Agarose gels have fairly large pore sizes and are used for separating larger DNA molecules while polyacrylamide gels are used to obtain high-resolution separations for smaller DNA molecules, usually below 500 or 1000 bp.

Forensic DNA typing methods use both types of gels. Restriction fragment length polymorphism (RFLP) methods use agarose gels to separate DNA fragments ranging in size from ~600 bp to ~23 000 bp. Low molecular weight DNA molecules are not well separated with agarose slab gels. On the other hand, PCR-amplified STR alleles, which range in size from ~100 bp to ~400 bp, are better served by polyacrylamide gels. In the case of some STR loci that contain microvariants, the high-resolution capability of polyacrylamide gels is essential for separating closely sized DNA molecules that may only differ by a single nucleotide.

AGAROSE GELS

Agarose is basically a form of seaweed and contains pores that are on the order of 2000 angstroms (Å) (200 nm) in diameter. Agarose gels are easily prepared by weighing out a desired amount of agarose powder and mixing it with the electrophoresis buffer. This mixture can be quickly brought to a boil by microwaving the solution whereupon the agarose powder goes into solution. After the solution cools down slightly, it is poured into a gel box to define the gel shape and thickness.

A comb is added to the liquid agarose before it cools to form wells with its teeth in the jelly-like substance that results after the gel 'sets'. Once the agarose has gelled, the comb is removed leaving behind little wells that can hold 5–10 μL of sample or more depending on the size of the teeth and the depth at which they were placed in the agarose gel. The comb teeth define the number of samples that can be loaded on to the gel as well as where the lanes will be located. There are predominantly two types of combs: square-tooth and sharkstooth.

Electrophoresis buffer is poured over the gel until it is fully submerged. Two buffers are commonly used with electrophoresis, Tris-acetate-EDTA (TAE) and Tris-borate-EDTA (TBE). Samples are mixed with a loading dye and carefully pipetted into each well of the submerged gel. This loading dye contains a mixture of bromophenol blue, a dark blue dye which helps to visually see the sample, and sucrose to increase the sample's viscosity and help it stay in the well prior to turning on the voltage and initiating electrophoresis.

The number of samples that can be run in parallel on the gel are defined by the number of teeth on the comb added to the gel before it sets (and hence the number of wells that will be created). Typically between 8 and 24 samples are run at a time on an agarose gel. Molecular weight standards are run in some of the lanes in order to estimate the size of each DNA sample following electrophoresis.

After the samples are loaded, a cover is placed over the gel box containing the submerged gel and the electrodes on either end of the gel are plugged into a power source. The anode (positive electrode) is placed on the end of the gel furthest from the wells to draw the DNA molecules through the gel material. Typically 100–600 V are placed across agarose gels that are 10–40 cm in length, creating electric field strengths of approximately 1–10 V/cm.

As the DNA molecules are drawn through the gel, they are separated by size, the smaller ones moving more quickly and easily through the gel pores. It might help to think of the DNA molecules as marathon runners with different abilities. They all start together at the beginning and then separate during the 'race' through the gel. The smaller DNA molecules move more quickly than the larger ones through the obstacles along the gel 'race course', and thus are further along when the voltage is turned off and the 'race' completed. When the separation is completed, the gel is scanned or photographed to record the results for examination and comparison.

POLYACRYLAMIDE GELS

Polyacrylamide (PA) gels have much smaller pore sizes (~100–200 Å) than agarose gels (~1500–2000 Å). The average pore size of a gel is an important factor in determining the ability of a slab gel to resolve two similarly sized DNA

Figure 9.2

Illustration of polyacryl-amide gel polymerization. The pore size of a gel is controlled by its degree of cross-linking, which depends on the propor-tions of acrylamide and bisacrylamide in the gel. Polymerization is typically induced by free radicals resulting from the chemical decomposition of ammonium persulfate. TEMED, a free radical stabilizer, is also added to the gel mixture to stabilize the polymerization process. A polyacrylamide gel is poured between two glass plates that define its dimensions. A spacer is placed between the plates to define the thickness of the gel. A typical gel size is 17 cm × 43 cm × 0.4 cm. DNA molecules flow through the polyacryl-amide gel matrix along the z-axis going into the page, much like flowing through a chain link fence with various sized holes.

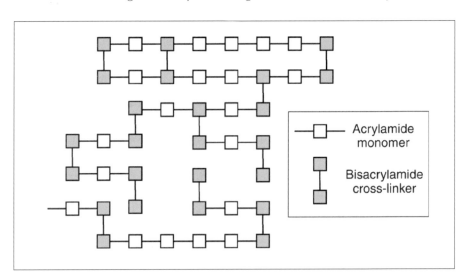

fragments. The pores in PA gels are chemically created with a cross-linking process involving acrylamide and bisacrylamide (Figure 9.2).

Polyacrylamide gels are chemically formed through polymerization of the monomeric acrylamide molecule in the presence of a variable quantity of the bisacrylamide cross-linker. The polymerization process is initiated by the generation of free radicals provided by ammonium persulfate and stabilized by the compound TEMED (N,N,N´,N´-tetramethylethylenediamine). This polymerization leads to the formation of long strands of acrylamide monomer with occasional cross-links provided by the bisacrylamide connector.

Polyacrylamide pore sizes can be decreased by increasing the overall concentration of acrylamide (both monomer plus cross-linker). The value of total acrylamide concentration in the gel solution is typically expressed as %T. The ratio of the monomer to the cross-linker may also be varied. The smallest pore sizes have been shown to occur when the cross-linker is 5% of the total acrylamide weight, or 5%C. A common gel solution used in STR allele separations is 5%T, 5%C. Another way this solution might be described is 5% acrylamide:bis(19:1).

One of the challenges in pouring or casting a slab gel is avoiding bubble formation. The polymerization process generates heat that can lead to bubbles forming in the gel. Gel mixtures are sometimes degassed under a vacuum for a short period of time prior to polymerization to remove any gases in the solution that might give rise to bubbles as the gel is solidifying. Sometimes bubbles occur in spite of great effort to avoid them. These gels may still be used as long as the bubbles are not in a lane where a sample will be run and/or do not interfere with the region of detection in fluorescence.

PA gels may be run in either a horizontal or a vertical format. The type of gel box defines the running format. Detection of DNA bands in polyacrylamide gels may be performed with fluorescent dyes or silver staining as will be described in Chapter 10.

NATIVE VERSUS DENATURING ELECTROPHORESIS CONDITIONS

Under normal conditions, the two complementary strands of DNA will remain together. Electrophoresis systems that perform the DNA separation while keeping the complementary strands together as double-stranded DNA are often referred to as 'native' or 'non-denaturing'. On the other hand, a separation system that possesses an environment capable of keeping the DNA strands apart as single-stranded DNA is usually referred to as a 'denaturing' system.

Generally better resolution between closely sized DNA molecules can be achieved with denaturing systems. This improved resolution is achieved because single-stranded DNA is more flexible than double-stranded DNA and therefore interacts with the sieving medium more effectively allowing closely sized molecules to be differentially separated. Additionally, natural conformation in DNA molecules, sometimes referred to as secondary structure, is eliminated in a denaturing environment.

To achieve a denaturing environment, chemicals, such as formamide and urea, may be used to keep the complementary strands of DNA apart from one another. The addition of 6 molar urea is a common technique for making a denaturing gel. Formamide and urea form hydrogen bonds with the DNA bases and prevent the bases from interacting with their complementary strand. The temperature of the separation or the pH of the solution may also be raised to aid in keeping the complementary strands of DNA apart.

A popular method for achieving denatured DNA strands (prior to electrophoresis) is to dilute the samples in 100% formamide. The samples are then heated to 95°C to denature the DNA strands, and then 'snap cooled' on ice by bringing them from the heated 95°C environment immediately to 0°C by placing them on ice.

PROBLEMS WITH GELS

The process of preparing a polyacrylamide gel involves a number of steps including cleaning and preparing the gel plates, combining the gel materials, pouring the gel, waiting for it to set up, and finally removing the comb. These steps are time consuming and rather labor intensive and represent mundane tasks in the laboratory. In addition, the acrylamide gel materials are known neurotoxins and need to be handled with care.

Precast gels have also become popular due to the time and labor involved with preparing the gel plates, pouring the gel, and waiting for it to set. However, one still has to load the DNA samples very carefully into each well (to prevent contamination from adjacent wells). The development of capillary electrophoresis has excited many DNA scientists because the tedious processes of gel pouring and sample loading have been automated with this technique.

CAPILLARY ELECTROPHORESIS

Capillary electrophoresis (CE) is a relatively new addition to the electrophoresis family. The first CE separations of DNA were performed just over a decade ago in the late 1980s. Since the introduction of new CE instrumentation in the mid-1990s, the technique has gained rapidly in popularity and for good reason. While slab-gel electrophoresis has been a proven technique for over 30 years, there are a number of advantages to analyzing DNA in a capillary format.

ADVANTAGES OF CE OVER SLAB GELS

First and foremost, the injection, separation, and detection steps can be fully automated, permitting multiple samples to be run unattended. In addition, only minute quantities of sample are consumed in the injection process and samples can be easily retested if needed. This is an important advantage for precious forensic specimens that often cannot be easily replaced.

Separation in capillaries may be conducted in minutes rather than hours due to higher voltages that are permitted with improved heat dissipation from capillaries. Another advantage is that quantitative information is readily available in an electronic format following the completion of a run. No extra steps such as scanning the gel or taking a picture of it are required. Lane tracking is not necessary since the sample is also contained within the capillary nor is the fear of cross-contamination from samples leaking over from adjacent wells a problem with CE.

DISADVANTAGES OF CE

The one major disadvantage of CE instruments is throughput. Owing to the fact that samples are analyzed sequentially one at a time, single capillary instruments are not easily capable of processing high numbers of samples or sample throughputs. As will be discussed in Chapter 15, however, capillary array systems have been developed to run multiple samples in parallel and those vastly improve the sample throughput.

CE instruments require a higher start up cost (more than $50 000) than slab-gel electrophoresis systems and this fact prohibits some laboratories from using them. Nevertheless, CE instruments are quickly becoming the principal workhorses in a number of forensic DNA typing laboratories because of their automation and ease of use.

COMPONENTS OF CE

The primary elements of a CE instrument include a narrow capillary, two buffer vials, and two electrodes connected to a high-voltage power supply. CE systems also contain a laser excitation source, a fluorescence detector, an autosampler to hold the sample tubes, and a computer to control the sample injection and detection (Figure 9.3). CE capillaries are made of fused silica (glass) and typically have an internal diameter of 50–100 µm and a length of 25–75 cm.

The same buffers that are used in gel electrophoresis may also be used with CE. However, instead of a gel matrix through which the DNA molecules pass, a viscous polymer solution serves as the sieving medium. Larger DNA molecules

Figure 9.3

Schematic of capillary electrophoresis instruments used for DNA analysis. The capillary is a narrow glass tube approximately 50 cm long and 50 μm in diameter. It is filled with a viscous polymer solution that acts much like a gel in creating a sieving environment for DNA molecules. Samples are placed into a tray and injected on to the capillary by applying a voltage to each sample sequentially. A high-voltage (e.g. 15 000 volts) is applied across the capillary after the injection in order to separate the DNA fragments in a matter of minutes. Fluorescent dye-labeled products are analyzed as they pass by the detection window and are excited by a laser beam. Computerized data acquisition enables rapid analysis and digital storage of separation results.

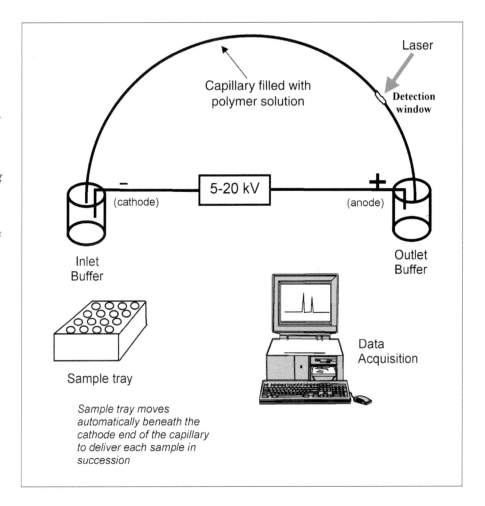

are retarded more by the linear, flexible polymer chains than smaller DNA fragments, which leads to a size-based separation analogous to the DNA passing through the pores in the cross-linked polyacrylamide gels discussed above.

Prior to injecting each sample, a new gel is 'poured' by filling the capillary with a fresh aliquot of the polymer solution. The CE can be thought of as a long, skinny gel that is only wide enough for one sample at a time. An important difference between CE and gels is that the electric fields are on the order of 10–100 times stronger with CE (i.e. 300 V/cm instead of 10 V/cm), which results in faster run times for CE.

Detection of the sample is performed automatically by the CE instrument by measuring the time span from sample injection to sample detection with a laser placed near the end of the capillary. Laser light is shined on to the capillary at a fixed position where a window has been burned in the coating of the capillary. DNA fragments are illuminated as they pass by this window in the capillary. As with gels, the smaller molecules will arrive at the detection point first followed by the larger molecules. Data from CE separations are plotted as a function of the relative fluorescence intensity observed from fluorescence emission of dyes passing the detector (see Chapter 10). The fluorescent emission signals from dyes attached to the DNA molecules can then be used to detect and quantify the DNA molecules passing the detector.

DNA SEPARATION MECHANISMS

Now that we have covered the two primary methods for DNA separations in use today, namely slab-gel electrophoresis and capillary electrophoresis, we will discuss briefly the theories behind DNA separations by electrophoresis.

With one phosphate group for every nucleotide unit, DNA molecules possess a constant charge to mass ratio. Thus, a piece of DNA that is ten nucleotide units long will feel the same force pulling on it when an electric field is applied to it as a DNA oligomer that is 100 nucleotide units in length. In order to resolve DNA fragments that differ in size, a sieving mechanism is required. The separation of DNA is therefore accomplished with gels or polymer solutions that retard larger DNA molecules as they pass through the separation medium. The smaller molecules can slip through the gel pores faster and thus migrate ahead of longer DNA strands as electrophoresis proceeds (Figure 9.4).

In the simplest sense, a gel may be considered as a molecular sieve with 'pores' that permit the DNA molecules to pass in a size-dependent manner because larger molecules are retarded more than smaller ones. Two primary mechanisms for DNA separations through gel pores have been described: the Ogston model, and reptation. These two theories are complementary as they operate in different size regimes. The Ogston model describes the behavior of DNA molecules that are smaller than the gel pores, while reptation describes the movement of larger DNA molecules (Figure 9.4).

OGSTON SIEVING

The Ogston model regards the DNA molecule as a spherical particle or coil like a small tangle of thread that is tumbling through the pores formed by the gel. Molecules move through the gel in proportion to their ability to find pores that are large enough to permit their passage. Smaller molecules migrate faster because they can pass through a greater number of pores. When DNA molecules are much larger than the mesh size of the gel sieving medium, the Ogston model predicts that the mobility (movement) of the molecules will go to zero.

Figure 9.4

Illustration of DNA separation modes in gel electrophoresis. Separation according to size occurs as DNA molecules pass through the gel, which acts as a molecular sieve (a). Ogston sieving and reptation are the two primary mechanisms used to describe the movement of DNA fragments through a gel (b).

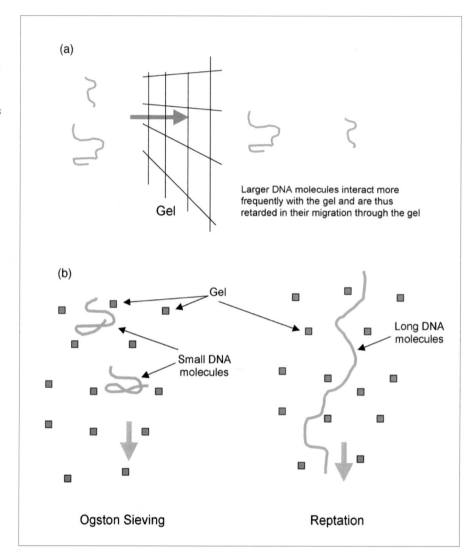

REPTATION

However, gel separations have been demonstrated with DNA fragments that are much larger than the predicted pore size of the gel. The reptation model for DNA separations views the DNA molecule as moving like a snake through the gel pores. DNA molecules become elongated like a straight length of thread and enter the gel matrix end on. Separation of sample components, such as two STR alleles, occurs as the DNA winds its way through the pores of the gel matrix.

ADDITIONAL COMMENTS ON ELECTROPHORETIC SEPARATIONS

Electrophoresis is a relative rather than an absolute measurement technique. The position of a DNA band on a gel has no meaning without reference to a size standard containing material with known DNA fragment sizes. Thus, samples are run on a gel side by side with molecular weight markers. For example, a DNA restriction digest might be used with a half-dozen or more fragments ranging in size from 100 bp to 1000 bp. A visual comparison can then be made to estimate the fragment size of the unknown sample based on which band it comes closest to since the samples were subjected to identical electrophoretic conditions. Alternatively, in multi-color fluorescent systems, an internal sizing standard can be run with each sample to calibrate the migration times of the DNA fragments of interest with a sample of known size (see Chapters 10 and 13).

The separation media that the DNA passes through, as well as the overall shape of the molecule and the electric field applied to the sample, influences the molecular movement (i.e. speed of separation for each component). The exact technique that one uses to separate the DNA molecules in a particular sample is dependent on the resolution required. The resolution capability of a separation system is dependent on a number of factors including the type of separation medium used and the voltage applied.

ADDITIONAL READING

Butler, J.M. (1995) *Sizing and Quantification of Polymerase Chain Reaction Products by Capillary Electrophoresis for Use in DNA Typing*. Ph.D. dissertation, University of Virginia.

Heller, C. (ed.) (1997) *Analysis of Nucleic Acids by Capillary Electrophoresis*. Braunschweig: Vieweg.

Martin, R. (1996) *Gel Electrophoresis: Nucleic Acids*. Oxford: Bios Scientific Publishers.

CHAPTER 10

DNA DETECTION METHODS: FLUORESCENT DYES AND SILVER STAINING

VARIOUS METHODS FOR DETECTING DNA MOLECULES

Over the years a number of methods have been used for detecting DNA molecules following electrophoretic separation. Early techniques involved radioactive labels and autoradiography. These methods were sensitive and effective but time consuming. In addition, the use of radioisotopes was expensive owing to the need for photographic films and supplies, and the extensive requirements surrounding the handling and disposal of radioactive materials.

In the past decade, methods such as silver staining and fluorescence techniques have gained in popularity for detecting short tandem repeat (STR) alleles owing to their low cost in the case of silver staining and their capability of automating the detection in the case of fluorescence. Table 10.1 reviews the various methods and instruments that have been used for detecting STR alleles. This chapter will focus primarily on fluorescence detection because it now dominates the forensic DNA community. Almost all commercially available STR typing kits involve the use of fluorescently labeled polymerase chain reaction (PCR) primers. However, we will briefly cover silver staining at the end of the chapter to provide what we hope will be a useful historical perspective for those who are using fluorescence detection.

FLUORESCENCE DETECTION

Fluorescence-based detection assays are widely used in forensic laboratories due to their capabilities for multi-color analysis as well as rapid and easy-to-use formats. Fluorescence measurements involve exciting a dye molecule and then detecting the light that is emitted from the excited dye. In the application to DNA typing with STR markers, the fluorescent dye is attached to a PCR primer that is incorporated into the amplified target region of DNA. Amplified STR alleles are visualized as bands on a gel or represented by peaks on an electropherogram. In this section, we will first discuss some of the basics surrounding fluorescence and then follow with a review of the methods used today for labeling DNA molecules, specifically the PCR products produced from STR markers.

Table 10.1

Detection methods and instruments used for analysis of STR alleles. A wide variety of fluorescence detection instrument platforms are listed.

Technique/Instrumentation	Comments	Reference
Fluorescence/ABI 373 or 377	Four different color dyes are used to label PCR products; peaks are measured during electrophoresis as they pass a laser that is scanning across the gel	Edwards *et al.* (1991), Frazier *et al.* (1996)
Fluorescence/ABI 310	Four ABI dyes are used to label PCR products; capillary electrophoresis version of ABI 377; most popular method in use today among forensic labs	Buel *et al.* (1998), Lazaruk *et al.* (1998)
Fluorescence/FMBIO scanner	Gel is scanned following electrophoresis with a 532 nm laser; typically used with three different dyes and PowerPlex STR kits	Schumm *et al.* (1995), Lins *et al.* (1998)
Fluorescence/ALF Sequencer	Automated detection similar to the ABI 377 but with only single color capability	Decorte and Cassiman (1996)
Fluorescence/LICOR	Near-IR dyes are used to label PCR products for automated detection similar to the ABI 377	Roy *et al.* (1996)
Fluorescence/scanner	SYBR Green stain (intercalating dye) of gel following electrophoresis; gel is scanned with 488 nm laser	Morin and Smith (1995)
Fluorescence/Beckman CE	PCR products are labeled with an intercalating dye during CE separation for single color detection	Butler *et al.* (1994)
Fluorescence/capillary arrays	Laser scans across multiple capillaries to detect fluorescently labeled PCR products	Wang *et al.* (1995), Mansfield *et al.* (1998)
Silver staining	Following electrophoresis, gel is soaked in silver nitrate solution; silver is reduced with formaldehyde to stain DNA bands	Budowle *et al.* (1995), Micka *et al.* (1996)
Direct blotting electrophoresis	Following run, gel bands are blotted on to a nylon membrane, fixed with UV light, and detected with digoxygenin	Berschick *et al.* (1993)
Autoradiography	P32-labeled dCTP incorporated into PCR products	Hammond *et al.* (1994)

IR = infrared; UV = ultraviolet.

BASICS OF FLUORESCENCE

As mentioned above, fluorescence measurements involve exciting a dye molecule and then detecting the light that is emitted from the excited dye. A molecule that is capable of fluorescence is called a *fluorophore*. Fluorophores come in a variety of shapes, sizes, and abilities. The ones that are primarily used in DNA labeling are dyes that fluoresce in the visible region of the spectrum, which consists of light emitted in the range of approximately 400–600 nm.

The fluorescence process is shown in Figure 10.1. In the first step, a photon ($h\nu_{ex}$) from a laser source excites a fluorophore electron from its ground energy state (S_o) to an excited transition state (S'_1). This electron then undergoes conformational changes and interacts with its environment resulting in the relaxed singlet excitation state (S_1). During the final step of the process, a photon ($h\nu_{em}$) is emitted at a lower energy when the excited electron falls back to its ground state. Because energy and wavelength are inversely related to one another, the emission photon has a higher wavelength than the excitation photon.

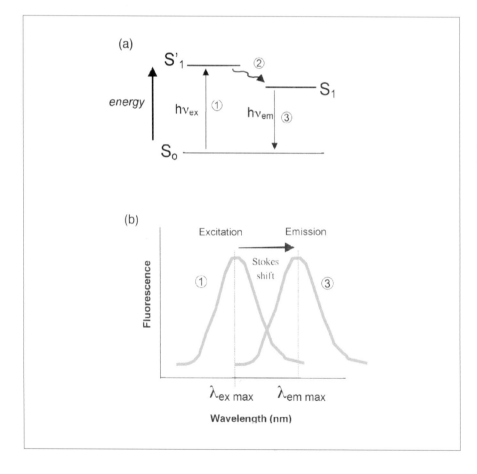

Figure 10.1

Illustration of the fluorescence process (a) and excitation/emission spectra (b). In the first step of the fluorescence process, a photon ($h\nu_{ex}$) from a laser source excites the fluorophore (dye molecule) from its ground energy state (S_o) to an excited transition state (S'_1). The fluorophore then undergoes conformational changes and interacts with its environment resulting in the relaxed singlet excitation state (S_1). During the final step of the process, a photon ($h\nu_{em}$) is emitted at a lower energy. Because energy and wavelength are inversely related to one another, the emission photon has a higher wavelength than the excitation photon.

The difference between the apex of the absorption and emission spectra is called the *Stokes shift*. This shift permits the use of optical filters to separate excitation light from emission light. Fluorophores have characteristic light absorption and emission patterns that are based upon their chemical structure and the environmental conditions. With careful selection and optical filters, fluorophores may be chosen with emission spectra that are resolvable from one another. As will be discussed later in the chapter, this capability permits the use of multiple fluorophores to measure several different DNA molecules simultaneously. The rate at which samples can be processed is much greater with multiple fluorophores than measurements involving a single fluorophore.

There are a number of factors that affect how well a fluorophore will emit light, or *fluoresce*. These factors include the following (Singer and Johnson 1997):

- *molar extinction coefficient:* the ability of a dye to absorb light;
- *quantum yield:* the efficiency with which the excited fluorophore converts absorbed light to emitted light;
- *photostability:* the ability of a dye to undergo repeated cycles of excitation and emission without being destroyed in the excited state, or experiencing 'photobleaching';
- *dye environment:* factors that affect fluorescent yield include pH, temperature, solvent, and the presence of quenchers, such as hemoglobin.

The overall fluorescence efficiency of a dye molecule depends on a combination of these four factors. For example, fluorescein dyes have a lower molar extinction coefficient than rhodamine dyes yet the fluorscein dyes fluoresce well because they have higher quantum yields. Thus, fluorescein dyes do not absorb light as well but make a better job of converting the absorbed light into emitted light. This fact points out that the brightness of a fluorophore is proportional to the product of the molar extinction coefficient and the quantum yield.

SELECTING THE OPTIMAL FLUOROPHORE FOR AN APPLICATION

Optimal dye selection requires consideration of the spectral properties of fluorescent labels in relation to the characteristics of the instrument used for detection (Singer and Johnson 1997). The intensity of the light emitted by a fluorophore is directly dependent on the amount of light that the dye has absorbed. Thus, the excitation source is very important in the behavior of a fluorophore. Other important instrument parameters to be considered include optical filters used for signal discrimination and the sensitivity and spectral response of the detector.

Lasers are an effective excitation source because the light they emit is very intense and at primarily one wavelength. Two lasers are primarily used to excite fluorescent dyes in the visible spectrum. The argon ion gas laser (Ar+) produces light at 488 nm and 514.5 nm (see Chapter 11). This laser is by far the most popular for applications involving fluorescent DNA labeling because more dyes are available that closely match its excitation capabilities. The other laser that is used is the solid-state Nd:YAG laser that produces a beam of light at 532 nm (see Chapter 12).

A significant advantage of fluorescent labeling over other methods is the ability to record two or more fluorophores separately using optical filters and a fluorophore separation algorithm known as a *matrix*. With this multicolor capability, components of complex mixtures can be labeled individually and identified separately in the same sample. Fluorescent signals are differentiated by using filters that block out light from adjacent regions of the spectrum. Signal discrimination by software matrix deconvolution of the various dye colors will be discussed later in this chapter.

A fluorescence detector is a photosensitive device that measures the light intensity emitted from a fluorophore. Detection of low-intensity light may be accomplished with a photomultiplier tube (PMT) or a charge-coupled device (CCD). In both cases, the action of a photon striking the detector is converted to an electric signal. The strength of the resultant current is proportional to the intensity of the incident light. This light intensity is typically reported in arbitrary units, such as relative fluorescence units (RFUs).

METHODS FOR LABELING DNA

Fluorescent labeling of PCR products may be accomplished in one of three ways: (1) incorporating a fluorescent dye into the amplicon through a 5′-end labeled oligonucleotide primer; (2) incorporating fluorescently labeled deoxynucleotides (dNTPs) into the PCR product; and (3) using a fluorescent intercalating dye to bind to the DNA (Mansfield and Kronick 1993). These three methods are illustrated in Figure 10.2.

Each method of labeling DNA has advantages and disadvantages. Intercalating dyes may be used following PCR and are less expensive than the other two methods. However, they can only be used to analyze DNA fragments in a single color, which means that all of the molecules must be able to be separated in terms of size. On the other hand, dye-labeled primers are popular because only a single strand of a PCR product is labeled, which simplifies data interpretation because the complementary DNA strand is not visible to the detector. Dye-labeled primers also enable multiple amplicons to be labeled simultaneously in an independent fashion.

Figure 10.2

Methods for fluorescently labeling DNA fragments. Double-stranded DNA molecules may be labeled with fluorescent intercalating dyes (a). The fluorescence of these dyes is enhanced upon insertion between the DNA bases. Alternatively a fluorescent dye may be attached to a nucleotide triphosphate and incorporated into the extended strands of a PCR product (b). The most common method of detecting STR alleles is the use of fluorescent dye labeled primers (c). These primers are incorporated into the PCR product to fluorescently label one of the strands.

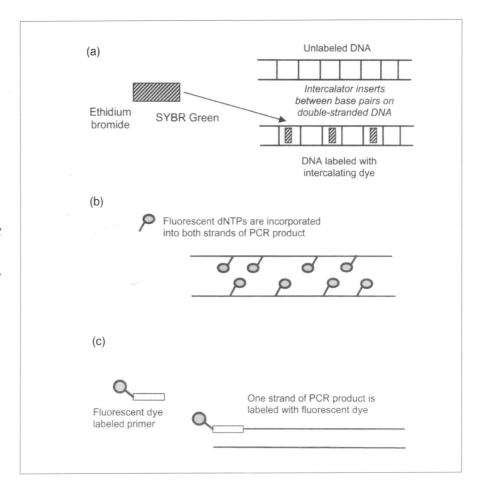

The addition of a fluorescent dye to a DNA fragment impacts the DNA molecule's electrophoretic mobility. This is because the physical size and shape of the dye changes the overall size of the dye–DNA conjugate. The ionic charge, which is present on the dye, also alters the charge to size ratio of the nucleic acid conjugate. Fluorescent dyes that are covalently coupled to STR primers slightly alter the electrophoretic mobility of a STR allele PCR product moving through a gel or capillary. However, software corrections are used to mitigate this problem. In addition, genotyping of alleles is always performed relative to allelic ladders that are labeled with the *same* fluorescent dye so that differences in dye mobilities do not impact allele calls.

SUMMARY OF FLUORESCENCE DETECTION

A laser strikes a fluorophore (dye) that is attached to the end of a DNA fragment. The fluorophore absorbs laser energy and then emits light at a lower energy (higher wavelength). Filters are used to collect only emitted light at a particular wavelength or range of wavelengths. Photomultiplier tubes or CCDs are used to collect and amplify the signal from the fluorophore and convert it to an electronic signal. These signals are measured in relative fluorescence units and make up the peaks seen in capillary electropherograms or gel bands.

Advantages of fluorescence detection methods include higher sensitivity and a broader dynamic range than comparable colorimetric detection methods (e.g. silver staining) and the capacity for simultaneous multi-parameter analysis of complex samples such as multiplex PCR products with different fluorescent labels.

FLUORESCENT DYES USED FOR STR ALLELE LABELING

Table 10.2 lists a number of fluorescent dyes that are commonly used to label PCR products for genotyping applications. The chemical names for the dyes are listed as well, along with their excitation and emission wavelengths. AmpFlSTR® kits from PE Biosystems use PCR primers that are labeled with the NHS-ester dyes 5-FAM, JOE, or NED (Perkin Elmer 1998). GenePrint® PowerPlex™ 1.1 and 2.1 kits from Promega Corporation use PCR primers labeled with fluorescein and tetramethyl rhodamine (TMR).

FAM and fluorescein fluoresces in the blue region of the visible spectrum, JOE in the green region, and NED and TMR in the yellow region. AmpFlSTR® kits utilize a fourth dye named ROX that fluoresces in the red region to label an

Dye	Chemical Name	Excitation Maximum (nm)	Emission Maximum (nm)
5-FAM	5-Carboxy fluorescein	493	522
JOE	6-Carboxy-2′,7′-dimethoxy-4′,5′-dichlorofluorescein	528	554
NED	*Proprietary to PE Biosystems*	553	575
ROX (CXR)	6-Carboxy-X-rhodamine	587	607
Fluorescein	Fluorescein	490	520
TMR (TAMRA)	*N,N,N′,N′*-Tetramethyl-6-carboxyrhodamine	560	583
TET	4,7,2′,7′-Tetrachloro-6-carboxyfluorescein	522	538
HEX	4,7,2′,4′,5′,7′-Hexachloro-6-carboxyfluorescein	535	553
SYBR Green (intercalator)	*Proprietary to Molecular Probes*	497	520

Table 10.2

Characteristics of commonly used fluorescent dyes in STR kits and other genotyping applications.

internal standard for DNA sizing purposes. PowerPlex™ STR kits use the red dye carboxy-X-rhodamine (CXR) for labeling their internal size standard. ROX and CXR are essentially the same dyes (Singer and Johnson 1997).

The 5-FAM, JOE, and NED dyes are fluorescein derivatives that have spectrally resolvable fluorescent spectra. The structures of four commonly used fluorescent dyes from PE Biosystems are shown in Figure 10.3. Because the structure of NED is proprietary to PE Biosystems, TAMRA, or tetramethyl rhodamine, has been included in its place for a yellow dye. A fifth dye should be available shortly from PE Biosystems, which will provide for another level of multiplexing.

The fluorescent emission spectra of the four ABI (Applied Biosystems Incorporated) dyes, 5-FAM, JOE, NED, and ROX, are shown in Figure 10.4. Each of the fluorescent dyes emits its maximum fluorescence at a different wavelength. This fact is used to design filters to capture the signal from each dye. The filters

Figure 10.3

ABI dyes used in four-color STR detection. The circled portion of the dye highlights the succinimidyl ester, which is used for dye attachment to the fluorescent oligo. In the AmpFlSTR kits, TAMRA has been replaced by NED (also a yellow dye). PowerPlex 1.1 and 2.1 STR kits use fluorescein and TMR, which are very similar to FAM and TAMRA, respectively. The red dye ROX is used to label an internal sizing standard and is the same as CXR used in PowerPlex kits.

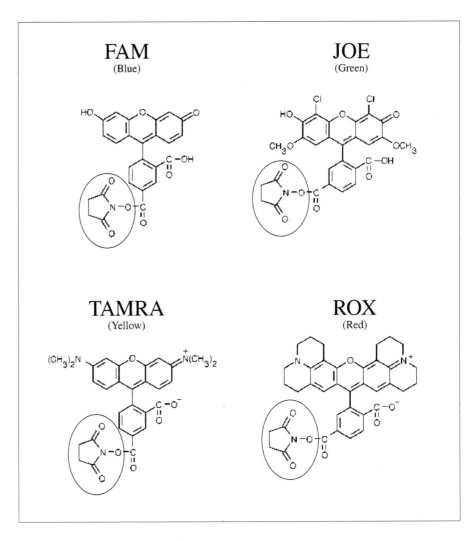

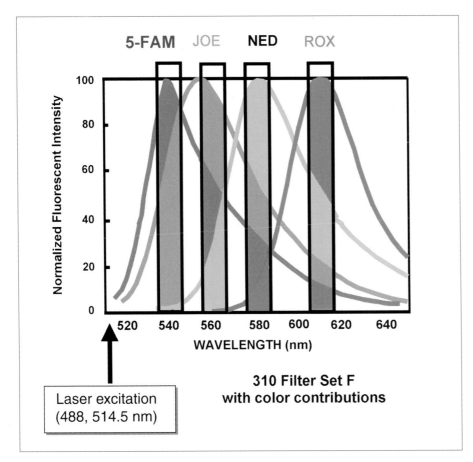

310 Filter Set F
with color contributions

Figure 10.4

Fluorescent emission spectra of ABI dyes used with AmpFlSTR kits. ABI 310 Filter Set F is represented by the four boxes centered on each of the four dye spectra. Each dye filter contains color contributions from adjacent overlapping dyes that must be removed by a matrix deconvolution. The dyes are excited by an argon ion laser, which emits light at 488 and 514.5 nm.

used to separate the various colors are shown as boxes centered on each of the four dye spectra. Note that there is considerable overlapping in color between several of the dyes in the filter regions. Blue and green have an especially high degree of overlap.

The dye sets for PowerPlex™ kits that are detected on the Hitachi FMBIO II fluorescent scanner (see Chapter 12) are shown in Figure 10.5. Notice that the fluorescence emission spectra for these three dyes have less spectral overlap because they are further apart.

Each dye set used must be matched to the instrument optics involved in detection as well as the excitation source. For example, the ABI Prism 310 uses an Argon ion (Ar+) laser with excitation wavelengths at 488 nm and 514 nm, while the FMBIO II uses a solid-state Nd:YAG laser with an excitation wavelength of 532 nm. PowerPlex 1.1 fluorescein-labeled primers, designed for FMBIO detection, are present in higher concentration than the same primers in PowerPlex 1.2, designed for ABI 310 detection, because of the different laser excitation wavelengths. Because the FMBIO laser is not as well suited for

Figure 10.5

Schematic of three-color detection using the Hitachi FMBIO Scanner System. These dyes and spectral filters (shown with boxes) are used for detection of STR alleles amplified with the Promega PowerPlex systems.

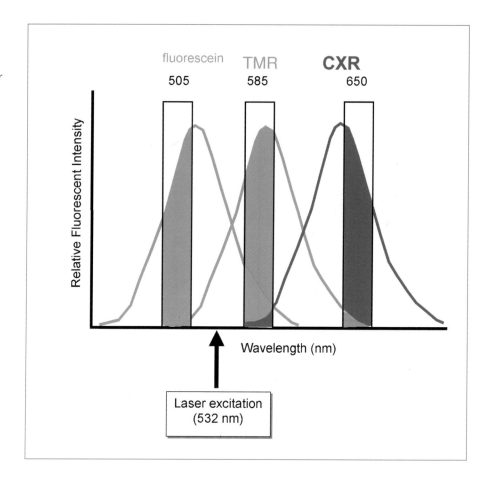

fluorescein dye excitation, more primer must be put in the PCR reaction to generate balanced product size compared to TMR-labeled amplicons.

When labeling DNA fragments with various dyes it is important to use appropriate concentrations of the dyes in order to obtain balanced signals between loci. For example, because NED has an excitation maximum that is further from the Ar+ 488/514 nm lines, more dye is required in order to obtain an equivalent signal to FAM.

ISSUES WITH FLUORESCENCE MEASUREMENTS

Multicomponent analysis is performed with a mathematical matrix that subtracts out the contribution of other dyes in each measured fluorescent dye. 'Color deconvolution' is another phrase to describe what this matrix does. When raw data are collected from a fluorescence-based detection platform, spectral overlap of different dyes must be accounted for in order to gain the capability to see the results from each dye individually.

One method of performing multicomponent analysis is to examine a standard set of DNA fragments labeled with each individual dye, known as matrix standard samples (Perkin Elmer Corporation 1998). Computer software then analyzes the data from each of the dyes and creates a matrix file to reflect the color overlap between the various fluorescent dyes. This matrix file table contains a table of numbers with four rows and four columns if there are four dyes that are being deconvoluted.

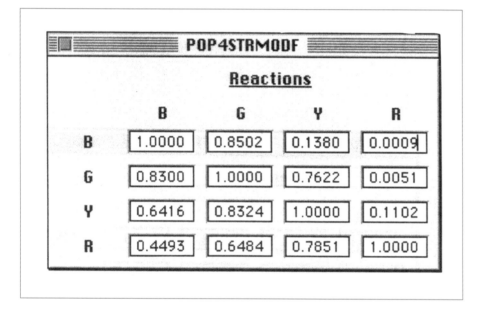

POP4STRMODF				
Reactions				
	B	**G**	**Y**	**R**
B	1.0000	0.8502	0.1380	0.0009
G	0.8300	1.0000	0.7622	0.0051
Y	0.6416	0.8324	1.0000	0.1102
R	0.4493	0.6484	0.7851	1.0000

Figure 10.6

Example of a matrix file table from an ABI Prism 310 instrument. These values are used by the GeneScan® Analysis Software to separate the various dye colors from one another. The letters B, G, Y, and R represent the dye colors blue, green, yellow, and red, respectively. All matrix files should have values of 1.0 on the diagonal from top left to bottom right. The other values in the table should all be less than 1.0. These values represent the amount of spectral overlap observed for each dye in each virtual detection filter. Matrix file values differ between instruments and even run conditions on a single instrument. Thus, a unique matrix file must be made for an instrument and a particular set of run conditions.

An example matrix from an ABI Prism 310 instrument may be seen in Figure 10.6. The values in this table represent the amount of spectral overlap observed for each dye in each color: blue (B), green (G), yellow (Y), and red (R). In the case of AmpFlSTR kits, the four fluorescent dyes are 5-FAM, JOE, NED, and ROX (Figure 10.4). Note that in the matrix file table (Figure 10.6), there are values of 1.0 on the diagonal from top left to bottom right and that all of the other values in the table are less than 1.0. These values represent the amount of spectral overlap observed for each dye. For example, the values in the B column are 1.000 (B), 0.8300 (G), 0.6416 (Y), and 0.4493 (R). Thus, in this example the most significant overlap is green into blue because 83% (0.8300) of the blue signal is made up of green on a normalized scale. Note that the emission spectra shown in Figure 10.4 also show the most overlap between the blue and green dyes.

Matrix files differ between instruments and even different run conditions on the same instrument because fluorescence of a dye is affected by the dye's environment. If the environmental conditions, such as temperature, pH, etc., change only very slightly, then the fluorescence behavior of the dyes will be altered. A matrix file should therefore be generated frequently to ensure good dye color separation and certainly any time the instrument conditions are altered, such as running samples in a different buffer system. As long as the electrophoresis conditions are constant from run to run, then the emission spectra of the dyes will be reproducible and spectral overlap can be accurately deciphered.

If the matrix color deconvolution does not work properly, then the baseline can be uneven, or a phenomenon known as 'pull-up' can occur. *Pull-up* is the result of a color bleeding from one spectral channel into another, usually because of off-scale peaks. The most common occurrence of pull-up involves small green peaks showing up under blue peaks that are off-scale. This occurs because of the significant overlap of the blue and green dyes seen in Figure 10.4. Samples can be diluted and analyzed again to reduce or eliminate the offending pull-up peak(s).

Raw data from a fluorescently labeled DNA sample are compared to the color-separated processed data in Figure 10.7. DNA fragments labeled with the yellow dye NED are shown in black. Multicomponent analysis is performed automatically with the GeneScan® Analysis Software using a mathematical matrix calculation.

FLUORESCENCE DETECTION PLATFORMS

As seen in Table 10.1, a number of fluorescence detection platforms exist and have been used for STR allele determination. The most popular detection platforms today for STR analysis in the United States are the ABI Prism 310 Genetic Analyzer and the FMBIO II gel scanner. These two instruments will be reviewed more extensively in Chapters 11 and 12, respectively. The ABI 310 and FMBIO II instruments have fundamental differences in their approach to detecting fluorescently labeled PCR products. In addition, specific STR kits have been designed for using each approach.

With the ABI 310 approach, detection is performed during electrophoresis (Figure 10.8). Other instruments listed in Table 10.1 that use a similar detection format as the ABI 310 include the ABI 373 or 377, the ALF DNA sequencer, and the LICOR systems. PE Applied Biosystems has prepared the Profiler Plus™ and COfiler™ STR kits to work on either the ABI 310 or ABI 377 detection platforms. These two kits cover the 13 core CODIS STR loci with three markers in common between the sets for concordance purposes (Figure 10.9).

With the FMBIO II or other gel-scanning systems, detection is performed following electrophoresis (Figure 10.10). Thus, many gels can be run offline and detected via rapid scanning on the FMBIO fluorescence imaging system.

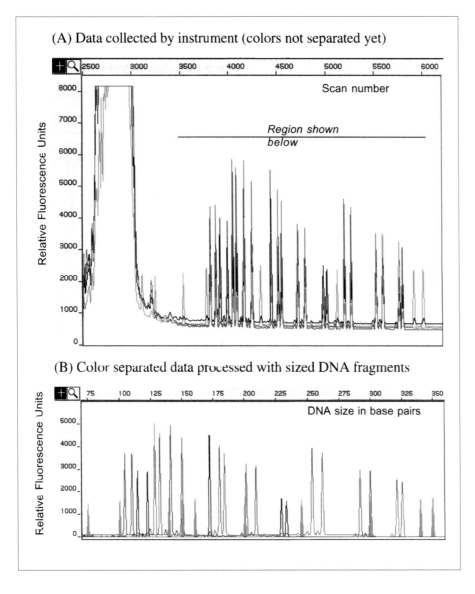

(A) Data collected by instrument (colors not separated yet)

Scan number

Region shown
below

(B) Color separated data processed with sized DNA fragments

DNA size in base pairs

Figure 10.7

STR data from ABI Prism 310 Genetic Analyzer. This sample was amplified with the AmpFlSTR SGM Plus kit. Raw data prior to color separation (a) compared with GeneScan 3.1 color-separated allele peaks (b). The red-labeled peaks are from the internal sizing standard GS500-ROX.

Promega Corporation has created two multiplex STR kits to work with the FMBIO II detection platform: PowerPlex™ 1.1 and PowerPlex™ 2.1 (Figure 10.11). These two kits also cover the 13 core CODIS STR loci with three STRs in common between the two kits for concordance purposes. These STRs are TH01, TPOX, and VWA and are outlined in Figure 10.11.

These two separation and detection approaches have differing abilities to separate STR alleles of various size ranges. Every DNA fragment travels the same distance when the detector is at a fixed point relative to the injection of the sample, as with the ABI 310. On the other hand, when separation and detection are separate steps, as with the FMBIO gel scanner, DNA fragments of different

Figure 10.8

Schematic illustration of the separation and detection of STR alleles with an ABI Prism 310 Genetic Analyzer.

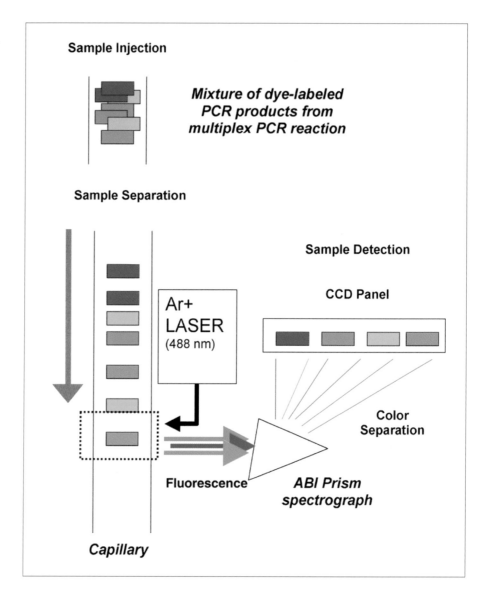

sizes travel different distances through the gel. Smaller molecular weight PCR products travel further through the gel and are thus better resolved from one another compared to the higher molecular weight species that only move a short distance through the gel before the electrophoresis is stopped and the gel is scanned.

SILVER STAINING

Silver staining of polyacrylamide gels has been useful for detecting small amounts of proteins and visualizing nucleic acids. Although not as commonly

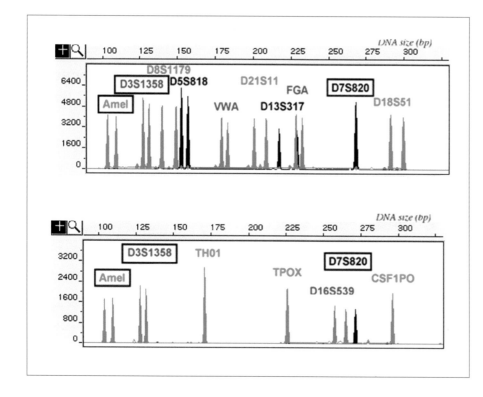

Figure 10.9

AmpFlSTR® Profiler Plus™ and COfiler™ STR data collected on an ABI 310 Capillary Electrophoresis System. The STR loci that are surrounded by a box are common to both multiplex mixes and are therefore useful as a quality assurance measure to demonstrate sample concordance.

used today, silver staining procedures were used for the first commercially available STR kits from Promega Corporation. Promega still supports silver-stain gel users. Silver-stain detection methods are still quite effective for laboratories that want to perform DNA typing for a much smaller startup cost. No expensive instruments are needed, simply a gel box for electrophoresis and some silver nitrate and other developing chemicals.

The procedure for silver staining is performed by transferring the gel between pans filled with various solutions that expose the DNA bands to a series of chemicals for staining purposes (Bassam *et al.* 1991). First, the gel is submerged in a pan of 0.2% silver nitrate solution. The silver binds to the DNA and is reduced with formaldehyde to form a deposit of metallic silver on the DNA molecules in the gel. A photograph is then taken of the gel to capture images of the silver-stained DNA strands and to maintain a permanent record of the gel. Alternatively, the gels themselves may be sealed and preserved.

ADVANTAGES AND DISADVANTAGES OF SILVER STAINING

Silver staining is less hazardous than radioactive detection methods, although not as convenient as fluorescence methods. Most reagents for silver staining are harmless and thus require no special precautions for handling. The primary

Figure 10.10

*Schematic of gel separation
and FMBIO II detection of
STR alleles.*

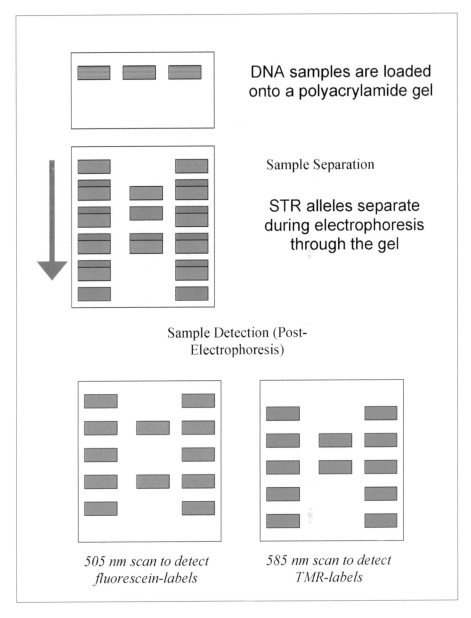

DNA samples are loaded
onto a polyacrylamide gel

Sample Separation

STR alleles separate
during electrophoresis
through the gel

Sample Detection (Post-
Electrophoresis)

*505 nm scan to detect
fluorescein-labels*

*585 nm scan to detect
TMR-labels*

advantage of silver staining is that the technique is inexpensive. The developing chemicals are readily available at low cost. The PCR products do not need any special labels, such as fluorescent dyes. The staining may be completed within half an hour and with a minimal number of steps. Sensitivity is approximately 100 times higher than that obtained with ethidium bromide staining (Merril *et al.* 1998). However, a major disadvantage to data interpretation is that both DNA strands may be detected in a denaturing environment leading to two bands for each allele. In addition, only one 'color' exists, which makes PCR product size differences the only method for multiplexing STR markers.

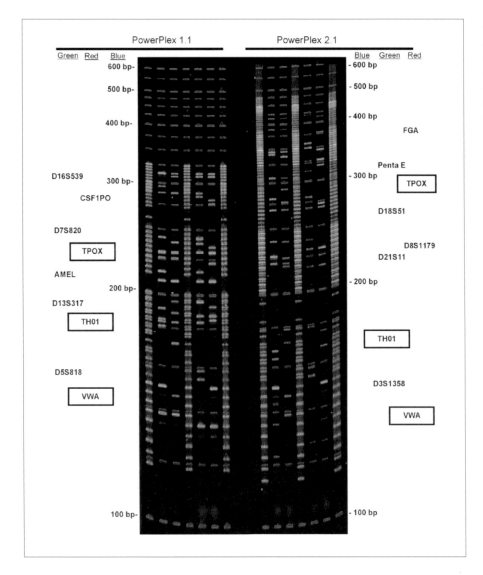

Figure 10.11

PowerPlex™1.1 and 2.1 data collected on a Hitachi FMBIO II Fluorescence Imaging System. Figure courtesy of Hitachi Genetic Systems.

REFERENCES

Bassam, B.J., Caetano-Anolles, G. and Gresshoff, P.M. (1991) *Analytical Biochemistry*, 1996, 80–83.

Berschick, P., Henke, L. and Henke, J. (1993) *Proceedings of the Fourth International Symposium on Human Identification.* Madison, WI: Promega Corporation, pp. 201–204.

Budowle, B., Baechtel, F.S., Comey, C.T., Giusti, A.M. and Klevan, L. (1995) *Electrophoresis*, 16, 1559–1567.

Buel, E., Schwartz, M. and LaFountain, M.J. (1998) *Journal of Forensic Science*, 43, 164–170.

Butler, J.M., McCord, B.R., Jung, J.M. and Allen, R.O. (1994) *BioTechniques*, 17, 1062–1070.

Decorte, R. and Cassiman, J.-J. (1996) *Electrophoresis*, 17, 1542–1549.

Edwards, A., Civitello, A., Hammond, H.A. and Caskey, C.T. (1991) *American Journal of Human Genetics*, 49, 746–756.

Frazier, R.R.E., Millican, E.S., Watson, S.K., Oldroyd, N.J., Sparkes, R.L., Taylor, K.M., Panchal, S., Bark, L., Kimpton, C.P. and Gill, P.D. (1996) *Electrophoresis*, 17, 1550–1552.

Hammond, H.A., Jin, L., Zhong, Y., Caskey, C.T. and Chakraborty, R. (1994) *American Journal of Human Genetics*, 55, 175–189.

Huang, N.E., Schumm, J.W. and Budowle, B. (1995) *Forensic Science International,* 71, 131–136.

Lazaruk, K., Walsh, P.S., Oaks, F., Gilbert, D., Rosenblum, B.B., Menchen, S., Scheibler, D., Wenz, H.M., Holt, C. and Wallin, J. (1998) *Electrophoresis*, 19, 86–93.

Lee, S.B., Buoncristiani, M., Schumm, J.W. and Wingeleth, D. (1995) *Proceedings of the Fifth International Symposium on Human Identification*. Madison, WI: Promega Corporation, pp. 104–111.

Lins, A.M., Micka, K.A., Sprecher, C.J., Taylor, J.A., Bacher, J.W., Rabbach, D., Bever, R.A., Creacy, S. and Schumm, J.W. (1998) *Journal of Forensic Sciences*, 43, 1178–1190.

Mansfield, E.S. and Kronick, M.N. (1993) *BioTechniques*, 15, 274–279.

Mansfield, E.S., Robertson, J.M., Vainer, M., Isenberg, A.R., Frazier, R.R., Ferguson, K., Chow, S., Harris, D.W., Barker, D.L., Gill, P.D., Budowle, B. and McCord, B.R. (1998) *Electrophoresis*, 19, 101–107.

Merril, C.R., Washart, K.M., and Allen, R.C. (1998) In: *Nucleic Acid Electrophoresis*. (D. Tietz, (ed.), New York: Springer.

Micka, K.A., Sprecher, C.J., Lins, A.M., Comey, C.T., Koons, B.W., Crouse, C., Endean, D., Pirelli, K., Lee, S.B., Duda, N., Ma, M. and Schumm, J.W. (1996) *Journal of Forensic Sciences*, 41, 582–590.

Morin, P.A. and Smith, D.G. (1995) *BioTechniques*, 19, 223–227.

Perkin Elmer Corporation (1998) *AmpFlSTR Profiler Plus PCR Amplification Kit User's Manual*. Foster City: PE Biosystems.

Roy, R., Steffens, D.L., Gartside, B., Jang, G.Y. and Brumbaugh, J.A. (1996) *Journal of Forensic Sciences*, 41, 418–424.

Schumm, J.W., Lins, A.M., Sprecher, C.J. and Micka, K.A. (1995) *Proceedings of the Sixth*

International Symposium on Human Identification. Madison, WI: Promega Corporation, pp. 10–19.

Singer, V.L. and Johnson, I.D. (1997) *Proceedings of the Eighth International Symposium on Human Identification.* Madison, WI: Promega Corporation, pp. 70–77.

Worley, J.M., Ma, M., Lee, S.B., Lins, A.M., Schumm, J.W. and Mansfield, E.S. (1994) *Proceedings of the Fifth International Symposium on Human Identification.* Madison, WI: Promega Corporation, pp. 109–117.

Wang, Y., Ju, J., Carpenter, B.A., Atherton, J.M., Sensabaugh, G.F. and Mathies, R.A. (1995) *Analytical Chemistry*, 67, 1197–1203.

CHAPTER 11

THE ABI PRISM 310 GENETIC ANALYZER

INTRODUCTION

Since its introduction in 1995 by PE Applied Biosystems, the ABI Prism 310 Genetic Analyzer has been an increasingly popular method for short tandem repeat (STR) typing in forensic DNA laboratories. A vast majority of forensic DNA laboratories within the United States use the ABI 310 for performing STR genotyping (Steadman 2000). In addition, the FBI Laboratory in Washington, DC performs its STR typing with the ABI 310.

The ABI 310 is a single capillary instrument with multiple color fluorescence detection that provides the capability of unattended operation. An operator simply loads a batch of samples in the 'autosampler', places a capillary and a syringe full of polymer solution in the instrument, and starts the 'run'. The data and genotype information are serially processed at the rate of approximately one sample every 30 minutes of operation. A major advantage of the technique for forensic laboratories is that the DNA sample is not fully consumed and may be retested if need be.

Many forensic scientists are using the ABI 310 without background knowledge of capillary electrophoresis (CE). This chapter reviews the theory and practice of capillary electrophoresis with a particular focus on the capabilities of the ABI Prism 310 Genetic Analyzer for genotyping STR markers. A few troubleshooting tips for the ABI 310 are also included.

EARLY WORK WITH CE AND STR TYPING

The first CE separations of STR alleles were performed in late 1992 using non-denaturing conditions with the polymerase chain reaction (PCR) products in a double-stranded form (McCord *et al.* 1993a, 1993b). Fluorescent intercalating dyes were used to visualize the DNA and to promote the resolution of closely spaced alleles. Internal standards were used to bracket the alleles in order to perform accurate STR genotyping. An allelic ladder was first run with the internal standards to calibrate the DNA migration times followed by analysis of the samples with the same internal standards (Butler *et al.* 1994). This internal sizing standard method involving a single fluorescent wavelength detector had to be used because multiple-color fluorescence CE instruments were not yet available. Since the commercialization of the ABI 310, internal standards labeled with a different color compared to the STR alleles can be used to perform the DNA size determinations and subsequent correlation to obtain the STR genotype.

Early on in the development of CE for DNA separations, one of the major concerns included sample preparation. PCR-amplified samples had to be dialyzed to remove salts that interfered with the injection of DNA fragments on to the CE column in order to observe the DNA with an ultraviolet (UV) detector. With the higher sensitivity of laser-induced fluorescence, sample preparation is no longer a major concern but does still play a role. Samples may be diluted in water or formamide and easily detected.

CAPILLARY ELECTROPHORESIS OF DNA

As discussed in Chapter 9, capillary electrophoresis involves the use of a narrow capillary filled with a polymer solution instead of a gel to perform the DNA size separation. The higher surface area to volume ratio in a capillary permits more efficient heat dissipation generated by the electrophoresis process and thus enables a higher separation voltage to be applied. Typical DNA separation times using CE are in the range of 5–30 minutes, compared to several hours for gel-based systems, because a higher voltage may be used. Most ABI 310 methods involve a separation voltage of 15 000 volts with a capillary length of 47 cm or 319 V/cm.

Polymer solutions have greatly aided DNA separations in capillaries. Prior to the injection of each new sample, a fresh portion of polymer solution is pumped into the capillary. This operation is analogous to pouring a new 'gel' automatically before each sample is loaded on the gel. The type and concentration of polymer solution used determines the resolution that may be obtained much in the same way that the percentage of cross-linking in polyacrylamide gels reflects the resolution capabilities of the electrophoretic system.

While CE is rapid on a per sample basis, it is a sequential technique where only one sample is analyzed at a time and is not as useful when trying to process large numbers of samples in parallel. Therefore, throughput is on the same time scale as, or even slower than, conventional gel electrophoresis methods. As will be discussed in a future section, capillary array systems with 96 capillaries in parallel have been developed to aid in high-throughput operations.

DNA samples are loaded on to the capillary by applying a fixed voltage for a defined period of time or by applying pressure to the sample and forcing a plug of sample to enter the inlet end of the capillary. In the case of the ABI 310, only the voltage application or 'electrokinetic' injection mode is available for injecting DNA samples.

COMPONENTS OF THE ABI 310

The basic components of the ABI Prism 310 Genetic Analyzer are illustrated in Figure 11.1. A capillary is located between the pump block and the inlet electrode. The capillary is filled with polymer solution through the pump block. A heated plate is used to heat the capillary to a specified temperature. Samples are placed in an autosampler tray that moves up and down to insert the sample on to the capillary and electrode for the injection process.

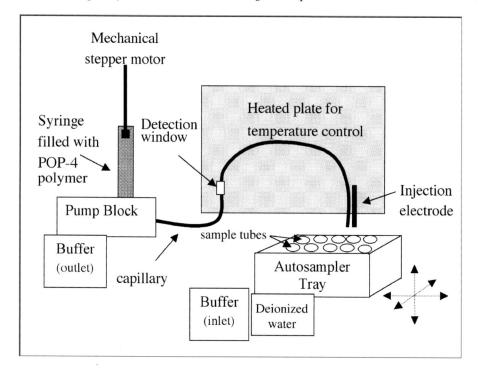

Figure 11.1

Schematic of ABI Prism 310 Genetic Analyzer. The capillary stretches between the pump block and the injection electrode. The mechanical stepper motor pushes polymer solution in the syringe into the pump block where it enters and then fills the capillary. Samples placed in the autosampler tray are sequentially injected on to the capillary. Electrophoretic separation occurs after each end of the capillary is placed in the inlet and outlet buffer and a voltage is applied across the capillary. A laser (not shown) is used to detect fluorescently labeled DNA fragments as they pass by the capillary detection window.

Prior to running any samples, the ABI 310 CE system must be readied for analysis. This preparation generally involves four steps:

1 putting a capillary in the instrument and aligning the detection window;
2 loading the polymer solution into a syringe and priming the system to remove any bubbles;
3 filling the buffer reservoirs so that current can flow between the electrodes and separations occur across the capillary;
4 placing deionized water in tubes that will be used for keeping the end of the capillary wet and cleaning off buffer salts before and after the injection process.

Each of these components plays an important role in the CE process and will be described in greater detail below.

THE CAPILLARY

At the core of a CE system is the capillary, which is a narrow glass tube that has an inner diameter of 50, 75, or 100 μm. Capillaries typically used for STR separations on the ABI 310 have an inner diameter of 50 μm. The outside of the capillary is usually coated with a plastic polyimide jacket to allow users to handle the capillary without it breaking. However, this coating is opaque and thus inhibits optical detection of anything passing through the interior of the capillary. A small capillary window is therefore needed to observe the separation products and is usually generated by burning away several millimeters of the polyimide coating. Capillary with windows already created in them may be purchased or a user can buy a long roll of capillary and burn their own detection windows. Once the fused silica (glass) tube is exposed, the window region must be handled carefully as it is easily breakable.

Two factors that are impacted by capillary length include peak resolution and separation time. Generally, the longer the capillary the better the resolution, but the greater the separation time. With CE, two capillary length measurements are important. The length to detector (L_{det}) is a measure of the distance from the capillary inlet where the DNA sample is injected to the detection window where the laser shines on the capillary and the fluorescent dyes are excited and detected. The total capillary length (L_{tot}) is the complete length of the capillary or, in other words, the distance from inlet to outlet buffer solutions when electrophoresis is occurring.

Varying the L_{tot} distance impacts the electric field strength that is applied to the CE system while shortening the L_{det} improves the separation speed. For optimal performance (i.e. highest resolution) with CE, it is best to have L_{det} as close to L_{tot} as possible. However, instrument space constraints keep L_{det} shorter than L_{tot} usually by 7 cm or more, primarily because the electrophoresis electrodes cannot be too close to the detection electronics. The detection window on the ABI 310 is fixed 11 cm from the outlet buffer. There is a minimum capillary length (L_{tot}) of approximately 41 cm (i.e. 30 cm L_{det}) with the ABI 310 Genetic Analyzer.

PE Applied Biosystems has made it easy for the user by supplying two lengths of capillary: 47 cm (36 cm to detector) and 61 cm (50 cm to detector). The shorter capillary is typically used for GeneScan applications, such as STR typing, where a faster separation speed is more important than resolution. The longer capillary is more effective for DNA sequencing, where a longer size range with single-base resolution is more desirable than rapid run times.

Capillaries used with the ABI 310 may or may not possess a covalently attached internal wall coating. Many capillaries used for CE are 'coated' by chemical derivatization to prevent a process known as electro-osmotic flow (EOF). Above pH 6, silica is negatively charged and thus the inside wall of a fused silica capillary will be covered by negative charges. EOF results from positive charges from the solution inside the capillary that form along the negatively charged capillary wall in what is known as the 'double layer'. Upon the application of an electric field, the mobile cations in the double layer migrate toward the cathode (inlet) and pull solution molecules in the same direction.

EOF is in the opposite direction, as electrophoretic migration of the DNA molecules and thus slows their progression through the capillary. EOF is highly dependent on environmental parameters, such as pH, temperature, voltage, and buffer viscosity. Thus, in order to obtain reproducible separations of DNA, EOF is removed by coating the inner wall of the capillary. There are two primary methods for coating the inner wall of a capillary: chemical derivatization of the charged silanol groups, or dynamic coating with a viscous polymer solution.

The capillaries typically used in the ABI 310 CE system are 'uncoated' meaning that the interior surface of the capillary does not have any chemical modifications to cover the charged silanol groups. However, the POP-4 polymer solution used for DNA separations dynamically coats the inside capillary wall and prevents EOF.

POLYMER SOLUTION

PE Applied Biosystems currently sells two polymer formulations for use with the ABI Prism 310 Genetic Analyzer. POP-4™ and POP-6™, which stands for Performance Optimized Polymer, are 4% and 6% concentrations of linear, uncross-linked dimethyl polyacrylamide, respectively. A high concentration of urea is also present in the polymer solution to help create an environment in the capillary that will keep the DNA molecules denatured.

POP-4 is a commercially available preparation of a flowable polymer [poly(N,N-dimethylacrylamide); DMA]. POP-4 contains 4% DMA homopolymer, 8 M urea, 5% 2-pyrrolidinone, and 100 mM N-Tris-(hydroxymethyl)methyl-3-aminopropane-sulfonic acid (TAPS) adjusted to pH 8.0 with NaOH (Rosenblum *et al.* 1997).

POP-4 is most commonly used for STR typing, while POP-6, which is more viscous and yields improved resolution at the expense of longer run times, is typically used for DNA sequencing applications. To prepare the CE system for use, approximately 600 or 700 μL are drawn up into a 1 mL syringe, which is placed in the ABI 310 instrument. Between 100 and 300 μL are often needed to prime the CE system and drive out any air bubbles. Several microliters are used between each DNA separation to refill the capillary for the next run. A full syringe can therefore last for 100 or more unattended injections prior to needing a refill.

ELECTROPHORESIS BUFFER

The electrophoresis buffer supplies the ions for conducting current across the capillary. If it is not properly replenished, the current can fluctuate affecting the DNA separation. PE Applied Biosystems supplies a 10X Genetic Analysis buffer with EDTA that is typically used in STR sample separations. The user simply dilutes the 10X buffer with nine times the volume of water to make a 1X solution. The 1X concentration of the Genetic Analysis buffer is 100 mM TAPs, 1 mM EDTA, pH 8.0 (Rosenblum *et al.* 1997). The electrophoresis buffer should be replaced after every set of about 100 sample injections.

OPERATION OF THE ABI 310 FOR GENOTYPING STR SAMPLES

The sample processing steps using the ABI 310 are illustrated in Figure 11.2. Samples are prepared and loaded into an autosampler tray. The user then enters the sample names and positions into a Sample Sheet, where comments concerning each sample may be entered along with the fluorescent dyes (blue, green, yellow, and red) in the sample. An internal sizing standard is also included in each sample and the appropriate color (usually red or yellow) needs to be indicated at this point.

Following the completion of the sample sheet, an injection list is then created and the sample sheet information imported into it. On the injection list, an operation module is selected for each sample. The typical module used for STR typing is 'GS STR POP4 (1 mL) F', which includes a default injection of 15 kV for 5 seconds and a separation voltage of 15 kV for 24 minutes.

SAMPLE PREPARATION

Following PCR amplification of forensic DNA samples using a commercially available STR typing kit, the resulting fluorescently labeled STR alleles need to be separated, sized, and genotyped. Samples are prepared for the ABI 310 by diluting them in a denaturant solution that helps disrupt the hydrogen bonds between the complementary strands of the PCR products. An internal standard is also added to each sample for sizing purposes. The samples are then heat denatured to separate the two strands of each PCR product and then loaded in the instrument for analysis.

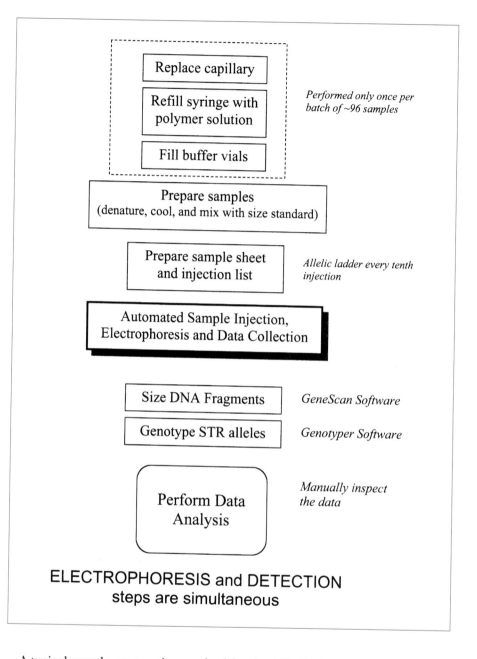

Figure 11.2
Sample processing steps using ABI 310 Genetic Analyzer.

A typical sample preparation method for the ABI 310 is as follows:

1. To a 0.5 mL tube, add 25 µL of deionized formamide.
2. Add 1 µL internal lane standard (GS350-ROX or GS500-ROX).
3. Add 1 µL PCR product amplified with AmpFlSTR kit or Promega PowerPlex 1.2.
4. Place grey septum on top of 0.5 mL tube.
5. Heat denature sample for 2–3 minutes at 95°C.

6   Snap cool the sample on ice for 2–3 minutes.

7   Place the sample in the 48-position autosampler tray (96-position trays also exist).

8   Place the autosampler tray in the ABI 310 instrument.

9   Enter the sample names into the ABI 310 sample sheet.

To simplify the sample preparation process and remove step 2, an equivalent amount of labeled internal lane standard may be added to a batch of deionized formamide. For example, if 50 samples were being prepared at a time, then 1250 μL of deionized formamide and 50 μL of GS500-ROX could be combined and 26 μL aliquoted to each sample tube. Regardless of whether the formamide and ROX-labeled internal standard are added separately or together, each sample tube contains ~27 μL, most of which is deionized formamide, and the PCR amplified sample has been diluted approximately 1:27 in the formamide. This dilution does two things. First, the high concentration of formamide helps keep the DNA stands denatured, especially after they are coaxed apart by heating to 95°C. Second, by diluting the PCR sample, the salts are also diluted which aids in the sample injection process.

For the same reason, it is important that the formamide be deionized. A good method for deionizing the formamide is the addition of an Amberlite ion exchange resin to the formamide. It is also a good idea to prepare a large batch of formamide and then aliquot it into single-use portions. Subjecting the formamide to freeze–thaw cycles can cause it to break down and form ionic byproducts that impact the injection process.

The salt content of a sample is very important in the CE electrokinetic injection process, as will be discussed later. Contaminating salts can come from either the formamide or the sample if it is not diluted enough. It should also be noted that deionized water can be used in the place of deionized formamide with the only caveat that samples may not be as stable after several days in water compared to formamide. A description of a procedure involving water instead of formamide for ABI 310 sample preparation has been published (Biega and Duceman 1999).

SAMPLE INJECTION

On the ABI 310 Genetic Analyzer, DNA samples are loaded into the capillary by electrokinetic injection. Each sample is placed in an analysis tube and then a voltage is applied to the sample to help draw it into the capillary opening. Electrokinetic injections selectively introduce a sample's charged species into the capillary. More sample material can be introduced into the capillary by simply increasing the voltage or the time applied. In order for this type of injection to work properly, the capillary and the electrode must both extend deep enough into the sample tube to interact fully with the solution in order to establish current flow during the application of the injection voltage. The standard injection on the default STR typing module is 15 000 V for 5 seconds.

Signal intensity may be increased by lengthening the sample injection time (e.g. from 5 to 10 or 15 seconds), dialyzing the sample on a filter membrane to remove salt from the solution (McCord *et al.* 1993a), or suspending the sample in deionized water (Butler 1995). *The peaks in a sample's fluorescent signal should be kept between 150 and 6000 relative fluorescence units (RFUs) on the ABI 310 for optimal results.* If the peaks are off-scale (above ~7500 RFUs), then the sample can be simply reinjected for less time, such as 2 seconds instead of the standard injection of 5 seconds, to bring the peaks back on scale.

Electrokinetic injections of DNA samples are highly dependent upon the levels of salt in the samples. These salt levels may be measured with a conductivity meter in terms of microsiemens (μS). The same sample with an identical amount of DNA that is diluted in formamide solutions with different conductivity results in vastly different sensitivity levels (Figure 11.3). As the salt level increases and the conductivity goes up, fewer DNA molecules are injected because they are competing with the salt ions to enter the capillary. In fact, the amount of DNA injected is inversely proportional to the ionic strength of the sample (Butler 1995). This differential sample injection due to salt content of the sample is from a process known as sample stacking.

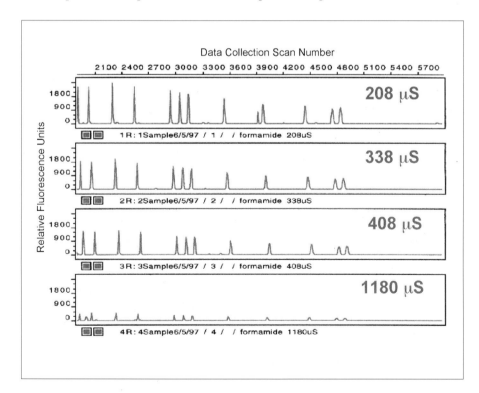

Figure 11.3

Results from ABI 310 using the same sample that has been diluted in different formamide solutions. Formamide solutions with higher conductivities (larger number of μS) result in less DNA being injected into the capillary. The sample is the GS350 ROX-labeled sizing standard. Figure courtesy of Bruce McCord, Ohio University.

Sample stacking is the process that results when samples are injected from a solution that has a lower ionic strength than the buffer inside the capillary. The buffer, for example, may be 100 mM in salts while the sample is less than 1 mM in ionic strength. When the electric field is applied during an electrokinetic injection, the resistance and field strength in the sample plug region increase because there are fewer ions to carry the current in the lower ionic strength sample. This causes the ions from the sample to migrate rapidly on to the capillary. As these sample ions enter a region where the polymer solution and buffer are at higher ionic strength, they stop moving as quickly and stack as a sharp band at the boundary between the sample plug and the electrophoresis buffer (Butler 1995).

One way to think of this sample stacking process is to imagine a flowing stream of water. When the banks are closer together, the water runs more rapidly than when the banks of the stream are further apart. By reducing the ionic strength of the DNA sample, the 'banks of the stream' are brought closer together and the sample rushes more quickly into the capillary. The amount of DNA that loads into the capillary during the period of time that the voltage is applied during an electrokinetic injection is thus a function of the sample's ionic strength.

Hence, samples prepared and diluted in water or formamide with a lower conductivity will give the highest degree of stacking. Formamide conductivity has a dramatic influence on the amount of DNA injected on to the capillary and therefore the sensitivity of the STR typing assay. In addition, the quality of the formamide has been shown to impact the resolution of closely spaced alleles such as the TH01 9.3 and 10 alleles that are 1 bp apart (Buel *et al.* 1998).

TEMPERATURE CONTROL

Room temperature fluctuations cause problems with proper sizing of STR alleles when using the ABI 310. Electrophoretic separations of STR samples are performed at a temperature of 60°C in order to minimize the formation of DNA secondary structure or intrastrand hybrid structures that impact the DNA separation (Wenz *et al.* 1998). DNA sizing is less precise at a lower temperature because of the DNA secondary structure that forms when the strands are not kept fully denatured. Variation in the run temperature will result in relative migration differences between the internal sizing standard DNA fragments and the STR alleles being measured and thus a change in the calculated size of the STR alleles. Because samples are run in a sequential fashion on a capillary system, maintaining a high degree of precision is essential in order to compare the allele sizes in an allelic ladder to those in the samples being analyzed.

The ABI 310 has a heated plate that is used to raise and maintain the temperature of the capillary. However, several centimeters of the capillary at both the inlet and outlet ends are exposed to the air and not directly in contact with the temperature-controlled plate. Maintaining the room temperature to a precision of less than ±1°C will improve the precision of DNA separations on the ABI 310. Future CE instruments will likely have improved temperature control to overcome these thermal fluctuation problems.

CAPILLARY MAINTENANCE AND STORAGE

In order for capillaries to be effective, they must be properly maintained. Capillary maintenance includes storing the ends of the capillary in water or buffer. If the capillary inlet and outlet dry out, then urea or other salts from the buffer will form crystals. Because the capillary openings are so narrow, even a very small crystal or particle from a solution can cause the capillary to clog. The best indicator of a clogged capillary is low current or no current when a voltage is placed across the capillary. Capillaries should be stored in deionized water when not in use for long periods of time.

BUFFER DEPLETION

Use of the same buffer over the course of a set of samples will result in a phenomenon known as buffer depletion. Ions move through the capillary due to the high voltage applied during electrophoresis. Positive ions will gather to the negatively charged electrode and negative ions will collect at the positively charged electrode during the course of electrophoresis. This ion movement results in an imbalance, referred to as buffer depletion. To correct this imbalance, the buffer is replenished or replaced on a regular basis. The buffer needs to be changed every day or two if the instrument is being used to its full capacity.

If the buffer is not replenished frequently, the DNA fragments will not separate as well due to ion depletion effects. The current will drop when the buffer becomes too depleted. For example, if the normal run current with a fresh buffer is 8 μA at 15 000 V then it will drop to 4–5 μA when the buffer becomes depleted. The current can thus serve as a useful diagnostic.

CAPILLARY FAILURE

Capillaries fail and need to be replaced after a number of sample injections. One of the primary reasons for capillary failure is that the dynamic coating on the inside wall of the capillary fails to work properly. Capillary failure is diagnosed by the presence of abnormally broad peaks that define a loss in resolution between closely spaced STR alleles. This loss in resolution is most likely the result of DNA and enzymes from the injected samples adhering to the capillary wall (Isenberg *et al.* 1998).

Capillaries can be removed from the ABI 310 and regenerated with consecutive washes of water, tetrahydrofuran, hydrochloric acid, and polymer solution (Madabhushi 1998). Margaret Kline at the National Institute of Standards and Technology (Gaithersburg, MD) has developed a capillary regeneration procedure that involves forcing several milliliters of deionized water and then a Tris–EDTA buffer through the capillary to remove any material that has bound to the inner wall. Of course the capillaries have to be removed from the instrument in order to perform this procedure. Capillary lifetimes of over 500 injections have been repeatedly demonstrated when using these wash steps. However, some laboratories may find it more convenient to just replace the capillary at around 100 injections as suggested by the manufacturer. Unfortunately, the ABI 310 does not permit an on-the-instrument wash that could be used to recondition a capillary and eliminate the need for frequent capillary replacement.

STEPS PERFORMED BY THE STANDARD MODULE

Instrument operation and data collection on the ABI 310 Genetic Analyzer is controlled by a series of steps and procedures that grouped together are referred to as a 'module'. The standard module used for STR typing is titled 'GS STR POP4 (1mL) F'. The steps for this module are listed below with an explanation for the purpose of each procedure.

Prior to starting the regular cycle of filling the capillary with polymer solution and injecting and separating DNA samples, several steps are performed in the standard module. First, the temperature on the capillary heating plate is brought up to 60°C to thermally equilibrate the capillary. The laser is turned on to full power (~10 mW). The autosampler platform is moved around in order to verify that the instrument is working well. The following steps are then performed with each sample that is analyzed on the ABI 310 capillary system.

- *Capillary fill* – polymer solution is forced into the capillary by applying a force to the syringe; the syringe position moves down by 5–10 revolutions or steps per injection with POP-4 and a 47 cm capillary. If the syringe moves significantly more than ten steps, then there is likely a leak in the pump block; if less, then the capillary may be plugged.
- *Pre-electrophoresis* – the separation voltage is raised to 10 000 V and run for 5 minutes. This step helps check for bubbles inside the capillary and helps to equilibrate the system for sample separation. If there are bubbles inside the capillary, the current will

remain at zero when the voltage is raised because ions are not flowing through the capillary.

- *Water wash of capillary* – capillary is dipped several times in deionized water to remove buffer salts that would interfere with the injection process.
- *Sample injection* – the autosampler moves to position A1 (or the next sample in the sample set) and is moved up on to the capillary to perform the injection. A voltage is applied to the sample and a few nanoliters of sample are pulled on to the end of the capillary. The default injection is 15 kV for 5 seconds.
- *Water wash of capillary* – capillary is dipped several times in waste water to remove any contaminating solution adhering to the outside of the capillary.
- *Water dip* – capillary is dipped in clean water (position 2) several times.
- *Electrophoresis* – autosampler moves to inlet buffer vial (position 1) and separation voltage is applied across the capillary. The injected DNA molecules begin separating through the POP-4 polymer solution.
- *Detection* – data collection begins. Raw data are collected with no spectral deconvolution of the different dye colors. The matrix is applied during Genescan analysis.

This entire process is accomplished in approximately 30 minutes per sample from one injection to the next assuming that the default time of 24 minutes for electrophoresis is used. The overall time for the capillary fill and pre-electrophoresis steps is about 6 minutes. DNA fragments up to approximately 400 bp in size should be through the capillary within 24 minutes of electrophoresis at 15 000 volts on a 47-cm capillary (320 V/cm).

ALTERNATIVE SOLUTIONS FOR HIGHER THROUGHPUT CAPABILITIES

Each ABI 310 instrument is capable of routinely analyzing about 8 000–10 000 sample injections per year. For laboratories desiring to process higher volumes of samples, multiple ABI 310 instruments or alternate analysis platforms may be used. Two alternatives include the ABI Prism 377 gel system and the ABI 3700 capillary array system.

The ABI Prism 377 involves the use of a thin polyacrylamide gel to separate the DNA molecules. Originally the ABI 377 instrument was designed to run 36 samples in parallel although 64 lane and 96 lane upgrades are now available with the ABI 377XL. STR samples can be separated in runs of 2–3 hours duration. Thus, three runs could be performed per day per instrument, with a potential throughput of about 72 000 lanes of data per year. The cost of an ABI 377 is approximately three times that of an ABI 310. The Forensic Science Service in England uses several dozen ABI 377s to perform their high-volume STR typing.

The ABI 3700, which is a 96-capillary array system, offers even higher potential throughput and automation than the ABI 377. Sample injection of 96 samples is performed in parallel. In a 24-hour period of unattended operation, more than 750 samples can be injected. Thus, approximately 190 000 sample injections can be theoretically processed per year. However, as of February 2000 routine STR typing of forensic samples has not been reported on the ABI 3700.

REFERENCES

Biega, L. A. and Duceman, B. W. (1999) *Journal of Forensic Sciences*, 44, 1029–1031.

Buel, E., Schwartz, M. and LaFountain, M. J. (1998) *Journal of Forensic Sciences*, 43, 164–170.

Butler, J. M. (1995) *Sizing and quantitation of polymerase chain reaction products by capillary electrophoresis for use in DNA typing*. Ph.D. dissertation, University of Virginia, Charlottesville.

Butler, J. M., McCord, B. R., Jung, J. M. and Allen, R. O. (1994) *BioTechniques*, 17, 1062–1070.

Isenberg, A. R., Allen, R. O., Keys, K. M., Smerick, J. B., Budowle, B. and McCord, B. R. (1998) *Electrophoresis*, 19, 94–100.

Lazaruk, K., Walsh, P. S., Oaks, F., Gilbert, D., Rosenblum, B. B., Menchen, S., Scheibler, D., Wenz, H. M., Holt, C., and Wallin, J. (1998) *Electrophoresis*, 19, 86–93.

Mansfield, E. S., Vainer, M., Enad, S., Barker, D. L., Harris, D., Rappaport, E. and Fortina, P. (1996) *Genome Research*, 6, 893–903.

McCord, B. R., Jung, J. M. and Holleran, E. A. (1993a) *Journal of Liquid Chromatography*, 16, 1963–1981.

McCord, B. R., McClure, D. L. and Jung, J. M. (1993b) *Journal of Chromatography* A, 652, 75–82.

Madabhushi, R.S. (1998) *Electrophoresis*, 19, 224–230.

Rosenblum, B.B., Oaks, F., Menchen, S. and Johnson, B. (1997) *Nucleic Acids Research*, 25, 3925–3929.

Steadman, G.W. (2000) *Survey of DNA Crime Laboratories, 1998*. Bureau of Justice Statistics, Special Report February 2000, US Department of Justice.

Wenz, H. M., Robertson, J. M., Menchen, S., Oaks, F., Demorest, D. M., Scheibler, D., Rosenblum, B. B., Wike, C., Gilbert, D. A. and Efcavitch, J. W. (1998) *Genome Research*, 8, 69–80.

CHAPTER 12

THE HITACHI FMBIO II
FLUORESCENCE IMAGING SYSTEM

An alternative solution to capillary systems for processing short tandem repeat (STR) samples is to run them on a polyacrylamide gel and then perform a post-electrophoresis fluorescent scan of the gel. Promega PowerPlex™ 1.1 and 2.1 STR kits have been made compatible with the Hitachi FMBIO II Fluorescence Imaging System. The STR amplicons are labeled with two different dyes, fluorescein and tetramethyl rhodamine (usually referred to as TMR), while a third dye, carboxy-X-rhodamine or CXR, is attached to an internal lane standard for DNA fragment sizing purposes.

FMBIO II FLUORESCENCE IMAGING SYSTEM

The FMBIO II Fluorescence Imaging System from Hitachi Genetic Systems (Alameda, CA) consists of a scanning unit that is controlled by a Macintosh computer and three software programs. The hardware for the system features a 20 mW solid-state Nd:YAG (neodinium yttrium aluminum garnet) laser that emits light at an excitation wavelength of 532 nm (Figure 12.1). The instrument can scan an area of 20 cm × 43 cm and has a reported linear dynamic range of four orders of magnitude. Two photomultiplier tubes are used for simultaneous detection of emitted light from two or more different fluorescent dyes. Band pass filters are used to achieve multi-color imaging.

Up to four filters can be stored in the instrument at any one time and accessed through the data collection software. The FMBIO II takes approximately 15–20 minutes to scan two dyes at once. In a typical scan of PowerPlex samples, the gel image is produced after electrophoresis using a 505 nm band-pass filter to detect amplification products containing a fluorescein label and a 585 nm band-pass filter to detect amplicons labeled with TMR. A 650 nm band-pass filter is used to observe the CXR-labeled internal size standard DNA fragments. These images can then be overlaid into a three-color image or viewed separately by color for closer inspection of the data.

Figure 12.1

Schematic of FMBIO II Fluorescence Imaging System. Following electrophoretic separation of STR alleles, a gel is placed in the FMBIO and scanned to reveal the presence of fluorescently labeled PCR products. The FMBIO utilizes a solid-state, green laser (1) to excite fluorophores at 532 nm using a polygon scanning mirror (2). The resulting fluorescent light signals emitted from the excited fluorophores attached to DNA fragments are then collected by two optical fiber arrays (3). Specific fluorescent dye signals are isolated using separate interference filters (4) and are converted to electrical signals with two photomultiplier tubes (5). Figure used with permission from Hitachi Genetic Systems web page.

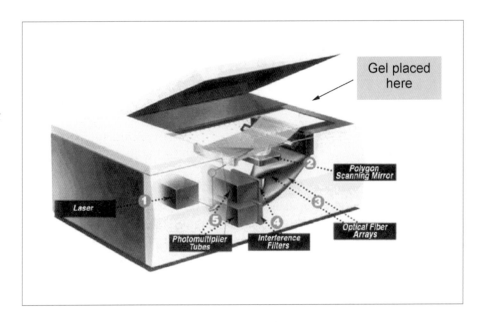

SOFTWARE PROGRAMS

The three software programs used in conjunction with the FMBIO scanner to perform STR genotyping include: (1) Read Image, (2) FMBIO® Analysis Software, and (3) STaR Call™ Genotyping Software. *Read Image* controls the scan area, scan resolution, and photomultiplier sensitivity as the FMBIO II scanning unit generates the digital image of the gel. The user can indicate which fluorescent emission filters to use and add comments to the scanned image. The scanned image for each fluorescent wavelength of the experimental data is converted into a 16-bit digital TIFF file and stored for future data analysis.

The generated gel data images are next examined by the *FMBIO® Analysis Software*, which performs functions such as DNA fragment sizing and quantification of peak height and area. DNA bands are sized through logarithmic comparison to size standards. Data can be displayed as either full gel images or electropherograms, which are a virtual slice through one of the gel lanes. The gel images can also be examined one color at a time following application of the color separation matrix.

The analysis software includes a DNA band finding program. Because of fluorescence intensity variation between gels and even within samples on a gel, this step requires some user review and editing of the data. An analyst manually evaluates each called DNA band. Stutter bands can be highlighted and edited out of the processed data or removed based on user-defined criteria in the genotyping software described below.

Once the DNA bands have been sized, the STR alleles are genotyped using *STaR Call™ Genotyping Software*. Band sizes from STR alleles are compared to sized alleles from allelic ladders run in adjacent lanes and converted to the appropriate genotype. Band sizes calculated by FMBIO® Analysis Software are imported into STaR Call™ and compared to values for each STR locus in a multiplex set. STR 'Lookup Tables' are exported to a Microsoft® Excel worksheet for evaluation of genotypes and manual confirmation that the expected size ranges are obtained for each allele. A 'lookup table' typically includes the DNA band size, STR allele call, and band quantification in the form of optical density (OD) units.

Based on comparison of DNA fragment sizes with allele ranges and allelic ladders, each band is assigned a locus name and repeat number. The program looks for bands with weaker intensities, assigns them as stutter products if they are one repeat unit less than a 'normal' allele, and appropriately excludes them from the final data output. All of these genotyping steps can be performed automatically by the software. However, the final genotype information is typically reviewed carefully in a manual fashion to insure that correct calls were made by the genotyping software.

SAMPLE PROCESSING ON THE FMBIO II

One of the downsides of performing sample processing with the FMBIO II is that the process involves the use of gel electrophoresis, which is more labor intensive than capillary electrophoresis. However, the FMBIO system can lead to higher sample throughputs per instrument. Unlike the ABI 310 capillary system that performs online detection during electrophoresis, a gel's image is captured *after* electrophoretic separation with the FMBIO II system. In other words, gels are run separately from the detection portion of the analysis with the FMBIO II approach (Figure 12.2). Therefore, with staggered start times, multiple gel electrophoresis systems can feed into a single FMBIO II Fluorescence Analysis System, leading to higher throughput for the cost of a single instrument. For example, the Bode Technology Group, a private contract DNA typing laboratory in Springfield, Virginia, runs on average 20 gels per day with each gel containing 25 samples plus allelic ladders and controls. Thus, in this case a single scanner can process 450 new samples every day.

GEL ELECTROPHORESIS

Gels must be poured, samples loaded, and electrophoresis conducted prior to scanning the samples. Gel sizes are typically 17 cm × 43 cm × 0.4 cm ('long gel') or 17 cm × 32 cm × 0.4 cm ('short gel'). The denaturing polyacrylamide gel

Figure 12.2

Sample processing steps using the Hitachi FMBIO II. Multiple gels can be prepared simultaneously and then quickly scanned after electrophoresis to improve sample throughput.

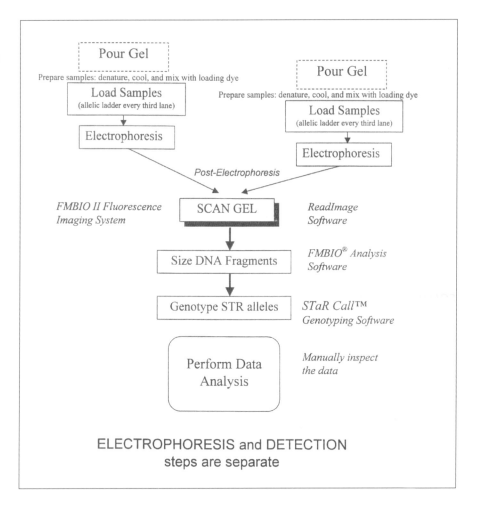

composition for PowerPlex 1.1 analysis is typically 4% polyacrylamide:bis (19:1), 7 M urea, and 0.5X Tris-Borate-EDTA (TBE) buffer (Micka *et al.* 1999). Alternatively, a 5% Long Ranger™ (FMC BioProducts, Rockland, ME) gel may be used with 7 M urea and 1X TBE (Lins *et al.* 1998). Precast gels, such as the 4.5% R3™ Precast Gels, are also available from Hitachi Genetic Systems (Micka *et al.* 1999). Gels can be re-used up to four times with similar performance if proper care is taken (Tereba *et al.* 1998).

The gels are usually run on a SA43 vertical electrophoresis apparatus (Life Technologies, Inc., Rockville, MD). A prerun at 60 W for 30–45 minutes is performed prior to loading the samples in order to warm the gel up to a plate temperature of 45°C to 50°C. The PCR-amplified STR alleles are then loaded on to the gel and separated for 60–90 minutes to resolve the DNA bands. A separation voltage of 60 V/cm is often used in order to resolve PowerPlex™ 1.1 STR alleles (Schumm *et al.* 1997).

SAMPLE PREPARATION FOR GEL LOADING

Samples are prepared by mixing 2 µL of the amplified sample with a 1 µL aliquot of the CXR-labeled fluorescent internal lane standard and 3 µL of Bromophenol blue loading solution (95% formamide, 0.05% bromophenol blue, 10 mM NaOH). This mixture is heated to 95°C for 2 minutes and then snap-cooled on ice to denature the DNA strands present in the sample. An aliquot of 2.5–3 µL of this sample is then loaded on to the appropriate lane of the gel (Schumm *et al.* 1997, Promega Corporation 1999). Allelic ladders are prepared in a similar fashion and loaded on to the gel every five or six lanes. Note that while internal lane standard 400 works to size PowerPlex 1.1 STR loci, the extra high molecular weight DNA bands in the internal lane standard 600 are needed to properly size the large alleles in Penta E and FGA STR systems.

SOLUTION FOR 13 CODIS STR LOCI

The Promega solution to the 13 CODIS STR loci currently involves the use of two STR kits. DNA samples are amplified and genotyped with eight STR markers in PowerPlex™ 1.1 and nine STR markers in 2.1 (Figure 12.3a, 12.3b). There are three STR systems in common between these two kits, namely VWA, TH01, and TPOX, in order to help verify sample concordance and avoid sample shuffling. The STaR Call™ 3.0 genotyping software automatically compares the three overlapping loci between the PowerPlex™ 1.1 and 2.1 systems, and highlights any non-agreeing alleles as an internal quality control check.

Samples amplified with both PowerPlex™ 1.1 and 2.1 are shown in Figure 12.3. The 505 nm scan that detects the fluoroscein-labeled PCR products is shown in Figure 12.3a, while the 585 nm scan that detects the tetramethyl rhodamine-labeled PCR products is shown in Figure 12.3b. Note that the PowerPlex™ 2.1 STR markers extend to a higher size range, almost 500 bp in size. The position of the STR locus impacts its resolution on the gel. Alleles from the D3S1358 STR locus travel further through the gel matrix and are therefore better resolved from one another compared to FGA alleles that are near the top of the gel. Thus, it is more difficult to distinguish off-ladder alleles within the FGA locus compared to the D3S1358 locus because the alleles are not spread apart as well.

The data file size needed to capture the information from a fluorescence scan of a gel is quite large. Owing to the different number of alleles and DNA size range, a typical gel scan of PowerPlex™ 1.1 is approximately 36 megabytes in size while a scan of a full PowerPlex™ 2.1 gel takes up approximately 48 megabytes for the storage of all information on that gel. A computer hard drive can fill up rather quickly with these image files necessitating the use of zip drives or magneto optical disk drives for data storage.

Figure 12.3 (a)

STR data collected from the 505 nm scan of a gel containing both PowerPlex™ 1.1 and 2.1 PCR-amplified samples. The fluorescein-labeled STR alleles are visualized in this scan. Two different samples are shown here with genotypes that differ at every locus. The number of repeat units represented in the allelic ladders for each STR locus is indicated next to the appropriate allele. Note that with the TH01 allelic ladder the 9.3 and 10 alleles are resolved indicating single base resolution in that portion of the gel electrophoretic separation. Figure courtesy of Hitachi Genetic Systems.

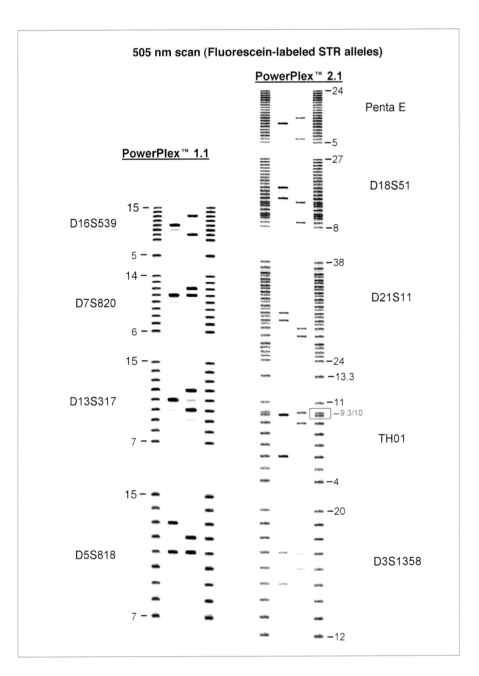

ISSUES WITH THE FMBIO II APPROACH

NUMBER OF SAMPLES PER GEL

The number of samples that may be run on each gel is flexible and depends on the comb used to form the sample loading wells. The Bode Technology Group uses a comb with 38 slots containing flat wells with intervening 'posts' that

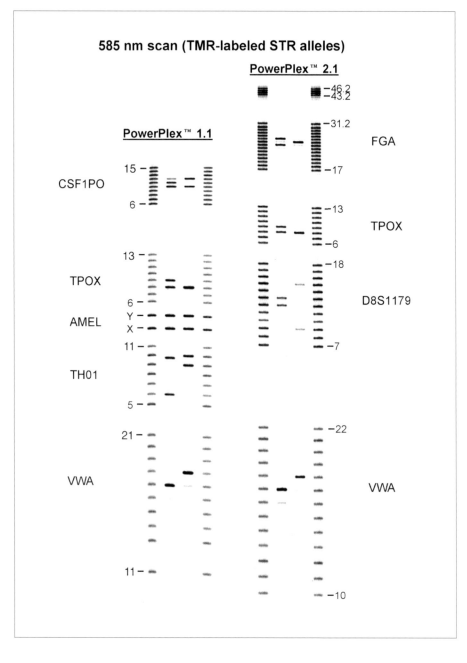

585 nm scan (TMR-labeled STR alleles)

Figure 12.3 (b)
STR data collected from the 585 nm scan of a gel containing both PowerPlex™ 1.1 and 2.1 PCR-amplified samples. The tetramethyl rhodamine (TMR)-labeled STR alleles are visualized in this scan. Two different samples are shown here with genotypes that differ at every locus (same as Figure 12.3a). The number of repeat units represented in the allelic ladders for each STR locus is indicated next to the appropriate allele. Note that the allelic ladders for VWA have different alleles for the PowerPlex™ 1.1 and 2.1 systems, yet the samples run exactly the same and may be used to provide concordance between PowerPlex™ 1.1 and 2.1 PCR amplifications. Figure courtesy of Hitachi Genetic Systems.

separate each loading well. Two slots are left empty on each end. Control lanes include a K562 sample, a reagent blank, a negative control, and a blind control sample for quality control purposes. The remaining 30 lanes are composed of five sets of allelic ladders and 25 test samples. Internal lane standards are loaded into each lane to enable size determination and allele calling of PCR products amplified at each STR locus (shown in blue in Figure 10.11).

GEL REUSE

Preparing, pouring, and polymerizing polyacrylamide gels can be tedious. Fortunately precast gels are available including the Hitachi R³™ Precast Gel Electrophoresis System or Long Ranger™ gels from FMC Bioproducts (Rockland, ME). In order to reduce the number of gels that have to be prepared to analyze a large set of samples, a method has been developed to reuse gels (Tereba *et al.* 1998).

After imaging a gel on the FMBIO II, it can be placed back in the gel box and electrophoresed in reverse for a short period of time to remove the DNA samples from the gel. Typically the gel reverse electrophoresis is performed for 15–30 minutes longer than the previous forward electrophoresis, in order to fully remove all of the DNA bands from the gel. The gel can then be reloaded with fresh samples and another set of data determined. Promega scientists have published protocols for the reuse of gels up to four or more times (Tereba *et al.* 1998, Micka *et al.* 1999).

Amazingly, the resolution of the gel does not degrade with this reuse. However, edge effects, such as 'frowning' of the outer lanes, become progressively worse with each run. With the use of internal lane standards though, the frowning effects do not impact the ability to size the unknown DNA fragments in the gel accurately. The reuse of gels for four or five times or even more over the period of several days translates to savings in terms of labor and reagent costs. The reuse of gels also minimizes the number of times that a laboratory has to clean the glass gel plates.

CLEANING GEL PLATES

A gel is poured between two glass plates. Any dust particles or other contaminants on the plates can interfere with the collection of fluorescence data by scattering the laser excitation or the fluorescence emission light. Cleaning glass plates is time consuming but essential to obtaining a good fluorescent signal with low background. Special low-fluorescence plates cost around $150 per pair compared to standard glass plates that are about $50 per pair.

When plates are cleaned, the gel has to be removed since it is bonded to one or both plates. The plates are often soaked to simplify the gel release. Cleaning usually takes about 5–10 minutes for a pair of plates once the gel has been removed.

DIFFERENT EXCITATION LASER

The FMBIO II uses a 532 nm laser wavelength to excite fluorescent dyes. The different laser excitation wavelength compared to the typical argon ion laser wavelengths of 488 nm and 514.5 nm means that the two dyes used to label STR alleles in the PowerPlex system are differentially excited causing the dye sensitivities to vary. This effect produces different relative intensities of the amplification products detected in the different instruments. Therefore, the primer concentrations were re-configured to make the amplification products from the PowerPlex systems compatible with the two instruments' different excitation/emission wavelengths (Lins *et al.* 1998). Hence, the primer concentrations in the PowerPlex™ 1.2 STR kit has been optimized for use on the ABI 310 while PowerPlex™ 1.1 and 2.1 kits have been designed for the FMBIO II.

COMPARISON OF FMBIO II WITH ABI 310 APPROACH

There are advantages and disadvantages to any approach taken for DNA typing. The instrument platforms covered in this chapter and the previous one, namely the FMBIO II Gel Imager and ABI Prism 310 Genetic Analyzer, are compared in Table 12.1. The steps surrounding the FMBIO are more labor intensive since the sample loading is not as automated as the ABI 310. However, the FMBIO is capable of about ten times the throughput of the ABI 310 on a per instrument basis.

Parameter	FMBIO II Gel Scanner	ABI Prism 310 CE System
STR kit solution for 13 CODIS core loci	PowerPlex™ 1.1 and 2.1 from Promega Corporation	Profiler Plus™ and COfiler™ from PE Biosystems
Fluorescent dyes detected	Fluorescein, TMR, CXR	5-FAM, JOE, NED, ROX
Laser wavelength used to excite fluorophores	532 nm (Nd:YAG solid-state laser)	488 nm and 514.5 nm (Argon ion gas laser)
Instrument cost	~$80 000	~$60 000
Batch size (including allelic ladders)	25 per gel (depends on comb used)	48 or 96 per tray
Sample throughput	20 or more gels/scanner/day (~450 samples/day)	48 samples/24 hour period
Sample data collection time	15 minutes to scan gel	~30 minutes per sample
Computer type (as of February 2000)	Macintosh®	Macintosh®
Data collection software	ReadImage	ABI 310 Data Collection
Peak sizing software	FMBIO® Analysis	GeneScan®
Genotyping software	STaR Call™	Genotyper®
Data File Size	~30 Mb/gel (~1 Mb/sample)	~200 kb/sample (GeneScan) ~100 kb/sample (Genotyper)

Table 12.1

Comparison of FMBIO II and ABI 310 detection formats.

Table 12.1
Continued

Parameter	FMBIO II Gel Scanner	ABI Prism 310 CE System
Accessories needed	Gel electrophoresis apparatus, glass gel plates, acrylamide, loading dye, comb	Capillary, POP-4 polymer, tubes, septa tube caps
Lifetime of gel or capillary for reuse	2–5 runs	~100–300 runs
Primary advantage of approach	Capable of high-volume sample processing because separation and detection are separate and many samples can be run in parallel on each gel	Automated sample processing with no gel pouring or sample loading required

REFERENCES

Lins, A.M., Micka, K.A., Sprecher, C.J., Taylor, J.A., Bacher, J.W., Rabbach, D., Bever, R.A., Creacy, S. and Schumm, J.W. (1998) *Journal of Forensic Sciences*, 43, 1168–1180.

Micka, K.A., Amiott, E.A., Hockenberry, T.L., Sprecher, C.J., Lins, A.M., Rabbach, D.R., Taylor, J.A., Bacher, J.W., Glidewell, D.E., Gibson, S.D., Crouse, C.A. and Schumm, J.W. (1999) *Journal of Forensic Sciences*, 44, 1243–1257.

Promega Corporation (1997) *GenePrint® Fluorescent STR Systems Technical Manual*. Madison, WI: Promega Corporation.

Promega Corporation (1999) *GenePrint® PowerPlex™ 2.1 System Technical Manual*. Madison, WI: Promega Corporation.

Schumm, J. W., Lins, A. M., Micka, K. A., Sprecher, C. J., Rabbach, D. and Bacher, J. W. (1996) *Proceedings of the First European Symposium on Human Identification*. Madison, WI: Promega Corporation, pp. 90–104.

Schumm, J.W., Sprecher, C.J., Lins, A.M., Micka, K.A., Rabbach, D.R., Taylor, J.A., Tereba, A. and Bacher, J.W. (1997) *Proceedings of the Eighth International Symposium on Human Identification*. Madison, WI: Promega Corporation, pp. 78–84.

Tereba, A., Micka, K.A. and Schumm, J.W. (1998) *BioTechniques*, 25, 892–897.

CHAPTER 13

STR GENOTYPING ISSUES

In Chapters 9 and 10, we discussed how short tandem repeat (STR) amplification products labeled with fluorescent dyes are separated and detected. In Chapters 11 and 12, we examined two commonly used instrument approaches for collecting the STR data. However, the data collection process leaves the analyst with only a series of peaks in an electropherogram or bands on a gel. The peak information (DNA size and quantity) must be converted into a common language that will allow data to be compared between laboratories. This common language is the sample genotype. This chapter will review the process of taking multi-color fluorescent peak information and converting it into STR genotypes.

A locus genotype is the allele, in the case of a homozygote, or alleles, in the case of a heterozygote, present in a sample for a particular locus and is normally reported as the number of repeats present in the allele. *A sample genotype or STR profile is produced by the combination of all of the locus genotypes into a single series of numbers.* This profile is what is entered into a case report or a DNA database for comparison purposes to other samples.

STR alleles from the same sample that are amplified with different primer sets or analyzed by different detection platforms will differ in size. However, by using locus-specific allelic ladders, such as those described in Table 5.4, allele peak sizes may be accurately converted into genotypes (Smith 1995). These genotypes then provide the universal language for comparing STR profiles.

THE GENOTYPING PROCESS

Sample data collected from either the ABI 310 or FMBIO II are in the form of peaks that represent the various STR alleles amplified from the DNA sample. These peaks are present at various locations in a sample's electropherogram and usually plotted as fluorescent signal intensity versus time passing the detector (in the case of the ABI 310) or position on the gel (in the case of the FMBIO II gel imager). The steps for converting those fluorescent peaks into an allele call are shown in Figure 13.1.

Figure 13.1

Genotyping process for STR allele determination. Software packages for DNA fragment analysis and STR genotyping perform much of the actual analysis, but extensive review of the data by trained analysts/examiners is often required.

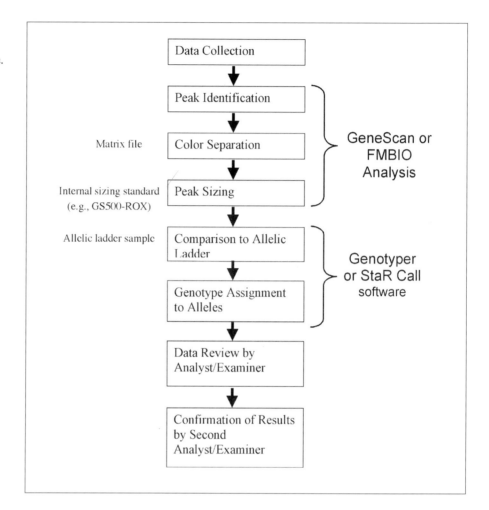

The multiplex STR kits in use today take advantage of multiple fluorescent dyes that can be spectrally resolved. The various dye colors are separated and the peaks representing DNA fragments are identified and associated with the appropriate color. The DNA fragments are then sized by comparison to an internal sizing standard (Figure 13.2). Finally, the PCR product sizes for the questioned sample are correlated to an allelic ladder that has been sized in a similar fashion with internal standards. The allelic ladder contains alleles of known repeat content and is used much like a measuring ruler to correlate the PCR product sizes to the number of repeat units present for a particular STR locus. From this comparison of the unknown sample with the known allelic ladder, the genotype of the unknown sample is determined.

SIZING DNA FRAGMENTS

DNA fragments represented by peaks in capillary electropherograms or bands on a gel can be sized relative to an internal size standard that is mixed with the DNA samples. The internal size standard is typically labeled with a different colored dye so that it can be spectrally distinguished from the DNA fragments of unknown size. In the case of the ABI 310 and AmpFlSTR kits, the internal standard is usually the GS500-ROX (Figure 13.2). This size standard contains 16 DNA fragments, ranging in size from 35 bp to 500 bp, that have been labeled with the red fluorescent dye ROX. For FMBIO users and PowerPlex kits, the internal lane standard ILS 600 is used (Figure 10.11). This size standard contains 22 DNA fragments, ranging in size from 60 bp to 600 bp, which have been labeled with the red fluorescent dye carboxy-X-rhodamine (CXR).

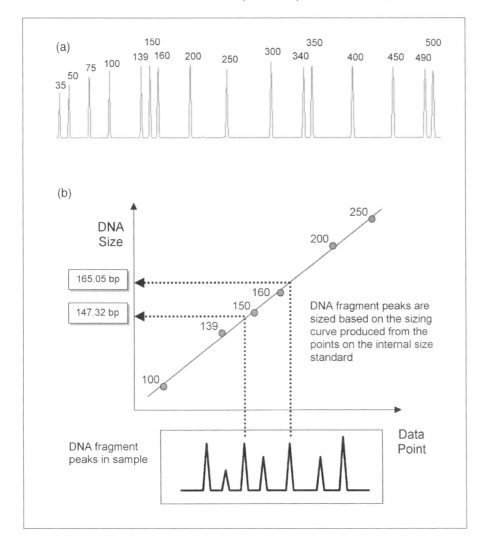

Figure 13.2

Peak sizing with DNA fragment analysis. An internal size standard, such as GS500-ROX (a), is analyzed along with the DNA sample and used to calibrate the peak data points to their DNA size (b). This standard is labeled with a different color fluorescent dye, in this case ROX (detected as red), so that it can be spectrally distinguished from the STR alleles which are labeled in other colors.

DNA FRAGMENT ANALYSIS AND GENOTYPING SOFTWARE

Fairly sophisticated software has been developed to take sample electrophoretic data rapidly through the genotyping process just described (Ziegle *et al.* 1992). For ABI 310 users (Chapter 11), this is done in two steps by two different software programs. GeneScan® software is used to spectrally resolve the dye colors for each peak and to size the DNA fragments in each sample. The resulting electropherograms are then imported into the second software program, Genotyper®. This program determines each sample's genotype by comparing the sizes of alleles observed in a standard allelic ladder sample to those obtained at each locus tested in the DNA sample.

Once GeneScan® processed electropherograms are imported into Genotyper®, a macro named 'Kazaam', that is specific for the STR loci and allelic ladders in each AmpFlSTR® kit, is initiated in Genotyper® actually to perform the allele calling. At this point, the analyst usually examines the peaks that have been called and based on their experience may or may not edit the calls made by the software. An allele table may then be created from the edited allele calls. Finally, the alleles may be exported to a spreadsheet program, such as Microsoft Excel, for further data analysis or uploading into a DNA database.

FMBIO II users (Chapter 12) perform automatic band calling, quantify peak heights and areas, and determine DNA band sizes through comparison to size standards with the FMBIO® Analysis Software. The analyst adjusts the color separation to obtain the best resolution between the dye labels. Gel bands in each color are then manually edited in order to make allele calls. Automated genotype calling from FMBIO STR data is performed with STaR Call™ Genotyping Software. This software takes the calculated STR allele base pair sizes and converts each peak into the appropriate allele call based on the fragment's calculated size compared to the calculated sizes of the alleles in the allelic ladder. Allele' look-up' tables in STaR Call™, which are basically Microsoft Excel spreadsheets, permit genotype information to be quickly reviewed and uploaded to a DNA database.

The genotypes for two samples shown earlier in the book (see Figure 1.3) are displayed in Figure 13.3. The output from Genotyper® 2.5 is split into the three dye colors: blue, green, and yellow. STR genotypes for a batch of samples are typically examined in Genotyper® software first by locus, from smallest to largest within a dye color, and then by dye color (blue, green, and finally yellow).

MANUAL INTERVENTION IN STR GENOTYPE DETERMINATIONS

While STR allele calls may be made in an automated fashion with either Genotyper® or STaR Call™, the resulting genotype information needs to be

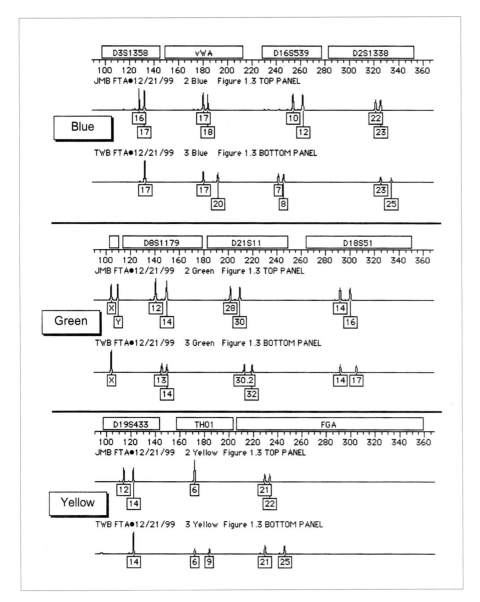

Figure 13.3

Genotype results on the two samples displayed in Figure 1.3 obtained with AmpFlSTR SGM Plus STR kit amplification and Genotyper 2.5 analysis.

examined manually by experienced analysts. Data analysis and review is essential for confirming STR results prior to making reports.

Software algorithms follow set parameters and criteria and hence can never be as effective at making difficult calls as a trained examiner. Strict guidelines for data interpretation should be in place to avoid problems with individual bias when the data are reviewed. However, there is always enough variation between data sets that not every situation can be covered by a predetermined rule.

Laboratories typically have two independent reads of the data by different operators. The genotypes must agree with each other before results will be reported or passed on for uploading to a DNA database. Likewise, a match between two samples is only reported if the two DNA profiles display the same pattern.

FACTORS AFFECTING GENOTYPING RESULTS

There are a number of issues that are important to obtaining accurate genotype results. Some issues are biology related and some are technology related. For example, the amount of stutter or incomplete 3′-nucleotide addition present are biology issues related to the amount of DNA template used in the PCR amplification. On the other hand, 'pull-up' artifacts and threshold issues result from the fluorescent technology and software used for genotyping the samples.

Three parts of the genotyping process illustrated in Figure 13.1 are crucial to the success of genotyping samples. These include the matrix file, the internal size standard, and the allelic ladder sample.

The *matrix file* is critical for proper color separation in an electropherogram. If the observed peaks are not associated with the proper dye label, then the sample genotype cannot be correctly determined. Matrix files are established by running samples that contain each of the dyes individually. The results of the individual dye runs are combined to form a mathematical matrix that is used to subtract the contribution of other colors in the overlapping spectra (see Chapter 10). A matrix is most accurate under consistent environmental conditions. Thus, if the electrophoresis buffer is changed, a new matrix should be established in order to obtain the most accurate color deconvolution between the different dyes.

The *internal size standard* is necessary for the proper sizing of DNA fragment peaks detected in an electropherogram. If any of the peaks in the size standard are below the peak detection threshold established in the data collection and analysis software, then the sizing algorithms will not work properly and STR alleles may be sized incorrectly. An analyst should check to make sure that the internal size standard peaks were all detected properly before proceeding to genotype the STR alleles in a sample.

The *allelic ladder* is the standard to which STR alleles are compared to obtain the sample genotype. The alleles in an allelic ladder need to be resolved from one another and above the peak detection threshold of the data collection and analysis software in order to correctly call STR alleles in unknown samples. The sizes obtained for each allele in the allelic ladder are used to make the final genotype determination in the unknown samples. Therefore, they must be determined correctly.

THE IMPORTANCE OF PRECISION IN ACCURATE GENOTYPING

STR genotyping is performed by comparison of the size of a sample's alleles to the size of alleles in allelic ladders for the same loci being tested in the sample. A high degree of precision is needed between multiple runs in order to make an accurate comparison of data from two runs, where one run is the allelic ladder standard and the other run is the questioned sample. The precision for a measurement system is determined by analyzing replicate samples or allelic ladders under normal operating conditions.

Precision for the separation and detection platform must be less than ±0.5 bp to distinguish accurately between microvariant (partial repeat) alleles and complete repeat alleles that differ by a single nucleotide (Gill *et al.* 1996). In general, the greater the molecular weight of the polymerase chain reaction (PCR) products, the larger the measurement error. Thus, alleles from larger STR loci such as FGA and D18S51 will generally have a larger size measurement variation than smaller STR loci such as D3S1358 and TH01.

For ABI 310 users, there is a reliance on a high degree of precision for run to run comparisons since a number of samples are run in a sequential fashion through the capillary between each injection of the allelic ladder (Lazaruk *et al.* 1998). Even though the samples are analyzed in parallel on a slab gel, a high degree of precision between samples run in different lanes is also necessary since an allelic ladder is only a few times on each gel.

The precision on an ABI 310 instrument is typically better than 0.1 bp (Wallin *et al.* 1998, Perkin Elmer Corporation 1998). However, a temperature variation of as little as 2 or 3°C over the course of a number of runs can cause allele peaks to migrate slightly differently from the internal sizing standard and therefore size differently over time. To alleviate this problem, the allelic ladder may be run more frequently (e.g. every 10 injections instead of every 20 injections) and the samples can be typed to the allelic ladder sample that was injected nearest them.

SIZING ALGORITHM ISSUES

The sizing of DNA fragments with internal standards is performed as illustrated in Figure 13.2. The most common algorithm used for determining the DNA fragment size is known as the local Southern method. This method uses the size of two peaks on either side of the unknown one being measured in order to make the calculations. Using the example in Figure 13.2, the '165.05 bp' peak size is determined with local Southern sizing by the position of the 150 bp and 160 bp peaks on the lower side and the position of the 200 and 250 bp peaks on the upper side.

The local Southern method works very well for accurate sizing of DNA fragments over the 100–450 bp size range necessary for STR alleles. However, there are some caveats that should be kept in mind that depend upon the internal size standard used. DNA fragment peaks that are larger than the internal sizing standard cannot be accurately determined. Nor can peaks that fall near the edge of the region defined by the internal sizing standard due to the fact that two peaks from the size standard are needed on either side of the unknown peak.

For the GS500-ROX internal standard commonly used with the AmpFlSTR kits, any unknown peaks falling above 490 bp or below 50 bp will not be sized with the local Southern method. Likewise, if the signal intensity for any of the calibration peaks in the internal sizing standard is too weak, then unknown peaks in that region will not be sized accurately.

OFF-LADDER ALLELES

Occasionally a sample may contain an allele that does not fall within 0.5 base pairs of an allele from the corresponding locus-specific allelic ladder (Gill *et al.* 1996). These alleles are designed as 'off-ladder' alleles or microvariants (see Chapter 6). The off-ladder allele peak may be larger or smaller than the alleles spanning the allelic ladder range or it may fall in between the rungs on the allelic ladder.

If the allele is sized to be less than the ladder, it may be designated as smaller than the smallest allele in the ladder used for genotyping purposes. For example, a CSF1PO allele sized below allele 6, which is the smallest in the ladder, would be designated CSF1PO <6. Likewise an allele sized above allele 15, the largest in the ladder, would be designated CSF1PO >15. Because the alleles in allelic ladders differ between manufacturers, an allele designation of '>15' from an amplification using one STR kit could be equivalent to an allele designation '16' from another.

Alleles that are sized between the rungs on an allelic ladder are usually designated by the number of bases beyond the allele just smaller than them. For example, a TH01 allele sized three bases larger than allele 8 would be designated TH01 8.3. It could also be referred to less specifically as TH01 8.*x*.

Off-ladder alleles can be verified by re-running the amplified product, re-amplifying the sample, or by amplifying the sample with single locus primers. Heterozygous samples with one 'normal' allele and one microvariant allele make it easy to confirm the microvariant. In this particular case, the normal allele with a full-length repeat sequence will fall in an allele bin from the allelic ladder, while the microvariant allele possessing a partial repeat sequence will fall between the allele bins created by the allelic ladder (see Figure 6.5). New microvariants are constantly being discovered as more samples are being analyzed around the world at various STR loci.

PARTIAL STR PROFILES

If the genomic DNA in a sample is severely degraded or PCR inhibitors are present, only a partial STR profile may be obtained. Usually the larger STR loci in a multiplex reaction, such as D18S51 and FGA, will be the first to fail on a degraded DNA sample. When only a partial profile is obtained, the significance of a match will be lower because there are fewer loci to compare.

MIXTURE INTERPRETATION

Mixtures of DNA from two or more individuals are common in some forensic cases and must be dealt with in the interpretation of the DNA profiles. In evaluating the evidence, an analyst must decide whether the source of the DNA in the questioned sample is from a single individual or more than one person. This may be accomplished by examination of the number of alleles detected at each locus as well as peak height ratios and/or band intensities on a gel. Occasionally extra peaks occur in the data that should not be confused with true alleles.

EXTRA PEAKS OBSERVED IN THE DATA

Electropherograms may contain extra peaks besides the primary target alleles of interest. These peaks can arise from a number of sources related to the biology of STRs and the technology of detecting fluorescently labeled amplification products. It is important to recognize these peaks and not make a false exclusion because of the presence of supposedly spurious peaks in one of the samples.

A laboratory needs to establish criteria to identify a true allele because a DNA typing analyst must decide which peaks contribute to a donor(s) profile(s) and which are due to an artifact. The following material is intended as a helpful guide to some of the commonly seen artifacts and should not be considered a comprehensive list for troubleshooting purposes.

BIOLOGY-RELATED ARTIFACT PEAKS

Stutter products are the most common source of additional peaks in an electropherogram of an STR sample. When STR loci are PCR-amplified, a minor product peak four bases ($n - 4$) shorter than the corresponding main allele peak is commonly observed (see Chapter 6). Validation studies conducted in a laboratory help define the maximum percent stutter for each locus. However, if the target allele peak is off-scale, then the stutter product can appear larger than it really is in relationship to the corresponding allele peak. For data interpretation, an upper-limit stutter percentage interpretational threshold can be set for each locus as three standard deviations above the highest stutter percentage observed at that locus (Perkin Elmer Corporation 1998).

Incomplete 3′(A) nucleotide addition results with amplifications containing too much DNA template or thermal cycling conditions that affect the optimization of the PCR reaction. The *Taq* DNA polymerase used for amplifying STR loci will catalyze the addition of an extra nucleotide, usually an 'A', on the 3′-end of double-stranded PCR products. The commercially available multiplex STR kits have been optimized to favor complete adenylation. However, when incomplete 3′-nucleotide addition occurs, 'split peaks' will result, sometimes referred to as +/−A, or N and N+1 peaks, and the allele of interest will be represented by two peaks one base pair apart. Genotyping software may inadvertently call one of these peaks an 'off-ladder' (microvariant) allele.

Three-banded patterns result from extra chromosomal fragments being present in a sample. These rare anomalies are detected by an extra peak at a single locus, as opposed to multiple loci as would likely be seen in a mixture. The three peaks will commonly all be of equal intensity but do not have to be (Crouse *et al.* 1999).

Mixed sample results are observed if more than one individual contributed to the DNA profile. Mixtures are readily apparent when multiple loci are examined. An analyst looks for higher than expected stutter levels, more than two peaks at a locus of equivalent intensity, or a severe imbalance in heterozygote peak intensities of greater than 30%. It is usually difficult to detect the minor contributor below a level of 1:20 compared to the major donor to the DNA profile.

TECHNOLOGY-RELATED ARTIFACT 'PEAKS'

Matrix (multicomponent) failure, sometimes referred to as 'pull-up' is a result of the inability of the detection instrument to properly resolve the dye colors used to label STR amplicons. This phenomenon is due to spectral overlap. A peak of another color is 'pulled-up' or 'bleeds through' as a result of exceeding the linear range of detection for the instrument (i.e. sample overloading). A matrix failure is observed as a peak-beneath-a-peak or as an elevation of the baselines for any color. Matrix standards may need to be re-run with the latest set of conditions and a new matrix generated by the software to correct this problem.

Dye blobs occur when fluorescent dyes come off of their respective primers and migrate independently through the capillary. These peaks are fairly broad and possess the spectrum of one of the dyes used for genotyping. These dye peaks are not reproducible and should not appear in the same position if the sample is re-injected on to the capillary.

Air bubbles, urea crystals, or voltage spikes can give rise to a false peak in the ABI 310. These peaks are usually sharp and appear equally intense throughout all four colors. These peaks are not reproducible and should not appear in the same position if the sample is re-injected on to the capillary.

Sample contaminants. Materials which fluoresce in the visible region of the spectrum (~500–600 nm) may interfere with DNA typing when using fluorescent scanners or one of the ABI PRISM systems by appearing as identifiable peaks in the electropherogram. In some early studies conducted by the Forensic Science Service (FSS), a number of fluorescent compounds were examined to determine their apparent mobility when electrophoresed in a polyacrylamide gel (Urquhart *et al.* 1994).

All of the compounds studied, which included antibiotics, vitamins, polycyclic aromatics, fluorescent brightners, and various textile dyes, could be removed with an organic extraction (i.e. phenol/chloroform, as is commonly used to extract DNA from cells). Interestingly enough, the Chelex method of DNA extraction (see Chapter 3) failed to remove all of the contaminating fluorescent peaks (Urquhart *et al.* 1994). Fortunately, these interfering peaks were usually wide and possessed a broader fluorescent spectrum, which made it fairly easy to distinguish them from the fluorescent dye-labeled PCR products. The FSS researchers concluded that the use of appropriate substrate controls or negative controls in PCR should alleviate this potential problem.

Several possible forensic scenarios exist where sample contaminants may be possible (Urquhart *et al.* 1994):

1   body fluid stains on dye materials from which the dye may leach during extraction;
2   body fluid stains on plant material, from which chlorophyll may co-extract with DNA;
3   blood or tissue samples from individuals with some pathological conditions, e.g. lead poisoning or some forms of porphyria, in which blood porphyrin levels are greatly elevated; and
4   bone or tooth samples from individuals who were treated with tetracycline-group antibiotics in their youth as growing bones and teeth are known to incorporate and accumulate these antibiotics.

DEVELOPING AN INTERPRETATION STRATEGY

A forensic DNA laboratory should develop its own STR interpretation guidelines based upon their own validation studies and results reported in the literature. Practical experience with instrumentation and results from performing casework are also important factors in developing an interpretation strategy.

- Conduct necessary validation studies (see Chapter 14) and gain experience in your laboratory.
- Utilize analyst's experience.
- Use literature references as a resource in understanding if an 'off-ladder' allele has been observed before. As a useful resource, we have included a list of all known alleles for the 13 CODIS STR loci as of January 2000 in Appendix I. A more up-to-date list can be found in the STRBase STR fact sheets for each STR locus or the non-published variant allele page (http://www.cstl.nist.gov/biotech/STRBase/var_tab.htm).

Validation studies will define observed stutter ratios for each locus, establish minimum peak heights, and define heterozygous peak ratios within a locus. When in doubt on a sample's correct result, the sample should be re-tested. This may be as simple as re-injecting it on the ABI 310 or putting another aliquot of the sample on the next gel. Even if sample re-testing involves re-extracting and/or re-amplifying the 'problem' sample, it is worthwhile in order to obtain an accurate result.

A MATCH OR NOT A MATCH: THAT IS THE QUESTION . . .

Generally, the process of comparing two or more samples is limited to one of three possible outcomes that are submitted in a case report:

1   *Match* – peaks between the compared STR profiles have the same genotypes and no unexplainable differences exist between the samples. Statistical evaluation of the significance of the match is usually reported with the match report.

2   *Exclusion* – the genotype comparison shows profile differences that can only be explained by the two samples originating from different sources.

3   *Inconclusive* – the data does not support a conclusion as to whether the profiles match. This finding might be reported if two analysts remain in disagreement after review and discussion of the data, and it is felt that insufficient information exists to support any conclusion.

In forensic DNA typing, if any one STR locus fails to match when comparing the genotypes between two or more samples, then the profiles between the questioned and reference sample will be declared a non-match, regardless of how many other loci match. Paternity testing is an exception to this because of the possibility of mutational events (see Chapter 6). When analyzing and reporting the results of parentage cases, an allowance for one possible mutation is often made. In other words, if 13 loci are used and the questioned parentage is included for all but one locus, the data from the non-inclusive allele will be attributed to a possible mutation.

In the end, interpretation of results in forensic casework is a matter of professional judgment and expertise. Interpretation of results within the context of a case is the responsibility of the case analyst with supervisors or technical leaders conducting a follow-up verification of the analyst's interpretation of the data as part of the technical review process. When coming to a final conclusion regarding a match or an exclusion between two or more DNA profiles, laboratory interpretation guidelines should be adhered to by both the case analyst and the supervisor. However, as experience using various analytical procedures grows, interpretation guidelines may evolve and improve. These guidelines should always be based on the use of proper controls and validated methods as described in the next chapter.

REFERENCES

Crouse, C., Rogers, S., Amiott, E., Gibson, S. and Masibay, A. (1999) *Journal of Forensic Sciences*, 44, 87–94.

Gill, P., Kimpton, C.P., Urquhart, A., Oldroyd, N.J., Millican, E.S., Watson, S.K. and Downes, T.J. (1995) *Electrophoresis*, 16, 1543–1552.

Gill, P., Urquhart, A., Millican, E.S., Oldroyd, N.J., Watson, S., Sparkes, R. and Kimpton, C.P. (1996) *International Journal of Legal Medicine*, 109, 14–22.

Lazaruk, K., Walsh, P.S., Oaks, F., Gilbert, D., Rosenblum, B.B., Menchen, S., Scheibler, D., Wenz, H.M., Holt, C. and Wallin, J. (1998) *Electrophoresis*, 19, 86–93.

Perkin Elmer Corporation (1998) *AmpFlSTR® Profiler Plus™ PCR Amplification Kit User's Manual.* Foster City: PE Applied Biosystems.

Smith, R.N. (1995) *BioTechniques*, 18, 122–128.

Urquhart, A., Chiu, C. T., Clayton, T. M., Downes, T., Frazier, R. R. E., Jones, S., Kimpton, C. P., Lareu, M. V., Millican, E. S., Oldroyd, N. J., Thompson, C., Watson, S., Whitaker, J. P. and Gill, P. (1994) *Proceedings of the Fifth International Symposium on Human Identification.* Madison, WI: Promega Corporation, pp. 73–83.

Wallin, J.M., Buoncristiani, M.R., Lazaruk, K., Fildes, N., Holt, C. and Walsh, P.S. (1998) *Journal of Forensic Sciences*, 43, 854–870.

Ziegle, J.S., Su, Y., Corcoran, K.P., Nie, L., Mayrand, P.E., Hoff, L.B., McBride, L.J., Kronick, M.N. and Diehl, S.R. (1992) *Genomics*, 14, 1026–1031.

CHAPTER 14

LABORATORY VALIDATION

Laboratories should adhere to high quality standards (such as those defined by TWGDAM and the DNA Advisory Board) and make every effort to be accredited for DNA work (by such organizations as ASCLD-LAB).

(NRC II Report, p. 4. Recommendation 3.1)

INTRODUCTION

IMPORTANCE OF QUALITY CONTROL

Any scientific test which results in information that may lead to the loss of liberty for an individual accused of a crime needs to be performed with utmost care. DNA typing is no exception. It is a multi-step, technical process that needs to be performed by qualified and effectively trained personnel to ensure that accurate results are obtained and interpreted correctly. When the process is conducted properly, DNA testing is a capable investigative tool for the law enforcement community with results that stand up to legal scrutiny in court.

Two topics are commonly referred to when discussing the importance of maintaining good laboratory practices to obtain accurate scientific results: quality assurance and quality control. *Quality assurance* (QA) refers to those planned or systematic actions necessary to provide adequate confidence that a product or service will satisfy given requirements for quality. *Quality control* (QC), on the other hand, usually refers to the day-to-day operational techniques and the activities used to fulfill requirements of quality.

Thus, an organization plans QA measures and performs QC activities in the laboratory. The forensic DNA community has long recognized the importance of quality control and, since early in the development of forensic DNA technology, has established organizations to recommend and oversee quality assurance guidelines and quality control measures.

DEFINITIONS

As we begin our discussion of laboratory validation, it is important to define several words that will be used frequently throughout the chapter. These words include validation, proficiency testing, laboratory accreditation, and the terms robust, reliable, and reproducible.

Validation refers to the process of demonstrating that a laboratory procedure is robust, reliable, and reproducible in the hands of the personnel performing the test in that laboratory. A *robust method* is one in which successful results are obtained a high percentage of the time and few, if any, samples need to be repeated. A *reliable method* refers to one in which the obtained results are accurate and correctly reflect the sample being tested. A *reproducible method* means that the same or very similar results are obtained each time a sample is tested. All three types of methods are important for techniques performed in forensic laboratories.

A *proficiency test*, as it relates to the DNA typing field, is an evaluation of a laboratory's performance in conducting DNA analysis procedures. These tests are performed periodically, usually on an annual or semi-annual basis, for each DNA analyst or examiner. Biological specimens with a previously determined DNA profile are submitted to the laboratory personnel being tested. The purpose of the test is to evaluate their ability to obtain a concordant result using the laboratory's approved *standard operating protocols* (SOPs).

The tests may be administered by someone else in the laboratory (*internal proficiency test*) or by an external organization (*external proficiency test*). If the test administered by an external organization is performed such that the laboratory personnel do not know that a test is being conducted, then it is termed a *blind external proficiency test*. A blind external proficiency test is generally considered the most effective at monitoring a laboratory's abilities but can be rather expensive and time consuming to arrange and conduct. Participation in a proficiency testing program is an essential part of a successful laboratory's quality assurance effort. Forensic laboratories develop their own proficiency testing program or establish one in cooperation with other laboratories.

A *laboratory audit* evaluates the entire operation of a laboratory. It is a systematic examination that may be conducted by the laboratory management or by an independent organization according to pre-established guidelines. A laboratory must possess standard operating protocols and adhere to them. Likewise, instruments and other equipment vital to the successful completion of a forensic DNA case must be maintained properly and personnel must be appropriately trained to perform their jobs. Records of an audit are maintained and serve to describe the findings of the audit and a course of action that may be taken to resolve any existing problems.

Laboratory accreditation results from a successful completion of an inspection or audit by an accrediting body. A list of major accrediting organizations that are recognized by the forensic DNA community is contained in the next section. Accreditation requires that the laboratory demonstrates and maintains good laboratory practices including chain-of-custody and evidence handling procedures.

The accreditation process generally involves several steps such as a laboratory self-evaluation, filing application and supporting documents to initiate the accreditation process, on-site inspection by a team of trained auditors, an inspection report, and an annual accreditation review report. The inspection evaluates the facilities and equipment, the training of the technical staff, the written operating and technical procedures, and the casework reports and supporting documentation of the applicant laboratory.

According to the DNA Advisory Board Standards (see Appendix III), all examiners who are actively engaged in DNA analysis need to undergo proficiency tests on at least a semi-annual basis (standard 13.1). Likewise, laboratory audits need to be conducted on an annual basis by the laboratory (standard 15.1) and on a biannual basis by an outside agency (standard 15.2).

ORGANIZATIONS INVOLVED IN ENSURING QUALITY AND UNIFORMITY OF DNA TESTING

A number of organizations exist around the world that work on a local, national, or international level to ensure that DNA testing is performed properly. The organizations are made up primarily of working scientists who want to coordinate their efforts to benefit the DNA typing community as a whole.

ORGANIZATIONS BASED IN THE UNITED STATES

The *Technical Working Group on DNA Analysis Methods* (TWGDAM) was established in November 1988 under Federal Bureau of Investigation (FBI) Laboratory sponsorship to aid forensic DNA scientists throughout North America. The first meeting consisted of 31 scientists representing 16 forensic laboratories in the United States and Canada and 2 research institutions. TWGDAM meetings were originally held twice a year at the FBI Academy in Quantico, Virginia, usually in January and July. More recently, public meetings have also been held in conjunction with scientific meetings such as the International Symposium on Human Identification, sponsored each year by Promega Corporation.

The original TWGDAM chairman was James Kearney of the FBI Laboratory who was followed by Bruce Budowle also of the FBI Laboratory. (In 1998 the TWGDAM name was changed to the Scientific Working Group on DNA Analysis Methods or SWGDAM. For additional information on SWGDAM, see: www.forswg.org/swgdamin.htm).

Over the years, several subcommittees have operated to bring recommendations before the TWGDAM group. These subcommittees have included the restriction fragment length polymorphism (RFLP), polymerase chain reaction

(PCR), Combined DNA Index System (CODIS), mitochondrial DNA, short tandem repeat (STR) interpretation, training, validation, and quality assurance/quality control working groups. TWGDAM issued guidelines for quality assurance in DNA analysis in 1989, 1991, and 1995.

Evolving technology and laboratory practices made it necessary to issue revisions in the quality assurance standards for DNA testing. These QA guidelines were originally intended to serve as a guide to laboratory managers in establishing their own QA program. However, the 1995 'Guidelines for a Quality Assurance Program for DNA Analysis' served as the *de facto* standards for forensic DNA testing until October 1998, when the ensuing DNA Advisory Board standards went into effect (see Appendix III).

The *DNA Advisory Board* (DAB) is a Congressionally mandated organization that was created and funded by the United States Congress DNA Identification Act of 1994. The first meeting of the DAB was held 12 May 1995, and chaired by Nobel laureate Dr Joshua Lederberg. The DAB consists of 13 voting members that include scientists from state, local, and private forensic laboratories; molecular geneticists and population geneticists not affiliated with a forensic laboratory; a representative from the National Institute of Standards and Technology; the chair of TWGDAM; and a judge. The DAB was created for a 5-year period to issue standards for the forensic DNA community. Following conclusion of the DAB's responsibilities, SWGDAM will operate as the group responsible for offering recommendations to the forensic community within the United States.

The *American Society of Crime Laboratory Directors* (ASCLD) and its Laboratory Accreditation Board (ASCLD/LAB) play an important role in the United States as well as internationally for laboratory accreditation programs. The ASCLD/LAB motto is 'quality assurance through inspection'. The Crime Laboratory Accreditation Program is a voluntary program in which any crime laboratory may participate to demonstrate that its management, operations, personnel, procedures and instruments meet stringent standards. The goal of accreditation is to improve the overall service of forensic laboratories to the criminal justice system. If a forensic laboratory is interested in becoming accredited, an ASCLD/LAB Accreditation Manual is available from the Executive Secretary for a fee. As of June 1999, ASCLD/LAB there were 182 accredited laboratories (not all for DNA). For additional information on ASCLD, visit its web site: www.ascld-lab.org.

The *National Forensic Science Training Center* (NFSTC) located in Orlando, Florida, has an accreditation program and offers to certify laboratories that comply with the TWGDAM/DAB guidelines. NFSTC accreditation is generally sought by contract service laboratories doing DNA database work since ASCLD/LAB accreditation is only available to forensic laboratories performing casework. For additional information on NFSTC, visit its web site: www.nsftc.org.

The *American Association of Blood Banks* (AABB) sets the national standards for laboratories performing DNA parentage testing. AABB provides accreditation for paternity testing laboratories. As of November 1999, there were 42 accredited paternity testing laboratories in the United States. For more information on AABB, visit their web site: www.aabb.org.

The *College of American Pathologists* (CAP) offers external proficiency testing to forensic and paternity testing laboratories as well as clinical laboratories. For further information on CAP, visit their web site: www.cap.org.

Cellmark Diagnostics, a forensic DNA testing laboratory, provides a proficiency test to help ensure ongoing laboratory quality. Their International Quality Assessment Scheme (IQAS) DNA Proficiency Test Program is designed for all laboratories conducting forensic DNA analysis. The proficiency tests consist of simulated forensic evidence case samples that are distributed four times a year. The Cellmark tests include questioned bloodstain and semen stain evidence along with known samples of blood. For more information on Cellmark Diagnostics, visit their web site: www.cellmark-labs.com.

The *Human Identity Trade Association* (HITA) is a non-profit organization that represents the interests of DNA companies and suppliers within the human identity market. HITA generally meets in conjunction with the International Symposium on Human Identification each fall. For additional information on HITA, visit the organization's web site: www.hita.org.

The *National Institute of Standards and Technology* (NIST) develops standard reference materials (SRMs) that may be used by forensic laboratories to calibrate and verify their analytical procedures. Under the new DAB guidelines, a laboratory is required to check its DNA procedures annually or whenever substantial changes are made to the protocol(s) against an appropriate and available NIST standard reference material or a standard traceable to a NIST standard (DAB standard 9.5). The various SRMs available from NIST are described below in the section on DNA standards. For additional information regarding NIST, visit its web site: www.nist.gov.

ORGANIZATIONS BASED IN EUROPE

The International Society for Forensic Genetics (ISFG) formerly known as the *International Society of Forensic Haemogenetics* (ISFH) is an international organization responsible for the promotion of scientific knowledge in the field of genetic markers analyzed with forensic purposes. The ISFG includes 830 members from 49 countries. Regular meetings are typically held biannually on an international level. Conference volumes were published under the title

Advances in Forensic Haemogenetics and are now entitled *Progress in Forensic Genetics.* Recommendations on forensic genetic analysis are also proposed as needed by an *ad hoc* DNA Commission. Three formal recommendations have come from this group regarding the use of STR markers (DNA Commission 1992, Bar *et al.* 1994, 1997). For additional information on ISFH, visit its web site: http://www.usc.es/~isfh/.

The *European Network of Forensic Science Institutes* (ENFSI) was started in 1995 to set standards for exchange of data between European member states and to be an accrediting body through conducting laboratory audits. As of early 2000, ENFSI has held 11 meetings and has participation from 20 countries in Europe.

The European forensic DNA community has an organization similar to SWGDAM named *EDNAP* (*European DNA Profiling Group*). EDNAP is effectively a working group of the ISFH and consists of representatives from more than a dozen European nations. EDNAP has conducted a series of interlaboratory studies on various STR markers to investigate the reproducibility of multiple laboratories in testing the same samples (see Table 14.1). These studies have demonstrated that, with the proper quality control measures, excellent reproducibility can be seen between forensic laboratories. For additional information on EDNAP, visit its web site: www.uni-mainz.de/FB/Medizin/Rechtsmedizin/ednap/ednap.htm.

Another European organization for standardizing forensic DNA methods is *STADNAP*, which is an acronym for Standardization of DNA Profiling Techniques in the European Union. The goals of STADNAP include defining criteria for the selection of forensic DNA typing systems used among the European countries, exchanging and comparing methods for unifying protocols used for DNA typing, and compiling reference allele frequency databases for European populations. For more information on STADNAP, visit its web site: www.stadnap.uni-mainz.de.

The *Interpol European Working Party on DNA Profiling* (IEWPDP) consists of DNA experts from Belgium, Czech Republic, Germany, Hungary, Italy, Netherlands, Norway, Slovakia, Spain, and the United Kingdom. IEWPDP makes recommendations concerning the use of DNA evidence in criminal investigations with the goal of facilitating a wider use of this technique in Europe. For example, Interpol recommended that the European standard set of STR loci include FGA, TH01, VWA, and D21S11.

ORGANIZATIONS FOR LATIN AMERICA AND IBERIAN PENINSULA

The *Grupo Iberoamericano de Trabajo en Analisis de DNA* (GITAD) was organized in 1998 to serve the needs of forensic DNA laboratories and institutions in Latin America and the two countries of the Iberian Peninsula, Spain and Portugal.

Much like SWGDAM and ENSFI, the primary objectives of GITAD include standardizing techniques, implementing a quality assurance/quality control system, and facilitating communication and training of laboratory personnel. For additional information regarding GITAD, visit their web site: members.xoom.com/GITAD/index.htm.

VALIDATION

Validation is a very important part of forensic DNA typing. Defense lawyers today rarely challenge the science behind DNA typing – rather they challenge the process by which the laboratory performs the DNA analysis. Thus, the scientific community must carefully document the validity of new techniques and technologies to ensure that procedures performed in the laboratory accurately reflect the examined samples. In addition, a laboratory must carefully document their technical procedures and policies for interpretation of data and follow them to guarantee that each sample is handled and processed appropriately.

STR VALIDATION

There are generally considered to be two stages to validation: developmental validation and internal validation. *Developmental validation* involves the testing of new STR loci or STR kits, new primer sets, and new technologies for detecting STR alleles. *Internal validation*, on the other hand, involves verifying that established procedures examined previously under the scrutiny of developmental validation (often by another laboratory) will work effectively in one's own laboratory. Developmental validation is typically performed by commercial STR kit manufacturers and large laboratories such as the FBI Laboratory, while internal validation is the primary form of validation performed in smaller local and state forensic DNA laboratories.

DEVELOPMENTAL VALIDATION STUDIES

The standard studies that are conducted to become 'TWGDAM Validated' are listed below with the 1995 TWGDAM Guideline numerical headings shown in parentheses. The purpose of each study is also enumerated.

- *Standard specimens* (4.1.5.1). DNA is isolated from different tissues and body fluids coming from the same individual and tested to make sure that the same type is observed. These studies are important because the blood from a suspect might be used to try and match semen found at a crime scene.

- *Consistency* (4.1.5.2). The measurement technique is evaluated repeatedly to assess the reproducibility of the method within and between laboratories. The power of DNA testing is only fully realized when results can be compared between laboratories in different areas or database samples that were analyzed some time before a crime was committed. Thus, results must be comparable across both distance and time. The use of internal sizing standards and allelic ladders has greatly improved the consistency of STR typing.

- *Population studies* (4.1.5.3). A set of anonymous samples that have been grouped by ethnicity is analyzed to determine allele frequencies for each major population group that exists in a forensic laboratory's vicinity. These allele frequencies are then used in reporting population statistics and calculating the probability of a random match.

- *Reproducibility* (4.1.5.4). Dried blood and semen stains are typed and compared to DNA profiles obtained from liquid samples. Samples from the same source should match. Obviously, this fact is important since a crime scene stain should match the reference blood sample of a suspect if he or she is the perpetrator of the crime.

- *Mixed specimen studies* (4.1.5.5). The ability of the DNA typing system to detect the various components of mixed specimens is investigated. Evidence samples in forensic cases often originate from more than one individual and thus it is essential that typing systems can detect mixtures. Several studies are typically conducted to define the limitations of the DNA typing system. Genomic DNA from two samples of known genotype is mixed in various ratios ranging from 50:1 to 1:50. The limit of detection for the minor component is determined by examining the profiles of the mock mixtures (see Chapter 7). Studies are also performed to examine the peak height ratios of heterozygote alleles within a locus and to determine the range of stutter percentages for each allele of each locus (see Chapter 6). The results of these relative peak height measurements can then be used to establish guidelines for separating a minor component of a mixture from the stutter product of a single source sample.

- *Environmental studies* (4.1.5.6). Samples of known genotype are environmentally stressed and examined to verify that the correct genotype is obtained. The environmental studies reflect the situations typical of a forensic case (i.e. exposure to sunlight, humidity, and temperature fluctuations).

- *Matrix studies* (4.1.5.7). Samples of known genotype are examined after contact with a variety of substrates commonly encountered in forensic cases. For example, blood and semen may be deposited on leather, denim, glass, metal, wool, or cotton as well as mixed with dyes and soil. DNA profiles from samples exposed to these substrates are carefully examined for non-specific artifacts and amplification failure at any of the loci studied.

- *Non-probative evidence* (4.1.5.8). DNA profiles are obtained from samples that are from forensic cases that have already been closed. These samples demonstrate that the DNA typing system being examined can handle real casework situations.

- *Non-human studies* (4.1.5.9). The DNA typing system being evaluated is subjected to non-human DNA to see if other biological sources could interfere with the ability to obtain reliable results on samples recovered from crime scenes. Primates, such as gorillas and chimpanzees, are typically tested along with domestic animals, such as horses, cattle, dogs, and cats. Bacteria and yeast, which can be prevalent at some crime scenes, are also tested. Most STR loci used for human identity testing are primate-specific, that is, they amplify in gorillas and chimps but not in dogs or cats. Bacteria, yeast, and most non-primates do not yield any detectable products with the STR kits currently available (Perkin Elmer Corporation 1998, Micka *et al.* 1999). The sex-typing marker amelogenin does amplify in a number of other species but with DNA fragments that are slightly smaller in size than the standard 106 and 112 bp for human X and Y alleles (Buel *et al.* 1995).

- *Minimum sample* (4.1.5.10). The minimum quantity of genomic DNA needed to obtain a reliable result is typically determined by examining a dilution series of a sample with a known genotype. For example, 10 ng, 5 ng, 2 ng, 1 ng, 0.5 ng, 0.25 ng, and 0.1 ng might be evaluated. Most protocols call for using at least 0.25–0.5 ng genomic DNA for PCR amplification to avoid allele dropout from stochastic effects during the PCR step or poor sensitivity during the detection phase of the analysis.

ADDITIONAL DEVELOPMENT AND INTERNAL VALIDATION STUDIES

- *Precision studies.* The calculated base pair sizes for STR allele amplification products are measured. All measured alleles should fall within a ±0.5 bp window around the measured size for the corresponding allele in the allelic ladder.

- *Stutter studies.* The percentage of observed stutter at each STR locus is examined by calculating the ratio of the stutter peak area and/or peak height compared to the corresponding allele peak area and height. Stutter values are derived from homozygotes and heterozygotes with alleles separated by at least two repeat units. The upper levels of stutter observed for each locus are then used to develop interpretation guidelines. Because the levels of stutter for each of the 13 CODIS STR loci have been described and usually fall below 10% of the allele peak area and height, many laboratories just use a standard 15% cut-off for interpreting stutter products. If the stutter peak is below 15% of the allele peak, it is ignored as a biological artifact of the sample. However, if it is above 15% then a possible mixture could be present in the sample.

- *Heterozygous peak height balance.* The peak heights of the smaller and the larger allele are compared typically by dividing the smaller sized allele peak height by the larger sized allele peak height. In other words, the height of the lower peak in relative fluorescence units is divided by the height of the higher peak (in relative flourescence units; RFUs). This peak height ratio is expressed as a percentage. The average heterozygote peak height ratio is usually greater than 90%, meaning that a heterozygous individual generally possesses well-balanced peaks. Ratios below 70% are rare in normal, unmixed samples (although primer point mutations can cause one of the alleles to not amplify as well, i.e. a partial null allele – see discussion on null alleles in Chapter 6).

■ *Annealing temperature studies*. These studies are conducted by running the amplification protocol with the annealing temperature either 2° above or 2° below the optimal temperature. Annealing temperature studies are important because thermal cyclers might not always be calibrated accurately and can drift over time if not maintained properly. Thus, an operator might think that the annealing temperature during each cycle is 59°C when in fact the thermal cycler is running hotter at 61°C. If any primers in the multiplex mix are not capable of withstanding slight temperature variation (i.e. they do not hybridize as well), then a locus could drop out or non-specific amplification products could arise.

■ *Cycle number studies*. The optimal PCR conditions (i.e. denaturing, annealing, and extension temperatures and times) are examined with a reduced number of cycles as well as a higher number of cycles than the standard protocol calls to evaluate the performance of the STR multiplex system. The sensitivity of detection of alleles for each locus is, of course, dependent on the quality of input DNA template. The cycle number studies permit a laboratory to determine the tolerance levels of a STR multiplex system with various amounts of DNA template. While a higher number of PCR cycles (e.g. 34 instead of 28) might be able to amplify very low levels of genomic DNA better, the likelihood of non-specific amplification products arising increases with higher numbers of PCR cycles.

PUBLICATION AND PRESENTATION OF VALIDATION RESULTS

Results of developmental validation studies are shared as soon as possible with the scientific community either through presentations at scientific professional meetings or publication in peer-reviewed journals. Rapid dissemination of information about these studies is important to the legal system that forensic science serves because the courts rely on precedence when ruling if DNA evidence is admissible.

The three most commonly used scientific journals for publishing validation studies and population results are the *International Journal of Legal Medicine*, *Forensic Science International*, and the *Journal of Forensic Sciences* (Figure 14.1). Scientific meetings where DNA typing validation studies are presented include the International Symposium on Human Identification (sponsored each fall by the Promega Corporation), the American Academy of Forensic Sciences (held each February), the Congress of the International Society of Forensic Haemogenetics (held in late summer bi-annually), and the International Association of Forensic Sciences (held every 3 years in August or September).

Several thorough developmental validation papers have been published that discuss results obtained from conducting the studies listed above for the AmpFlSTR® Blue STR kit (Wallin *et al.* 1998) and the PowerPlex™ 1.1/amelo-

Publisher: Springer-Verlag.,
Postfach 105280
D-69042 Heidelberg, Germany
Editor: B. Brinkmann
Web site:
http://link.springer-
ny.com/link/service/journals/00414/
index.htm

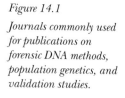

Figure 14.1

Journals commonly used for publications on forensic DNA methods, population genetics, and validation studies.

Publisher: American Society for Testing and Materials, 100 Barr Harbor Drive, West Conshohocken, PA 19428-2959 USA
Editor: R.E. Gaensslen
Web site:
http://www.aafs.org/Journal.htm

Publisher: Elsevier Science, 655 Avenue of the Americas, New York, NY 10010-5107 USA
Editor: P. Saukko
Web site:
http://www.elsevier.com:80/inca/publications/st
ore/5/0/5/5/1/2/

genin STR multiplex system (Micka *et al.* 1999). In addition, validation studies have been published on the Forensic Science Service quadruplex (Lygo *et al.* 1994) and Second Generation Multiplex (Sparkes *et al.* 1996) as well as multiplex systems developed by the Royal Canadian Mounted Police (Fregeau *et al.* 1999). In all cases, multiplex STR profiling systems were found to yield reliable, reproducible, and robust results.

INTERNAL VALIDATION OF ESTABLISHED PROCEDURES

In order to meet TWGDAM/DAB Guidelines for quality assurance, forensic DNA laboratories conduct the following tests as part of the process of becoming 'validated'. These studies demonstrate that DNA typing results can be consistently and accurately obtained by the laboratory personnel involved in the testing.

Validation studies are performed with each new DNA typing system that is developed and used. For example, a laboratory may be validated with the PowerPlex™ 1.1 kit but it would need to perform additional validation studies when expanding its capabilities to amplifying the STR loci included in the PowerPlex™ 2.1 kit.

Typical studies for an internal validation include reproducibility, precision measurements for sizing alleles, and sensitivity (e.g. 50 ng down to 20 pg) studies along with mixture analysis and non-probative casework samples. Sizing precision studies are also conducted, where the calculated allele sizes in base pairs is plotted against the size deviation from the corresponding allele in the allelic ladder with which the genotype was determined (Wallin *et al.* 1998). If a high degree of precision cannot be maintained due to laboratory conditions such as temperature fluctuations, then samples may not be able to be genotyped accurately.

Each forensic laboratory develops or adopts *standard operating protocols* that give a detailed listing of all the materials required to perform an assay as well as the exact steps required to complete the experiment successfully. In addition, SOPs list critical aspects of the assay that must be monitored carefully. SOPs are followed exactly when performing forensic DNA casework.

INTER-LABORATORY TESTS

Inter-laboratory tests are the means by which multiple laboratories compare results and demonstrate that the methods used in one's own laboratory are reproducible in another laboratory. These tests are essential to demonstrate consistency in results from multiple laboratories, especially since DNA databases are now used where many laboratories contribute to the DNA profile information (see Chapter 16).

Since 1994, the European DNA Profiling Group has conducted a series of inter-laboratory evaluations on various STR loci and methodologies used for analyzing them. A listing of the first seven published EDNAP reports that deal with STR markers may be found in Table 14.1. Each study involved the examination of 5–7 bloodstains that were distributed to multiple laboratories (usually a dozen or more) to test their ability to obtain consistent results. In all cases where simple STR loci were tested, consistent results were obtained. However, complex STR markers, such as ACTBP2 (SE33), often gave inconsistent results (Gill *et al.* 1994, 1998). Thus, STRs with complex repeat structures are not recommended for use in DNA databases at this time where results are submitted from multiple laboratories.

In the United States several inter-laboratory studies have been performed. The first large test with commercial kits was conducted by the National Institute of Standards and Technology and involved 34 laboratories that evaluated the three STRs, TH01, TPOX, and CSF1PO, in a multiplex amplification format (Kline *et al.* 1997). This study concluded that, as long as locus-specific allelic ladders were used, a variety of separation and detection methods could be used to obtain equivalent genotypes for the same samples.

Study Number	STR Loci Examined	Protocols Provided?	Primers/ Ladders Provided?	Number of Laboratories Involved	Reference
1	TH01, ACTBP2	For PCR	Both	14	Gill *et al.* (1994)
Result: TH01 worked well in all laboratories, ACTBP2 exhibited variable sizing with different electrophoresis systems					
2	TH01, VWA, FES/FPS, F13A1	For PCR	Both	30	Kimpton *et al.* (1995)
Result: Fluorescent multiplex results were robust but problems existed with allele designations at FES/FPS and F13A1 when alternative detection methods were used					
3	TH01, VWA	No	No	16	Andersen *et al.* (1996)
Result: All allele designations matched those of the originating laboratory; achieved despite variation in amplification, electrophoresis, and detection systems used					
4	D21S11, FGA	No	Ladders only	16	Gill *et al.* (1997)
Result: Comparable results were obtained from all laboratories despite the fact that various primers and protocols were utilized; the key to standardization with more complex STR loci is to use a common allelic ladder					
5	ACTBP2, APOAI1, D11S554	Yes	Primers and ladder for ACTBP2	7	Gill *et al.* (1998)
Result: ACTBP2 showed good reproducibility between laboratories (<0.15 bp measured size difference); greater than expected variation with APOAI1 and D11S554 – they need locus-specific ladders					
6	D12S391, D1S1656	Yes	Both	7, 12	Gill *et al.* (1998)
Result: Excellent reproducibility between seven laboratories for D12S391 and 12 laboratories for D1S1656; demonstrated the need to use ±0.5 bp windows centered on the appropriate allelic ladder marker					
7	DYS385	Yes	Both	14	Schneider *et al.* (1999)
Result: Reproducible results may be obtained with a variety of separation and detection systems					

Table 14.1

European DNA profiling group (EDNAP) collaborative studies regarding DNA typing with STR markers. The purpose of these studies was to explore whether uniformity of DNA profiling results could be achieved between European laboratories.

As described in Chapter 5, the FBI Laboratory sponsored a STR Project from which the 13 core STR loci where chosen for inclusion in the Combined DNA Index System. A total of 22 DNA typing laboratories were involved in this project, where a series of samples was systematically examined by the various laboratories. More recently, a DNA quantification and mixture study was conducted by NIST to evaluate the differential extraction capabilities of the participating laboratories.

DNA STANDARD REFERENCE MATERIALS

The National Institute of Standards and Technology, part of the US Department of Commerce, is responsible for developing national and international standard reference materials. These SRM sets are generally used to validate a laboratory's measurement capability, calibrate instrumentation, and troubleshoot protocols (Reeder 1999). Hundreds of SRMs are available from NIST but three in particular apply directly to the forensic DNA typing community. These are SRM 2390, SRM 2391a, and SRM 2392.

The recently issued DNA Advisory Board standard 9.5 (1998) states: 'The laboratory shall check its DNA procedures annually or whenever substantial changes are made to the protocol(s) against an appropriate and available NIST standard reference material or standard traceable to a NIST standard.'

A review of the various SRM materials that are now available is given below.

RFLP TESTING STANDARD: SRM 2390

SRM 2390, entitled DNA Profiling Standard (RFLP-based typing methods), was released in August 1992 and is intended for use in standardizing forensic and paternity testing quality assurance procedures for RFLP testing that uses *Hae*III restriction enzymes as well as instructional law enforcement and non-clinical research purposes.

It contains two well-characterized human DNA samples: a female cell line (K562) and a male source (TAW). Both samples are available in three forms: as a cell pellet (3×10^6 cells), an extracted genomic DNA (~200 ng/μL), and a *Hae*III restriction digest (pre-cut DNA; 25 ng/μL). A molecular weight marker for DNA sizing purposes and six quantification standards (250 ng, 100 ng, 50 ng, 25 ng, 12.5 ng, and 6 ng) are also included as is agarose for slab-gel preparation.

Certified values for the DNA band sizes are available for five commonly used RFLP markers. These markers (and VNTR probes) are D2S44 (YNH24), D4S139 (PH30), D10S28 (TBQ7), D1S7 (MS1), and D17S79 (V1). The certified values represent the pooled results from analyses performed at NIST and 28 collaborating laboratories and come with calculated uncertainties.

PCR-BASED TESTING STANDARD: SRM 2391a

SRM 2391a, entitled PCR-based DNA Profiling Standard, was released in December 1999. It is an updated version of the original SRM 2391 that became available in 1995 and includes certified values for new STR loci. SRM 2391a is intended for use in standardizing forensic and paternity testing quality assurance procedures involving PCR-based genetic testing as well as instructional law enforcement and non-clinical research purposes.

It contains 12 components of well-characterized DNA in two forms: genomic DNA and DNA to be extracted from cells spotted on filter paper. There are ten genomic DNA samples all at a concentration of 1 ng/μL (20 μL volume). Cell lines 9947A and 9948 are included on a 6 mm Scleicher & Schull 903 filter paper circle spotted with 5×10^4 cells. The cells permit a laboratory to test its ability to perform DNA extraction while the genomic DNA materials may be used to verify reliable PCR amplification and detection technologies.

Certified genotype values for the 12 SRM components are listed for the FBI's CODIS 13 STR loci (CSF1PO, D3S1358, D5S818, D7S820, D8S1179, D13S317, D16S539, D18S51, D21S11, FGA, TH01, TPOX, and VWA) as well as additional STR loci F13A01, F13B, FES/FPS, LPL, Penta D, Penta E, D2S1338, and D19S433. These STR markers are all available in commercial kits from either Promega Corporation or PE Biosystems. Certified values for the genetic loci HLA-DQA1, PolyMarker, D1S80, and amelogenin are also described for the 12 components.

MITOCHONDRIAL DNA TESTING STANDARD: SRM 2392

SRM 2392, entitled Mitochondrial DNA Sequencing (Human) Standard, was released in December 1999. This SRM is intended to provide quality control when performing the PCR and sequencing human mitochondrial DNA (mtDNA) for forensic investigations, medical diagnosis, or mutation detection as well as to serve as a control when PCR amplifying and sequencing any DNA sample.

It contains three components of well-characterized human DNA: extracted DNA from cell-culture line CHR (60 μL DNA at 1 ng/μL), extracted DNA from cell-culture line 9947A (60 μL DNA at 1 ng/μL), and cloned DNA from the CHR HV1 region (10 μL DNA at 100 ng/μL).

Certified sequence information of two entire mtDNA templates (CHR and 9947A) are listed with information on all 16 569 bp compared to the Anderson reference sequence. The HV1 CHR clone contains a 'C-stretch' which is difficult to sequence. A list of 58 unique primer sets that were designed to amplify any portion or the entire human mtDNA genome is also included.

QUALITY CONTROL FOR COMMERCIAL SOURCES OF MATERIALS

In the early days of STR typing, forensic laboratories put together their own PCR mixes, primer sets, and allelic ladders. This meant that variation existed in the materials used for various laboratories and sometimes in the interpretation of a sample's genotype. Laboratories often had to spend a significant amount of time preparing the allelic ladders and verifying that each lot of primer mix worked appropriately. Today, most forensic DNA laboratories use commercially available STR kits that provide a uniform set of materials and protocols for the community. Thus, the primary responsibility of performing quality control on the STR amplification reagents has fallen on the commercial manufacturers.

Production of STR kits by commercial manufacturers requires extensive quality control. A fluorescent dye is attached to one primer for each locus amplified by the multiplex STR kit. Each primer must be purified and combined in the correct amount in order to produce a balanced amplification. Variation in this primer mix production can affect locus-to-locus balance in the multiplex amplification. In addition, allelic ladders must also be produced on a large scale and be well characterized, since they serve as the standard for performing the DNA typing experiments with unknown samples. As they may be needed in some situations, *Certificates of Analysis* are available upon request from STR kit manufacturers for court purposes. The certificate confirms that the specific combination of components that comprise a given kit lot number perform together to meet the stated performance (Perkin Elmer Corporation 1998).

REFERENCES

Andersen, J., Martin, P., Carracedo, A., Dobosz, M., Eriksen, B., Johnsson, V., Kimpton, C., Kloosterman, A., Konialis, C., Kratzer, A., Phillips, P., Mevag, B., Pfitzinger, H., Rand, S., Rosen, B., Schmitter, H., Schneider, P. and Vide, M. (1996) *Forensic Science International*, 78, 83–93.

Bar, W., Brinkmann, B., Lincoln, P., Mayr, W.R. and Rossi, U. (1994) *International Journal of Legal Medicine*, 107, 159–160.

Bar, W., Brinkmann, B., Budowle, B., Carracedo, A., Gill, P., Lincoln, P., Mayr, W. and Olaisen, B. (1997) *International Journal of Legal Medicine*, 110, 175–176.

Buel, E., Wang, G. and Schwartz, M. (1995) *Journal of Forensic Sciences*, 40, 641–644.

Crouse, C. and Schumm, J.W. (1995) *Journal of Forensic Sciences*, 40, 952–956.

DNA Advisory Board, Federal Bureau of Investigation, US Department of Justice (1998) *Quality Assurance Standards for Forensic DNA Testing Laboratories.*

DNA Recommendations (1992) *International Journal of Legal Medicine,* 105, 63–64.

Fregeau, C.J., Bowen, K.L. and Fourney, R.M. (1999) *Journal of Forensic Sciences,* 44, 133–166.

Gill, P., Kimpton, C., D'Aloja, E., Andersen, J.F., Bär, W., Brinkmann, B., Holgerssen, S., Johnsson, V., Kloosterman, A.D., Lareu, M.V, Nellemann, L., Pfitzinger, H., Phillips, C.P., Schmitter, H., Schneider, P.M. and Stenersen, M. (1994) *Forensic Science International,* 65, 51–59.

Gill, P., d'Ajola, A., Andersen, J., Dupuy, B., Jangblad, M., Johnsson, V., Kloosterman, A.D., Kratzer, A., Lareu, M.V., Meldegaard, M., Philips, C., Pfitzinger, H., Rand, S., Sabatier, M., Scheithauer, R., Schmitter, H., Schneider, P.M. and Vide, M.C. (1997) *Forensic Science International,* 86, 25–33.

Gill, P., d'Aloja, E., Dupuy, B., Eriksen, B., Jangblad, A., Johnsson, V., Kloosterman, A.D., Lareu, M.V., Mevag, B., Morling, N., Phillips, C., Pfitzinger, H., Rand, S., Sabatier, M., Scheithauer, R., Schmitter, H., Schneider, P.M., Skita, I. and Vide, M.C. (1998) *Forensic Science International,* 98, 193–200.

Kimpton, C., Gill, P., D'Aloja, E., Andersen, J.F., Bär, W., Holgerssen, S., Jacobsen, S., Johnsson, V., Kloosterman, A.D., Lareu, M.V., Nellemann, L., Pfitzinger, H., Phillips, C.P., Rand, S., Schmitter, H., Schneider, P.M., Stenersen, M. and Vide, M.C. (1995) *Forensic Science International,* 71, 137–152.

Kline, M.C., Duewer, D.L., Newall, P., Redman, J.W., Reeder, D.J., and Richard, M. (1997) *Journal of Forensic Sciences,* 42, 897–906.

Lygo, J.E., Johnson, P.E., Holdaway, D.J., Woodroffe, S., Whitaker, J.P., Clayton, T.M., Kimpton, C.P., and Gill, P. (1994) *International Journal of Legal Medicine,* 107, 77–89.

Micka, K.A., Amiott, E.A., Hockenberry, T.L., Sprecher, C.J., Lins, A.M., Rabbach, D.R., Taylor, J.A., Bacher, J.W., Glidewell, D.E., Gibson, S.D., Crouse, C.A. and Schumm, J.W. (1999) *Journal of Forensic Sciences,* 44, 1243–1257.

National Research Council (1996) *NRC II: The Evaluation of Forensic DNA Evidence.* Washington, DC: National Academy Press.

Perkin Elmer Corporation (1998) *AmpFlSTR® Profiler Plus™ PCR Amplification Kit User's Manual.* Foster City: Perkin Elmer Corporation.

Reeder, D.J. (1999) *Archives of Pathology and Laboratory Medicine,* 123, 1063–1065.

Schneider, P.M., d'Aloja, E., Dupuy, B.M., Eriksen, B., Jangblad, A., Kloosterman, A.D., Kratzer, A., Lareu, M.V., Pfitzinger, H., Rand, S., Scheithauer, R., Schmitter, H., Skitsa, I.,

Syndercombe-Court, D. and Vide, M.C. (1999) *Forensic Science International*, 102, 159–165.

Sparkes, R., Kimpton, C., Watson, S., Oldroyd, N., Clayton, T., Barnett, L., Arnold, J., Thompson, C., Hale, R., Chapman, J., Urquhart, A., and Gill, P. (1996) *International Journal of Legal Medicine*, 109, 186–194.

TWGDAM (1989) *Crime Lab Digest,* 16, 40–59.

TWGDAM (1991) *Crime Lab Digest,* 18, 44–75.

TWGDAM (1995) *Crime Lab Digest,* 22, 21–43.

Wallin, J.M., Buoncristiani, M.R., Lazaruk, K.D., Fildes, N., Holt, C.L. and Walsh, P.S. (1998) *Journal of Forensic Sciences*, 43, 854–870.

NEW TECHNOLOGIES AND AUTOMATION

We live in an age of rapid discovery in biotechnology. New technologies that were only imagined a few years ago are now reality. Furthermore, DNA sequence information is becoming available at an unprecedented rate. This information is leading us to a better understanding of human genetic diversity. While it is impossible to predict where the forensic DNA community will be 5 or 10 years from now, there are some new technologies that deserve recognition and that will be reviewed briefly in this chapter. The advantages of automation in large-scale testing operations, such as are done for construction of DNA databases, will also be discussed.

NEW DNA SEPARATION/GENOTYPING TECHNOLOGIES

Most DNA testing in the United States is currently performed in small public forensic laboratories, each consisting of less than a dozen scientists devoted to DNA analysis. However, with the development of several new technologies that will be discussed below, it is conceivable that in the future large-scale operations might become more prevalent for DNA database work. In addition, some DNA tests may be performed at the crime scene with hand-held or portable devices. Thus, this section has been broken up into technological developments that will aid crime-scene DNA testing and large-scale testing for DNA database development. Some methods are extensions of current fluorescence-based technology and other techniques involve completely novel technology.

PORTABLE DEVICES FOR POSSIBLE CRIME SCENE INVESTIGATIONS

Microfabrication techniques revolutionized the integrated circuit industry 20 years ago and have brought the world ever faster and more powerful computers. These same microfabrication methods are now being applied to develop miniature, microchip-based laboratories, or so-called 'labs-on-a-chip'. Miniaturizing the sample preparation and analysis steps in forensic DNA typing could lead to devices that permit investigation of biological evidence at a crime scene, or more rapid and less expensive DNA analysis in a more conventional laboratory setting. We will focus here on three areas of ongoing research for miniature DNA analysis instruments: microchip capillary electrophoresis (CE) devices, miniature thermal cyclers, and hybridization arrays.

Microchip CE Devices

The primary advantage of analyzing DNA in a miniature CE device is that shorter channels, or capillaries, lead to faster DNA separations. Instead of using a 30-cm long glass capillary tube to perform the DNA separation, microchip CE devices are typically glass microscope slides with narrow channels etched into them that are 10–50 μm deep by 50 μm wide and several centimeters long. A glass coverplate is bonded on top of the etched channels in order to create a sealed separation channel (Woolley and Mathies 1994). Alternatively, injection-molded plastic may be used (McCormick *et al.* 1997).

Separation speeds that are 10–100 times faster than conventional electrophoresis may be obtained with this approach. Using a 2-cm separation distance (compared to 36-cm for an ABI 310 capillary), tetranucleotide short tandem repeat (STR) alleles were separated in as little as 30 seconds (Schmalzing *et al.* 1997). Microchip CE systems are being developed with multi-color detection formats. These systems should therefore be compatible with commercially available STR kits. Figure 15.1 shows a simultaneous two-color analysis of polymerase chain reaction (PCR) products from the eight loci in the PowerPlex™ 1.1 STR kit (Schmalzing *et al.* 1999). This separation was performed in less than 2½ minutes.

In order to obtain ultrafast DNA separations, the injection plug must be narrow and short compared to the separation length. DNA separations in less than 30 seconds have also been demonstrated with short capillaries using a fast ramp power supply for rapid injections (Muller *et al.* 1998). Research is ongoing to improve separation speeds and ease of use with the hope that in the near future microchip CE devices will be used routinely for rapid DNA analyses.

A capillary array microplate device has been constructed with 96 separation channels in order to scale up the number of samples processed at a single time. These devices are capable of separating 96 different samples in less than 2 minutes (Shi *et al.* 1999). Although the DNA separation parameters need improvement before this particular 96-channel microplate can resolve closely spaced STR alleles, the device demonstrates that rapid DNA separations are feasible in a highly parallelized format.

Miniature Thermal Cyclers

Sample preparation devices are also shrinking in size. In particular, miniature thermal cyclers are being developed for performing PCR. These devices are being microfabricated with silicon reaction chambers (Northrup *et al.* 1998). A

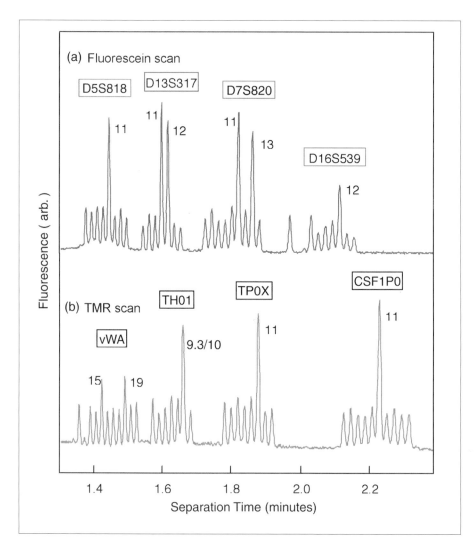

Figure 15.1

Rapid microchip CE separation of the eight STR loci from PowerPlex 1.1 (Schmalzing et al. 1999). The electrophero-grams from scanning each color of a simultaneous two-color analysis are divided. The PCR-amplified sample is mixed with the allelic ladders prior to injection to provide a frame of reference for genotyping the sample. The allele calls for each locus are listed next to the corresponding peak. Figure courtesy of Dr Daniel Ehrlich, Whitehead Institute.

major advantage of miniaturizing the PCR thermal cycling process is the potential for lower reagent consumption and thus reduction in the cost of an analysis. In addition, more rapid thermal cycling times are possible because the PCR reaction mixture can be heated and cooled quickly. Since the reaction volume is smaller, it takes less time to thermally equilibrate the PCR reaction.

The miniature analytical thermal cycler instrument (MATCI) developed at Lawrence Livermore National Laboratory weighs only 35 pounds, fits in a medium-sized briefcase, and is powered by 13 rechargeable batteries. The MATCI system has been used to successfully amplify DQA1 alleles and a STR triplex consisting of the D3S1358, VWA, and FGA loci (Belgrader *et al.* 1998). A 25 μL PCR reaction was performed with 30 cycles in about 42 minutes using MATCI compared to 2.5 hours on a PE9600 thermal cycler. The MATCI has also been used in conjunction with time-of-flight mass spectrometry to complete a STR genotyping assay in less than 50 minutes (Ross *et al.* 1998).

Ultimately, the combination of sample preparation in a miniature thermal cycling device coupled to rapid DNA analysis on a microchip CE device may be the future. A microfabricated PCR reactor has been coupled to a micro-capillary electrophoresis chip to perform a rapid PCR-CE analysis in less than 20 minutes (Woolley *et al.* 1996). In this particular case, a PCR amplification of a single amplicon involving 30 cycles was performed in 15 minutes and was imme-diately followed by a high-speed CE chip separation in 83 seconds.

A similar type of online, automated DNA amplification and separation has also been performed with a larger scale CE system (Swerdlow *et al.* 1997). In this case, the total time from extracted DNA to result was 20 minutes – 8 minutes for thermal cycling, 4 minutes for purification, and 8 minutes for electrophoresis. It may well be that in the not too distant future DNA results, from biological sample to STR profile, may be routinely obtained in under an hour.

STR Determination by Hybridization Arrays

Nanogen Inc. (San Diego, CA) has developed another microchip-based assay that appears promising for rapid STR allele determination. This assay involves the use of a silicon microchip composed of an arrayed set of electrodes that act as independent test sites (Figure 15.2). Electric potentials can be directed to each test site, which contains a unique DNA probe for hybridization (Sosnowski *et al.* 1997a).

A DNA hybridization assay is conducted by washing a DNA sample over the chip and seeing where it binds on the array. PCR-amplified samples will bind or hybridize to their complementary probe sequence. An 'electronic stringency' can then be applied to each probe site by simply adjusting the electric field strength. Samples that are not a perfect match for the probe will be denatured and driven away from the probe.

Since each test site is separate from the others on the spatial array of probes, a signal obtained from a particular position on the probe array indicates which sequence has bound to the probe. Fluorescent probes may be added to the DNA molecules for detection purposes. Software then reads the array position versus fluorescent signal and interprets the data to determine the sequence present in the DNA samples being measured.

In order to measure which STR alleles are present at a particular locus, a chip is prepared that contains known alleles for that locus. Each probe position on the chip has a different allele attached (Figure 15.2b). Thus, in order to have the capability of measuring eight alleles at the TPOX locus (e.g. 6–13 repeats), eight different probe sites are required.

The STR hybridization assay involves two probes that bind to the STR repeat

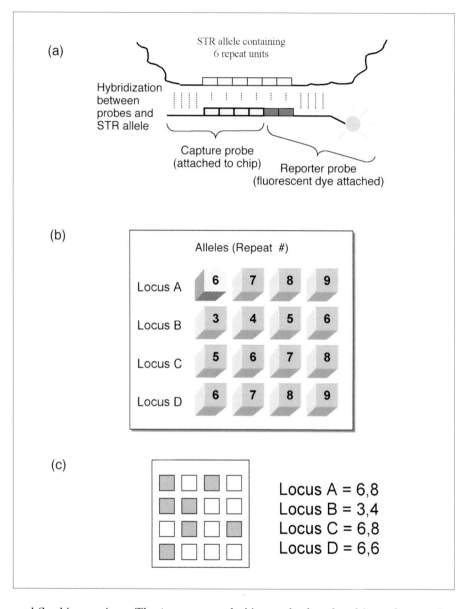

Figure 15.2

Schematic of nanogen STR hybridization chip assay. The assay illustrated in (a) involves a capture probe oligo-nucleotide that is attached at a unique location on the chip (b). The capture probe hybridizes to the appropriate STR allele by binding to the repeat region and 30–40 bases of the flanking region. A reporter probe containing 1–3 repeat units, some flanking sequence and a fluorescent dye hybridizes to the STR allele and generates a fluorescent signal at the probe site that can be interpreted to yield the sample's genotype (c). Multiple STR loci may be probed on the same chip with one probe site existing for each allele.

and flanking regions. The 'capture probe' is attached to the chip at the test site and captures the PCR-amplified STR allele when the sample is added to the chip. The 'reporter probe' contains the fluorescent dye and thus enables the detection of the STR allele bound to the particular site defined by the capture probe (Figure 15.2a). The unique sequences on either side of the repeat make it possible to have discrimination between alleles of different STR loci with the same repeat sequence.

A sample's genotype is assessed by observing the positions that give a fluorescent signal once the PCR product has hybridized to its corresponding capture probe(s). The read-out provides a genotype that corresponds to the number of repeats present in the sample even though no size-based separation has been performed (Figure 15.2c). Thus, samples measured with this hybridization assay can be compared to results obtained from a conventional DNA separation of the STR alleles. Nanogen has conducted several successful sample correlation tests with the Bode Technology Group, a private forensic laboratory located in Springfield, Virginia (Sosnowski *et al.* 1997b).

INSTRUMENTS FOR LARGE-SCALE DNA DATABASE TESTING

As the demand for DNA typing results increases, particularly with the national DNA databases being developed around the world (see Chapter 16), instrumentation capable of high-volume sample processing will become more prevalent. In this section, we will review two technologies that show great promise for high-throughput DNA typing. These technologies include capillary array electrophoresis and time-of-flight mass spectrometry.

Capillary Array Electrophoresis Instruments

In Chapter 9, we discussed the advantages of capillary electrophoresis due to its capability for automated injection, separation, and detection of samples. However, one of the major disadvantages of single capillary instruments is that sample throughput is limited because samples are processed sequentially rather than in parallel as on a gel. Parallel CE separations may be performed though by placing a number of capillaries next to each other to form a capillary array electrophoresis (CAE) system. Each capillary in the array then would be analogous to a lane of a gel, although without the problems of lane tracking on the gel.

In 1999, two-capillary 96-array electrophoresis systems became commercially available: the ABI 3700 from PE Biosystems (Foster City, CA) and the MegaBACE from Molecular Dynamics/Amersham Pharmacia Biotech (Sunnyvale, CA). These instruments were developed to meet the large-scale sequencing needs of the Human Genome Project. Both the ABI 3700 and MegaBACE instruments have 96 capillaries in parallel and are capable of sequencing more than 500 nucleotides in each capillary every 2 or 3 hours. These CAE instruments can potentially analyze more than 1000 samples every 24 hours and will most likely be applied in a routine fashion to forensic DNA database samples in the near future. In fact, the literature contains several published reports demonstrating effective STR typing with capillary array electrophoresis instruments (Wang *et al.* 1995, Mansfield *et al.* 1996, 1998).

An appealing advantage of using capillary array instruments is that the same STR amplification kits can be used. The same four-color fluorescent detection capabilities exist with commercially available CAE instruments. Thus, STR data from a lower throughput method such as the ABI 310 can be compared in the future to data collected with a higher throughput technique involving capillary arrays.

MALDI-TOF Mass Spectrometry

Another instrument platform capable of large-scale sample processing is time-of-flight mass spectrometry. Mass spectrometry is a versatile analytical technique that involves the detection of ions and the measurement of their mass-to-charge ratio. Owing to the fact that these ions are separated in a vacuum environment, the analysis times can be extremely rapid, on the order of seconds. Combined with robotic sample preparation, time-of-flight mass spectrometry offers the potential for processing thousands of DNA samples on a daily basis.

In order to get the DNA molecules into the gas phase for analysis in the mass spectrometer, a technique known as matrix-assisted laser desorption-ionization (MALDI) is used. When MALDI is coupled with time-of-flight mass spectrometry, this measurement technique is commonly referred to as MALDI-TOF-MS. Figure 15.3 shows a schematic of the MALDI-TOF-MS process.

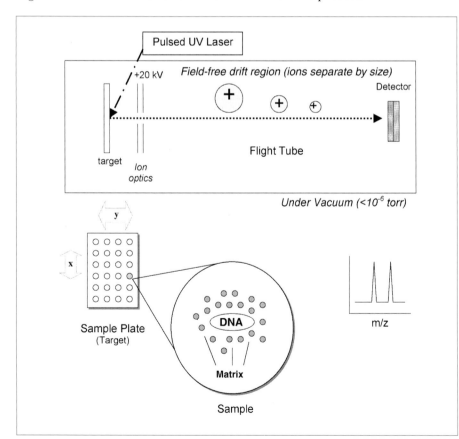

Figure 15.3

Schematic of MALDI time-of-flight mass spectrometry. DNA samples are mixed with a matrix compound and dried as individual spots on a sample plate. The sample plate is then introduced to the vacuum environment of the mass spectrometer. A small portion of the sample is ionized by an ultraviolet (UV) laser pulse and the generated ions are accelerated through the ion optics. The ions separate by size as they pass down the flight tube. The mass-to-charge ratio (m/z) of each ion is detected as it impacts the detector.

The analysis of DNA using MALDI-TOF-MS proceeds as follows. A liquid DNA sample is combined with an excess of a matrix compound, such as 3-hydroxy-picolinic acid (Butler *et al.* 1998). These samples are spotted on to a metal or silicon plate. As the sample air dries, the DNA and matrix co-crystallize. The sample plate is then introduced into the vacuum environment of the mass spectrometer for analysis. A rapid laser pulse initiates the ionization process. The matrix molecules that surround the DNA protect it from fragmentation during the ionization process.

Each pulse of the laser initiates ionization of the sample and the subsequent separation of ions in the flight tube (Figure 15.3). The DNA ions travel to the detector in a matter of several hundred microseconds as they separate based on their mass. However, it takes several seconds to analyze each sample because multiple laser pulses are taken and averaged to form the final mass spectrum. Samples are analyzed sequentially by moving the sample plate underneath a fixed laser beam. Sample plates are now commercially available that can hold 384 (or more) samples at a time. Each sample plate can be analyzed in less than 1 hour depending on the number of laser shots collected for each sample and the pulse rate of the laser.

Time-of-flight mass spectrometry has the potential to bring DNA sample processing to a new level in terms of high-throughput analysis. However, there are several challenges for analysis of PCR products, such as STRs, using MALDI-TOF-MS. The most significant problem is that resolution and sensitivity in the mass spectrometer are diminished when either the DNA size or the salt content of the sample is too large.

However, STR markers have been successfully analyzed via MALDI-TOF mass spectrometry by redesigning the PCR primers to be closer to the repeat region, and thereby reducing the size of the amplified alleles (Ross and Belgrader 1997, Ross *et al.* 1998, Butler *et al.* 1998). The mass spectrum of an allelic ladder for the STR locus TH01, shown in Figure 15.4, demonstrates that STR alleles may be effectively detected with MALDI-TOF-MS. These alleles are 105 bp smaller than corresponding alleles amplified with AmpFlSTR® kit primers for the TH01 STR locus.

Another benefit to MALDI-TOF-MS besides sample analysis speed is accuracy. In fact, the high degree of accuracy for sizing STR alleles using this technique permits reliable typing without the use of an allelic ladder (Butler *et al.* 1998). Allelic ladders as well as internal sizing standards are necessary in electrophoretic separation systems to adjust for minor variations in peak migration times due to fluctuations in temperature and voltage (see Chapter 9).

With mass spectrometry, the actual mass of the DNA molecule is being measured, making it a more accurate technique than a relative size measurement as in electrophoresis. In fact, STR allele measurements taken almost a year

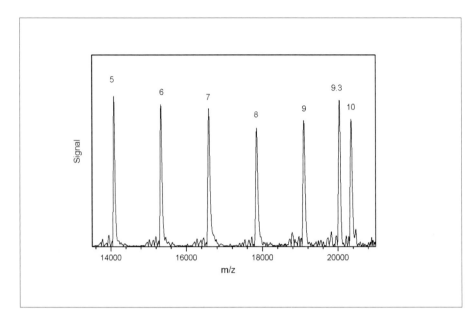

Figure 15.4

Mass spectrum of a TH01 allelic ladder obtained with a time-of-flight mass spectrometer (Butler et al. 1998). The ladder contains alleles 5, 6, 7, 8, 9, 9.3, and 10. It was generated by re-amplifying an AmpFlSTR® Green I allelic ladder mix using primers that bind close to the repeat region. The PCR product size of allele 10 is 83 bp with a measured mass of 20 280 Da. The separation time in the mass spectrometer for allele 10 is only 204 microseconds! The allele 9.3 and allele 10 peaks, which are a single nucleotide apart, differ by 1.5 microseconds on a separation time scale and can be fully resolved with this method.

apart on different instruments produced virtually identical masses (Butler and Becker 1999). Furthermore, a comparison study of MALDI-TOF-MS results with over 1000 STR alleles measured by conventional fluorescent methods using an ABI 310 demonstrated an excellent correlation between the two methods (Butler and Becker 1999).

Unfortunately, the expense of the MALDI-TOF-MS system, which is of the order of several hundred thousand dollars, and the previous wide-scale acceptance of fluorescent methodologies will likely keep mass spectrometry from becoming a major player in forensic DNA analysis of STR markers. However, it is an effective means for analysis of single nucleotide polymorphisms (SNPs) and may have a role to play in forensic DNA analysis as SNPs become more widely accepted.

SNP ANALYSIS SYSTEMS

Although the primary focus of this book is on currently used STR markers, we think it would be valuable to mention technologies for analysis of SNP markers that are likely to be used by the forensic community in the not-to-distant future (see Chapter 8). SNPs have potential forensic value because numerous markers are being discovered that are population-specific and have a low mutation rate. In addition, SNPs can be highly multiplexed, can be made quite small to withstand degraded DNA samples, and can be simpler tools than STRs with which to interpret mixtures because there are no stutter artifacts.

Table 15.1 lists a number of techniques that have been used to analyze SNPs.

Table 15.1
SNP analysis techniques.

Method	Description	References
Genetic bit analysis	Primer extension with ddNTPs is detected with a colorimetric assay in a 96-well format	Nikiforov *et al.* (1994)
Direct sequencing	PCR products are sequenced and compared to reveal SNP sites	Kwok *et al.* (1994)
Denaturing high-performance liquid chromatography (HPLC)	Two PCR products are mixed and injected on an ion-paired reversed-phase HPLC; single base differences in the two amplicons will be revealed by extra heteroduplex peaks	Hecker *et al.* (1999)
TaqMan 5′-nuclease assay	A fluorescent probe consisting of reporter and quencher dyes is added to a PCR reaction; amplification of a probe-specific product causes cleavage of the probe and generates an increase in fluorescence	Livak (1999)
Fluorescence polarization	Primer extension across the SNP site with dye-labeled ddNTPs; monitoring changes in fluorescence polarization reveals which dye is bound to the primer	Chen *et al.* (1999)
Mass spectrometry	Primer extension across the SNP site with ddNTPs; mass difference between the primer and extension product is measured to reveal nucleotide(s) present	Haff and Smirnov (1997), Li *et al.* (1999)
High-density arrays (Affymetrix chip)	Thousands of oligonucleotide probes are represented at specific locations on a microchip array; fluorescently labeled PCR products hybridize to complementary probes to reveal SNPs	Wang *et al.* (1998), Sapolsky *et al.* (1999)
Electronic dot-blot (Nanogen chip)	Potential SNP alleles are placed at discrete locations on a microchip array; an electric field at each point in the array is used to control hybridization stringency	Sosnowski *et al.* (1997a), Gilles *et al.* (1999)
Molecular beacons	Hairpin stem on oligonucleotide probe keeps fluorophore and its quencher in contact until hybridization to DNA target, which results in fluorescence	Giesendorf *et al.* (1998)
Oligonucleotide ligation assay (OLA)	Colorimetric assay in microtiter 96-well format involving ligation of two probes if the complementary base is present	Delahunty *et al.* (1996)
T_m-shift genotyping	Allelic-specific PCR is performed with a GC-tail attached to one of the forward allele-specific primers; amplified allele with GC-tailed primer will exhibit a melting curve at a higher temperature	Germer and Higuchi (1999)

For example, genetic bit analysis (GBA) has been used by Gene Screen (Dallas, TX) and Laboratory Corporation of America (Burlington, NC) to genotype multiple SNP markers for paternity applications. As the Human Genome Project and new commercial ventures continue to improve SNP analysis, the testing of multiple SNP sites will become less expensive and easier to perform. In the future, SNP detection platforms may be used in conjunction with fluorescent STR results to establish DNA profiles of forensic casework samples. Some technologies, such as mass spectrometry and microchip array hybridization using electronic stringency, are capable of performing analysis on both STR and SNP markers.

LABORATORY AUTOMATION

Laboratory automation is an important topic, especially since the demand for forensic DNA testing is increasing. Laboratories will take on more cases and have much larger amounts of samples to type because of DNA database laws. While the type of laboratory automation that is currently used by DNA typing laboratories varies widely from little to none, in the future automation will likely play an increasing role in primarily two areas: liquid handling and data analysis.

LIQUID HANDLING ROBOTS

There are a number of liquid handling tasks performed in DNA typing laboratories during the DNA extraction, PCR setup, and PCR amplification analysis steps. These liquid handling tasks are typically performed with manual pipettors by a DNA technician or analyst. Small volumes of liquids are repeatedly moved from one tube to another. These repetitive tasks can lead to mistakes as laboratory personnel become tired or careless.

By introducing automated liquid handling with robotics, the level of human error can be greatly reduced. Computers and robotics do the same task the same way time after time without becoming tired. The challenge though lies in setting up the automation and maintaining it (Hale 1999). The most likely place where liquid handling automation will be used in the future is with the high-volume sample processing of convicted offender samples for computer DNA databases (see Chapter 16).

There are a number of popular liquid-handling robotic systems that are commercially available. Beckman Coulter, Hamilton Company, MWG Biotech, Rosys, and Tecan market popular liquid-handling robots. Appendix IV contains contact information with these manufacturers. Each robotic system has different capabilities and should be carefully assessed in order to meet the needs and goals of one's own laboratory environment.

SAMPLE TRACKING PROGRAMS

Managing large amounts of data becomes a problem for many laboratories as they scale up their efforts. Computer databases are often developed to aid in tracking samples and results obtained. Sample tubes can be bar-coded and tracked through the analysis process. An example of efforts in this area is the Overlord System developed at the Forensic Science Service (FSS) (Hopwood *et al.* 1997). The FSS Overlord program is a laboratory information management system (LIMS) and aids sample tracking as well as overall control of the different robotic stations. LIMS systems are rather expensive and are typically used only by laboratories with very high sample volumes.

STR INTERPRETATION PROGRAMS

One of the highest labor efforts in typing STRs is the data interpretation. In many cases, more time is actually spent evaluating the STR profiles than preparing and collecting the data on the sample. New software is being developed to address these issues. These programs include TrueAllele developed by Mark Perlin of Cybergenetics and STRess developed by the Forensic Science Service in England.

TrueAllele is a commercially available allele-calling program from Cybergenetics that uses quantification and deconvolution algorithms to improve STR allele calls based upon quality measures (Palsson *et al.* 1999). TrueAllele is written in Matlab and runs with Macintosh, Windows, or UNIX-based systems. This program has an advantage over the Genotyper® or STaR Call™ software packages in that TrueAllele provides a quality measure for every allele call. The quality value assigned by TrueAllele ranges between 0.0 and 1.0 and reflects a peak's height, shape, and stutter pattern (Palsson *et al.* 1999). The selection criteria used by the program are empirically derived through review of many STR profiles. TrueAllele is being primarily used for microsatellite disease-linkage studies where hundreds of thousands of genotypes are gathered to decipher chromosomal locations of disease genes.

The FSS has developed a data interpretation program called STRess (STR Expert System Suite) to aid their STR profile processing. Interpretation guidelines drawn from approximately 100 000 samples processed by the FSS and used by experienced operators were incorporated into the programming of STRess (Gill *et al.* 1996, Dunbar *et al.* 1998). FSS genotyping guidelines require that all samples are genotyped by two independent operators to ensure accuracy of DNA typing results followed by a third operator to review allele calls and confirm that they are concordant. The aim of STRess was to reduce the amount of manual effort needed to evaluate the STR data by replacing one of the genotype analysts. The FSS has estimated that incorporating the STRess program into routine analysis has resulted in a 40% time savings (Dunbar *et al.* 1998). Thus, improved data analysis software will likely play an important role in the future of DNA typing with STR markers.

UNIQUE CHALLENGES WITH FORENSIC DNA AND NEW TECHNOLOGIES

DNA separations for the purposes of STR genotyping have been primarily conducted to date with electrophoresis, either in the form of slab gels or capillary instruments. However, a number of new methods are under development in research laboratories around the world. These methods involve techniques such as miniature electrophoresis separation systems, hybridization techniques, and mass spectrometry, all of which have been discussed briefly here. We can expect that these new technologies will make DNA typing faster, cheaper, and easier to perform. In the not too distant future, portable systems may be in use that would permit a rapid DNA test right at the crime scene. In addition, large laboratory centers will be able to perform thousands or even hundreds of thousands of DNA tests per day.

However, the adoption of new technology by the forensic DNA community takes time for several reasons. First and foremost, methods need to be carefully validated to ensure that results with a new technology are accurate and reproducible (see Chapter 14). Second, methods should yield comparable results to current technologies so that genotype information can be compared over time. The development of large DNA databases make it necessary to have a constant currency so that convicted offender samples have been analyzed with the same DNA markers as crime scene samples (see Chapter 16). A new set of markers or a new form of sample analysis, unless it gives an equivalent result to current technology, must have clear advantages and be very inexpensive to overcome legacy data in large DNA databases.

With the continued progress in biotechnology around the world will come better and better methods for DNA typing methods used in forensic DNA laboratories. We can expect that future DNA testing technologies will include the following desirable characteristics:

- improved capabilities for multiplex PCR, i.e. the ability to amplify more regions of the DNA simultaneously in order to improve further the number of markers examined and therefore the discrimination power of the test;
- more rapid separation/detection technology;
- more automated sample processing and data analysis/interpretation;
- less expensive sample analysis;
- accurate, robust methods.

REFERENCES

Belgrader, P., Smith, J.K., Weedn, V.W. and Northrup, M.A. (1998) *Journal of Forensic Science*, 43, 315–319.

Butler, J.M. and Becker, C.H. (1999) *Improved analysis of DNA short tandem repeats with time-of-flight mass spectrometry.* Final Report on NIJ Grant 97-LB-VX-0003. Washington, DC: National Institute of Justice.

Butler, J.M., Li, J., Shaler, T.A., Monforte, J.A. and Becker, C.H. (1998) *International Journal of Legal Medicine*, 112, 45–49.

Chen, X., Levine, L. and Kwok, P.-Y. (1999) *Genome Research*, 9, 492–498.

Delahunty, C., Ankener, W., Deng, Q., Eng, J. and Nickerson, D.A. (1996) *American Journal of Human Genetics*, 58, 1239–1246.

Dunbar, H.N., Sparkes, R.L., Hopwood, A.J., Pinchin, R. and Watson, S.K. (1998) *Proceedings of the Second European Symposium on Human Identification*. Madison, WI: Promega Corporation, pp. 55–58.

Germer, S. and Higuchi, R. (1999) *Genome Research*, 9, 72–78.

Giesendorf, B.A.J., Vet, J.A.M., Tyagi, S., Mensink, E.J.M.G., Trijbels, F.J.M. and Blom, H.J. (1998) *Clinical Chemistry*, 44, 482–486.

Gill, P., Urquhart, A., Millican, E., Oldroyd, N., Watson, S., Sparkes, R. and Kimpton, C. (1996) *International Journal of Legal Medicine*, 109, 14–22.

Gilles, P.N., Wu, D.J., Foster, C.B., Dillon, P.J. and Chanock, S.J. (1999) *Nature Biotechnology*, 17, 365–370.

Haff, L.A. and Smirnov, I.P. (1997) *Genome Research*, 7, 378–388.

Hale, A.N. (1999) Building realistic automated production lines for genetic analysis. In: *Automation: Genomic and Functional Analyses* (Craig, A.G. and Hoheisel, J.D., eds), Methods in Microbiology, Volume 28, Chapter 5, pp. 93–129. San Diego: Academic Press.

Hecker, K.H., Taylor, P.D. and Gjerde, D.T. (1999) *Analytical Biochemistry*, 272, 156–164.

Hopwood, A., Brookes, J., Shariff, A., Cage, P., Tatum, E., Mirza, R., Crook, M., Brews, K. and Sullivan, K. (1997) *Proceedings of the Eighth International Symposium on Human Identification*. Madison, WI: Promega Corporation, pp. 20–24.

Kwok, P.-K., Carlson, C., Yager, T.D., Ankener, W. and Nickerson, D.A. (1994) *Genomics*, 23, 138–144.

Li, J., Butler, J.M., Tan, Y., Lin, H., Royer, S., Ohler, L., Shaler, T.A., Hunter, J.M., Pollart, D.J., Monforte, J.A. and Becker, C.H. (1999) *Electrophoresis* 20, 1258–1265.

Livak, K.J. (1999) *Genetic Analysis*, 14, 143–149.

Mansfield, E.S., Vainer, M., Enad, S., Barker, D.L., Harris, D., Rappaport, E. and Fortina, P. (1996) *Genome Research,* 6, 893–903.

Mansfield, E.S., Robertson, J.M., Vainer, M., Isenberg, A.R., Frazier, R.R., Ferguson, K., Chow, S., Harris, D.W., Barker, D.L., Gill, P.D., Budowle, B. and McCord, B.R. (1998) *Electrophoresis*, 19, 101–107.

McCormick, R., Nelson, R.J., Alonso-Amigo, M.G., Benvegnu, D.J. and Hooper, H.H. (1997) *Analytical Chemistry*, 69, 2626–2630.

Muller, O., Minarik, M. and Foret, F. (1998) *Electrophoresis*, 19, 1436–1444.

Nikiforov, T.T., Rendle, R.B., Goelet, P., Rogers, Y-H., Kotewicz, M.L., Anderson, S., Trainor, G.L. and Knapp, M.R. (1994) *Nucleic Acids Research*, 22, 4167–4175.

Northrup, M.A., Benett, B., Hadley, D., Landre, P., Lehew, S., Richards, J. and Stratton, P. (1998) *Analytical Chemistry*, 70, 918–922.

Palsson, B., Palsson, F., Perlin, M., Gudbjartsson, H., Stefansson, K. and Gulcher, J. (1999) *Genome Research*, 9, 1002–1012.

Ross, P.L. and Belgrader, P. (1997) *Analytical Chemistry*, 69, 3966–3972.

Ross, P.L., Davis, P.A. and Belgrader, P. (1998) *Analytical Chemistry*, 70, 2067–2073.

Sapolsky, R.J., Hsie, L., Berno, A., Ghandour, G., Mittmann, M. and Fan, J.-B. (1999) *Genetic Analysis*, 14, 187–192.

Schmalzing, D., Koutny, L., Adourian, A., Belgrader, P., Matsudaira, P. and Ehrlich, D. (1997) *Proceedings of the National Academy of Sciences, USA*, 94, 10273–10278.

Schmalzing, D., Koutny, L., Chisholm, D., Adourian, A., Matsudaira, P. and Ehrlich, D. (1999) *Analytical Biochemistry*, 270, 148–152.

Shi, Y., Simpson, P.C., Scherer, J.R., Wexler, D., Skibola, C., Smith, M.T. and Mathies, R.A. (1999) *Analytical Chemistry*, 71, 5354–5361.

Sosnowski, R.G., Tu, E., Butler, W.F., O'Connell, J.P. and Heller, M.J. (1997a) *Proceedings of the National Academy of Sciences USA*, 94, 1119–1123.

Sosnowski, R.G., Canter, D., Duhon, M., Feng, L., Muralihar, M., Radtkey, R., O'Connell, J., Heller, M. and Nerenberg, M. (1997b) *Proceedings of the Eighth International Symposium on Human Identification*. Madison, WI: Promega Corporation, pp. 119–125.

Swerdlow, H., Jones, B.J. and Wittwer, C.T. (1997) *Analytical Chemistry*, 69, 848–855.

Wang, Y., Ju, J., Carpenter, B.A., Atherton, J.M., Sensabaugh, G.F. and Mathies, R.A. (1995) *Analytical Chemistry*, 67, 1197–1203.

Wang, D.G., Fan, J.-B., Siao, C.-J. *et al.* (1998) *Science*, 280, 1077–1082.

Woolley, A.T. and Mathies, R.A. (1994) *Proceedings of the National Academy of Sciences, USA*, 91, 11348–11352.

Woolley, A.T., Hadley, D., Landre, P., deMello, A.J., Mathies, R.A. and Northrup, M.A. (1996) *Analytical Chemistry*, 68, 4081–4086.

CHAPTER 16

COMBINED DNA INDEX SYSTEM (CODIS) AND THE USE OF DNA DATABASES

INTRODUCTION

On 13 October 1998, the Federal Bureau of Investigation (FBI) officially launched its nationwide DNA database. This database, named the COmbined DNA Index System or CODIS, linked all 50 states in the United States with the capability to search criminal DNA profiles in a similar fashion as the FBI fingerprint database. Since the first national DNA database was established in the United Kingdom in 1995, DNA databases around the world have revolutionized the ability to use DNA profile information to link crime scene evidence to perpetrators.

These databases are effective because a majority of crimes are committed by repeat offenders. In fact, 60% of those individuals released from prison for violent offenses and subsequently released were re-arrested for a similar offense in less than 3 years (McEwen and Reilly 1994). This chapter will discuss the DNA databases being used in the United States and throughout the world to stop violent criminals, such as the introductory case reviewed in Chapter 1.

VALUE OF DNA DATABASES

Information sharing has always been crucial to successful law enforcement. Good information can solve crimes and ultimately save lives. DNA databases are just beginning to serve as valuable tools in aiding law enforcement investigations. Their effectiveness will grow as the size of the database becomes larger. These databases can be used to locate suspects in violent crime cases that would otherwise never have been solved. Consider the sexual assault case described in Chapter 1. Without the Virginia DNA database, the rapist would probably have avoided detection.

A second important role that DNA databases, or data banks, can serve is to make associations between groups of unsolved cases. Criminals do not honor the same geographical boundaries that law enforcement personnel do. Crimes committed in Florida can be linked to ones committed in Virginia through an effective national DNA database.

However, DNA profile information must be in the database for it to be of value. Today tremendous sample backlogs exist in the United States – meaning that samples have been collected but are waiting analysis and entry into CODIS. Hundreds of thousands of samples await short tandem repeat (STR) typing. Efforts are being made to correct this sample backlog problem. Hopefully in a few years, crime scene samples can be quickly analyzed and uploaded for a rapid and effective search against a comprehensive national DNA database. However, the establishment of an effective DNA database requires time and full coopera-tion between forensic DNA laboratories, the law enforcement community, and government policy makers.

ESTABLISHING A NATIONAL DNA DATABASE

Implementing a national DNA database is no small task. A number of features must be in place before the database can be established and actually be effective. These are listed below:

- a commitment on the part of each state to provide samples for the DNA database;
- a common set of DNA markers or standard core so that results can be compared between all samples entered into the database;
- standard software and computer formats so that data can be transferred between laboratories;
- quality standards so that everyone can rely on results from each laboratory.

The technology of forensic DNA databases basically involves three parts: (1) the collection of known specimens; (2) analyzing those specimens and placing their DNA profiles in a computer database; and (3) subsequent comparison of unknown profiles obtained from crime scene evidence with the known profiles in the computer database.

All 50 states within the United States have now enacted legislation to establish a DNA databank containing profiles from individuals convicted of specific crimes. Law enforcement agencies search these databanks for matches with DNA profiles from biological evidence of unsolved crimes. Using these databanks, law enforcement agencies have been successful in identifying suspects in cases that would likely be unsolvable by any other means.

A number of other countries around the world have also launched national DNA databases. The earliest national DNA data bank, and so far the most effective, was created in the United Kingdom in 1995. In less than 5 years, more than 500 000 DNA profiles have been entered into the database, which has aided more than 50 000 criminal investigations (Werrett and Sparkes 1998).

COMBINED DNA INDEX SYSTEM (CODIS)

The FBI started CODIS as a pilot project in 1990 that served just 14 state and local laboratories. It took several years to gather enough DNA profiles from convicted offenders to reach the critical mass necessary to obtain matches for crime scene evidence. During the 1990s, the number of samples in CODIS grew to several hundred thousand. In addition, the number of laboratories submitting data increased. As of November 1999, CODIS software was installed in more than 100 public laboratories around the United States, giving them the capability to submit DNA profiles to a national DNA database.

Within CODIS there are two primary sample indexes: convicted offender samples and forensic casework samples. There is also a population file with DNA types and allele frequency data from anonymous persons intended to represent major population groups found in the United States (Budowle and Moretti 1998). These databases are used to estimate statistical frequencies of DNA profiles.

DNA profile information inputted into CODIS over the years has included restriction fragment length polymorphism (RFLP) loci and polymerase chain reaction (PCR)-based markers HLA-DQA1, PolyMarker, and D1S80. More recently, the 13 CODIS core STR loci are required for data entry into the NDIS system (Budowle *et al.* 1998). These 13 STR markers were reviewed in Chapter 5 and provide a random match probability of approximately 1 in 100 trillion.

CODIS is not a criminal history information database but rather a system of pointers that provides only the information necessary for making matches. Only a unique identifier and the DNA profiles for a sample, such as the 13 STR loci shown in Table 16.1, are stored in CODIS. No personal information, criminal history information, or case-related information is contained within CODIS.

When CODIS identifies a potential match, the laboratories responsible for the matching profiles are notified and they contact each other to validate or refute the match (Niezgoda and Brown 1995). After the match has been confirmed by qualified DNA analysts, which often involves retesting of the matching convicted offender DNA sample, laboratories may exchange additional information, such as names and phone numbers of criminal investigators and case details. If a match is obtained with the Convicted Offender index, the identity and location of the convicted offender is determined and an arrest warrant procured.

The primary metric for CODIS is the 'hit', which is defined as a match between two or more DNA profiles that provides the police with an investigative lead that would not otherwise have developed. As of January 2000, there have been more than 600 hits for CODIS allowing hundreds of crimes to be linked and solved around the United States. Because the number of hits is largely related to the size of the database, as CODIS continues to grow, so will its value.

Table 16.1

Example of the STR profile information stored in the CODIS DNA Database for a single sample. Note that there is no personal information that can be used to link an individual to his or her DNA profile. The two alleles for each STR marker are placed in separate columns labeled value 1 and value 2. For markers with homozygous results, both value 1 and value 2 are the same, see for example CSF1PO. The information in the 'sample info' field can be related to a known individual only by the originating forensic DNA laboratory.

Sample Info	Sample #	Category	Tissue Type	Tissue Form	Population
F130	1	Convicted Offender	Blood	Stain	Caucasian
Marker	**Value 1**	**Value 2**	**Date**	**Time**	
AMEL	X	Y	15-FEB-2000	17:38:30	
CSF1PO	10	10	15-FEB-2000	17:38:30	
D13S317	11	14	15-FEB-2000	17:38:30	
D16S539	9	11	15-FEB-2000	17:38:30	
D18S51	14	16	15-FEB-2000	17:38:30	
D21S11	28	30	15-FEB-2000	17:38:30	
D3S1358	16	17	15-FEB-2000	17:38:30	
D5S818	12	13	15-FEB-2000	17:38:30	
D7S820	9	9	15-FEB-2000	17:38:30	
D8S1179	12	14	15-FEB-2000	17:38:30	
FGA	21	22	15-FEB-2000	17:38:30	
TH01	6	6	15-FEB-2000	17:38:30	
TPOX	8	8	15-FEB-2000	17:38:30	
VWA	17	18	15-FEB-2000	17:38:30	

LEVELS OF CODIS

The COmbined DNA Index System is composed of local, state, and national levels (Figure 16.1). All three levels contain the convicted offender and casework indexes and the population data file. The software is configurable to support any RFLP or PCR DNA markers. At the local level or Local DNA Index System (LDIS), investigators can input their DNA profiles and search for matches with local cases. All forensic DNA records originate at the local level and are 'uploaded' or transmitted to the state and national levels.

Each participating state has a single laboratory that functions as the State DNA Index System (SDIS) to manage information at the state level. SDIS enables exchange and comparison of DNA profiles within a state and is usually operated by the agency responsible for maintaining a state's convicted offender DNA database program.

The National DNA Index System (NDIS) manages nationwide information in a single repository maintained by the FBI Laboratory. Participating states submit their DNA profiles in order to have searches performed on a national level. The role of NDIS is to search casework and offender indexes, manage candidate matches, and return results of matches to the local LDIS level.

When NDIS was first activated in October 1998, there were 119 000 offender

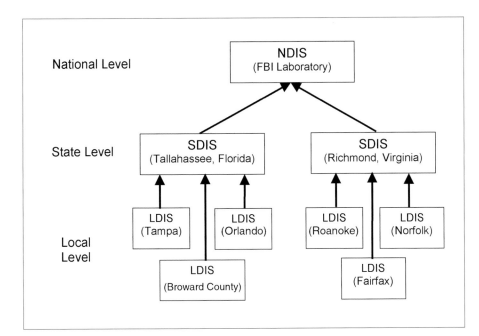

Figure 16.1

Schematic of the three tiers in the combined DNA index system (CODIS). DNA profile information begins at the local level, or local DNA index system (LDIS), and then can be uploaded to the state level, or state DNA index system (SDIS), and finally to the national level, or national DNA index system (NDIS). Each local or state laboratory maintains its portion of CODIS while the FBI Laboratory maintains the national portion (NDIS).

profiles and 5000 forensic casework profiles from nine states. By December 1999, a little over a year later, 21 states and the FBI had inputted 211 673 offender profiles and 11 112 forensic profiles. Most of the original DNA profiles result from RFLP markers. However, laboratories in the United States are now converting to the 13 core STR loci, and all future samples will be typed with these STRs.

In order for a state to have its DNA profiles included in the national DNA index system, a memorandum of understanding must be signed whereby the state DNA laboratories agree to adhere to FBI issued quality assurance standards. A complete DNA profile of four RFLP markers or the 13 core STR loci is required for submission of convicted offender information to the National DNA Index System. There must also be a minimum number of loci included in the casework DNA profile: at least three CODIS RFLP loci or 10 of the 13 CODIS STR loci before uploading the information to NDIS. The lower number of loci needed for casework DNA profiles comes from recognition that degraded DNA samples obtained from forensic cases may not yield results at every marker even though analysis is attempted with those DNA markers.

CJIS WAN

Public crime laboratories in the United States are connected via the FBI's Criminal Justice Information Services Wide Area Network (CJIS WAN) through T1 lines capable of transmitting 1.5 megabytes of information per second. CJIS

WAN provides internet-like connectivity but without the security risk. This network is an intranet with access only permitted to participating laboratories. The National DNA Index System computers are protected by firewalls to maintain a high degree of security. The hub of CJIS WAN is located in Clarksburg, West Virginia.

Each state pays for their end of the system. The computer equipment for a state system costs around $15 000–25 000. The FBI Laboratory provides the CODIS software and maintains the equipment for the national system. SDIS and LDIS laboratories sign memorandums of understandings with the FBI. CODIS users agree to adhere to FBI-issued quality assurance standards (see Appendix III) and to submit to NDIS audits.

CONVICTED OFFENDER SAMPLES VS. FORENSIC CASEWORK SAMPLES

For a criminal DNA database to be successful, both convicted offender DNA samples must be entered and crime scene material from cases where there is no suspect must be tested. Because the demand for DNA testing is surpassing the ability of public forensic laboratories to perform the tests, private contract laboratories are now being used to reduce the sample backlogs for convicted offender samples.

Private DNA typing laboratories can have a higher throughput capacity because the focus is on running samples rather than performing casework and testifying in court. In addition, all of the convicted offender samples are in the same format (i.e. liquid blood) which improves the capability for automating the DNA typing process. On the other hand, forensic cases can involve the examination of a dozen or more pieces of biological evidence from a variety of formats (e.g. semen stains, bloodstains, etc.), which makes them much more complex.

Since July 1998, the Virginia Department of Forensic Sciences DNA laboratory system has outsourced many of its convicted offender samples (Pederson 1999). By November 1999, the Bode Technology Group, a contract service laboratory located in Springfield, Virginia, had analyzed more than 100 000 samples. Convicted offender samples were analyzed at a rate of approximately 2000 samples per week (Pederson 1999). This rapid growth in the Virginia DNA database led directly to the hit that solved the rape case discussed in Chapter 1.

To ensure that analysis of convicted offender samples by contract laboratories is performed in a reliable fashion, the DNA Advisory Board issues guidelines for analysis of convicted offender samples. These guidelines became effective in April 1999. Appendix III contains a copy of the contract laboratory guidelines in a format that directly compares them with the guidelines for quality assurance of forensic casework samples.

IMPORTANT ISSUES FOR DNA DATABASES

There are a number of important issues for DNA databases. These issues include security of the information contained in them, the ability to perform rapid searches and effective matches from large numbers of entries, maintaining the quality of the inputted data, and handling changes in technology. Both computer and DNA technologies are constantly improving at a rapid rate. DNA databases have to be flexible enough to handle this change. Legacy data must be maintained or the value of the database will be diminished.

PRIVACY ISSUES

One of the major challenges for maintaining a DNA database is the issue of privacy and security of the information stored in the database. Blood samples contain genetic information that could be used against an individual or their family if not handled properly. The issue of privacy is approached in two ways. First, the DNA markers, such as the 13 CODIS core STR loci, are in non-coding regions of the DNA and are not known to have any association with a genetic disease or any other genetic predisposition. Thus, the information in the database is only useful for human identity testing.

Second, no names of individuals or other characterizing data is stored with the DNA profiles. The National DNA Index System of CODIS only references the sources of the DNA profiles, such as Orange County Sheriff's Office or Palm Beach County Crime Laboratory. Specific case data are secured and controlled by local law enforcement agencies (Spalding 1995). Thus, only the crime laboratory that submitted the DNA profile has the capability to link the DNA results with a known individual.

Another important facet to the privacy and security of the information in DNA databases is the fact that access to CODIS is solely for law enforcement purposes. There are strict penalties for anyone using the information or samples for any purpose other than law enforcement including a $100 000 fine for unauthorized disclosures of information on any sample (McEwen 1995).

MAINTAINING QUALITY CONTROL OF DATA

The old adage of 'garbage in, garbage out' applies with any database containing information that will be probed regularly. If the DNA profiles entered into a DNA database are not accurate, then they will be of little value for making a meaningful match. The high quality of data going into a DNA database is ensured by requiring laboratories to follow quality assurance guidelines

(Appendix III), to submit to audits of their procedures, and by conducting regular proficiency tests of analysts.

SEARCH AND MATCH ALGORITHMS

As DNA databases grow in size, they become more valuable as an intelligence tool, but they also become more of a challenge to search rapidly. In addition, because the STR kits used by the various manufacturers may have different primer binding regions for the same loci, null alleles could result with one primer set and not the other (Walsh 1998). This would result in an apparent discrepancy between results obtained with one STR kit versus another. Lower stringency search algorithms may be used to address this issue.

For example, the CODIS search algorithm and match criteria can be loosened on a search using 26 possible alleles from the 13 STRs by only requiring a match at 25 out of 26 possible alleles.

Differences in measurement capabilities of laboratories, particularly in their ability to detect microvariant (off-ladder) alleles, make it important to have allele equivalency capabilities in the search algorithm. Thus, a TH01 allele 8.3 measured in one laboratory can be matched with an allele 8.x or allele 9 measured in another laboratory.

SAMPLE COLLECTION FROM CONVICTED OFFENDERS

One of the facts about DNA databases that is not often considered is the sample collection process. Law enforcement personnel have to extract blood or obtain a saliva sample from incarcerated felons that are not always cooperative. In some cases, extraordinary efforts including force is required to persuade felons to submit to a blood draw (Spalding 1995). Collecting the actual samples can be a challenge considering the fact that the convicted offenders know that their blood or saliva could be used to catch them committing other crimes in the future or match them to previous unsolved crimes they committed.

WORKING UNKNOWN SUSPECT CASES

Crime laboratories must work cases that have no suspect in order to take full advantage of DNA databases. Convicted offender samples can be typed in large batches because large numbers come into the laboratory together and they are in the same format, such as liquid blood. Casework samples, on the other hand, present a different kind of challenge. Each case requires significant up-front work including evidence handling, locating DNA within the submitted evidence, and extraction of DNA from different types of substrates. Often sample mixtures must be dealt with and interpreted. Multiple pieces of evidence may also be involved in a case. In addition, significant work is required after analysis of the samples. Laboratory reports must be written and court testimony may be required.

In spite of the time and effort required to obtain results on crime scene samples, it is working these cases that make DNA databases effective. Law enforcement agencies must be encouraged to collect and submit evidence to the nation's crime laboratories. In some cases, thousands of rape kits are sitting in police evidence rooms that are not submitted to crime laboratories.

MEASURING THE SUCCESS OF A DATABASE

The purpose of DNA databases is to solve crimes that would otherwise be unsolvable. A common method of measuring the effectiveness of CODIS or any other DNA database is in what is referred to as a 'hit'. A hit is a confirmed match between two or more DNA profiles discovered by the database search. Within CODIS, hits may occur at a local (LDIS), state (SDIS), or national (NDIS) level.

Hits fall into two different categories. A forensic hit occurs when two or more forensic casework samples are linked at LDIS, SDIS, or NDIS. These types of hits are sometimes called case-to-case hits and are especially important to solving serial crimes. An offender hit occurs when one or more forensic samples are linked to a convicted offender sample. These types of hits are sometimes referred to as case-to-offender hits. Either type of hit contributes to the bottom-line performance metric of a DNA database – the number of criminal investigations aided.

DNA DATABASE LAWS

DNA databases work because most criminals are repeat offenders (McEwen and Reilly 1994). If their DNA profile can be entered into the system early in their criminal career, then they can be identified when future crimes are committed. Serial crimes can also be linked effectively with a computer database. Ultimately, the value of the DNA database is in its ability to apprehend criminals that are not direct suspects in a case and to prevent further victims from crimes committed by those individuals.

CRIMES FOR INCLUSION IN A STATE DNA DATABASE

As of June 1998, all 50 states in the United States had passed legislation requiring convicted offenders to provide samples for DNA databasing. However, each state has different requirements as to what types of offenses are considered for DNA sample collection. The requirements for having to donate a blood sample range from all felons to strictly sex offenses. The trend is for laws that require a DNA sample submission for any felony crime. Table 16.2 includes a summary list of the qualifying offenses for entry into a state's DNA database and the number of states within the United States that fall into each category as of late 1999.

Table 16.2

US state DNA database laws and qualifying offenses for DNA collection (Herkenham 1999).

Offenses	Number of States
Sex offenses	50
Offenses against children	41
Murder	36
Assault and battery	27
Attempts	25
Juveniles	24
Kidnapping	22
Robbery	20
Burglary	14
All Felonies	5

Some state DNA database statutes specify exactly how the sample will be taken while others simply require any biological sample containing DNA. California, for example, requires two specimens of blood, a saliva sample and right thumb and full palm print impression for verifying identity of the submitting convicted offender (Herkenham 1999). The law for South Carolina, on the other hand, asks only for a suitable sample from which DNA may be obtained.

The ability of state and local forensic DNA laboratories to improve their capabilities for DNA analysis, especially with the STR technology described in this book, has been greatly aided by federal funding. The DNA Identification Act of 1994 provided approximately $40 million in federal matching grants to aid states in DNA analysis activities. This funding has been a great benefit to forensic DNA laboratories, which are typically understaffed and underfunded. While a convicted offender backlog of several hundred thousand samples exists in the United States as of early 2000, efforts are underway to alleviate this sample backlog within the next few years.

NATIONAL DNA DATABASES AROUND THE WORLD

National DNA databases are being used in many countries around the world. The same STR markers are being used in many instances. This fact will permit international collaboration on cases that warrant them. The pioneering national DNA database was formed in April 1995 in the United Kingdom. Since the debut of this database, more than 500 000 convicted felon DNA profiles have been processed by the United Kingdom's Forensic Science Service

(Werrett and Sparkes 1998). Their original database involved six STR loci and the amelogenin gender identification marker with a random match probability of approximately 1 in 50 million. In 1999, the set of STR markers was expanded with the availability of the AmpFlSTR® SGM Plus™ kit to include ten STRs and amelogenin with a random match probability of approximately 1 in 3 trillion (see Chapter 5). The United Kingdom database has been used to solve more than 50 000 crimes and has definitely demonstrated its value as an important tool for law enforcement.

REFERENCES

Budowle, B. and Moretti, T.R. (1998) *Proceedings of the Ninth International Symposium on Human Identification.* Madison, WI: Promega Corporation, pp. 64–73.

Budowle, B., Moretti, T.R., Niezgoda, S.J. and Brown, B.L. (1998) *Proceedings of the Second European Symposium on Human Identification.* Madison, WI: Promega Corporation, pp. 73–88.

Coffman, D. (1998) *Proceedings of the Ninth International Symposium on Human Identification.* Madison, WI: Promega Corporation, p. 63.

Herkenham, M.D. (1999) *State DNA Database Statues: Summary of Provisions.* US Department of Justice.

McEwen, J.E. (1995) *American Journal of Human Genetics*, 56, 1487–1492.

McEwen, J.E. and Reilly, P.R. (1994) *American Journal of Human Genetics*, 54, 941–958.

Niezgoda, S.J. (1997) *Proceedings of the Eighth International Symposium on Human Identification.* Madison, WI: Promega Corporation, pp. 48–49.

Niezgoda, S.J. and Brown, B. (1995) *Proceedings of the Sixth International Symposium on Human Identification.* Madison, WI: Promega Corporation, pp. 149–153.

Pederson, J. (1999) *Profiles in DNA* (Promega Corporation) 3, 3–7 .

Scheck, B. (1994) *American Journal of Human Genetics*, 54, 931–933.

Spalding, V.B. (1995) *Proceedings of the Sixth International Symposium on Human Identification.* Madison, WI: Promega Corporation, pp. 137–148.

Walsh, P.S. (1998) *Journal of Forensic Science*, 43, 1103–1104.

Werrett, D.J. and Sparkes, R. (1998) *Proceedings of the Ninth International Symposium on Human Identification.* Madison, WI: Promega Corporation, pp. 55–62.

BIOLOGY, TECHNOLOGY
AND GENETICS

CHAPTER 17

DNA TESTING IN HIGH-PROFILE CASES

DNA typing procedures have been routinely performed in public and private laboratories for the past decade. However, the vast majority of the general public was not widely exposed to the power of DNA information until the O.J. Simpson case, which began in 1994. This final chapter will review the DNA evidence in a number of high-profile cases that involved the use of DNA markers and technology described in this book. The facts of each situation will be described in the context of the biology, technology, and genetics for the forensic DNA typing involved. In some of the cases, even our perceptions of history have been changed by DNA evidence.

Each of the cases that will be reviewed in this chapter illustrates important concepts that can benefit the reader's understanding of the entire process of forensic DNA testing. From the O.J. Simpson case, we see the importance of proper evidence collection and sample preservation as well as careful handling in the laboratory to prevent the possibility of any contamination. The DNA evidence in the cases of the Romanovs (the last Russian Tsar and his family), the Unknown Soldier, and Thomas Jefferson all helped change our perception of history. The Romanovs and the Unknown Soldier involved the use of mitochondrial DNA sequence matches from bone fragments while the Thomas Jefferson case utilized newly available Y chromosome markers to track paternal lineages over a 200-year period through living relatives.

We have also chosen to highlight two mass disasters where STR typing proved to be a valuable means for identifying human remains. In these cases, STR typing was successfully performed in spite of heavy damage inflicted by a high-temperature fire (Branch Davidian compound in Waco, Texas, April 1993) or severe water damage (airplane crash of Swissair Flight 111 near Nova Scotia, September 1998).

CRIMINAL INVESTIGATIONS

O.J. SIMPSON AND DNA EVIDENCE IN THE 'TRIAL OF THE CENTURY'

On the night of 12 June 1994, Nicole Brown Simpson and Ronald Goldman were found brutally murdered at Nicole's home. A few days later Nicole's ex-husband, Orenthal James (O.J.) Simpson, was picked up by Los Angeles police officers and became the chief suspect in the murder investigation. Owing to O.J. Simpson's successful football career and popularity, the case immediately drew the public's attention. Over 100 pieces of biological evidence were gathered from the crime scene consisting primarily of blood droplets and stains. DNA samples were sent to three laboratories for testing. Over the summer months of 1994, the Los Angeles Police Department (LAPD) DNA Laboratory, the California Department of Justice (CA DOJ) DNA Laboratory in Berkeley, and a private contract laboratory from Maryland named Cellmark Diagnostics performed the DNA testing using both restriction fragment length polymorphism (RFLP) and polymerase chain reaction (PCR) techniques. A list of the RFLP and PCR markers examined in this high-profile case is contained in Table 17.1 [no short tandem repeats (STRs) were examined].

The so-called 'Trial of the Century', *People of the State of California v. Orenthal James Simpson*, began in the fall of 1994. O.J. Simpson hired a legal 'dream team', which worked hard to acquit their client. O.J.'s defense team knew that the DNA evidence was the most powerful thing going against the football star and vigorously attacked the collection of the biological material from the crime scene. Through accusations of improper sample collection and handling as well as police conspiracies and laboratory contamination, the defense team managed to introduce a degree of 'reasonable doubt'. After a lengthy and exhausting trial, the jury acquitted O.J. Simpson on 3 October 1995.

There were seven sets of bloodstains collected by the LAPD and analyzed by the three DNA laboratories mentioned above. These sets of samples are reviewed in Table 17.2 along with the challenges put forward by the defense

Table 17.1

DNA markers examined in the O.J. Simpson case by the three forensic laboratories involved in the case (Weir 1995). The arrows show corresponding markers that were used by the different laboratories. There was complete agreement with results between the laboratories. No STR markers were examined by any of the laboratories as this case occurred prior to the routine use of STRs in the United States.

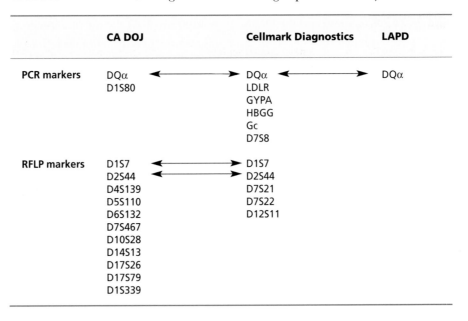

	CA DOJ	Cellmark Diagnostics	LAPD
PCR markers	DQα ⟷	DQα ⟷	DQα
	D1S80	LDLR	
		GYPA	
		HBGG	
		Gc	
		D7S8	
RFLP markers	D1S7 ⟷	D1S7	
	D2S44 ⟷	D2S44	
	D4S139	D7S21	
	D5S110	D7S22	
	D6S132	D12S11	
	D7S467		
	D10S28		
	D14S13		
	D17S26		
	D17S79		
	D1S339		

team. For each sample, the statistics for the odds of a random match ranged from 1 in 40 when only PCR testing with the DQ-alpha marker was evaluated to more than 1 in 40 billion when all RFLP markers were examined.

To gain a better understanding of the magnitude of the DNA testing conducted in the O.J. Simpson case, 61 items of evidence were received by CA DOJ from LAPD (Sims *et al.* 1995). From these evidence items, 108 samples were extracted in 22 sets and tested alongside 21 quality control samples that were co-extracted and 24 extraction reagent blanks. These extraction reagent blanks were performed to verify that no contamination was introduced in the CA DOJ laboratory.

The acquittal verdict goes to show that DNA evidence is not always understood and can be quite complex to explain to the general public. Expert witnesses have the challenge of presenting the difficult subjects of DNA biology, technology, and genetics and jury members must make sense of concepts such as contamination and mixture analysis that can be fairly complex. From a scientific point of view, the results from the three testing laboratories agreed and more than a score of DNA markers were examined with no exclusions between the crime scene samples and Mr Simpson.

Table 17.2

Summary of the DNA evidence in the O.J. Simpson trial (Levy 1996).

Samples/Location (Date collected)	Number of Samples Collected	DNA Match	Defense Challenge
Blood drops at Nicole Brown's home (June 13)	5 drops leading away from house	Simpson	Heavy degradation of the "real" killer's DNA; tampering with evidence "swatches"; sample contamination during laboratory investigation
Stains on rear gate at Brown's home (July 3)	3 stains	Simpson	Samples planted by rogue police officers prior to collection
Stains in O.J.'s Bronco (June 14)	5 stains around vehicle; bloody footprint; stain on center console	Simpson in 5 stains; Brown in footprint; Simpson/Goldman mixture on console	Simpson's DNA present for reasons unrelated to the crime; Detective Mark Fuhrman planted the blood footprint; Laboratory controls failed on console mixture analysis
Second collection of stains in O.J.'s Bronco (August 26)	3 stains	Mixture of Simpson, Brown, and Goldman	Blood planted in the vehicle between the crime and the collection
Stains at Simpson's home (June 13)	2 drops in driveway, 1 in foyer, 1 in master bedroom	Simpson	Simpson bled at these locations for reasons unrelated to the crime
Socks found in Simpson's bedroom (June 13)	Multiple stains	Simpson and Brown	Blood planted after the socks were collected
Bloody glove found on the grounds of Simpson's home (June 13)	15 stains identified	Goldman, Simpson, and Brown alone or as mixture	Glove was removed from murder scene and planted by Detective Mark Fuhrman; Simpson's DNA was present because of laboratory contamination

To their credit, the defense team focused on the evidence collection and preservation as the most important issues in the trial rather than attacking the validity of DNA testing. They implicated the LAPD in planting some of O.J. Simpson's liquid blood reference sample collected on June 13th – the day after the murders took place. Furthermore, the defense attacked the manner in which the evidence was handled in the LAPD DNA laboratory and alleged that contamination of the evidence samples by O.J.'s reference blood sample resulted from sloppy work and failure to maintain sterile conditions in the laboratory.

The contamination allegation became the focus of their arguments because much of the evidence had been handled, opened, and supposedly contaminated in the LAPD laboratory before it was packed up and sent to other laboratories for further testing. Thus, according to the defense, no matter how carefully the samples were handled by the CA DOJ DNA Laboratory or Cellmark Diagnostics, their testing results would not reflect the actual evidence from the crime scene. Since the samples were supposedly tainted by the LAPD laboratory, the defense argued that the evidence should not be considered conclusive. However, the sheer number of DNA samples that typed to O.J. makes it hard to believe that some random laboratory error made it possible to obtain such overwhelming incriminating results.

BENEFITS FROM THE O.J. SIMPSON TRIAL

Since the conclusion of the O.J. Simpson trial in 1995, forensic DNA laboratories have improved their vigilance in conducting DNA evidence collection and performing the testing in a manner that is above reproach. Because PCR is an extremely sensitive technology, laboratories practicing the technique need to take extraordinary measures to prevent contamination in the laboratory. Hence, the value of laboratory accreditation and routine proficiency tests to verify that a laboratory is conducting its investigations in a proper and professional manner (see Chapter 14).

The issuance of the DNA Advisory Board (DAB) Quality Assurance Standards (see Appendix III) has helped raise the professional status of forensic DNA testing. It is noteworthy that, in a systematic analysis of circumstances normally encountered during casework, no PCR contamination was ever noted according to a recent study (Scherczinger *et al.* 1999). Significant contamination occurred only with gross deviations from basic preventative protocols, such as those outlined in the DAB Guidelines, and could not be generated by simple acts of carelessness.

In addition to the direct DNA work conducted for the O.J. Simpson case, bloodstain samples were examined to see if EDTA, a blood preservative, could be detected. EDTA is a common preservative customarily added to blood collection tubes to prevent clotting of reference samples drawn from suspects of violent crimes. Therefore its presence in a bloodstain from a crime scene would be an indication of evidence tampering or planting. No EDTA was found in the collected crime scene samples in the O.J. Simpson case. This analysis was made possible through new analytical methods involving the use of liquid chromatography/mass spectrometry developed at the Federal Bureau of Investigation (FBI) Laboratory to detect low levels of EDTA in dried bloodstains (Miller *et al.* 1997).

While it is certainly an advantage to have new techniques at the disposal of forensic scientists, such as those developed to determine low levels of EDTA, arguably the most important outcome of the O.J. Simpson trial was the renewed emphasis placed on DNA evidence collection.

THE BLUE DRESS AND THE CLINTON–LEWINSKY AFFAIR

This next section highlights how a simple DNA test can impact on world events. In 1998, independent counsel Kenneth Starr was investigating allegations that US President William Jefferson Clinton had a sexual relationship with a young White House intern, Monica Lewinsky. President Clinton had publicly denied the allegations quite emphatically and at that time there was no concrete evidence to the contrary.

During the course of the investigation, a dark blue dress belonging to Monica Lewinsky was brought to the FBI Laboratory for examination. Semen was identified on evidence item Q3243, as the dress was cataloged. The unknown semen stain was quickly examined with seven RFLP single locus probes. Late on the evening of 3 August 1998, a reference blood sample was drawn from President Clinton for comparison purposes (Woodward 1999).

As in the O.J. Simpson case, conventional RFLP markers were used to match the sample of President Clinton's blood to the semen stain on Monica Lewinski's dress. At the time these samples were run in the FBI Laboratory (early August 1998), STR typing methods were being validated but were not yet in routine use within the FBI's DNA Analysis Unit. High molecular weight DNA from the semen stain (FBI specimen Q3243-1) and President Clinton's blood (FBI specimen K39) was digested with the restriction enzyme *Hae*III. A seven-probe match was obtained at the RFLP loci D2S44, D17S79, D1S7, D4S139, D10S28, D5S110, and D7S467.

This match was reported in the following manner: 'Based on the results of these seven genetic loci, specimen K39 (CLINTON) is the source of the DNA obtained from specimen Q3243-1, to a reasonable degree of scientific certainty' (Grunwald and Adler 1999). The random match probability was calculated to be on the order of 1 in 7.8 trillion when compared to a Caucasian population database.

When faced with this indisputable DNA evidence, President Clinton recanted his earlier statements that he had not had 'sexual relations' with Miss Lewinsky. The DNA results along with other evidence and testimony resulted in the impeachment of President Clinton on 19 December 1998. This physical evidence played an important role in demonstrating that a sexual relationship had existed between Miss Lewinsky and William Jefferson Clinton, the President of the United States. Although he was later acquitted during the Senate impeachment trial and completed his second term in office, President Clinton's career will always be tainted by the semen stain on the blue dress.

HISTORICAL INVESTIGATIONS

The ability of DNA technology to be a silent witness from the grave has greatly aided several important historical investigations in the past decade. In the next two sections, we will examine how unknown human remains came to be identified by comparison to living relatives. In particular, the maternal inheritance characteristic of mitochondrial DNA (see Chapter 8) was used to identify the remains of the Romanovs, the last Russian royal family, as well as some of the remains resting in the Tomb of the Unknown Soldier at Arlington National Cemetery.

IDENTIFYING THE REMAINS OF THE LAST RUSSIAN CZAR

Russian Czar (or Tsar) Nicholas II and his family were removed from power and murdered during the Bolshevik revolution of 1918. They were shot by a firing squad, doused with sulfuric acid to render their bodies unrecognizable, and disposed of in a shallow pit under a road. Their remains were lost to history until July 1991 when nine skeletons were uncovered from a shallow grave near Ekaterinburg, Russia. A number of forensic tests were attempted involving computer-aided reconstructions and odontological analysis, but as the facial areas of the skulls were destroyed, classical facial identification techniques were difficult at best and not conclusive.

The Chief Forensic Medical Examiner of the Russian Federation turned to the Forensic Science Service in the United Kingdom to carry out DNA-based analysis of the remains for purposes of identification. Five STR markers (VWA, TH01, F13A1, FES/FPS, and ACTBP2) were used to examine the nine skeletons. Approximately 1 g of bone from each of the skeletons yielded about 50 pg of DNA, just enough for PCR amplification of several STR markers. As can be seen in Figure 17.1, the remains of the Romanov family members consisting

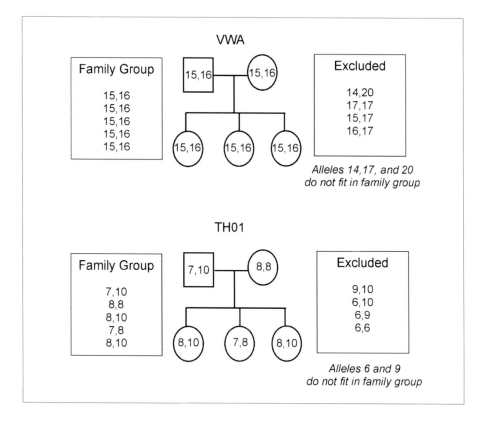

Figure 17.1

Grouping of STR genotypes from nine skeletons uncovered at the Romanov grave. The genotypes obtained from the nine samples at the STR loci VWA and TH01 are depicted here (see Gill et al. 1994). Similar genotypes are combined as a 'family group' while those that differ are listed in an 'excluded' group. A postulated pedigree is shown in the middle for each locus to demonstrate that the children have alleles that are inherited from their parents. The 'excluded' group includes three servants and a family doctor who were massacred with the Romanov family. Sex typing of the samples using the amelogenin assay identified four males and five females. The Romanov's son Alexei and one of their daughters (possibly Anastasia) were missing from the grave.

of the Tsar, the Tsarina, and three children were distinguishable from those of three servants and the family doctor by their STR genotypes.

While the STR analysis served to establish family relationships between the remains through comparing matching alleles, a link still had to be made with a known descendant of the Romanov family to verify that the remains were indeed those of the Russian royal family. Mitochondrial DNA analysis was used to answer this question.

Mitochondrial DNA (mtDNA) was extracted from the femur of each skeleton and sequenced. Blood samples were then obtained from maternally related descendants of the Romanov family and sequenced in the same manner. His Royal Highness Prince Philip, Duke of Edinburgh and husband of the present British Queen Elizabeth, is a grand nephew of unbroken maternal descent from Tsarina Alexandra (Figure 17.2). His blood sample thus provided the comparison to confirm the sibling status of the children and the linkage of the mother to the Tsarina's family. The sequences of all 740 tested nucleotides from the mtDNA control region matched between HRH Prince Philip and the putative Tsarina and the three children.

The mtDNA sequence from the putative Tsar was compared with two relatives of unbroken maternal descent from Tsar Nicholas II's grandmother, Louise of

Figure 17.2

Lineage of the Romanov family. The individuals represented by blue are maternal relatives of the Tsarina Alexandra while those shown in red are maternal relatives of Tsar Nicholas II. Living maternal relatives Prince Philip (for Tsarina) and Xenia Cheremeteff-Sfiri (for Tsar) served as family reference samples. The mtDNA mitotype for each reference sample is listed with the nucleotide changes relative to their position in the Anderson sequence. Tsar Nicholas II and his brother Georgij Romanov both exhibited a heteroplasmic T/C at mtDNA position 16169, which differed from the homoplasmic T found in Xenia Cheremeteff-Sfiri (Ivanov et al. 1996). Prince Philip's mitotype matched the remains of the Tsarina and her children while Xenia's mitotype matched the remains of the Tsar at all positions except the heteroplasmic position 16169 (Gill et al. 1994).

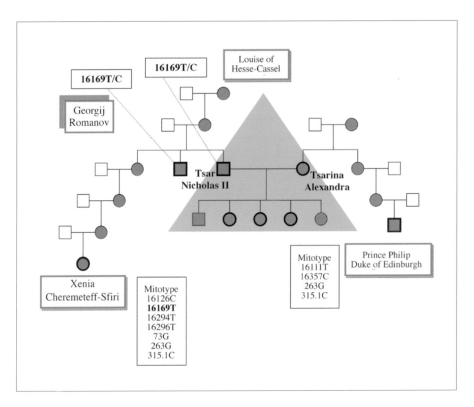

Hesse-Cassel. The two relatives had the same mtDNA sequence as the putative Tsar with the exception of a single nucleotide at position 16169. At this position, the putative Tsar's sample had a mixture of two nucleotides (T and C), a condition known as heteroplasmy (see Chapter 8), while the blood samples of relatives had only a T nucleotide.

To further confirm the putative Tsar's remains, the brother of Nicholas II, Grand Duke of Russia Georgij Romanov, was exhumed and tested by the Armed Forces DNA Identification Laboratory (Ivanov *et al.* 1996). Heteroplasmy was found again at the identical nucleotide site within the mtDNA sequence. Owing to the extreme rarity of this heteroplasmy happening by chance between two unrelated individuals, the remains of Tsar Nicholas II and his family were declared authentic and laid to rest in Red Square with a funeral fit for a royal family.

ANNA ANDERSON: WAS SHE THE MISSING ANASTASIA?

A separate chapter of the Romanov story was addressed at about this same time again using DNA evidence. The fact that at least one of the children was missing from the gravesite has for years fueled the fire of mystery around the missing daughter Anastasia. Among the people that have come forward claiming to be

Anastasia, a lady named Anna Anderson Manahan, who resided for many years in Charlottesville, Virginia, had perhaps the most convincing story.

In order to test a DNA sample from Mrs Manahan, who had died and been cremated in 1984, a 20-year-old paraffin-imbedded tissue sample was obtained from a hospital in Charlottesville where it had been stored since a biopsy was taken some time earlier. Her STR and mtDNA sequence profiles were compared with the Romanov DNA results and failed to match (Gill *et al.* 1995). Thus, the claim of Anna Anderson was put to rest but the historical mystery surrounding the missing daughter Anastasia remains unsolved.

IDENTIFYING REMAINS FROM THE TOMB OF THE UNKNOWN SOLDIER

On 30 June 1998, US Secretary of Defense William Cohen announced to the world that DNA technology had been used to identify the Vietnam Unknown in the Tomb of the Unknown Soldier located in Arlington National Cemetery. The remains of First Lieutenant Michael J. Blassie, United States Air Force, were identified through the use of mtDNA. An exact match across 610 nucleotides of the polymorphic mtDNA control region was obtained between Jean Blassie, Michael's mother, and a sample extracted from the bone fragments removed from the Tomb of the Unknown Soldier (Holland and Parsons 1999). At the same time, eight other possible soldiers were excluded because family reference samples did not match.

Michael Blassie was an Air Force Academy graduate and the oldest of five children who grew up in St Louis, Missouri. Lieutenant Blassie arrived in Vietnam in January 1972 and was flying his 132nd mission when his A-37B attack jet was shot down on 11 May 1972, outside An Loc, a hotly contested South Vietnamese village near the Cambodian border. Intense fighting in the area prevented the site from being searched and his remains were not recovered until almost 5 months later. By this time only four ribs, the right humerus and part of the pelvis remained along with some personal items, including Blassie's identification card. The remains were sent to the Army's Central Identification Laboratory in Hawaii where they remained for 8 years designated as 'believed to be Michael Blassie'. In 1980, a military review board changed the designation on the remains to 'unknown' and the identification card found with the body had vanished.

The Tomb of the Unknown Soldier was first opened in 1921 to honor soldiers who had died in World War I. On the tomb are inscribed the words 'Here rests in honored glory an American soldier known but to God'. Within this hallowed ground lie four servicemen, the unknown soldiers of World War I, World War II, the Korean War and the Vietnam War. These unknown soldiers are guarded 24 hours a day at Arlington National Cemetery by a sentinel from the 3rd US

Infantry. The World War II and Korean War unknowns were selected from about 8500 and 800 unidentifiable remains, respectively, and were entombed on Memorial Day 1958. The Vietnam War casualty was authorized in 1973 for enshrinement, but it was not filled for 11 more years. To honor a Vietnam veteran on Memorial Day 1984, one of the few available unknown remains was selected for enshrinement and honored in a ceremony led by President Ronald Reagan. There the remains of the Vietnam Unknown lay until 14 May 1998, when they were disinterred in a solemn ceremony and transported to the Armed Forces Institute of Pathology for investigation. So sacred is the tomb and the memory of the soldiers resting there, that it has only been opened four times: in 1921 for World War I, in 1958 for World War II and Korean, in 1984 for Vietnam, and in 1998 to remove the Vietnam remains for DNA testing.

Throughout the month of June 1998, mtDNA sequence information was recovered from the skeletal material (pelvis) and analyzed by scientists at the Armed Forces DNA Identification Laboratory (AFDIL) located in Rockville, Maryland. Maternal relatives from eight possible American casualties near An Loc were also evaluated as family reference samples. The mtDNA sequence content from positions 16024–16365 (HVI) and positions 73–340 (HVII) on the polymorphic control region were evaluated. Only a complete match was observed between Jean Blassie (Michael's mother) and the skeletal remains disinterred from the Tomb of the Unknown Soldier. Because of this positive identification, the Blassies were permitted to bury Lieutenant Blassie's remains at Jefferson Barracks National Cemetery located in St Louis, Missouri. This ceremony was conducted on 11 July 1998, and brought closure to the Blassie family.

MEASURES TO PREVENT ANY MORE UNKNOWN AMERICAN SOLDIERS

The United States Armed Forces is currently making an effort to prevent there ever being another 'unknown soldier' from wartime casualties. Today, reference bloodstains are collected from every soldier that enters the US Armed Forces. A repository of over 2.5 million samples now exists in Gaithersburg, Maryland. In the event of a casualty where dental records or fingerprints cannot be used to identify the individual, then DNA testing on the remains can be compared to the reference bloodstain for the soldier or group of soldiers in question.

MASS DISASTER INVESTIGATIONS

In addition to identifying wartime casualties, DNA testing is used for disaster victim identification in the event of a mass disaster such as a plane crash or a fire. Often these types of mass disasters leave human remains that are literally in pieces. Body parts can be separated from one another and the remains commingled, making identification without DNA techniques virtually impossible. DNA testing can identify each portion of the remains, provided that there is a surviving family member to contribute a reference sample for comparison purposes. Reference samples can also be obtained from biological material left on personal items of the deceased, such as a toothbrush, comb, or razor.

WACO BRANCH DAVIDIAN FIRE

On 19 April 1993, the Mount Carmel Branch Davidian compound in Waco, Texas, burned during a raid by FBI agents. Over 80 individuals died, and their remains were severely damaged following a high-temperature fire. While approximately half of these individuals could be identified by dental or fingerprint comparison and anthropological and pathological findings, the rest had to be identified based on information that could only be provided by DNA analysis. This was the first mass disaster investigation where DNA analysis with STR markers was used.

The Armed Forces DNA Identification Laboratory (AFDIL) and the Forensic Science Service Laboratory in England (FSS) analyzed these samples by examining a variety of DNA markers including HLA DQ alpha, AmpliType PM, D1S80, amelogenin sex-typing, mitochondrial DNA sequencing, and four STR loci (TH01, F13A1, FES/FPS, VWA). Without the use of PCR-based DNA typing procedures, specifically STR markers, approximately half of the individuals who perished in the Mount Carmel Compound of Branch Davidians would not have been identified.

AFDIL received 242 samples from the Mount Carmel Branch Davidian compound representing 82 sets of human remains (DiZinno *et al.* 1994). Blood-stained cards from living relatives were also tested to serve as reference samples for the unknowns. From the badly burned bodies, usable tissue was often not available, in which case portions of rib bones were removed and the DNA extracted.

Body identifications were made by matching observed sample genotypes with predicted possible genotypes obtained from using results of relatives' reference blood samples and information gathered from family trees. This approach is basically a reverse paternity analysis where the parent genotypes are used to predict the child's genotype. A total of 26 positive identifications were made using the family tree matching approach (Clayton *et al.* 1995). A shortage of relatives prevented the identification of the other bodies. These results highlight the need for reference samples in order to take full advantage of DNA testing in mass disaster situations.

SWISSAIR FLIGHT 111

On the evening of 2 September 1998, while *en route* to Geneva, Switzerland, from New York City, Swissair Flight 111 crashed into the Atlantic Ocean not far from Halifax, Nova Scotia. All 229 people on board (214 passengers and 15 crew members) were killed. The plane went down about 10 km from land, requiring the wreckage to be raised from a depth of more than 60 m (~180 feet) of water.

Over the next few weeks, a large task force of investigators collected human remains from the crash scene. These remains were carefully collected and subsequently identified for two important reasons. First, without a reason for the plane falling from the sky, criminal activity was a possibility. The plane's manifest listed 229 people on board. But were they all who they claimed to be? Any discrepancy from that number could be a sign of terrorist activity. A missing individual or an extra passenger that could not be accounted for might have been a terrorist with a bomb.

The second important reason for identifying the victims of any mass disaster is to bring closure to the living relatives. If the remains of their loved ones can be identified, then something can be given back to the living relatives for burial and memorial purposes. However, one of the challenges for identifying the remains of airline crashes is that often entire families travel together. In this case, closely related individuals have to be distinguished from each other and sometimes without the benefit of a living relative to act as a reference sample.

In the case of the 229 victims of the Swissair Flight 111 tragedy, a number of methods were used to identify the victims. These methods included fingerprints, dental records, X-ray evaluation, and DNA testing. Only one body was intact enough for visual identification. DNA testing played an important role in this investigation because of the lack of fingerprint and dental records on many of the victims.

A total of 147 victims could be identified by means other than DNA. For example, 1020 fingers were recovered from the crash site. However, these fingers allowed only 43 victims to be identified based on their fingerprints because only a small percentage of the victims had fingerprint records that could be located. Police visited the homes of the victims and tried to recover latent fingerprints from objects that they may have handled. These efforts led to the recovery of over 200 latent prints that were used to identify 33 of 43 victims mentioned above. An effective method of initial identification involved dental records, which were used to positively identify 102 of the victims and enable a certificate of death to be issued. Dental comparisons provided the fastest identification when reference samples were available. However, DNA analysis was the most effective method of identification overall, especially when crash scene victims were not intact.

Concurrent to other efforts to identify the crash victims, DNA testing was performed by the Royal Canadian Mounted Police (RCMP). DNA analysis was performed by four RCMP laboratories from across Canada and the Ontario Provincial forensic laboratory, each contributing a vital and specific subset of data. The DNA identification process was coordinated by the DNA Methods and Database Section in Ottawa. This team of more than 50 DNA scientists consisted of members of the Biology sections of the RCMP Forensic Laboratories located in Halifax, Regina, Vancouver and Ottawa and the Centre for Forensic Sciences in Toronto. DNA typing with the STR markers described in this book was used to help identify all 229 people on board Swissair Flight 111. In every case where other forms of identification were performed, DNA analysis helped confirm and support those results.

Two separate identification issues were addressed by DNA testing. First, recovered human remains showing identical STR genotypes were associated, and second, each passenger was identified through comparisons of human remains with the reference samples isolated from personal effects of the victims or reference blood samples submitted by relatives of the victims. In many cases, DNA analysis was the only means by which the samples could be positively identified.

Over 2400 human remains were recovered from the crash site of which 1277 were analyzed by DNA testing. These samples were analyzed along with 310 reference samples from relatives that were submitted on FTA paper blood cards (see Chapter 3) to be genotyped and used in a relational database (Figure 17.3). In addition, 89 personal effects, such as toothbrushes and hair from combs were taken from the homes of 47 victims because no relatives were available to serve as a reference. One of the challenges of collecting the reference samples was the fact that the living relatives were from 21 different countries. The FTA kit enabled rapid blood collection and room temperature delivery of the reference samples, and aided the successful completion of the investigation.

The AmpFlSTR® Profiler Plus™ STR markers D3S1358, VWA, FGA, D8S1179, D21S11, D18S51, D5S818, D13S317, and D7S820 were the primary means of identifying the remains, although additional STR loci TH01, TPOX, CSF1PO, and D16S539 from the AmpFlSTR® COfiler™ kit were used to gain a higher power of discrimination (Fregeau *et al.* 1999). COfiler amplifications were performed on 118 crash scene remains and 129 'known' reference comparison samples. The crash scene samples were analyzed in approximately 1 week using either the 9 STRs from Profiler Plus™ or all 13 STRs from Profiler Plus™ and COfiler™. The challenge of making appropriate associations between the samples took a little longer. Genotypes of all 229 victims were compared to genotypes of all other victims and family relatives, which represented 71 490

Figure 17.3

Strategy for disaster victim identification in the Swissair Flight 111 crash scene investigation. Most samples were tested with nine STRs and amelogenin using the AmpFlSTR® Profiler Plus™ kit and then four additional STRs were added with the COfiler™ kit as needed to obtain a higher power of discrimination between closely related individuals. The relational database compared genotypes of 1277 crash scene samples to genotypes of all 229 victims and family relatives, a total of 71 490 genotype comparisons (Leclair et al. 1999).

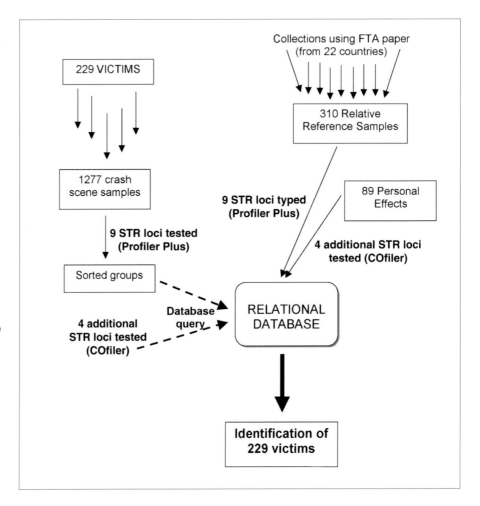

genotype comparisons (Leclair *et al.* 1999). The comparison of reference sample genotypes to questions involved over 180 000 comparisons because more known sample genotypes existed for cross-comparison purposes.

Traditional parentage trios with both living parents were encountered for only 25% of the 229 victims. Even more challenging was the fact that 43 families of 2–5 individuals were present among the victims. A pair of identical twins was also present on the plane and could not be individually identified with DNA testing. Nevertheless, the DNA testing led to confident kinship analysis in the case of 218 victims for whom reference samples from close relatives or personal effects were submitted (Leclair *et al.* 1999).

The efforts of the RCMP demonstrated a successful model for how a mass disaster investigation should be conducted. Tremendous cooperation is required from forensic laboratories, law enforcement personnel and family members of victims, often from a number of countries, in order to identify the victims of mass disasters successfully. The need for readily available reference samples was also highlighted by this investigation. In fact, a formal recommendation was made from the RCMP to the Canadian Transport Safety Board for all airline personnel and any private citizens who are frequent fliers to have fingerprints and DNA samples made available for identification purposes if ever the need arises. These records cannot be stored by the police but rather could be maintained by the airline or stored in an individual's safety deposit box. Of the 229 victims of Swissair Flight 111, all 229 were positively identified, an astounding success compared to previously used conventional identification techniques and one that would not have been possible without the power of DNA typing with STR markers.

THE THOMAS JEFFERSON–SALLY HEMINGS AFFAIR

The final section of this chapter examines the use of Y-chromosome information to discern historical clues about the connection between President Thomas Jefferson and his slave, Sally Hemings. This case demonstrates the power of DNA information in historical investigations due to the fact that the DNA in our cells holds clues about our ancestors.

In 1802, a year after becoming President of the United States, Thomas Jefferson was publicly accused by a Richmond, Virginia, newspaper of fathering a child by his slave, Sally Hemings. While it is uncertain how this accusation arose, the connection between Thomas Jefferson and his slave Sally Hemings has been a source of controversy for almost 200 years.

Then, in November 1998, the prestigious scientific journal *Nature* published a report that introduced DNA evidence into this historical controversy (Foster *et al.* 1998). The report entitled 'Jefferson fathered slave's last child' used Y-chromosome DNA markers to trace the Jefferson male line to a descendant of Sally Hemings's youngest son, Eston Hemings. The study involved 19 samples collected from living individuals who represented the Jefferson and Hemings line as well as other people who potentially could have been Jefferson's offspring or the father of Eston Hemings. These samples were tested at 19 different sites on the Y chromosome.

TRACKING DOWN LIVING RELATIVES

The study began in 1996 when Dr Eugene Foster, a retired pathology professor, began tracking down living male-line relatives of President Thomas Jefferson. In order to show whether or not President Jefferson had fathered a child with Sally Hemings, direct male descendants were needed from both the Jefferson and the Hemings lines. Unfortunately, Jefferson's only legitimate son died in infancy. His two daughters who lived to adulthood obviously did not carry his Y chromosome and therefore their descendants were not useful in this study. There were two other possibilities for direct male-line descendants, Thomas Jefferson's brother Randolph and his father's brother Field.

The last of the direct male descendants of Jefferson's brother Randolph died in the 1920s or 1930s, so Dr Foster turned to the relatives of President Jefferson's paternal uncle, Field Jefferson. Seven living descendants of Field Jefferson were located. Five of them agreed to cooperate in the study and had their blood drawn for Y-chromosome marker testing purposes.

On the Hemings side of the equation, it was even more difficult to come up with an abundance of living male relatives. Sally Hemings had at least six and possibly seven children: Harriet (1795–1797), Beverly (1798–post 1822), Harriet (1801–post 1822), an unnamed daughter (1799–1800), Madison (1805–1877), and Eston (1808–1856). According to the oral history of the descendants of Thomas Woodson (1790–1879), he was Sally Hemings's first child. Sally's son, Beverly, and daughter, Harriet, are listed as dying post 1822 because they disappeared into white society in the Washington, DC area in the year 1822.

Of the three known male sons from Sally Hemings, only descendants of Madison and Eston could possibly be located since Beverly's fate is unknown. Madison's Y-chromosome line ended in the mid-1800s when one of his three sons vanished into white society and the other two had no children. Thus, Eston Hemings descendants remained the last chance to find a male-line descendant of the man who fathered Sally Hemings's children.

Eston Hemings was born 21 May 1808, at Monticello, where he lived until President Jefferson's death in 1826 at which time he was freed. Eventually he married and moved to Ohio and finally to Madison, Wisconsin, where he died and was buried in 1856. Eston assumed the surname of Jefferson when he left Virginia and gave everyone the impression that he was white because of his light skin color.

Eston Hemings Jefferson had two sons and a daughter. His youngest son, Beverly Jefferson, lived from 1838–1908 and had one son. This son, Carl Smith Jefferson, lived from 1876 to 1941 and had two sons, William Magill Jefferson (1907–1956) and Carl Smith Jefferson, Jr. (1910–1948). Only William had a son. This son, John Weeks Jefferson was born in 1946. As the *only* living male descendant of Eston Hemings, John Weeks Jefferson's blood was drawn to help answer the question of whether or not President Thomas Jefferson was Eston Hemings's father (Murray and Duffy 1998).

ADDITIONAL SAMPLES GATHERED FOR THIS STUDY

Several additional samples were gathered to serve as controls in this study and to address potential paternity questions. Thomas Woodson, who was mentioned earlier as possibly the first child born to Sally Hemings, was an African American whose first known appearance in the documentary record is from a deed issued in 1807. He moved from Virginia to Ohio where he lived as a successful farmer until his death in 1879. His descendants now number over 1400 and are scattered across the United States (Murray and Duffy 1998). According to Woodson family tradition, he was the oldest child of Thomas Jefferson and Sally Hemings, born in 1790 shortly after Sally returned to Monticello from France (Monticello 2000). While there were no supporting documents for the claim of Thomas Woodson's family, Dr Foster collected blood samples from five of his living descendants to help confirm or disprove this family tradition.

Another important set of samples for testing was gathered from direct male-line descendants of Samuel and Peter Carr, who were Thomas Jefferson's nephews, the sons of his sister. According to Thomas Jefferson's grandchildren, Thomas Jefferson Randolph and Ellen Coolidge, Samuel and Peter Carr were the fathers of the children of Sally Hemings and her sister (Monticello 2000). Dr Foster collected three blood samples from living descendants of John Carr, the grandfather of Samuel and Peter Carr.

Finally, five male descendants from several old-line Virginia families around Charlottesville were sampled to serve as control samples. These controls were tested to provide a 'background' signal with the idea that potential similarities in the Y-chromosome tests due to geographic proximity needed to be eliminated (Murray and Duffy 1998).

THE Y-CHROMOSOME MARKERS EXAMINED

DNA samples from each of the 19 blood specimens gathered by Dr Foster were carefully extracted by a pathologist at the University of Virginia (Murray and Duffy 1998). The DNA samples were coded by Dr Foster and then taken to England, where researchers at Oxford University examined them. Eventually the team of scientists involved expanded to include researchers from the University of Leicester in England and Leiden University in the Netherlands. A variety of tests were run independently at these three locations (Foster *et al.* 1998).

The Y-chromosome markers used in this study are listed in Table 17.3. Chapter 8 in this book contains more information on many of these DNA markers. In all, there were 19 Y-chromosome markers examined in this study. These included 11 STRs, 7 SNPs (single nucleotide polymorphisms or bi-allelic markers), and 1 minisatellite MSY1, which proved to be the most polymorphic marker.

All 19 regions of the Y chromosome examined in this study matched between the Jefferson and Hemings descendants. These DNA results were viewed by Dr

DNA Marker Tested	Field Jefferson Male-Line	Eston Hemings Male-Line	John Carr Male-Line	Thomas Woodson Male-Line
Number of individuals typed	5	1	3	5
Y STR loci				
DYS19	15	15	14 ⬅	14 ⬅
DYS388	12	12	12	12
DYS389A	4	4	5 ⬅	5 ⬅
DYS389B	11	11	12 ⬅	11
DYS389C	3	3	3	3
DYS389D	9	9	10 ⬅	10 ⬅
DYS390	11	11	11	11
DYS391	10	10	10	13 ⬅
DYS392	15	15	13 ⬅	13 ⬅
DYS393	13	13	13	13
DXYS156Y	7	7	7	7
Y SNP loci	(0 = ancestral state; 1 = derived state)			
DYS287 (YAP)	0	0	0	0
SRYm8299	0	0	0	0
DYS271 (SY81)	0	0	0	0
LLY22g	0	0	0	0
Tat	0	0	0	0
92R7	0	0	1 ⬅	1 ⬅
SRYm1532	1	1	1	1
Minisatellite locus				
MSY1	(3)– 5	(3)– 5		
	(1)–14	(1)–14	(1)–17 ⬅	(1)–16 ⬅
	(3)–32	(3)–32	(3)–36 ⬅	(3)–27 ⬅
	(4)–16	(4)–16	(4)–21 ⬅	(4)–21 ⬅

Foster and his co-authors as evidence for President Thomas Jefferson fathering the last child of Sally Hemings (Foster *et al.* 1998). Interestingly, the John Carr and Thomas Woodson's male lines differed significantly from the Jefferson–Hemings results (Table 17.3). At least 7 of the 19 tested DNA markers gave different results. Thus, Thomas Jefferson could not be linked as the father of Thomas Woodson, nor were Samuel Carr or Peter Carr the father of Eston Hemings. The results of the Virginia old-line families were not reported, presumably because these samples served their purpose as effective controls and revealed no unusual Y-chromosome patterns.

In this study, Y-chromosome markers demonstrated their usefulness in monitoring paternal transmission of genetic information by tracing the male lineage of Thomas Jefferson across 15 generations (Figure 17.3). The ability to connect Y-chromosome DNA information across the generation gaps meant that living relatives could be used in this investigation rather than disturbing the almost 200-year-old burial site of President Jefferson.

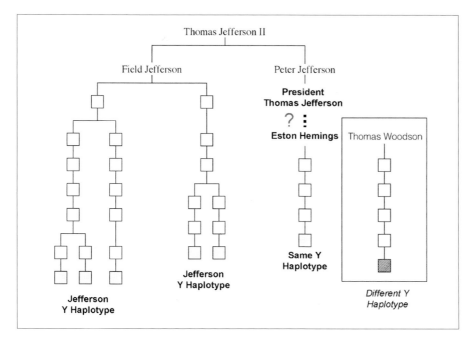

Figure 17.4

Ancestry of Thomas Jefferson and Eston Hemings male lines. The shaded boxes represent the samples tested by Foster et al. *(1998) in their Jefferson Y-chromosome study. A male descendant of Eston Hemings, son of Thomas Jefferson's slave Sally Hemings, was found to have a Y-chromosome haplotype that matched male descendants of Field Jefferson, President Thomas Jefferson's uncle. A male descendant of Thomas Woodson, claimed by some to be descended from Jefferson, had a different Y haplotype and therefore could not have been a Jefferson.*

ALTERNATIVE SCENARIOS

Shortly after the results of Dr Foster's study were announced, an alternative scenario was proposed. Could some other male Jefferson have fathered Eston Hemmings? All the results in this study conclusively show is that there is a genetic match between descendants of Eston Hemings and Thomas Jefferson's uncle, Field Jefferson. Was it historically possible for another male Jefferson to have fathered Sally Hemings's children? The Thomas Jefferson Memorial Foundation, a private, non-profit organization established in 1923 that owns and operates Monticello with the goal of preservation and education, conducted a year-long investigation into the historical record.

According to this careful historical investigation, 25 adult male descendants of Thomas Jefferson's father Peter and his uncle Field lived in Virginia during the 1794–1807 period of Sally Hemings's pregnancies (Monticello 2000). Most of them lived over 100 miles from Monticello and make no appearance in Thomas Jefferson's correspondence documents. Several male Jeffersons, including President Jefferson's brother Randolph and his sons, did live in the area of Monticello and visited occasionally. However, the historical records fail to indicate that any of these individuals were present at Monticello 9 months before the births of Sally Hemings's children. This information, combined with the fact that Thomas Jefferson was present at Monticello during the time of conception of each of Sally Heming's six children, led to the 26 January 2000 Thomas Jefferson Memorial Foundation report that he was the father of all of Sally Hemings's children (Monticello 2000).

REFERENCES

Clayton, T.M., Whitaker, J.P. and Maguire, C.N. (1995) *Forensic Science International,* 76, 7–15.

DiZinno, J., Fisher, D., Barritt, S., Clayton, T., Gill, P., Holland, M., Lee, D., McGuire, C., Raskin, J., Roby, R., Ruderman, J. and Weedn, V. (1994) *Proceedings from the Fifth International Symposium on Human Identification.* Madison, WI: Promega Corporation, pp. 129–135.

Foster, E.A., Jobling, M.A., Taylor, P.G., Donnelly, P., de Knijff, P., Mieremet, R., Zerjal, T. and Tyler-Smith, C. (1998) *Nature,* 396, 27–28.

Fregeau, C.J., Leclair, B., Bowen, K., Elliot, J., Borys, S. and Fourney, R. (1999) *Abstracts for the 18th International Congress of the International Society of Forensic Haemogenetics,* San Francisco, August 17–21, 1999, p. 149.

Gill, P., Ivanov, P.L., Kimpton, C., Piercy, R., Benson, N., Tully, G., Evett, I., Hagelberg, E. and Sullivan, K. (1994) *Nature Genetics,* 6, 130–135 .

Gill, P., Kimpton, C., Aliston-Greiner, R., Sullivan, K., Stoneking, M., Melton, T., Nott, J., Barritt, S., Roby, R.K., Holland, M.M. and Weedn, V.W. (1995) *Nature Genetics,* 9, 9–10 .

Grunwald, L. and Adler, S.J. (eds) (1999) *Letters of the Century: America 1900–1999.* New York: The Dial Press, p. 673.

Holland, M.M. and Parsons, T.J. (1999) *Forensic Science Review,* 11, 21–50.

Ivanov, P.L., Wadhams, M.J., Roby, R.K., Holland, M.M., Weedn, V.W. and Parsons, T.J. (1996) *Nature Genetics,* 12, 417–420.

Leclair, B., Fregeau, C.J., Bowen, K.L., Borys, S.B., Elliot, J. and Fourney, R.M. (1999) *Abstracts for the 18th International Congress of the International Society of Forensic Haemogenetics,* San Francisco, August 17–21, 1999, p. 10.

Levy, H. (1996) O.J. Simpson: What the blood really showed. In: *And the Blood Cried Out,* pp. 157–188. NY: Basic Books.

Miller, M.L., McCord, B.R., Martz, R. and Budowle, B. (1997) *Journal of Analytical Toxicology,* 21, 521–528.

Monticello (2000) *Thomas Jefferson Memorial Foundation Research Committee Report on Thomas Jefferson and Sally Hemings,* January 26, 2000; available at http://www. monticello.org.

Murray, B. and Duffy, B. (1998) *US News and World Report,* November 9, 1998, pp. 59–63.

Scherczinger, C.A., Ladd, C., Bourke, M.T., Adamowicz, M.S., Johannes, P.M., Schercziger, R., Beesley, T. and Lee, H.C. (1999) *Journal of Forensic Sciences,* 44, 1042–1045.

Sims, G., Montgomery, R., Myers, S. and Konzak, K. (1995) *Proceedings of the Sixth International Symposium on Human Identification.* Madison, WI: Promega Corporation, pp. 116–117.

Weir, B.S. (1995) *Nature Genetics,* 11, 365–368.

Woodward, B. (1999) *Shadow: Five Presidents and the Legacy of Watergate.* New York: Simon & Schuster.

APPENDIX I

REPORTED STR ALLELES: SIZES AND SEQUENCES

EXPLANATION OF INFORMATION INCLUDED IN THE FOLLOWING TABLES

This appendix material describes the reported alleles for the 13 short tandem repeat (STR) loci most commonly used in the United States and around the world. Note that the number of alleles present for a particular locus is an indication of the polymorphic nature of that marker and its value for use in human identity testing. Thus, FGA is more useful than TPOX because it possesses more alleles and there is a greater chance that two individuals selected at random would have different genotypes at FGA than at TPOX.

STR alleles are named based on the number of full repeat units that they contain with partial repeats (i.e. microvariants) being designated by the number of full repeats, a decimal, and the number of nucleotides present in the partial repeat in accordance with International Society of Forensic Haemogenetics (ISFH) recommendations (1994). The polymerase chain reaction (PCR) product size for each of the possible alleles is listed based on the commercial STR kit used to amplify the particular locus. Different commercially available STR kits produce different DNA fragment sizes due to the fact that their primers hybridize to different positions in the flanking regions of the STR sequence. Hence, we have calculated the expected DNA fragment sizes (based on their actual sequence) for all reported alleles if one uses the designated Promega kit or the PE Applied Biosystems kit. These PCR product sizes are listed without any nontemplate addition, i.e. they are in the '–A' rather than the '+A' form. *STR allele sizes measured in a laboratory may also vary from the actual sequence-based size listed here due to the internal sizing standard used and the particular electrophoretic conditions.*

The common repeat sequence motif for each STR locus is listed according to ISFH recommendations (1997). In most cases, the sequence changes in the repeat region are the only variation occurring and the flanking sequences remain constant. However, variation in the flanking sequence is also a possibility. Finally, we have listed the reference where each new allele (and its sequence, if published) has been described. As more and more samples are analyzed using these STR loci, we recognize that new (rare) alleles will be discovered and that this listing will quickly become outdated. We encourage the reader to consult the STRBase variant allele listing (http://www.cstl.nist.gov/biotech/strbase/var_tab.htm) and to contribute newly discovered alleles so that they may be categorized for fellow workers in this field. The complete sequence for one of the alleles listed for each locus may be found by using the GenBank accession number listed for that locus or by checking the reference sequence in STRBase (http://www.cstl.nist.gov/biotech/strbase/seq_info.htm).

CSF1PO
GenBank Accession: X14720 (allele 12). PCR product sizes of observed alleles

Allele (Repeat #)	Promega PowerPlex 1.1	ABI COfiler (w/o + A)	Repeat Structure $[AGAT]_n$	Reference
6	291 bp	280 bp	$[AGAT]_6$	COfiler
7	295 bp	284 bp	$[AGAT]_7$	Huang *et al.* (1995)
8	299 bp	288 bp	$[AGAT]_8$	Puers *et al.* (1993)
9	303 bp	292 bp	$[AGAT]_9$	Puers *et al.* (1993)
9.1	304 bp	293 bp	Not published	STRBase
10	307 bp	296 bp	$[AGAT]_{10}$	Puers *et al.* (1993)
10.1	308 bp	297 bp	Not published	STRBase
10.3	310 bp	299 bp	Not published	Lazaruk *et al.* (1998)
11	311 bp	300 bp	$[AGAT]_{11}$	Puers *et al.* (1993)
12	315 bp	304 bp	$[AGAT]_{12}$	Puers *et al.* (1993)
12.1	316 bp	305 bp	Not published	Budowle and Moretti (1998)
13	319 bp	308 bp	$[AGAT]_{13}$	Puers *et al.* (1993)
14	323 bp	312 bp	$[AGAT]_{14}$	Puers *et al.* (1993)
15	327 bp	316 bp	$[AGAT]_{15}$	COfiler
16	331 bp	320 bp	$[AGAT]_{16}$	STRBase

15 observed alleles

FGA
GenBank Accession: M64982 (allele 21). PCR product sizes of observed alleles

Allele (Repeat #)	Promega PowerPlex 2.1	ABI Profiler Plus (w/o + A)	Repeat Structure $[TTTC]_3$ TTTT TTCT $[CTTT]_n$ CTCC $[TTCC]_2$	Reference
12.2	308 bp	196 bp	Not published	SGM Plus
13	310 bp	198 bp	Not published	SGM Plus
15	318 bp	206 bp	$[TTTC]_3$TTTT TTCT$[CTTT]_7$CTCC$[TTCC]_2$	Barber *et al.* (1996)
16	322 bp	210 bp	$[TTTC]_3$TTTT TTCT$[CTTT]_8$CTCC$[TTCC]_2$	SGM Plus
16.1	323 bp	211 bp	$[TTTC]_3$TTTT TTCT$[CTTT]_5$T $[CTTT]3$CTCC$[TTCC]_2$	Griffiths *et al.* (1998)
16.2	324 bp	212 bp	$[TTTC]_3$TTTT TT $[CTTT]_9$CTCC$[TTCC]_2$	SGM Plus
17	326 bp	214 bp	$[TTTC]_3$TTTT TTCT$[CTTT]_9$CTCC$[TTCC]_2$	Barber *et al.* (1996)
17.1	327 bp	215 bp	Not published	SGM Plus
17.2	328 bp	216 bp	Not published	SGM Plus
18	330 bp	218 bp	$[TTTC]_3$TTTT TTCT$[CTTT]_{10}$CTCC$[TTCC]_2$	Barber *et al.* (1996)

Allele (Repeat #)	Promega PowerPlex 2.1	ABI Profiler Plus (w/o + A)	Repeat Structure [TTTC]$_3$ TTTT TTCT [CTTT]$_n$ CTCC [TTCC]$_2$	Reference
18.1	331 bp	219 bp	Not published	SGM Plus
18.2	332 bp	220 bp	[TTTC]$_3$TTTT TT [CTTT]$_{11}$CTCC[TTCC]$_2$	Barber *et al.* (1996)
19	334 bp	222 bp	[TTTC]$_3$TTTT TTCT[CTTT]$_{11}$CTCC[TTCC]$_2$	Barber *et al.* (1996)
19.1	335 bp	223 bp	Not published	SGM Plus
19.2	336 bp	224 bp	[TTTC]$_3$TTTT TT [CTTT]$_{12}$CTCC[TTCC]$_2$	SGM Plus
19.3	337 bp	225 bp	Not published	SGM Plus
20	338 bp	226 bp	[TTTC]$_3$TTTT TTCT[CTTT]$_{12}$CTCC[TTCC]$_2$	Barber *et al.* (1996)
20.1	339 bp	227 bp	Not published	SGM Plus
20.2	340 bp	228 bp	[TTTC]$_3$TTTT TT [CTTT]$_{13}$CTCC[TTCC]$_2$	Barber *et al.* (1996)
20.3	341 bp	229 bp	Not published	SGM Plus
21	342 bp	230 bp	[TTTC]$_3$TTTT TTCT[CTTT]$_{13}$CTCC[TTCC]$_2$	Barber *et al.* (1996)
21.2	344 bp	232 bp	[TTTC]$_3$TTTT TT [CTTT]$_{14}$CTCC[TTCC]$_2$	SGM Plus
22	346 bp	234 bp	[TTTC]$_3$TTTT TTCT[CTTT]$_{14}$CTCC[TTCC]$_2$	Barber *et al.* (1996)
22.1	347 bp	235 bp	Not published	SGM Plus
22.2	348 bp	236 bp	[TTTC]$_3$TTTT TT [CTTT]$_{15}$CTCC[TTCC]$_2$	Barber *et al.* (1996)
22.3	349 bp	237 bp	Not published	Gill *et al.* (1996)
23	350 bp	238 bp	[TTTC]$_3$TTTT TTCT[CTTT]$_{15}$CTCC[TTCC]$_2$	Barber *et al.* (1996)
23.2	352 bp	240 bp	[TTTC]$_3$TTTT TT [CTTT]$_{16}$CTCC[TTCC]$_2$	Barber *et al.* (1996)
23.3	353 bp	241 bp	Not published	SGM Plus
24	354 bp	242 bp	[TTTC]$_3$TTTT TTCT[CTTT]$_{16}$CTCC[TTCC]$_2$	Barber *et al.* (1996)
24.1	355 bp	243 bp	Not published	SGM Plus
24.2	356 bp	244 bp	[TTTC]$_3$TTTT TT [CTTT]$_{17}$CTCC[TTCC]$_2$	Barber *et al.* (1996)
24.3	357 bp	245 bp	Not published	SGM Plus
25	358 bp	246 bp	[TTTC]$_3$TTTT TTCT[CTTT]$_{17}$CTCC[TTCC]$_2$	Barber *et al.* (1996)
25.1	359 bp	247 bp	Not published	SGM Plus
25.2	360 bp	248 bp	[TTTC]$_3$TTTT TT [CTTT]$_{18}$CTCC[TTCC]$_2$	SGM Plus
25.3	361 bp	249 bp	Not published	SGM Plus
26	362 bp	250 bp	[TTTC]$_3$TTTT TTCT[CTTT]$_{18}$CTCC[TTCC]$_2$	Barber *et al.* (1996)
26.1	363 bp	251 bp	Not published	SGM Plus
26.2	364 bp	252 bp	[TTTC]$_3$TTTT TT [CTTT]$_{19}$CTCC[TTCC]$_2$	SGM Plus
27	366 bp	254 bp	[TTTC]$_3$TTTT TTCT[CTTT]$_{19}$CTCC[TTCC]$_2$	Barber *et al.* (1996)
27′	366 bp	254 bp	[TTTC]$_3$TTTT TTCT[CTTT]$_{13}$CCTT[CTTT]5CTCC [TTCC]$_2$	Griffiths *et al.* (1998)
27.1	367 bp	255 bp	Not published	SGM Plus
27.2	368 bp	256 bp	[TTTC]$_3$TTTT TT [CTTT]$_{20}$CTCC[TTCC]$_2$	SGM Plus
27.3	369 bp	257 bp	Not published	SGM Plus
28	370 bp	258 bp	[TTTC]$_3$TTTT TTCT[CTTT]$_{20}$CTCC[TTCC]$_2$	Barber *et al.* (1996)
28.1	371 bp	259 bp	Not published	SGM Plus
28.2	372 bp	260 bp	[TTTC]$_3$TTTT TT [CTTT]$_{21}$CTCC[TTCC]$_2$	SGM Plus
29	374 bp	262 bp	[TTTC]$_3$TTTT TTCT[CTTT]$_{15}$CCTT[CTTT]5CTCC [TTCC]$_2$	Barber *et al.* (1996)
29.2	376 bp	264 bp	Not published	SGM Plus
30	378 bp	266 bp	[TTTC]$_3$TTTT TTCT[CTTT]$_{16}$CCTT[CTTT]$_5$CTCC [TTCC]$_2$	Griffiths *et al.* (1998)
30.2	380 bp	268 bp	[TTTC]$_3$TTTT TT [CTTT]$_{14}$[CTTC]$_3$[CTTT]$_3$CTCC [TTCC]$_4$	Barber *et al.* (1996)
31	382 bp	270 bp	Not published	SGM Plus
31.2	384 bp	272 bp	[TTTC]$_4$TTTT TT [CTTT]$_{15}$[CTTC]$_3$ [CTTT]$_3$CTCC [TTCC]$_4$	Griffiths *et al.* (1998)
32	386 bp	274 bp	Not published	SGM Plus
32.2	388 bp	276 bp	[TTTC]$_4$TTTT TT [CTTT]$_{16}$[CTTC]$_3$ [CTTT]$_3$CTCC [TTCC]$_4$	Griffiths *et al.* (1998)
33.2	392 bp	280 bp	[TTTC]$_4$TTTT TT [CTTT]$_{17}$[CTTC]$_3$ [CTTT]$_3$CTCC [TTCC]$_4$	Griffiths *et al.* (1998)
34.2	396 bp	284 bp	[TTTC]$_4$TTTT TT [CTTT]$_{18}$[CTTC]$_3$ [CTTT]$_3$CTCC [TTCC]$_4$	Barber *et al.* (1996)
35.2	400 bp	288 bp	Not published	SGM Plus

Allele (Repeat #)	Promega PowerPlex 2.1	ABI Profiler Plus (w/o + A)	Repeat Structure [TTTC]$_3$ TTTT TTCT [CTTT]$_n$ CTCC [TTCC]$_2$	Reference
42.2	428 bp	316 bp	[TTTC]$_4$TTTT TT [CTTT]$_8$ [CTGT]$_4$[CTTT]$_{13}$ [CTTC]$_3$[CTTT]$_3$ CTCC[TTCC]$_4$	Griffiths *et al.* (1998)
43.2	432 bp	320 bp	[TTTC]$_4$TTTT TT [CTTT]$_8$[CTGT]5[CTTT]$_{13}$[CTTC]$_4$ [CTTT]$_3$CTCC[TTCC]$_4$	Griffiths *et al.* (1998)
44.2	436 bp	324 bp	[TTTC]$_4$TTTT TT [CTTT]$_{11}$[CTGT]$_3$[CTTT]$_{14}$ [CTTC]$_3$[CTTT]$_3$CTCC[TTCC]$_4$	Griffiths *et al.* (1998)
45.2	440 bp	328 bp	[TTTC]$_4$TTTT TT [CTTT]$_{10}$[CTGT]$_5$[CTTT]$_{13}$ [CTTC]$_4$[CTTT]$_3$CTCC[TTCC]$_4$	Griffiths *et al.* (1998)
46.2	444 bp	332 bp	[TTTC]$_4$TTTT TT [CTTT]$_{12}$[CTGT]$_5$[CTTT]$_{13}$ [CTTC]$_3$[CTTT]$_3$CTCC[TTCC]$_4$	Barber *et al.* (1996)
47.2	448 bp	336 bp	[TTTC]$_4$TTTT TT [CTTT]$_{12}$[CTGT]$_5$[CTTT]$_{14}$ [CTTC]$_3$[CTTT]$_3$CTCC[TTCC]$_4$	Griffiths *et al.* (1998)
48.2	452 bp	340 bp	[TTTC]$_4$TTTT TT [CTTT]$_{14}$[CTGT]$_3$[CTTT]$_{14}$ [CTTC]$_4$[CTTT]$_3$CTCC[TTCC]$_4$	Griffiths *et al.* (1998)
49.2	456 bp	344 bp	Not published	SGM Plus
50.2	460 bp	344 bp	[TTTC]$_4$TTTT TT [CTTT]$_{14}$[CTGT]$_4$[CTTT]$_{15}$ [CTTC]$_4$[CTTT]$_3$CTCC[TTCC]$_4$	Griffiths *et al.* (1998)
51.2	464 bp	348 bp	Not published	SGM Plus

69 observed alleles

TH01

GenBank Accession: D00269 (allele 9). PCR product sizes of observed alleles

Allele (Repeat #)	Promega PowerPlex 1.1	Promega PowerPlex 2.1	ABI COfiler (w/o + A)	Repeat Structure [AATG]$_n$ Other strand: [TCAT]$_n$	Reference
3	171 bp	152 bp	160 bp	[AATG]$_3$	Espinheira *et al.* (1996)
4	175 bp	156 bp	164 bp	[AATG]$_4$	Griffiths *et al.* (1998)
5	179 bp	160 bp	168 bp	[AATG]$_5$	Brinkmann *et al.* (1996b)
5.3	182 bp	163 bp	171 bp	Not published	SGM Plus
6	183 bp	164 bp	172 bp	[AATG]$_6$	Brinkmann *et al.* (1996b)
6.1	184 bp	165 bp	173 bp	Not published	SGM Plus
6.3	186 bp	167 bp	175 bp	[AATG]3ATG[AATG]$_3$	Klintschar *et al.* (1998)
7	187 bp	168 bp	176 bp	[AATG]$_7$	Brinkmann, Sajantila *et al.* (1996)
7.1	188 bp	169 bp	177 bp	Not published	SGM Plus
7.3	190 bp	171 bp	179 bp	Not published	SGM Plus
8	191 bp	172 bp	180 bp	[AATG]$_8$	Brinkmann *et al.* (1996b)
8.3	194 bp	175 bp	183 bp	[AATG]5ATG[AATG]$_3$	Brinkmann *et al.* (1996b)
9	195 bp	176 bp	184 bp	[AATG]$_9$	Brinkmann *et al.* (1996b)
9.3	198 bp	179 bp	187 bp	[AATG]$_6$ATG[AATG]$_3$	Brinkmann *et al.* (1996b)
10	199 bp	180 bp	188 bp	[AATG]$_{10}$	Brinkmann *et al.* (1996b)
10.3	202 bp	183 bp	191 bp	[AATG]$_6$ATG[AATG]$_4$	Brinkmann *et al.* (1996b)
11	203 bp	184 bp	192 bp	[AATG]$_{11}$	Brinkmann *et al.* (1996b)
12	207 bp	188 bp	196 bp	[AATG]$_{12}$	Van Oorschot *et al.* (1994)
13.3	214 bp	195 bp	203 bp	[AATG][AACG][AATG]$_8$ ATG[AATG]$_3$	Gene *et al.* (1996, Griffiths *et al.* (1998)
14	215 bp	196 bp	204 bp	Not published	SGM Plus

20 observed alleles

TPOX

GenBank Accession: M68651 (allele 11). PCR product sizes of observed alleles

Allele (Repeat #)	Promega PowerPlex 1.1	Promega PowerPlex 2.1	ABI COfiler (w/o + A)	Repeat Structure [AATG]$_n$	Reference
5	220 bp	258 bp	213 bp	Not published	STRBase
6	224 bp	262 bp	217 bp	[AATG]$_6$	COfiler
7	228 bp	266 bp	221 bp	[AATG]$_7$	Amorim *et al.* (1996)
8	232 bp	270 bp	225 bp	[AATG]$_8$	Puers *et al.* (1993)
9	236 bp	274 bp	229 bp	[AATG]$_9$	Puers *et al.* (1993)
10	240 bp	278 bp	233 bp	[AATG]$_{10}$	Puers *et al.* (1993)
11	244 bp	282 bp	237 bp	[AATG]$_{11}$	Puers *et al.* (1993)
12	248 bp	286 bp	241 bp	[AATG]$_{12}$	Puers *et al.* (1993)
13	252 bp	290 bp	245 bp	[AATG]$_{13}$	Amorim *et al.* (1996)
14	256 bp	294 bp	249 bp	[AATG]$_{14}$	Huang *et al.* (1995)

10 observed alleles

VWA

GenBank Accession: M25858 (allele 18). PCR product sizes of observed alleles

Allele (Repeat #)	Promega PowerPlex 1.1	ABI Profiler Plus (w/o + A)	Repeat Structure [TCTA] [TCTG]$_{3-4}$ [TCTA]$_n$	Reference
10	123 bp	152 bp	TCTA TCTG TCTA [TCTG]$_4$[TCTA]$_3$	Griffiths *et al.* (1998)
11 (13')*	127 bp	156 bp	TCTA[TCTG]$_3$[TCTA]$_7$	Brinkmann *et al.* (1996b)
12	131 bp	160 bp	TCTA[TCTG]$_4$[TCTA]$_7$	Griffiths *et al.* (1998)
13	135 bp	164 bp	[TCTA]$_2$[TCTG]$_4$[TCTA]$_3$TCCA[TCTA]$_3$	Griffiths *et al.* (1998)
13 (15)	135 bp	164 bp	TCTA[TCTA]$_4$[TCTA]$_8$TCCATCTA	Brinkmann *et al.* (1996b)
13 (15")	135 bp	164 bp	TCTA[TCTA]$_4$[TCTA]$_{10}$	Brinkmann *et al.* (1996b)
14 (16")	139 bp	168 bp	TCTA[TCTG]$_4$[TCTA]$_{11}$	Brinkmann *et al.* (1996b)
14' (16''')	139 bp	168 bp	TCTA TCTG TCTA[TCTG]$_4$[TCTA]$_3$TCCA[TCTA]$_3$	Brinkmann *et al.* (1996b)
14"	139 bp	168 bp	TCTA [TCTG]$_5$[TCTA]$_3$TCCA[TCTA]$_3$	Lins *et al.* (1998)
15 (17)	143 bp	172 bp	TCTA[TCTG]$_4$[TCTA]$_{10}$TCCATCTA	Brinkmann *et al.* (1996b)
15 (17')	143 bp	172 bp	TCTA[TCTG]$_3$[TCTA]$_{11}$TCCATCTA	Brinkmann *et al.* (1996b)
15.2	145 bp	174 bp	[TCTA]$_2$[TCTG]$_4$[TCTA]$_5$T--A[TCTA]$_4$	Gill *et al.* (1995)
16 (18)	147 bp	176 bp	TCTA[TCTG]$_4$[TCTA]$_{11}$TCCATCTA	Brinkmann *et al.* (1996b)
16 (18')	147 bp	176 bp	TCTA[TCTG]$_3$[TCTA]$_{12}$TCCATCTA	Brinkmann *et al.* (1996b)
16.1	148 bp	177 bp	Not published	STRBase
17 (19)	151 bp	180 bp	TCTA[TCTG]$_4$[TCTA]$_{12}$TCCATCTA	Brinkmann *et al.* (1996b)
18 (20)	155 bp	184 bp	TCTA[TCTG]$_4$[TCTA]$_{13}$TCCATCTA	Brinkmann *et al.* (1996b)
18' (20')	155 bp	184 bp	TCTA[TCTG]$_5$[TCTA]$_{12}$TCCATCTA	Brinkmann *et al.* (1996b)
18.2	157 bp	186 bp	Not published	SGM Plus
18.3	158 bp	187 bp	Not published	SGM Plus
19 (21)	159 bp	188 bp	TCTA[TCTG]4$_4$[TCTA]$_{14}$TCCATCTA	Brinkmann *et al.* (1996b)
19.2	161 bp	190 bp	Not published	SGM Plus
20 (22)	163 bp	192 bp	TCTA[TCTG]$_4$[TCTA]$_{15}$TCCATCTA	Brinkmann *et al.* (1996b)
21 (23)	167 bp	196 bp	TCTA[TCTG]$_4$[TCTA]$_{16}$TCCATCTA	Brinkmann *et al.* (1996b)
22 (24)	171 bp	200 bp	TCTA[TCTG]$_4$[TCTA]$_{17}$TCCATCTA	Brinkmann *et al.* (1996b)
23	175 bp	204 bp	Not published	SGM Plus
24	179 bp	208 bp	Not published	SGM Plus
25	183 bp	212 bp	Not published	SGM Plus

*Allele designations shown in parentheses come from Brinkmann *et al.* 1996b
28 observed alleles

D3S1358

GenBank Accession: None (sequence available in STRBase). PCR product sizes of observed alleles

Allele (Repeat #)	Promega PowerPlex 2.1	ABI Profiler Plus (w/o + A)	Repeat Structure [TCTA] [TCTG]$_{2-3}$ [TCTA]$_n$	Reference
8	99 bp	97 bp	Not published	STRBase
9	103 bp	101 bp	Not published	SGM Plus
10	107 bp	105 bp	Not published	SGM Plus
11	111 bp	109 bp	Not published	SGM Plus
12	115 bp	113 bp	Not published	SGM Plus
13	119 bp	117 bp	TCTA[TCTG]$_2$[TCTA]$_{10}$	Mornhinweg *et al.* (1998)
14	123 bp	121 bp	TCTA[TCTG]$_2$[TCTA]$_{11}$	Szibor *et al.* (1998)
15	127 bp	125 bp	TCTA[TCTG]$_3$[TCTA]$_{11}$	Szibor *et al.* (1998)
15'	127 bp	125 bp	TCTA[TCTG]$_2$[TCTA]$_{12}$	Szibor *et al.* (1998)
15.2	129 bp	127 bp	Not published	SGM Plus
16	131 bp	129 bp	TCTA[TCTG]$_3$[TCTA]$_{12}$	Szibor *et al.* (1998)
16'	131 bp	129 bp	TCTA[TCTG]$_2$[TCTA]$_{13}$	Mornhinweg *et al.* (1998)
16.2	133 bp	131 bp	Not published	Budowle *et al.* (1997)
17	135 bp	133 bp	TCTA[TCTG]$_3$[TCTA]$_{13}$	Szibor *et al.* (1998)
17'	135 bp	133 bp	TCTA[TCTG]$_2$[TCTA]$_{14}$	Mornhinweg *et al.* (1998)
17.1	136 bp	134 bp	Not published	SGM Plus
18	139 bp	137 bp	TCTA[TCTG]$_3$[TCTA]$_{14}$	Szibor *et al.* (1998)
18.3	142 bp	140 bp	Not published	STRBase
19	143 bp	141 bp	TCTA[TCTG]$_3$[TCTA]$_{15}$	Mornhinweg *et al.* (1998)
20	147 bp	145 bp	TCTA[TCTG]$_3$[TCTA]$_{16}$	Mornhinweg *et al.* (1998)

20 observed alleles

D5S818

GenBank Accession: G08446 (allele 11). PCR product sizes of observed alleles

Allele (Repeat #)	Promega PowerPlex 1.1	ABI Profiler Plus (w/o + A)	Repeat Structure [AGAT]$_n$	Reference
7	119 bp	134 bp	[AGAT]$_7$	Lins *et al.* (1998)
8	123 bp	138 bp	[AGAT]$_8$	Lins *et al.* (1998)
9	127 bp	142 bp	[AGAT]$_9$	Lins *et al.* (1998)
10	131 bp	146 bp	[AGAT]$_{10}$	Lins *et al.* (1998)
11	135 bp	150 bp	[AGAT]$_{11}$	Lins *et al.* (1998)
12	139 bp	154 bp	[AGAT]$_{12}$	Lins *et al.* (1998)
13	143 bp	158 bp	[AGAT]$_{13}$	Lins *et al.* (1998)
14	147 bp	162 bp	[AGAT]$_{14}$	Lins *et al.* (1998)
15	151 bp	166 bp	[AGAT]$_{15}$	Lins *et al.* (1998)
16	155 bp	170 bp	Not published	Profiler Plus

10 observed alleles

D7S820
GenBank Accession: G08616 (allele 12). PCR product sizes of observed alleles

Allele (Repeat #)	Promega PowerPlex 1.1	ABI Profiler Plus (w/o + A)	Repeat Structure [GATA]$_n$	Reference
5	211 bp	253 bp	Not published	STRBase
6	215 bp	257 bp	[GATA]$_6$	Lins *et al.* (1998)
6.3	218 bp	260 bp	Not published	Profiler Plus
7	219 bp	261 bp	[GATA]$_7$	Lins *et al.* (1998)
7.3	222 bp	264 bp	Not published	STRBase
8	223 bp	265 bp	[GATA]$_8$	Lins *et al.* (1998)
8.1	224 bp	266 bp	Not published	STRBase
8.2	225 bp	267 bp	Not published	STRBase
9	227 bp	269 bp	[GATA]$_9$	Lins *et al.* (1998)
9.1	228 bp	270 bp	Not published	STRBase
9.3	230 bp	272 bp	Not published	STRBase
10	231 bp	273 bp	[GATA]$_{10}$	Lins *et al.* (1998)
10.1	232 bp	274 bp	Not published	STRBase
10.3	234 bp	276 bp	Not published	STRBase
11	235 bp	277 bp	[GATA]$_{11}$	Lins *et al.* (1998)
11.1	236 bp	278 bp	Not published	STRBase
12	239 bp	281 bp	[GATA]$_{12}$	Lins *et al.* (1998)
12.1	240 bp	282 bp	Not published	STRBase
13	243 bp	285 bp	[GATA]$_{13}$	Lins *et al.* (1998)
13.1	244 bp	286 bp	Not published	STRBase
14	247 bp	289 bp	[GATA]$_{14}$	Lins *et al.* (1998)
15	251 bp	293 bp	Not published	Profiler Plus

22 observed alleles

D8S1179 (listed as D6S502 in early papers)
GenBank Accession: G08710 (allele 12). PCR product sizes of observed alleles

Allele (Repeat #)	Promega PowerPlex 2.1	ABI Profiler Plus (w/o + A)	Repeat Structure [TCTR]$_n$	Reference
7	203 bp	123 bp	[TCTA]$_7$	Griffiths *et al.* (1998)
8	207 bp	127 bp	[TCTA]$_8$	Barber and Parkin (1996)
9	211 bp	131 bp	[TCTA]$_9$	Barber and Parkin (1996)
10	215 bp	135 bp	[TCTA]$_{10}$	Barber and Parkin (1996)
11	219 bp	139 bp	[TCTA]$_{11}$	Barber and Parkin (1996)
12	223 bp	143 bp	[TCTA]$_{12}$	Barber and Parkin (1996)
13	227 bp	147 bp	[TCTA]$_1$[TCTG]$_1$[TCTA]$_{11}$	Barber and Parkin (1996)
14	231 bp	151 bp	[TCTA]$_2$[TCTG]$_1$[TCTA]$_{11}$	Barber and Parkin (1996)
15	235 bp	155 bp	[TCTA]$_2$[TCTG]$_1$[TCTA]$_{12}$	Barber and Parkin (1996)
16	239 bp	159 bp	[TCTA]$_2$[TCTG]$_1$[TCTA]$_{13}$	Barber and Parkin (1996)
17	243 bp	163 bp	[TCTA]$_2$[TCTG]$_2$[TCTA]$_{13}$	Barber and Parkin (1996)
18	247 bp	167 bp	[TCTA]$_2$[TCTG]$_1$[TCTA]$_{15}$	Barber and Parkin (1996)
19	251 bp	171 bp	[TCTA]$_2$[TCTG]$_2$[TCTA]$_{15}$	Griffiths *et al.* (1998)

13 observed alleles

D13S317
GenBank Accession: G09017 (allele 13). PCR product sizes of observed alleles

Allele (Repeat #)	Promega PowerPlex 1.1	ABI Profiler Plus (w/o + A)	Repeat Structure [TATC]$_n$	Reference
5	157 bp	193 bp	Not published	Profiler Plus
7	165 bp	201 bp	[TATC]$_7$	Lins *et al.* (1998)
7.1	166 bp	202 bp	Not published	STRBase
8	169 bp	205 bp	[TATC]$_8$	Lins *et al.* (1998)
8.1	170 bp	206 bp	Not published	STRBase
9	173 bp	209 bp	[TATC]$_9$	Lins *et al.* (1998)
10	177 bp	213 bp	[TATC]$_{10}$	Lins *et al.* (1998)
10'	177 bp	213 bp	[TATC]$_{10}$ AATC	Lins *et al.* (1998)
11	181 bp	217 bp	[TATC]$_{11}$	Lins *et al.* (1998)
12	185 bp	221 bp	[TATC]$_{12}$	Lins *et al.* (1998)
13	189 bp	225 bp	[TATC]$_{13}$	Lins *et al.* (1998)
14	193 bp	229 bp	[TATC]$_{14}$	Lins *et al.* (1998)
15	197 bp	233 bp	[TATC]$_{15}$	Lins *et al.* (1998)
16	201 bp	237 bp	Not published	STRBase

14 observed alleles

D16S539
GenBank Accession: G07925 (allele 11). PCR product sizes of observed alleles

Allele (Repeat #)	Promega PowerPlex 1.1	ABI COfiler (w/o + A)	Repeat Structure [GATA]$_n$	Reference
5	264 bp	233 bp	[GATA]$_5$	Lins *et al.* (1998)
8	276 bp	245 bp	[GATA]$_8$	Lins *et al.* (1998)
9	280 bp	249 bp	[GATA]$_9$	Lins *et al.* (1998)
10	284 bp	253 bp	[GATA]$_{10}$	Lins *et al.* (1998)
11	288 bp	257 bp	[GATA]$_{11}$	Lins *et al.* (1998)
12	292 bp	261 bp	[GATA]$_{12}$	Lins *et al.* (1998)
13	296 bp	265 bp	[GATA]$_{13}$	Lins *et al.* (1998)
13.3	299 bp	268 bp	Not published	STRBase
14	300 bp	269 bp	[GATA]$_{14}$	Lins *et al.* (1998)
15	304 bp	273 bp	[GATA]$_{15}$	Lins *et al.* (1998)

10 observed alleles

D18S51
GenBank Accession: L18333 (allele 13). PCR product sizes of observed alleles

Allele (Repeat #)	Promega PowerPlex 2.1	ABI Profiler Plus (w/o + A)	Repeat Structure [AGAA]$_n$	Reference
7	286 bp	264 bp	Not published	SGM Plus
8	290 bp	268 bp	[AGAA]$_8$	Griffiths *et al.* (1998)
9	294 bp	272 bp	[AGAA]$_9$	Barber and Parkin (1996)
9.2	296 bp	274 bp	Not published	SGM Plus
10	298 bp	276 bp	[AGAA]$_{10}$	Barber and Parkin (1996)
10.2	300 bp	278 bp	Not published	SGM Plus
11	302 bp	280 bp	[AGAA]$_{11}$	Barber and Parkin (1996)
12	306 bp	284 bp	[AGAA]$_{12}$	Barber and Parkin (1996)
12.2	308 bp	286 bp	Not published	SGM Plus
13	310 bp	288 bp	[AGAA]$_{13}$	Barber and Parkin (1996)
13.1	311 bp	289 bp	Not published	STRBase
13.2	312 bp	290 bp	[AGAA]$_{13}$AG	Barber and Parkin (1996)
14	314 bp	292 bp	[AGAA]$_{14}$	Barber and Parkin (1996)
14.2	316 bp	294 bp	[AGAA]$_{14}$AG	Barber and Parkin (1996)
15	318 bp	296 bp	[AGAA]$_{15}$	Barber and Parkin (1996)
15.1	319 bp	297 bp	Not published	SGM Plus
15.2	320 bp	298 bp	[AGAA]$_{15}$AG	Barber and Parkin (1996)
15.3	321 bp	299 bp	Not published	SGM Plus
16	322 bp	300 bp	[AGAA]$_{16}$	Barber and Parkin (1996)
16.2	324 bp	302 bp	Not published	SGM Plus
16.3	325 bp	303 bp	Not published	SGM Plus
17	326 bp	304 bp	[AGAA]$_{17}$	Barber and Parkin (1996)
17.1	327 bp	305 bp	Not published	SGM Plus
17.2	328 bp	306 bp	[AGAA]$_{17}$AG	Gill *et al.* (1996)
17.3	329 bp	307 bp	Not published	SGM Plus
18	330 bp	308 bp	[AGAA]$_{18}$	Barber and Parkin (1996)
18.1	331 bp	309 bp	Not published	SGM Plus
18.2	332 bp	311 bp	Not published	SGM Plus
19	334 bp	312 bp	[AGAA]$_{19}$	Barber and Parkin (1996)
19.2	336 bp	314 bp	[AGAA]$_{19}$AG	Gill *et al.* (1996)
20	338 bp	316 bp	[AGAA]$_{20}$	Barber and Parkin (1996)
20.1	339 bp	317 bp	Not published	SGM Plus
20.2	340 bp	318 bp	Not published	SGM Plus
21	342 bp	320 bp	[AGAA]$_{21}$	Barber and Parkin (1996)
21.2	344 bp	322 bp	Not published	SGM Plus
22	346 bp	324 bp	[AGAA]$_{22}$	Barber and Parkin (1996)
22.1	347 bp	325 bp	Not published	STRBase
23	350 bp	328 bp	[AGAA]$_{23}$	Barber and Parkin (1996)
23.1	351 bp	329 bp	Not published	SGM Plus
24	354 bp	332 bp	[AGAA]$_{24}$	Barber and Parkin (1996)
25	358 bp	336 bp	[AGAA]$_{25}$	Barber and Parkin (1996)
26	362 bp	340 bp	[AGAA]$_{26}$	Barber and Parkin (1996)
27	366 bp	344 bp	[AGAA]$_{27}$	Barber and Parkin (1996)

43 observed alleles

D21S11
GenBank Accession: M84567 (allele 24.2). PCR product sizes of observed alleles

Allele (Repeat #)	Promega PowerPlex 2.1	ABI Profiler Plus (w/o + A)	Repeat Structure [TCTA]*n* [TCTG]*n* {[TCTA]₃ TA [TCTA]₃ TCA [TCTA]₂ TCCATA} [TCTA]*n* TA TCTA	Reference
24 (53)*	203 bp	186 bp	[TCTA]₄[TCTG]₆{43bp}[TCTA]₆	Griffiths *et al.* (1998)
24.2 (54)	205 bp	188 bp	[TCTA]₅[TCTG]₆ {[TCTA]₃ TCA [TCTA]₂ TCCA TA}[TCTA]₉	Griffiths *et al.* (1998)
25 (55)	207 bp	190 bp	[TCTA]₄[TCTG]₃{43bp}[TCTA]₁₀	Schwartz et al. (1996)
25.2 (56)	209 bp	192 bp	[TCTA]₅[TCTG]₆ {[TCTA]₃TCA [TCTA]₂ TCCA TA}[TCTA]₁₀	Griffiths *et al.* (1998)
26 (57)	211 bp	194 bp	[TCTA]₄[TCTG]₆{43bp}[TCTA]₈	Moller *et al.* (1994)
26.1	212 bp	195 bp	Not published	SGM Plus
26.2	213 bp	196 bp	Not published	STRBase
27 (59)	215 bp	198 bp	[TCTA]₄[TCTG]₆{43bp}[TCTA]₉	Moller *et al.* (1994)
27' (59)	215 bp	198 bp	[TCTA]₆[TCTG]₅{43bp}[TCTA]₈	Schwartz *et al.* (1996)
27" (59)	215 bp	198 bp	[TCTA]₅[TCTG]₅{43bp}[TCTA]₉	Griffiths *et al.* (1998)
27.2	217 bp	200 bp	Not published	SGM Plus
27.3	218 bp	201 bp	Not published	SGM Plus
28 (61)	219 bp	202 bp	[TCTA]₄[TCTG]₆{43bp}[TCTA]₁₀	Moller *et al.* (1994)
28'	219 bp	202 bp	[TCTA]₅[TCTG]₆{43bp}[TCTA]₉	Zhou *et al.* (1997)
28.2 (62)	221 bp	204 bp	[TCTA]₄[TCTG]₆{43bp}[TCTA]₁₀	Griffiths *et al.* (1998)
28.2'	221 bp	204 bp	[TCTA]₅[TCTG]₆{43bp}[TCTA]₈ TA TCTA	Zhou *et al.* (1997)
28.3	222 bp	205 bp	Not published	SGM Plus
29 (63)	223 bp	206 bp	[TCTA]₄[TCTG]₆{43bp}[TCTA]₁₁	Griffiths *et al.* (1998)
29' (63)	223 bp	206 bp	[TCTA]₆[TCTG]₅{43bp}[TCTA]₁₀	Zhou *et al.* (1997)
29.1	224 bp	207 bp	Not published	SGM Plus
29.2 (64)	225 bp	208 bp	[TCTA]₅[TCTG]₅{43bp}[TCTA]₁₀ TA TCTA	Zhou *et al.* (1997)
29.3	226 bp	209 bp	Not published	SGM Plus
30 (65)	227 bp	210 bp	[TCTA]₄[TCTG]₆{43bp}[TCTA]₁₂	Schwartz *et al.* (1996)
30' (65)	227 bp	210 bp	[TCTA]₅[TCTG]₆{43bp}[TCTA]₁₁	Zhou *et al.* (1997)
30" (65)	227 bp	210 bp	[TCTA]₆[TCTG]₅{43bp}[TCTA]₁₁	Griffiths *et al.* (1998)
30''' (65)	227 bp	210 bp	[TCTA]₆[TCTG]₆{43bp}[TCTA]₁₀	Brinkmann *et al.* (1996a)
30.1	228 bp	211 bp	Not published	SGM Plus
30.2 (66)	229 bp	212 bp	[TCTA]₅[TCTG]₆{43bp}[TCTA]₁₀TA TCTA	Griffiths *et al.* (1998)
30.2' (66)	229 bp	212 bp	[TCTA]₅[TCTG]₅{43bp}[TCTA]₁₁ TA TCTA	Schwartz *et al.* (1996)
31 (67)	231 bp	214 bp	[TCTA]₅[TCTG]₆{43bp}[TCTA]₁₂	Griffiths *et al.* (1998)
31' (67)	231 bp	214 bp	[TCTA]₆[TCTG]₅{43bp}[TCTA]₁₂	Moller *et al.* (1994)
31"	231 bp	214 bp	[TCTA]₆[TCTG]₆{43bp}[TCTA]₁₁	Zhou *et al.* (1997)
31''' (67)	231 bp	214 bp	[TCTA]₇[TCTG]₅{43bp}[TCTA]₁₁	Schwartz *et al.* (1996)
31.1	232 bp	215 bp	Not published	SGM Plus
31.2 (68)	233 bp	216 bp	[TCTA]₅[TCTG]₆{43bp}[TCTA]₁₁ TA TCTA	Griffiths *et al.* (1998)
31.3	234 bp	217 bp	Not published	SGM Plus
32 (69)	235 bp	218 bp	[TCTA]₆[TCTG]₅{43bp}[TCTA]₁₃	Griffiths *et al.* (1998)
32' (69)	235 bp	218 bp	[TCTA]₅[TCTG]₆{43bp}[TCTA]₁₃	Zhou *et al.* (1997)
32.1	236 bp	219 bp	Not published	SGM Plus
32.2 (70)	237 bp	220 bp	[TCTA]₅[TCTG]₆{43bp}[TCTA]₁₂ TA TCTA	Griffiths *et al.* (1998)
32.2' (70)	237 bp	220 bp	[TCTA]₄[TCTG]₆{43bp}[TCTA]₁₃ TA TCTA	Brinkmann *et al.* (1996a)
32.2" (70)	237 bp	220 bp	[TCTA]₅[TCTG]₆{[TCTA]₂TA[TCTA]₃TCA [TCTA]₂TCCA TA}[TCTA]₁₃ TA TCTA	Brinkmann *et al.* (1996a)
32.3	238 bp	221 bp	Not published	SGM Plus
33 (71)	239 bp	222 bp	[TCTA]₅[TCTG]₆{43bp}[TCTA]₁₄	Zhou *et al.* (1997)
33.2 (72)	241 bp	224 bp	[TCTA]₅[TCTG]₆{43bp}[TCTA]₁₃ TA TCTA	Griffiths *et al.* (1998)
33.2' (72)	241 bp	224 bp	[TCTA]₆[TCTG]₅{43bp}[TCTA]₁₃ TA TCTA	Brinkmann *et al.* (1996a)
33.2" (72)	241 bp	224 bp	[TCTA]₆[TCTG]₆{43bp}[TCTA]₁₂ TA TCTA	Brinkmann *et al.* (1996a)

Allele (Repeat #)	Promega PowerPlex 2.1	ABI Profiler Plus (w/o + A)	Repeat Structure [TCTA]$_n$ [TCTG]$_n$ {[TCTA]$_3$ TA [TCTA]$_3$ TCA [TCTA]$_2$ TCCATA} [TCTA]$_n$ TA TCTA	Reference
33.3	242 bp	225 bp	[TCTA]$_5$[TCTG]$_6${43bp}[TCTA]$_8$ TCA [TCTA]$_3$ TCA [TCTA]$_2$ TA TCTA	Brinkmann *et al.* (1996a)
34 (73)	243 bp	226 bp	[TCTA]$_5$[TCTG]$_6${43bp}[TCTA]$_{15}$	Zhou *et al.* (1997)
34' (73)	243 bp	226 bp	[TCTA]$_{10}$[TCTG]$_5${43bp}[TCTA]$_{11}$	Brinkmann *et al.* (1996a)
34.2 (74)	245 bp	228 bp	[TCTA]$_5$[TCTG]$_6${43bp}[TCTA]$_{14}$ TA TCTA	Griffiths *et al.* (1998)
34.3	246 bp	229 bp	[TCTA]$_5$[TCTG]$_6${43bp}[TCTA]$_{10}$ TCA [TCTA]$_4$ TA TCTA	Brinkmann *et al.* (1996a)
35 (75)	247 bp	230 bp	[TCTA]$_{10}$[TCTG]$_5${43bp}[TCTA]$_{12}$	Griffiths *et al.* (1998)
35' (75)	247 bp	230 bp	[TCTA]$_{11}$[TCTG]$_5${43bp}[TCTA]$_{11}$	Brinkmann *et al.* (1996a)
35.1	248 bp	231 bp	Not published	STRBase
35.2 (76)	249 bp	232 bp	[TCTA]$_5$[TCTG]$_6${43bp}[TCTA]$_{15}$TA TCTA	Zhou *et al.* (1997)
35.3	250 bp	233 bp	Not published	SGM Plus
36 (77)	251 bp	234 bp	[TCTA]$_{11}$[TCTG]$_5${43bp}[TCTA]$_{12}$	Griffiths *et al.* (1998)
36' (77)	251 bp	234 bp	[TCTA]$_{10}$[TCTG]$_5${43bp}[TCTA]$_{13}$	Brinkmann *et al.* (1996a)
36" (77)	251 bp	234 bp	[TCTA]$_{10}$[TCTG]$_6${43bp}[TCTA]$_{12}$	Brinkmann *et al.* (1996a)
36.2	253 bp	236 bp	[TCTA]$_5$[TCTG]$_6${43bp}[TCTA]$_{16}$ TA TCTA	Zhou *et al.* (1997)
36.3	254 bp	237 bp	Not published	SGM Plus
37 (78)	255 bp	238 bp	[TCTA]$_{11}$[TCTG]$_5${43bp}[TCTA]$_{13}$	Griffiths *et al.* (1998)
37' (78)	255 bp	238 bp	[TCTA]$_9$[TCTG]$_{11}${43bp}[TCTA]$_{12}$	Brinkmann *et al.* (1996a)
37.2	257 bp	240 bp	Not published	SGM Plus
38 (79)	259 bp	242 bp	[TCTA]$_{13}$[TCTG]$_5${43bp}[TCTA]$_{12}$	Griffiths *et al.* (1998)
38' (79)	259 bp	242 bp	[TCTA]$_9$[TCTG]$_{11}${43bp}[TCTA]$_{12}$	Brinkmann *et al.* (1996a)
38" (79)	259 bp	242 bp	[TCTA]$_{10}$[TCTG]$_{11}${43bp}[TCTA]$_{13}$	Brinkmann *et al.* (1996a)
38''' (79)	259 bp	242 bp	[TCTA]$_{11}$[TCTG]$_{11}${43bp}[TCTA]$_{11}$	Brinkmann *et al.* (1996a)
38.2	261 bp	244 bp	Not published	SGM Plus

*Allele designations shown in parentheses come from Urquhart *et al.* 1994.
70 observed alleles

REFERENCES

Amorim, A., Gusmao, L. and Prata, M. J. (1996) *Advances in Forensic Haemogenetics*, 6, 486–488.

Barber, M.D., McKeown, B.J. and Parkin, B.H. (1996) *International Journal of Legal Medicine*, 108, 180–185.

Barber, M.D. and Parkin, B.H. (1996) *International Journal of Legal Medicine*, 109, 62–65.

Brinkmann, B., Meyer, E. and Junge, A. (1996a) *Human Genetics*, 98, 60–64.

Brinkmann, B., Sajantila, A., Goedde, H.W., Matsumoto, H., Nishi, K. and Wiegand, P. (1996b) *European Journal of Human Genetics*, 4, 175–182.

Budowle, B. and Moretti, T.R. (1998). *Proceedings of the Ninth International Symposium on Human Identification.* Madison, WI: Promega Corporation, pp. 64–73.

Budowle, B., Nhari, L.T., Moretti, T.R., Kanoyangwa, S.B., Masuka, E., Defenbaugh, D.A. and Smerick, J.B. (1997) *Forensic Science International*, 90, 215–221.

Espinheira, R., Geada, H., Ribeiro, T. and Reys, L. (1996) *Advances in Forensic Haemogenetics*, 6, 528.

Gene, M., Huguet, E., Moreno, P., Sanchez, C., Carracedo, A. and Corbella, J. (1996) *International Journal of Legal Medicine*, 108, 318–320.

Gill, P., Kimpton, C. P., Urquhart, A., Oldroyd, N., Millican, E.S., Watson, S.K. and Downes, T.J. (1995) *Electrophoresis*, 16, 1543–1552.

Gill, P., Urquhart, A., Millican, E.S., Oldroyd, N.J., Watson, S., Sparkes, R. and Kimpton, C.P. (1996) *International Journal of Legal Medicine*, 109, 14–22.

Griffiths, R.A.L., Barber, M.D., Johnson, P.E., Gillbard, S.M., Haywood, M.D., Smith, C.D., Arnold, J., Burke, T., Urquhart, A. and Gill, P. (1998) *International Journal of Legal Medicine*, 111, 267–272.

Huang, N.E., Schumm, J.W. and Budowle, B. (1995) *Forensic Science International*, 71, 131–136.

Lazaruk, K., Walsh, P.S., Oaks, F., Gilbert, D., Rosenblum, B.B., Menchen, S., Scheibler, D., Wenz, H.M., Holt, C. and Wallin, J. (1998) *Electrophoresis*, 19, 86–93.

Klintschar, M., Kozma, Z., Al Hammadi, N., Fatah, M.A. and Nohammer, C. (1998) *International Journal of Legal Medicine*, 111, 107–109.

Lins, A.M., Micka, K.A., Sprecher, C.J., Taylor, J.A., Bacher, J.W., Rabbach, D., Bever, R.A., Creacy, S. and Schumm, J.W. (1998) *Journal of Forensic Science*, 43, 1178–1190.

Luis, J., Liste, I. and Caeiro, B. (1994) *Advances in Forensic Haemogenetics*, 5, 366–368.

Moller, A., Meyer, E. and Brinkmann, B. (1994) *International Journal of Legal Medicine*, 106, 319–323.

Mornhinweg, E., Luckenbach, C., Fimmers, R. and Ritter, H. (1998) *Forensic Science International*, 95, 173–178.

Perkin Elmer Corporation (1998) *AmpFlSTR® COfiler™ PCR Amplification Kit User's Bulletin*. Foster City: PE Applied Biosystems.

Perkin Elmer Corporation (1998). *AmpFlSTR® Profiler Plus™ PCR Amplification Kit User's Manual*. Foster City: PE Applied Biosystems.

Perkin Elmer Corporation. (1999). *AmpFlSTR® SGM Plus™ PCR Amplification Kit User's Manual*. Foster City: PE Applied Biosystems.

Puers, C., Lins, A. M., Sprecher, C. J., Brinkmann, B. and Schumm, J. W. (1993) *Proceedings of the Fourth International Symposium on Human Identification.* Madison, WI: Promega Corporation, pp. 161–172.

Schwartz, D. W. M., Dauber, E. M., Glock, B. and Mayr, W. R. (1996) *Advances in Forensic Haemogenetics,* 5, 622–625.

STRBase variant allele report; http://www.cstl.nist.gov/biotech/strbase/var_tab.htm.

Szibor, R., Lautsch, S., Plate, I., Bender, K. and Krause, D. (1998) *International Journal of Legal Medicine,* 111, 160–161.

Urquhart, A., Kimpton, C.P., Downes, T.J. and Gill, P. (1994) *International Journal of Legal Medicine,* 107, 13–20.

van Oorschot, R.A.H., Gutowski, S.J. and Robinson, S.L. (1994) *International Journal of Legal Medicine,* 107, 121–126.

Zhou, H.G., Sato, K., Nishimaki, Y., Fang, L. and Hasekura, H. (1997) *Forensic Science International,* 86, 109–188.

As part of the process of validating new forensic DNA markers, family studies are typically conducted to demonstrate that these DNA markers are inherited properly according to Mendelian rules. The Centre d'Etude du Polymorphisme Humain (CEPH), located in France, has collected DNA from 61 large families of Utah Mormon, Venezuelan, and Amish descent. Each family set contains three generations: four grandparents, two parents, and a number of sons and daughters. These CEPH family DNA sets are ideal for studying inheritance patterns and may be purchased from Coriell Cell Repositories (see the following URL on the World Wide Web; http://locus.umdnj.edu/nigms/ceph/cephkits.html).

We have included here in this appendix the genotyping results for CEPH reference family #13293 (see Figure A.1), which is a Utah Mormon family with four grandparents, two parents, five sons, and two daughters. These 13 DNA samples were typed at all 13 CODIS STR loci using the ABI Prism® 310 Genetic Analyzer and the AmpFlSTR® Profiler Plus™ and COfiler™ kits. The alleles from each grandparent have been colored separately. The color block around each allele in the offspring illustrates the source of that particular allele. Thus, allele inheritance patterns can be easily seen based on the color of a particular allele call compared to the grandparents. Note that none of the sons and daughters share the same DNA profile across the 13 CODIS STR loci. There is effective shuffling of the alleles with each generation. No mutations at any of the STR markers were observed in this data set.

Figure A.1: CEPH Utah Pedigree 13293.

PGF = paternal grandfather   MGF = maternal grandfather   S = son

PGM = paternal grandmother   MGM = maternal grandmother   D = daughter

F = father   M = mother

CEPH Utah Pedigree 13293

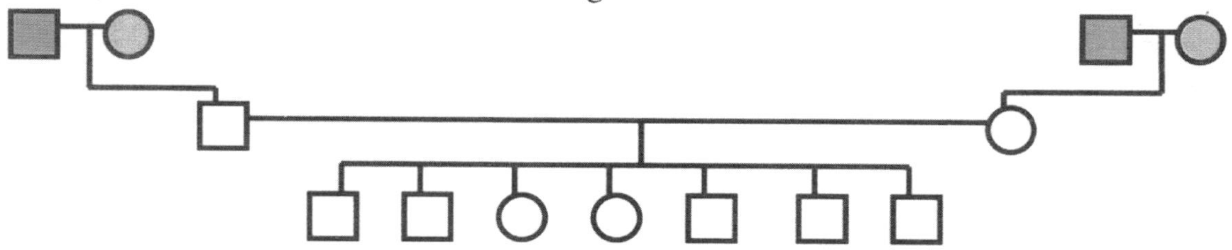

Marker	PGF	PGM	F	S1	S2	D1	D2	S3	S4	S5	M	MGF	MGM
CSF1PO	11,12	10,10	10,12	12,13	12,12	10,12	10,12	12,13	12,12	12,12	12,13	12,13	10,13
FGA	20,22	20,21	20,20	20,21	20,24	20,24	20,24	20,24	20,24	20,21	21,24	21,24	21,22
TH01	9.3,9.3	7,9	9,9.3	8,9	8,9.3	8,9	8,9	8,9	8,9	8,9	8,8	6,8	7,8
TPOX	8,8	8,8	8,8	8,8	8,8	8,8	8,8	8,8	8,8	8,8	8,8	8,8	8,9
VWA	16,16	17,19	16,17	16,17	16,17	17,17	16,16	16,17	17,17	16,17	16,17	16,16	16,17
D3S1358	14,15	17,18	14,18	15,18	16,18	14,15	14,15	15,18	15,18	16,18	15,16	15,16	15,17
D5S818	10,12	10,12	10,12	11,12	12,13	10,13	10,11	12,13	11,12	12,13	11,13	11,12	9,13
D7S820	13,13	9,11	9,13	9,12	9,9	9,9	9,13	9,12	12,13	12,13	9,12	9,11	9,12
D8S1179	12,13	11,13	13,13	13,13	10,13	10,13	13,13	10,13	13,13	13,13	10,13	10,13	13,13
D13S317	9,13	9,10	9,10	10,12	10,11	9,12	10,11	10,11	10,12	9,11	11,12	11,12	11,12
D16S539	12,13	12,13	13,13	12,13	13,13	12,13	13,13	12,13	13,13	13,13	12,13	9,13	12,12
D18S51	13,13	13,14	13,13	12,13	13,13	13,13	12,13	13,13	13,13	13,13	12,13	13,17	12,12
D21S11	29,29	28,29	29,29	29,32.2	29,32.2	29,32.2	29,32.2	29,32.2	29,32.2	29,32.2	32.2,32.2	30,32.2	28,32.2
AMEL	X,Y	X,X	X,Y	X,Y	X,Y	X,X	X,X	X,Y	X,Y	X,Y	X,X	X,Y	X,X

DNA ADVISORY BOARD
QUALITY ASSURANCE STANDARDS

The following information has been previously published and is available directly from the US Department of Justice, Federal Bureau of Investigation (FBI). However, we felt it would be a valuable addition to this book to include these documents in their entirety so that they could be readily accessible to the reader. The DNA Advisory Board (DAB) was established by the Director of the FBI under the DNA Identification Act of 1994 to operate for a period of 5 years and consists of 13 voting members. One of the primary purposes of the DAB was to recommend standards for quality assurance in conducting analysis of DNA and to provide guidance to forensic analysts performing those DNA analyses. The following national standards supersede the TWGDAM Guidelines for purposes of certifications required to receive federal funding and to participate in the US National DNA Index System. Two sets of standards have been issued by the DAB. The first set, which became effective on 1 October 1998, was directed towards forensic DNA laboratories conducting casework investigations. The second set, which became effective on 1 April 1999, is directed at government laboratories performing convicted offender DNA databasing. We have merged both documents (as they contain many redundant points) and list any unique items from the convicted offender DNA databasing laboratory standards in italics.

DNA ADVISORY BOARD
QUALITY ASSURANCE STANDARDS FOR FORENSIC
DNA TESTING LABORATORIES *FOR CONVICTED*
OFFENDER DNA DATABASING LABORATORIES

PREFACE

Throughout its deliberation concerning these quality standards, the DNA Advisory Board recognized the need for a mechanism to ensure compliance with the standards. An underlying premise for these discussions was that accreditation would be required to demonstrate compliance with the standards and therefore assure quality control and a quality program. Accordingly, the Board recommends that forensic laboratories performing DNA analysis seek such accreditation with all deliberate speed. Additionally, the Board strongly encourages the accrediting bodies to begin positioning themselves to accommodate the increasing demand for accreditation.

PROPOSED MECHANISM TO RECOMMEND CHANGES TO STANDARDS

Once the Director of the FBI has issued standards for quality assurance for forensic DNA testing, the DNA Advisory Board may recommend revisions to such standards to the FBI Director, as necessary. In the event that the duration of the DNA Advisory Board is extended beyond March 10, 2000 by the FBI Director, the Board may continue to recommend revisions to such standards to the FBI Director. In the event that the DNA Advisory Board is not extended by the FBI Director after March 10, 2000, the Technical Working Group on DNA Analysis Methods [TWGDAM] may recommend revisions to such standards to the FBI Director, as necessary.

EFFECTIVE DATE

These standards shall take effect October 1, 1998.
These Quality Assurance Standards for Convicted Offender DNA Databasing Laboratories take effect April 1, 1999.

QUALITY ASSURANCE STANDARDS FOR FORENSIC DNA TESTING LABORATORIES

INTRODUCTION

Forensic DNA identification analysis currently involves forensic casework and convicted offender analyses. These complementary functions demand adherence to the highest analytical standards possible to protect both public safety and individual rights. Separate standards have been drafted for laboratories performing these functions. This separation is an acknowledgment of the differences in the nature or type of sample, the typical sample quantity and potential for reanalysis, and specialization that may exist in a laboratory. Standards for convicted offender laboratories, in some instances, are less stringent than those performing forensic casework analyses, but in no case should the two documents be interpreted as conflicting.

This document consists of definitions and standards. The standards are quality assurance measures that place specific requirements on the laboratory. Equivalent measures not outlined in this document may also meet the standard if determined sufficient through an accreditation process.

REFERENCES

American Society of Crime Laboratory Directors-Laboratory Accreditation Board (ASCLD-LAB). ASCLD-LAB Accreditation Manual, January 1994, and January 1997.

Federal Bureau of Investigation, Quality Assurance Standards for Forensic DNA Testing Laboratories (1998).

International Standards Organization (ISO)/International Electrotechnical Commission (IEC), ISO/IEC Guide 25-1990, (1990) American National Standards Institute, New York, NY.

Technical Working Group on DNA Analysis Methods, 'Guidelines for a Quality Assurance Program for DNA Analysis,' Crime Laboratory Digest, April 1995, Volume 22, Number 2, pp. 21–43.

42 Code of Federal Regulations, Chapter IV (10-1-95 Edition), Health Care Financing Administration, Health and Human Services.

1. SCOPE

The standards describe the quality assurance requirements that a *government* laboratory, which is defined as a facility in which forensic DNA testing is performed (*convicted offender DNA testing is regularly performed*), should follow to ensure the quality and integrity of the data and competency of the laboratory. These standards do not preclude the participation of a laboratory, by itself or in collaboration with others, in research and development, on procedures that have not yet been validated.

2. DEFINITIONS

As used in these standards, the following terms shall have the meanings specified:

(a) Administrative review is an evaluation of the report and supporting documentation for consistency with laboratory policies and for editorial correctness.

(b) Amplification blank control consists of only amplification reagents without the addition of sample DNA. This control is used to detect DNA contamination of the amplification reagents.

(c) Analytical procedure is an orderly step-by-step procedure designed to ensure operational uniformity and to minimize analytical drift.

(d) Audit is an inspection used to evaluate, confirm, or verify activity related to quality.

   Batch is a group of samples analyzed at the same time.

(e) Calibration is the set of operations which establish, under specified conditions, the relationship between values indicated by a measuring instrument or measuring system, or values represented by a material, and the corresponding known values of a measurement.

   CODIS is the Combined DNA Index System administered by the FBI. It houses DNA profiles from convicted offenders, forensic specimens, population samples and other specimen types.

(f) Critical reagents are determined by empirical studies or routine practice to require testing on established samples before use on evidentiary samples in order to prevent unnecessary loss of sample.

(g) Commercial test kit is a pre-assembled kit that allows the user to conduct a specific forensic DNA test.

   Convicted offender is an individual who is required by statute to submit a standard sample for DNA databasing.

   Convicted offender database (CODIS) manager or custodian (or equivalent role, position, or title as designated by the laboratory director) is the person responsible for administration and security of the laboratory's CODIS.

   Convicted offender standard sample is biological material collected from an individual for DNA analysis and inclusion into CODIS. See also database sample.

Critical equipment or instruments are those requiring calibration prior to use and periodically thereafter.

Database sample is a known blood or standard sample obtained from an individual whose DNA profile will be included in a computerized database and searched against other DNA profiles.

(h) Examiner/analyst *(or equivalent role, position, or title as designated by the laboratory director)* is an individual who conducts and/or directs the analysis of forensic casework samples, interprets data and reaches conclusions.

(i) Forensic DNA testing is the identification and evaluation of biological evidence in criminal matters using DNA technologies.

(j) Known samples are biological material whose identity or type is established.

(k) Laboratory is a *government* facility in which forensic DNA testing *(convicted offender DNA testing)* is performed *or a government facility who contracts with a second entity for such testing.*

(l) Laboratory support personnel *(or equivalent role, position, or title as designated by the laboratory director)* are individual(s) who perform laboratory duties and do not analyze evidence samples.

(m) NIST is the National Institute of Standards and Technology.

(n) Polymerase Chain Reaction (PCR) is an enzymatic process by which a specific region of DNA is replicated during repetitive cycles which consist of (1) denaturation of the template; (2) annealing of primers to complementary sequences at an empirically determined temperature; and (3) extension of the bound primers by a DNA polymerase.

(o) Proficiency test sample is biological material whose DNA type has been previously characterized and which is used to monitor the quality performance of a laboratory or an individual.

(p) Proficiency testing is a quality assurance measure used to monitor performance and identify areas in which improvement may be needed. Proficiency tests may be classified as:

1 Internal proficiency test is one prepared and administered by the laboratory;
2 External proficiency test, which may be open or blind, is one which is obtained from a second agency.

(q) Qualifying test measures proficiency in both technical skills and knowledge.

(r) Quality assurance includes the systematic actions necessary to demonstrate that a product or service meets specified requirements for quality.

(s) Quality manual is a document stating the quality policy, quality system and quality practices of an organization.

(t)   Quality system is the organizational structure, responsibilities, procedures, processes and resources for implementing quality management.

(u)   Reagent blank control consists of all reagents used in the test process without any sample. This is to be used to detect DNA contamination of the analytical reagents.

(v)   Reference material (certified or standard) is a material for which values are certified by a technically valid procedure and accompanied by or traceable to a certificate or other documentation, which is issued by a certifying body.

(w)   Restriction Fragment Length Polymorphism (RFLP) is generated by cleavage by a specific restriction enzyme and the variation is due to restriction site polymorphism and/or the number of different repeats contained within the fragments.

(x)   Review is an evaluation of documentation to check for consistency, accuracy, and completeness.

(y)   Second agency is an entity or organization external to and independent of the laboratory and which performs forensic DNA *(DNA identification)* analysis.

(z)   Secure area is a locked space (for example, cabinet, vault or room) with access restricted to authorized personnel.

(aa)   Subcontractor is an individual or entity having a transactional relationship with a laboratory.

(bb)   Technical manager or leader (or equivalent position or title as designated by the laboratory system) is the individual who is accountable for the technical operations of the laboratory.

(cc)   Technical review is an evaluation of reports, notes, data, and other documents to ensure an appropriate and sufficient basis for the scientific conclusions. This review is conducted by a second qualified individual.

(dd)   Technician *(or equivalent role, position, or title as designated by the laboratory director)* is an individual who performs analytical techniques on evidence samples under the supervision of a qualified examiner/analyst and/or performs DNA analysis on samples for inclusion in a database. Technicians do not evaluate or reach conclusions on typing results or prepare final reports.

(ee)   Traceability is the property of a result of a measurement whereby it can be related to appropriate standards, generally international or national standards, through an unbroken chain of comparisons.

(ff)   Validation is a process by which a procedure is evaluated to determine its efficacy and reliability for forensic casework analysis *(DNA analysis)* and includes:

   1   Developmental validation is the acquisition of test data and determination of conditions and limitations of a new or novel DNA methodology for use on forensic samples.
   2   Internal validation is an accumulation of test data within the laboratory to demonstrate that established methods and procedures perform as expected in the laboratory.

3. QUALITY ASSURANCE PROGRAM

STANDARD 3.1 The laboratory shall establish and maintain a documented quality system that is appropriate to the testing activities.

3.1.1 The quality manual shall address at a minimum:
- (a) Goals and objectives
- (b) Organization and management
- (c) Personnel Qualifications and Training
- (d) Facilities
- (e) Evidence control *(Sample control)*
- (f) Validation
- (g) Analytical procedures
- (h) Calibration and maintenance
- (i) Proficiency testing
- (j) Corrective action
- (k) Reports *(Documentation)*
- (l) Review
- (m) Safety
- (n) Audits

4. ORGANIZATION AND MANAGEMENT

STANDARD 4.1 The laboratory shall:

(a) Have a managerial staff with the authority and resources needed to discharge their duties and meet the requirements of the standards in this document.

(b) Have a technical manager or leader who is accountable for the technical operations. *(Have a CODIS manager or custodian who is accountable for CODIS operations).*

(c) Specify and document the responsibility, authority, and interrelation of all personnel who manage, perform or verify work affecting the validity of the DNA analysis.

5. PERSONNEL

STANDARD 5.1 Laboratory personnel shall have the education, training and experience commensurate with the examination and testimony provided. The laboratory shall:

5.1.1 Have a written job description for personnel to include responsibilities, duties and skills.

5.1.2 Have a documented training program for qualifying all technical laboratory personnel.

5.1.3 Have a documented program to ensure technical qualifications are maintained through continuing education.

    5.1.3.1 Continuing education – the technical manager or leader, *(CODIS manager or custodian)* and examiner/analyst(s) must stay abreast of developments within the field of DNA typing by reading current scientific literature and by attending seminars, courses, professional meetings or documented training sessions/classes in relevant subject areas at least once a year.

5.1.4 Maintain records on the relevant qualifications, training, skills and experience of the technical personnel.

STANDARD 5.2 The technical manager or leader shall have the following:

5.2.1 <u>Degree requirements:</u> The technical manager or leader of a laboratory shall have at a minimum a Master's degree in biology-, chemistry- or forensic science-related area and successfully completed a minimum of 12 semester or equivalent credit hours of a combination of undergraduate and graduate course work covering the subject areas of biochemistry, genetics and molecular biology (molecular genetics, recombinant DNA technology), or other subjects which provide a basic under-standing of the foundation of forensic DNA analysis as well as statistics and/or pop-ulation genetics as it applies to forensic DNA analysis.

    5.2.1.1 The degree requirements of section 5.2.1 may be waived by the American Society of Crime Laboratory Directors (ASCLD) or other organization des-ignated by the Director of the FBI in accordance with criteria approved by the Director of the FBI. This waiver shall be available for a period of two years from the effective date of these standards. The waiver shall be permanent and portable.

5.2.2 <u>Experience requirements:</u> A technical manager or leader of a laboratory must have a minimum of three years of forensic DNA laboratory experience *(relevant problem solving or related analytical laboratory experience).*

5.2.3 Duty requirements:

    5.2.3.1 <u>General:</u> manages the technical operations of the laboratory.

    5.2.3.2 <u>Specific duties</u>
        (a) Is responsible for evaluating all methods used by the laboratory and for proposing new or modified analytical procedures to be used by examiners.
        (b) Is responsible for technical problem solving of analytical methods and for the oversight of training, quality assurance, safety and proficiency testing in the laboratory.

    5.2.3.3 The technical manager or leader shall be accessible to the laboratory to provide onsite, telephone or electronic consultation as needed.

STANDARD 5.3 *CODIS manager or custodian shall have the following:*

5.3.1 <u>Degree requirements:</u> A CODIS manager or custodian shall have, at a minimum, a Bachelor's degree in a natural science or computer science.

5.3.2 <u>Experience requirements:</u> A CODIS manager or custodian shall have a working knowledge of computers, computer networks, and computer database management, with an understanding of DNA profile interpretation.

5.3.3 *Duty requirements:*
   (a) *Is the system administrator of the laboratory's CODIS network and is responsible for the security of DNA profile data stored in CODIS.*
   (b) *Is responsible for oversight of CODIS computer training and quality assurance of data.*
   (c) *Has the authority to terminate the laboratory's participation in CODIS in the event of a problem until the reliability of the computer data can be assured. The state CODIS manager or custodian has this authority over all CODIS sites under his/her jurisdiction.*

STANDARD 5.3 Examiner/analyst shall have:

5.3.1 *Degree requirements: An examiner/analyst shall have,* at a minimum a BA/BS *(Bachelor's)* degree or its equivalent degree in biology-, chemistry- or forensic science-related area and must have successfully completed college course work (graduate or undergraduate level) covering the subject areas of biochemistry, genetics and molecular biology (molecular genetics, recombinant DNA technology) or other subjects which provide a basic understanding of the foundation of forensic DNA analysis, as well as course work and/or training in statistics and population genetics as it applies to forensic DNA analysis.

5.3.2 *Experience requirements: An examiner/analyst shall have* a minimum of six (6) months of forensic DNA laboratory experience, including the successful analysis of a range of samples typically encountered in forensic case work prior to independent case work analysis using DNA technology.

5.3.3 *An examiner/analyst shall have* successfully completed a qualifying test before beginning independent casework responsibilities.

STANDARD 5.4 Technician shall have:

5.4.1 On the job training specific to their job function(s).

5.4.2 Successfully completed a qualifying test before participating in forensic DNA typing responsibilities.

STANDARD 5.5 Laboratory support personnel shall have:

5.5.1 Training, education and experience commensurate with their responsibilities as outlined in their job description.

6. FACILITIES

STANDARD 6.1 The laboratory shall have a facility that is designed to provide adequate security and minimize contamination. The laboratory shall ensure that:

6.1.1 Access to the laboratory is controlled and limited.

6.1.2 Prior to PCR amplification, evidence examinations, *liquid sample examinations,* DNA extractions, and PCR setup are conducted at separate times or in separate spaces.

6.1.3 Amplified DNA product is generated, processed and maintained in a room(s) separate from the evidence examination, *liquid blood examinations,* DNA extractions and PCR setup areas.

6.1.4 A robotic work station may be used to carry out DNA extraction and amplification in a single room, provided it can be demonstrated that contamination in minimized and equivalent to that when performed manually in separation rooms.

6.1.4 The laboratory follows written procedures for monitoring, cleaning and decontaminating facilities and equipment.

7. EVIDENCE CONTROL (SAMPLE CONTROL)

STANDARD 7.1 The laboratory shall have and follow a documented evidence (*sample inventory*) control system to ensure the integrity of physical evidence. This system shall ensure that:

7.1.1 Evidence is *(Offender samples are)* marked for identification.

7.1.2 Chain of custody for all evidence is maintained.

7.1.2 Documentation of sample identity, collection, receipt, storage, and disposition is maintained.

7.1.3 The laboratory follows documented procedures that minimize loss, contamination, and/or deleterious change of evidence.

7.1.4 The laboratory has secure areas for evidence storage *(sample storage including environmental control consistent with the form or nature of the sample).*

STANDARD 7.2 Where possible, the laboratory shall retain or return a portion of the evidence sample or extract.

7.2.1 The laboratory shall have a procedure requiring that evidence sample/extract(s) are stored in a manner that minimizes degradation.

8. VALIDATION

STANDARD 8.1 The laboratory shall use validated methods and procedures for forensic casework analyses *(DNA analyses).*

8.1.1 Developmental validation that is conducted shall be appropriately documented.

8.1.2 Novel forensic DNA methodologies shall undergo developmental validation to ensure the accuracy, precision and reproducibility of the procedure. The developmental validation shall include the following:

    8.1.2.1 Documentation exists and is available which defines and characterizes the locus.

    8.1.2.2 Species specificity, sensitivity, stability and mixture studies are conducted.

    8.1.2.3 Population distribution data are documented and available.

        8.1.2.3.1 The population distribution data would include the allele and genotype distributions for the locus or loci obtained from relevant populations. Where appropriate, databases should be tested for independence expectations.

8.1.3 Internal validation shall be performed and documented by the laboratory.

    8.1.3.1 The procedure shall be tested using known and non-probative evidence samples *(known samples only)*. The laboratory shall monitor and document the reproducibility and precision of the procedure using human DNA control(s).

    8.1.3.2 The laboratory shall establish and document match criteria based on empirical data.

    8.1.3.3 Before the introduction of a procedure into forensic casework *(database sample analysis)*, the analyst or examination team shall successfully complete a qualifying test.

    8.1.3.4 Material modifications made to analytical procedures shall be documented and subject to validation testing.

8.1.4 Where methods are not specified, the laboratory shall, wherever possible, select methods that have been published by reputable technical organizations or in relevant scientific texts or journals, or have been appropriately evaluated for a specific or unique application.

9. ANALYTICAL PROCEDURES

STANDARD 9.1 The laboratory shall have and follow written analytical procedures approved by the laboratory management/technical manager.

9.1.1 The laboratory shall have a standard operating protocol for each analytical technique used.

9.1.2 The procedures shall include reagents, sample preparation, extraction, equipment, and controls, which are standard for DNA analysis and data interpretation.

9.1.3 The laboratory shall have a procedure for differential extraction of stains that potentially contain semen.

STANDARD 9.2 The laboratory shall use reagents that are suitable for the methods employed.

9.2.1 The laboratory shall have written procedures for documenting commercial supplies and for the formulation of reagents.

9.2.2 Reagents shall be labeled with the identity of the reagent, the date of preparation or expiration, and the identity of the individual preparing the reagent.

9.2.3 The laboratory shall identify critical reagents *(if any)* and evaluate them prior to use in casework. These critical reagents include but are not limited to: *(THIS LAST PORTION NOT IN CONVICTED OFFENDER DATABASING STANDARDS)*

(a)   Restriction enzyme
(b)   Commercial kits for performing genetic typing
(c)   Agarose for analytical RFLP gels
(d)   Membranes for Southern blotting
(e)   K562 DNA or other human DNA controls
(f)   Molecular weight markers used as RFLP sizing standards
(g)   Primer sets
(h)   Thermostable DNA polymerase

STANDARD 9.3 The laboratory shall have and follow a procedure for evaluating the quantity of the human DNA in the sample where possible. *(NOT IN CONVICTED OFFENDER DATABASING STANDARDS)*

9.3.1 For casework RFLP samples, the presence of high molecular weight DNA should be determined.

STANDARD 9.4 The laboratory shall monitor the analytical procedures using appropriate controls and standards.

9.4.1 The following controls shall be used in RFLP casework analysis:

9.4.1.1 Quantitation standards for estimating the amount of DNA recovered by extraction. *(When required by the analytical procedure, standards for estimating the amount of DNA recovered by extraction shall be used.)*

9.4.1.2 K562 as a human DNA control. (In monitoring sizing data, a statistical quality control method for K562 cell line shall be maintained.)

9.4.1.3 Molecular weight size markers to bracket known and evidence samples. *(Molecular weight size markers to bracket samples on an analytical gel. No more than five lanes shall exist between marker lanes.)*

9.4.1.4 A Procedure *shall be available* to monitor the completeness of restriction enzyme digestion. *(Interpretation of the autorad/lumigraph is the ultimate method of assessment but a test gel or other method may be used as necessary.)*

9.4.2 The following controls shall be used for PCR casework analysis *(database analysis)*:

9.4.2.1 Quantitation standards, which estimate the amount of human nuclear DNA recovered by extraction. *(When required by the analytical procedure, standards which estimate the amount of human nuclear DNA recovered by extraction shall be used.)*

9.4.2.2 Positive and negative amplification controls.

9.4.2.3 Reagent blanks. *(Contamination controls.)*

    9.4.2.3.1 Samples extracted prior to the effective date of these standards without reagent blanks are acceptable as long as other samples analyzed in the batch do not demonstrate contamination.

9.4.2.4 Allelic ladders and/or internal size makers for variable number tandem repeat sequence PCR based systems.

STANDARD 9.5 The laboratory shall check its DNA procedures annually or whenever substantial changes are made to the protocol(s) against an appropriate and available NIST standard reference material or standard traceable to a NIST standard.

STANDARD 9.6 The laboratory shall have and follow written general guidelines for the interpretation of data.

9.6.1 The laboratory shall verify that all control results are within established tolerance limits.

9.6.2 Where appropriate, visual matches shall be supported by a numerical match criterion. *(NOT IN CONVICTED OFFENDER DATABASING STANDARDS)*

9.6.3 For a given population(s) and/or hypothesis of relatedness, the statistical interpretation shall be made following the recommendations 4.1, 4.2 or 4.3 as deemed applicable of the National Research Council report entitled 'The Evaluation of Forensic DNA Evidence' (1996) and/or court directed method. These calculations shall be derived from a documented population database appropriate for the calculation. *(NOT IN CONVICTED OFFENDER DATABASING STANDARDS)*

10. EQUIPMENT CALIBRATION AND MAINTENANCE

STANDARD 10.1 The laboratory shall use equipment suitable for the methods employed.

STANDARD 10.2 The laboratory *(shall identify critical equipment and)* shall have a documented program for calibration of instruments and equipment.

10.2.1 Where available and appropriate, standards traceable to national or international standards shall be used for the calibration.

10.2.1.1 Where traceability to national standards of measurement is not applicable, the laboratory shall provide satisfactory evidence of correlation of results.

10.2.2 The frequency of the calibration shall be documented for each instrument requiring calibration. Such documentation shall be retained in accordance with applicable Federal or state law.

STANDARD 10.3 The laboratory shall have and follow a documented program to ensure that instruments and equipment are properly maintained.

10.3.1 New *(critical)* instruments and equipment, or *(critical)* instruments and equipment that have undergone repair or maintenance, shall be calibrated before being used in casework analysis.

10.3.2 Written records or logs shall be maintained for maintenance service performed on instruments and equipment. Such documentation shall be retained in accordance with applicable Federal or state law.

11. REPORTS

STANDARD 11.1 The laboratory shall have and follow written procedures for taking and maintaining case notes to support the conclusions drawn in laboratory reports. *(The laboratory shall have and follow written procedures for generating and maintaining documentation for database samples.)*

11.1.1 The laboratory shall maintain, in a case record, all documentation generated by examiners related to case analyses. *(The laboratory shall have written procedures for the release of database sample information.)*

11.1.2 Reports according to written guidelines shall include: *(NOT IN CONVICTED OFFENDER DATABASING STANDARDS)*

(a) Case identifier
(b) Description of evidence examined
(c) A description of the methodology
(d) Locus
(e) Results and/or conclusions
(f) An interpretative statement (either quantitative or qualitative)
(g) Date issued
(h) Disposition of evidence
(i) A signature and title, or equivalent identification, of the person(s) accepting responsibility for the content of the report.

11.1.3 The laboratory shall have written procedures for the release of case report information. *(NOT IN CONVICTED OFFENDER DATABASING STANDARDS)*

12. REVIEW

STANDARD 12.1 The laboratory shall conduct administrative and technical reviews of all case files and reports to ensure conclusions and supporting data are reasonable and within the constraints of scientific knowledge. *(The laboratory shall have and follow written procedures for reviewing database sample information, results, and matches.)*

12.1.1 The laboratory shall have a mechanism in place to address unresolved discrepant conclusions between analysts and reviewer(s).

STANDARD 12.2 The laboratory shall have and follow a program that documents the annual monitoring of the testimony of each examiner *(laboratory personnel)*.

13. PROFICIENCY TESTING

STANDARD 13.1 Examiners and other personnel designated by the technical manager or leader who are actively engaged in DNA analysis shall undergo, at regular intervals of not to exceed 180 days, external proficiency testing in accordance with these standards. Such external proficiency testing shall be an open proficiency testing program.

13.1.1 The laboratory shall maintain the following records for proficiency tests:
(a) The test set identifier.
(b) Identity of the examiner.

(c) Date of analysis and completion.
(d) Copies of all data and notes supporting the conclusions.
(e) The proficiency test results.
(f) Any discrepancies noted.
(g) Corrective actions taken.
Such documentation shall be retained in accordance with applicable Federal or state law.

13.1.2 The laboratory shall establish at a minimum the following criteria for evaluation of proficiency tests:
(a) All reported inclusions are correct or incorrect.
(b) All reported exclusions are correct or incorrect.
(c) All reported genotypes and/or phenotypes are correct or incorrect according to consensus genotypes/phenotypes or within established empirically determined ranges.
(d) All results reported as inconclusive or uninterpretable are consistent with written laboratory guidelines. The basis for inconclusive interpretations in proficiency tests must be documented.
(e) All discrepancies/errors and subsequent corrective actions must be documented.
(f) All final reports are graded as satisfactory or unsatisfactory. A satisfactory grade is attained when there are no analytical errors for the DNA profile typing data. Administrative errors shall be documented and corrective actions taken to minimize the error in the future.
(g) All proficiency test participants shall be informed of the final test results.

14. CORRECTIVE ACTION

STANDARD 14.1 The laboratory shall establish and follow procedures for corrective action whenever proficiency testing discrepancies and/or casework *(analytical)* errors are detected.

14.1.1 The laboratory shall maintain documentation for the corrective action. Such documentation shall be retained in accordance with applicable Federal or state law.

15. AUDITS

STANDARD 15.1 The laboratory shall conduct audits annually in accordance with the standards outlined herein.

15.1.1 Audit procedures shall address at a minimum:
(a) Quality assurance program
(b) Organization and management
(c) Personnel
(d) Facilities
(e) Evidence control *(Sample control)*
(f) Validation
(g) Analytical procedures
(h) Calibration and maintenance
(i) Proficiency testing
(j) Corrective action
(k) Reports *(Documentation)*

(l) Review
(m) Safety
(n) Previous audits

15.1.2 The laboratory shall retain all documentation pertaining to audits in accordance with relevant legal and agency requirements.

STANDARD 15.2 Once every two years, a second agency shall participate in the annual audit.

16. SAFETY

STANDARD 16.1 The laboratory shall have and follow a documented environmental health and safety program.

17. SUBCONTRACTOR OF ANALYTICAL TESTING FOR WHICH VALIDATED PROCEDURES EXIST

STANDARD 17.1 A laboratory operating under the scope of these standards will require certification of compliance with these standards when a subcontractor performs forensic DNA *(convicted offender DNA)* analyses for the laboratory.

17.1.1 The laboratory will establish and use appropriate review procedures to verify the integrity of the data received from the subcontractor *including but not limited to:*
(a) *Random reanalysis of samples.*
(b) *Visual inspection and evaluation of results/data.*
(c) *Inclusion of QC samples.*
(d) *On-site visits.*

APPENDIX IV

SUPPLIERS OF DNA ANALYSIS EQUIPMENT, PRODUCTS, OR SERVICES

Company Name	Street Address	Contact Information	Products/Services
Affiliated Genetics	P.O. Box 870247, Woods Cross, UT 84087-0247	800-362-5559 Fax: 801-298-3352 www.affiliatedgenetics.com	Paternity testing
Affymetrix	3380 Central Expressway, Santa Clara, CA 95051	408-731-5503 Fax: 408-481-0422 www.affymetrix.com	GeneChip DNA hybridization products
American Type Culture Collection (ATCC)	10801 University Boulevard, Manassas, VA 20110-2209	703-365-2700 Fax: 703-365-2750 www.atcc.org	Genomic DNA and cell cultures for research purposes
Amersham Pharmacia Biotech, Inc.	SE-751 84 Uppsala, Sweden 800 Centennial Avenue, P.O. Box 1327, Piscataway, NJ 08855-1327	Tel: +46 (0) 18 612 00 00 Fax: 46 (0) 18 612 12 00 USA Office: Tel: 732-457-8000 Fax: 732-457-0557 www.apbiotech.com	Molecular biology supplies; analysis instrumentation; ALF DNA Sequencer
Analytical Genetic Testing Center, Inc.	7808 Cherry Creek South Drive #201, Denver, CO 80231	800-204-4721 Fax: 303-750-2171 www.geneticid.com	Paternity testing, forensic DNA analysis, expert witness services
ASCLD-LAB	3200 34th Street South, St Petersburg, FL 33711	727-549-6067 Fax: 727-549-6070 www.ascld-lab.org	Crime laboratory accreditation and audits
Baltimore Rh Typing Laboratory Inc.	400 West Franklin Street, Baltimore, MD 21201	800-765-5170 Fax: 410-383-0938 www.rhlab.com	Paternity testing
Beckman Coulter, Inc.	4300 N. Harbor Blvd, Fullerton, CA 92834	714-871-4848 Fax: 714-773-8283 www.beckmancoulter.com	Analysis instrumentation and robotics for liquid handling
Biosynthesis Inc.	612 East Main St, Lewisville, TX 75057	800-227-0627 Fax: 972-420-0442 www.biosyn.com	Oligo synthesis, molecular biology products, paternity testing
Bode Technology Group	7364 Steel Mill Drive, Springfield, VA 22150	703-644-1200 Fax: 703-644-7730 www.bodetech.com	Contract forensic DNA testing and research

Company Name	Street Address	Contact Information	Products/Services
CBR Laboratories, Inc. Parentage Testing	800 Huntington, Boston, MA 02115	800-850-2466 Fax: 617-278-3493 www.cbrlabs.baweb.com	Paternity testing
Cellmark Diagnostics, Inc.	20271 Goldenrod Lane #101, Germantown, MD 20876	800-USA-LABS Fax: 301-428-4877 www.cellmark-labs.com	Forensic and paternity testing; DNA databanking services
Columbia Laboratory Services	3990 Sheridan St, #202, Hollywood, FL 33021	800-952-2181 Fax: 954-964-3442 www.columbialab.com	Paternity testing
Commonwealth Biotechnology Inc.	601 Biotech Drive, Richmond, VA 23235	800-735-9224 Fax: 804-648-2641 www.cbi-biotech.com	Paternity testing; contract research; oligo synthesis
Coriell Institute for Medical Research	401 Haddon Avenue, Camden, NJ 08103	856-966-7377 Fax: 856-964-0254 arginine.umdnj.edu	Genomic DNA samples and cell cultures for genetic research reagents; CEPH family samples
Cybergenetics, Inc.	160 N. Craig St., Suite 210, Pittsburgh, PA 15213	888-FAST-MAP Fax: 412-683-3005 www.cybgen.com	Software for automated genotyping
DNA Diagnostics Center Paternity Testing	205-C Corporate Ct, Fairfield, OH 45014	800-613-5768 www.dnacenter.com	Paternity testing
Fairfax Identity Laboratories	3025 Hamaker Court #203, Fairfax, VA 22031	800-848-IDNA www.fairfaxidlab.com	Paternity testing; DNA databanking services
FMC Bioproducts	191 Thomaston St, Rockland, ME 04841	207-594-3400 Fax: 207-594-3426 www.bioproducts.com	LongRanger gels; agarose gel materials
Gene Codes Corporation	640 Avis Drive Suite 300, Ann Arbor, MI 48108	800-497-4939 Fax: 734-769-7074 www.genecodes.com	Software for DNA sequencing
Genelex Corporation	2203 Airport Way South, Seattle, WA 98134-2027	800-523-6427 Fax: 206-382-6277 www.genelex.com	Forensic and paternity testing
Gene Screen	2600 Stemmons Freeway #133, Dallas, TX 75207	800-DNA-TEST Fax: 214-634-3322 www.genescreen.com	Forensic and paternity testing
Genetica DNA Laboratories, Inc.	8740 Montgomery Road, Cincinnati, OH 45236	800-433-6848 Fax: 513-985-9983 www.genetica.com	Paternity testing
Genetic Profiles Corporation	6122 Nancy Ridge Dr, # 205, San Diego, CA 92121	800-551-7763 Fax: 619-623-0842 www.geneticprofiles.com	Paternity testing

Company Name	Street Address	Contact Information	Products/Services
Hamilton Company	4970 Energy Way, Reno, NV 89502	800-648-5950 Fax: 775-856-7259 www.hamiltoncomp.com	Robotic pipetting stations
Hitachi Genetic Systems	1201 Harbor Bay Parkway, Alameda, CA 94502	800-624-6176 Fax: 510-337-2099 www.hitachi-soft.com/gs	Genetic analysis instrumentation; FMBIO II
Identigene, Inc.	7400 Fannin, Suite 1222, Houston, TX 77054	800-DNA-TYPE Fax: 713-798-9595 www.identigene.com	Paternity testing
Identity Genetics, Inc.	801 32nd Ave, Brookings, SD 57006	800-861-1054 Fax: 605-697-5306 www.identitygenetics.com	Paternity testing
Identity Link, Inc.	606 Idol Drive, Suite 2, High Point, NC 27262	800-325-5465 Fax: 336-885-3045 www.identitylink.com	Paternity testing
J&W Scientific	91 Blue Ravine Road, Folsom, CA 95630	916-985-7888 Fax: 916-985-1101 www.jandw.com	Capillaries for CE
Kiva Genetics Inc.	2375 Garcia Ave, Mountain View, CA 94043	650-210-3500 Fax: 650-934-9375 www.kivagenetics.com	CE microchip devices; DNA testing services
Laboratory Corporation of America	1447 York Court, Burlington, NC 27215	800-742-3944 336-584-5171 www.labcorp.com	Forensic and paternity testing
Lark Technologies, Inc.	9441 West Sam Houston Parkway South, Suite 103, Houston, TX 77099	800-288-3720 Fax: 713-464-7492 www.lark.com	Molecular biology contract research; Sequencing service
LICOR	4308 Progressive Ave, Lincoln, NE 68504	800-645-4267 Fax: 402-467-2819 bio.licor.com	Instruments for genetic analysis
Lifecodes Corporation	550 West Ave, Stamford, CT 06902	800-543-3263 Fax: 203-328-9599 www.lifecodes.com	Forensic and paternity testing; HLA typing
Life Technologies Inc. (Gibco BRL)	9800 Medical Center Drive, PO Box 6482, Rockville, MD 20849 - 6482	800-338-5772 Fax: 301-610-8699 www.lifetech.com	Molecular biology products
Long Beach Genetics	2384 E. Pacifica Place, Rancho Dominguez, CA 90220	800-824-2699 Fax: 310-632-9424 www.lbgenetics.com	Paternity testing
Memorial Blood Centers of Minnesota Paternity Laboratory	2304 Park Ave, South Minneapolis, MN 55404	612-871-3300 Fax: 612-872-3689 www.mbcm.org	Paternity testing

Company Name	Street Address	Contact Information	Products/Services
Micro Diagnostics, Inc. (Lifecodes Corp.)	1400 Donelson Pike #A-15, Nashville, TN 37217	615-360-5000 Fax: 615-360-5003 www.microdx.com	Forensic and paternity testing
Midland Certified Reagent Company	3112-A West Cuthbert Ave, Midland, TX 79701	800-247-8766 Fax: 915-694-2387 www.mcrc.com	Oligo synthesis
Millipore Corporation	80 Ashby Road, Bedford, MA 01730	800-MILLIPORE Fax: 781-533-3110 www.millipore.com	DNA separation/purification products
Misonix Inc.	1938 New Highway, Farmingdale, NY 11735	800-645-9846 Fax: 516-694-9412 www.misonix.com	PCR laminar flow hoods
Mitotyping Technologies, LLC	1981 Pine Hall Drive, State College, PA 16801	814-861-0676 Fax: 814-861-0576 www.mitotyping.com	Mitochondrial DNA testing
MJ Research	590 Lincoln Street, Waltham, MA 02451	888-PELTIER Fax: 617-923-8080 www.mjresearch.com	Thermal cyclers and PCR consumables
Molecular Dynamics	928 East Arques Ave, Sunnyvale, CA 94086-4520	800-333-5703 Fax: 408-773-1493 www.mdyn.com	Gel imaging instruments and capillary array systems
MWG Biotech	4170 Mendenhall Oaks Parkwy, High Point, NC 27265	336-812-9995 Fax 336-812-9983 www.mwgbiotech.com	Oligo synthesis; genetic analysis equipment; thermal cyclers; robotics for liquid handling
Myriad Genetic Laboratories	320 Wakara Way, Salt Lake City, UT 84108	800-469-7423 801-584-3600 www.myriad.com	DNA databanking services; high-volume genetic and clinical testing
Nanogen, Inc.	10398 Pacific Center Court, San Diego, CA 92121	858-410-4600 Fax: 858-410-4848 www.nanogen.com	Microchip devices for DNA analysis
NFSTC	3200 34th Street South, St Petersburg, FL 33711	727-549-6067 Fax: 727-549-6070 www.nfstc.org	Forensic laboratory accreditation and training programs
Operon Technologies	1000 Atlantic Avenue #108, Alameda, CA 94501	800-688-2248 Fax: 510-865-5255 www.operon.com	Oligo synthesis
Paternity Testing Corporation	3501 Berrywood Drive, Columbia, MO 65201	888-837-8322 Fax: 573-442-9870 www.ptclabs.com	Paternity testing
PE Applied Biosystems	850 Lincoln Centre Drive, Foster City, CA 94404	800-345-5224 Fax: 650-638-5884 www.pebio.com/fo	STR typing kits; thermal cyclers; analysis instrumentation; genotyping software; ABI 310 and 377

Company Name	Street Address	Contact Information	Products/Services
PRO-DNA Diagnostic Inc.	5345 de l'Assumption #125, Montreal, Quebec H1T 4B3, Canada	800-236-9670 Fax: 514-899-9669 www.proadn.com	Paternity testing
Promega Corporation	2800 Woods Hollow Road, Madison, WI 53711	800-356-9526 Fax: 608-277-2516 www.promega.com	STR typing kits; DNA extraction kits
Qiagen, Inc.	28159 Stanford Ave, Valencia, CA 91355	800-426-8157 Fax: 800-718-2056 www.qiagen.com	DNA isolation products; sample preparation robotics
Rainin Instrument Company, Inc.	5400 Hollis St, Emeryville, CA 94608	800-472-4646 Fax: 510-652-8876 www.rainin.com	Pipetting products and services
ReliaGene Technologies, Inc.	5525 Mounes St #101, New Orleans, LA 70123	800-256-4106 www.reliagene.com	Paternity and forensic testing; DNA databanking and mtDNA services
Research Genetics	2130 Memorial Parkway, Huntsville, AL 35801	800-533-4363 Fax: 256-536-9016 www.resgen.com	Molecular biology products; custom genotyping; oligo synthesis
Roche Molecular Biochemicals	PO Box 50414, Indianapolis, IN 46250	800-262-1640 Fax: 800-428-2883 biochem.roche.com	Molecular biology supplies
Rosys Inc.	11 Parkway Circle, New Castle, DE 19720	302-326-0433 Fax: 302-326-0492 www.rosys.ch	Robotics for liquid handling
Sigma Chemical Company	3050 Spruce St, St Louis, MO 63103	314-771-5765 www.sigma.com	Molecular biology supplies
TECAN US, Inc.	4022 Stirrup Creek Dr, #310, Durham, NC 27703	800-338-3226 Fax: 919-361-5201 www.tecan-us.com	Robotics for liquid handling
Transgenomic, Inc.	5600 South 42nd St, Omaha, NE 68107	800-369-2822 Fax: 402-733-1932 www.transgenomic.com	Instruments for genetic analysis
University of North Texas Health Sciences Center DNA Identity Laboratory	3500 Camp Bowie Blvd, Fort Worth, TX 76107	800-687-5301 www.hsc.unt.edu/dna/ paternity.html	Paternity testing
Whatman Fitzco	5600 Pioneer Creek Drive, Maple Plain, MN 55357	800-367-8760 Fax: 612-479-2880 www.fitzcoinc.com	FTA paper for DNA storage and extraction

* United States unless otherwise indicated.

AUTHOR INDEX

SUBJECT INDEX